The *Complete Review* Guide
to Contemporary
World Fiction

[handwritten note] thank you so much for starting the int'l books club. Bravo! Ivonne

[handwritten note] thanks for running this club! Clare

[handwritten note] Dear Kylie, Thanks for leading us in this world of literature! so much fun! Natalie

[handwritten note] Thank you! It was fun joining in! Best, Amy

[handwritten note] Dear Kylie thank you for organizing this International Book Club. It's been fun! Sandra

[handwritten note] Dear Kylie — I love this group! Thank you for creating it. I look forward to it every month! Ruth

[handwritten note] Dear Kylie! Thank you so much for organizing this group. Looking forward to many more interesting discussions in the future. Mark

The *Complete Review* Guide to Contemporary World Fiction

M. A. ORTHOFER

COLUMBIA UNIVERSITY PRESS NEW YORK

Columbia University Press
Publishers Since 1893
New York   Chichester, West Sussex
cup.columbia.edu

Library of Congress Cataloging-in-Publication Data
Names: Orthofer, M. A., 1964– compiler.
Title: The Complete Review guide to contemporary world fiction /
[compiled by] M. A. Orthofer.
Description: New York : Columbia University Press, [2016] |
Includes bibliographical references and index.
Identifiers: LCCN 2015034501 | ISBN 9780231146746 (cloth :
acid-free paper) | ISBN 9780231146753 (pbk : acid-free paper) |
ISBN 9780231518505 (e-book)
Subjects: LCSH: Fiction—History and criticism. | Fiction—
Translations into English—Bibliography.
Classification: LCC PN3491 .C626 2016 | DDC 809.3—dc23
LC record available at http://lccn.loc.gov/2015034501

∞

Columbia University Press books are printed
on permanent and durable acid-free paper.
This book is printed on paper with recycled content.
Printed in the United States of America

c 10 9 8 7 6 5 4 3 2 1
p 10 9 8 7 6 5 4 3 2 1

COVER DESIGN: *Noah Arlow*

References to Web sites (URLs) were accurate at the time of
writing. Neither the author nor Columbia University Press
is responsible for URLs that may have expired or changed
since the manuscript was prepared.

CONTENTS

The *Complete Review* Guide
to Contemporary
World Fiction

Introduction

More than anywhere else in the world, it is domestic fiction that dominates bookstore shelves, best-seller lists, and media and review coverage in the United States. Tens of thousands of new works of fiction are published annually here, the vast majority by American authors. Most of the rest were also originally written in English, and only a few hundred are translated works of fiction.[1] In almost every other country, foreign literature occupies a central and prominent position, but in the United States it seems to sit far more precariously on the fringes.

Because American authors provide an enormous amount and variety of work, American readers are arguably spoiled for choice even without resorting to fiction from abroad. With novels and stories set in every imaginable locale—terrestrial, cosmic, or simply in the mind's eye—and styles ranging from the most accessible to the willfully experimental, American fiction could well cover it all. Yet even though the work of writers who speak and write in the same language as their readers do is more approachable than that of those with backgrounds in very different literary traditions, foreign literature can offer entirely new dimensions and perspectives. Publishers and readers may gravitate to the familiar and the local out of convenience, habit, or sheer indolence, but great literature and great books know no borders.

Over the years, there has been an ebb and flow of interest in contemporary foreign fiction in the United States. In recent decades, writing from abroad has not garnered as much attention as it perhaps should, yet at the beginning of the twenty-first century a far greater and more interesting variety of such fiction is more readily accessible than ever before, just waiting to be discovered and read. Although the large publishers continue to be somewhat reluctant to publish works in translation, there has been an explosion of innovative new ventures exploring new models of publishing translations, complementing an established group of smaller publishers that have found success in focusing largely or exclusively on fiction in translation. The emergence of English as the undisputed *lingua franca* of the twenty-first century has also led to its widespread use by writers abroad, producing a greater selection of books that do not have to clear the hurdle of translation to reach English-speaking readers. As a result, we may be entering a golden age of literary dissemination and exposure, with more books than ever, from more places than ever, available in English. *The Complete Review Guide to Contemporary World Fiction* leads readers into and through this rapidly expanding world.

The Internet has made information about foreign authors and their work, as well as a great deal of the work itself, much more readily accessible. When I founded the Complete Review (complete-review.com) in 1999, one of my goals was to take advantage of the Internet's tremendous reach and connectivity. Suddenly, book reviews from print publications, new online resources, and individual readers from across the world were just a link away. Beyond reviews, an enormous amount of literary coverage, in both local languages and English, has been made available, from traditional newspaper stories to discussions in online forums to blogs devoted to every imaginable facet of reading. Professional websites— publishers' foreign rights pages, the sites of national organizations promoting local literature abroad such as the French Publishers' Agency or the Finnish Literature Exchange, and the sites of international literary agencies—provide additional up-to-date information and insights into contemporary fiction from many nations. The Complete Review (website) is designed to help connect readers to much of this information. Ironically, though, one of the shortcomings of this and most other Internet resources is its tremendous scope. With reviews of well over three thousand titles on the site, each with links to additional reviews and information available online, the Complete Review provides a great deal of in-depth coverage. While this breadth is helpful when seeking precise information, the bigger picture often remains elusive.

As a print and an e-book, *The Complete Review Guide to Contemporary World Fiction* provides an entry point and a more general overview of various nations' literatures, as well as a foundation to help readers navigate what is available on the Internet. An appendix to *The Complete Review Guide* and the accompanying website (www.complete-review.com/guide) also offer an extensive list of additional resources, both in print and online.

Owing to the huge volume of what is published each year in America and the United Kingdom, foreign and translated fiction is easily lost. Moreover, those publishers that specialize in fiction in translation generally cannot compete with the large publishers' marketing budgets, and only a few major print review outlets devote significant space to translated fiction. Although the Internet has been a boon to both those seeking information about international writing and examples of it, its greatest use is for those looking for specific rather than general information. Printed reference works on foreign fiction also abound, but most are limited to a very narrow slice of literature, from a certain country or area, period, or genre. Detailed information about specific works, authors, or national literatures is often easy to find, but surprisingly few resources supply broader overviews in manageable form. I wrote this book to fill this void.

In providing an overview of the most interesting and significant contemporary fiction from around the world, *The Complete Review Guide* hopes to lead readers to new stories, voices, and places.

The Complete Review Guide is organized geographically, with the books and authors arranged by nation and region. Because writers and their fiction move across many borders and languages, national origin, domicile, and language are only rudimentary categories by which to arrange writers. Designations can often be questioned, as even an author whose output is as neatly divided as Vladimir Nabokov's proves difficult to fit into any single national category: he wrote first in Russian while living in exile in Berlin and then in English after moving first to the United States and then to Switzerland. The classification of authors in *The Complete Review Guide* is necessarily frequently subjective, but I have tried to make it as logical and utilitarian as possible, and regardless of where authors are categorized, I address their cross-cultural connections when discussing their lives and work. While there is always a clear nexus between author and locale in *The Complete Review Guide*, attributions to one nation or another should not be taken as definitive determinations.

In *The Complete Review Guide*, authors are assigned to specific locales according to—in order of significance—the language in which they write, their domicile (previous or original as well as current), the subject matter of their fiction, and their reputation. Given the possible combinations, beginning with writers who continue to write in more than one language, I had to make compromises, but overall these general organizing principles should allow for the most straightforward global overview. Longtime American or Canadian residents who continued to write in their mother tongue and whose work is largely about their native country, such as Josef Škvorecký (the former Czechoslovakia) or Alain Mabanckou (Congo-Brazzaville) are included in the sections on their country of birth, whereas those who have switched to writing in English (such as Aleksandar Hemon) and whose writing also features American locales, are generally included in the section on the United States. In many cases, especially for those who write in English, subject matter and reputation can tip the balance: the longtime American resident Chinua Achebe clearly must be considered a Nigerian author. In some cases, the decision is largely based on popular reputation (and how an author is marketed): Roberto Bolaño left

Chile in his teens and spent almost all his (writing) life in Mexico and Spain, yet he is generally considered a Chilean author and hence is categorized as such in *The Complete Review Guide*.

The amount of fiction available to English-speaking readers from different areas of the world varies greatly. Countries in which English is a literary language are at an obvious advantage, as translation continues to be a stumbling block for many publishers. While some languages are relatively well represented in translation—many of the European languages, especially French, as well as, more recently, Arabic and Chinese—there remain vast areas of the world from which barely any fiction is translated, as well as some with currently very little literary production of any kind. Although *The Complete Review Guide* reflects what is available to English-speaking readers, I also have tried to offer insights into the entire global scene.

Even with regard to the fiction available to English-speaking readers, *The Complete Review Guide* gives precedence to global inclusivity. The space devoted to discussing American and British literature could be expanded many times over, but given the widespread familiarity with it, as well as the many alternative sources of information available, I believed it better to devote this space to examples from lesser-known regions and other languages. It is a difficult balance to strike: important and worthwhile works from closer to home have been left out, while isolated examples from some countries that are mentioned are not necessarily literature of the first rank but help shape a fuller picture of world literature.

The Complete Review Guide to Contemporary World Fiction is emphatically a *reader's* guide for an English-speaking audience. One consequence, however, is that introducing only works that are available in English can distort the view of national literatures, as there are many languages from which only a limited number of texts have been translated. Many nations' fiction is highly evolved, but because only a tiny amount of it is available in English, it may seem underdeveloped.

Another drawback is the time lag, often large, between the original publication of books written in foreign languages and their availability in English. For the most part, only Nobel laureates and a few popular authors writing in widely translated languages such as French or Spanish see their works translated into English within a year or two of their initial publication. Hence "contemporary" necessarily becomes a flexible and relative term. In addition, there are large historical gaps in many national literatures that are only now being filled for English-speaking readers, with older classics and perennially popular works finally appearing in translation. These integral pieces of national literary traditions provide a context that makes newer work more accessible, and while they themselves are not strictly contemporary, they may be entirely new to English-speaking audiences. Thus, *The Complete Review Guide* focuses on fiction written after 1945 but does not ignore everything that came before, and in the cases of lesser-known literary traditions, it fills important gaps.

WORLD LITERATURE NOW

Well into the twentieth century, American literary fashion was dictated to a large extent by Continental tastes, so contemporary European fiction then occupied a much more prominent place in the United States. The great nineteenth-century British, French, and Russian novels and the broader variety of early-twentieth-century fiction found readers throughout Europe as well as America, and the classics of that period have retained that foothold. However, by the middle of the twentieth century, what seemed to be an inevitable trend toward internationalization slowed and ended. Like economic globalization, literary globalization boomed at the close of the nineteenth century and withered during the Great Depression and its aftermath. In this new era of nationalism and suspicion of the foreign, the movement of contemporary literature across borders was drastically curtailed. It was not just a matter of xenophobia. Political conditions and then World War II affected literary production in many countries. Ideology—especially the rise of Stalinism and Nazism—stifled writing in major literary centers such as Russia and Germany, only partially countered by those nations' dissident writers. In China, novelists were almost completely silenced during the entire Maoist era. World War II and then the Cold War also had an impact on what was produced and read throughout the world, with national variations of political correctness playing a significant role in determining what could be written, published, and imported.

Throughout the world, this wariness of the foreign was largely reversed with the next great wave of economic globalization that came in the second half of the twentieth century, especially as it accelerated after the end of the Cold War.

Since the end of World War II, the amount of fiction written and published worldwide has snowballed, though at very different rates. In some of the world's most populous nations, most notably the People's Republic of China and Indonesia, very few novels by native authors were published until the last decades of the twentieth century.[2] However, in recent years, domestic literary production in these two countries, particularly China, has swelled to incredible proportions. African nations and India have seen slower, steadier growth, marked by regional and linguistic variations: English-language writing and publishing, in particular, have expanded rapidly in India since the 1980s.[3] In Africa, though, many areas still have an underdeveloped literary and publishing infrastructure, limiting production. During the Cold War, the state-controlled publishing industries of Eastern Europe and the Soviet Union churned out a great deal of fiction (supplemented by a low-circulation but influential *samizdat* market), but with the collapse of Communism, state support for publishing fell dramatically, and a free market led to local works being displaced by an enormous inflow of foreign fiction—a trend that is only slowly being reversed.[4] The Arabic market for both publishing and selling books remains fragmented, but since the turn of the century, the amount of fiction available has greatly increased.

With their historical, linguistic, and cultural connections to the nations they colonized, England and France have become revitalized literary centers through which the fiction from much of the world is channeled. The more insular Great Britain long remained slightly apart from the active Continental scene, which has a vigorous and well-supported culture of translation, and it still does not have quite the same diversity found in France and some of the other European countries. But an enormous variety of English-language fiction by writers from the Commonwealth nations moves through here, and translation is now more widely fostered.

The European continent remains by far the most active area of literature moving across borders and languages. With often generous government subsidies, a wide range of books, from the popular to the more literary, have been translated.[5] Elsewhere, publishers and readers have become more receptive to a greater variety of foreign-language fiction. Single-language markets have become more inclusive as national barriers are broken down, whether in the Arabic-speaking world or Latin America. In India, after the rapid rise of English-language fiction in the late twentieth century, readers are becoming reacquainted with contemporary fiction written in other Indian languages. And in China, the delayed influx of foreign fiction has had a strong impact. In all these cases, exposure to so much more foreign and translated literature has inspired and stimulated local writers and increased the production of domestic fiction.

Globalization has not been uniform. Fiction from some areas, such as parts of Southeast Asia, is only slowly becoming part of the international literary scene. While English-language fiction from India is widely available elsewhere, fiction translated from regional languages has not yet attracted much notice abroad.[6] Other countries have had setbacks as well: Russian-language fiction attracts considerably less interest abroad than it did in Soviet times, and fiction from Japan— still one of the world's largest economies—has been pushed far from the literary center stage, with little beyond *manga* (comics), some genre fiction, and only a few authors besides Haruki Murakami currently attracting much notice abroad.

Although totalitarian regimes have generally been less tolerant of creative writing, some have, albeit in carefully controlled conditions, encouraged it. Nonetheless, state-sanctioned literature has historically had only limited (if any) appeal and value: the stronger the official approval is, the more turgid the fiction will be is a reliable rule of thumb.

The best writing from countries governed by totalitarian regimes tends to come from those in opposition to them, with works by dissidents and exiles also more readily finding publishers and audiences abroad.

The most controlling large-scale totalitarian regimes have now either disappeared (the Soviet Union) or are increasingly seeing their efforts at censorship subverted. Even though Chinese authorities still regularly ban books, these often appear underground, online, and abroad, limiting the effectiveness of official suppression. Elsewhere, government interference still has an enormous distorting effect on what is published domestically, but the number of countries where it greatly inhibits literary culture has been shrinking rapidly as democratic reform has spread.

Economic factors continue to play a role in the development and maintenance of domestic literary cultures. Those countries in which the overwhelming majority of citizens have little discretionary income, as is still the case in much of Africa and parts of Asia, tend to have underdeveloped publishing industries and book distribution networks (whether via bookshops or libraries). In many of these nations, the situation is exacerbated by government control of and interference in the institutions that foster the promotion and circulation of literature. Such circumstances make it difficult for a local writing culture to become established and sustain itself. Nevertheless, now more than ever, writing is emerging from all corners and the farthest reaches of the globe. Authors from totalitarian and impoverished countries have greater opportunities to publish and travel abroad, allowing works from countries like Cuba and Iran, as well as many African nations, to circulate abroad even if they cannot be widely distributed domestically.

As recent cultural trends have demonstrated, democracy and freedom of expression are clearly conducive to a dynamic—though arguably not always serious—literary culture. Popular fiction has flourished in countries that have made the transition from restrictive to democratic rule in recent decades, from Spain to South Korea. Economic growth and technological innovation have also contributed to the dramatic increase in the amount of writing available to growing numbers of readers. Print-on-demand technology and new distribution channels have made self-publishing viable, and by 2008 more titles were being released in this form than by traditional publishers in the United States,[7] a trend that will surely be repeated sooner rather than later throughout the world. Similarly, the Internet and e-readers have enabled the instant and widespread distribution of content and could lead to great changes in the amount of reading matter available. In some cases, new approaches to writing have evolved from new technology, including the rise of the so-called cell-phone novel (*keitai shōsetsu*) in Japan, which has now spread to other countries as well.

Creative writing is thriving across the world, but quantity, of course, does not guarantee quality. Concerns about the dumbing-down of literature, especially as more of it becomes available, are expressed in country after country. The influx of popular fiction originally written in English—mainly American commercial fiction—in countries around the world after World War II distorted domestic markets, as these books easily outsold most local offerings. In many countries, local writers have reclaimed at least part of the market, and some have begun to enjoy similar success abroad, but—so the argument goes—often at the cost of lower standards, as they imitate popular American formulas or embrace the lowest common local denominator.

Greater exposure to more kinds of fiction, however, not only has led to the imitation of American-style best sellers but also has inspired authors to borrow, adapt, and combine other approaches, invigorating local writing across much of the world. Occasionally, the popularity of literary trends such as the Salman Rushdiesque strain of magical realism, with its national-historical sweep, may seem to get out of hand, but more often they just are getting too much attention. Adding to the richness of today's literary scene is the recent revitalization of genre fiction, adding to a body of work that is more challenging and entertaining than in previous eras. Needless to say, there are fluctuations as literary schools get into ruts and genres are worked to death before eventually springing back to life. But in the big—the global—picture, literary culture, at least as measured by what is being produced, seems healthier than ever before. (The debate about reading culture is a different matter.)

THE RISE OF ENGLISH

The spread of English has had a substantial effect on world literature and what is available to readers. Even though it has been a boon to those who read English, the reluctance of major U.S. and British presses to publish books in translation threatens to expand the already sizable divide between fiction written in English and fiction originally written in another language.

Indeed, English has become the language of choice even for writers in countries where others are more widely spoken, especially in Britain's former colonies. English also remains the most popular choice among writers who have left their homelands and turned to writing in a second language. French also remains a popular second language, embraced by writers including Milan Kundera, Shan Sa, and Dai Sijie. Many other languages, from German to Japanese, have also been adopted by foreign writers. While some bilingual authors continue to write in more than one language, almost none who started writing in English have turned away from it. The American-born Prix Goncourt–winning author Jonathan Littell, who wrote his first novel in English, is one of the exceptions, abandoning English for French. Kenyan author Ngũgĩ wa Thiong'o first achieved success with works he wrote in English, but he later became a strong proponent of writing in indigenous languages and now practices what he preaches, writing in Gikuyu (but also translating many of his works into English himself).

The practical reasons for writers to turn to English are obvious, given the enormous potential audience for English-language fiction. In addition, English versions of books, in the original or translation, are the common currency for international publishers seeking foreign titles, as it is the most widely understood language. Many of the translations from and into other languages—especially less widely spoken languages—are through English.

English has become so dominant that the English-language originals of some popular titles—J. K. Rowling's *Harry Potter* books, the latest books by Dan Brown—have appeared near the top of domestic best-seller lists even in countries like France and Germany where local fiction is thriving and translations reach the market very quickly. In the Netherlands, publishers have found it necessary to publish works by locally popular authors such as John Irving, Donna Tartt, and J. M. Coetzee in their Dutch translations before the English originals are available anywhere else, in order to prevent the otherwise inevitable cannibalization of domestic sales.

This trend toward an increasing percentage of fiction being written in English seems likely to continue, as does the reliance on English translations of foreign works in the movement of fiction among other languages. Whereas American and British publishers—other than those specializing in translated fiction—still are often reluctant to invest in translated works, publishers in other parts of the world have begun expanding their range. India and southern Africa have seen a concerted effort to translate more works from regional languages—some of them with tens or even hundreds of millions of speakers—into English. Other parts of Africa, as well as other countries where English is one of several languages widely used, are likely to follow suit. This will make many more works available, even if they are unlikely to figure prominently in the American and British literary spheres.

Meanwhile, France, in particular, continues to play a significant role in the spread of world literature because of its ties to its former colonies (and the widespread use of French throughout the world); because as in much of Europe, translation is more generously supported; and because French publishers and readers still seem more receptive to fiction in translation than their American and British counterparts do. Germany plays a smaller, similar role, especially as a conduit for writing from eastern Europe and Scandinavia. In addition, the annual Frankfurt Book Fair, at which each year a different nation showcases its literature as the guest of honor, leads to more multifarious translations into German (even though most book deals at the fair are transacted in English).

It also is noteworthy that in the United States and Great Britain, translation and creative writing, at least of fiction, tend to be considered almost entirely separate spheres. Even though many contemporary American and British poets and playwrights regularly translate foreign poetry and plays into English, very few English-speaking novelists translate prose from other languages. The majority of the best-known and most prolific modern-day prose translators into English—including Ralph Manheim, Edith Grossman, Gregory Rabassa, Michael Henry Heim, and Anthea Bell—do not write fiction and are known solely as translators. Tiina Nunnally is one of the rare authors who has a greater following as a translator, while Lydia Davis and Tim Parks are among the few writers who have achieved some measure of success and popularity for their translations and their fiction. Some other authors also publish translations regularly, including J. M. Coetzee, Paul Auster, and Harry Mathews, but much of the work they focus on tends to be outside the mainstream. In contrast, translations by novelists are commonplace in many other countries and cultures. In languages with smaller domestic markets, translation is often a way for authors to supplement their income, but even in larger markets, many successful authors are involved in translation. Haruki Murakami has translated American classics such as *The Catcher in the Rye* and *The Great Gatsby*, as well as the works of Raymond Carver, Raymond Chandler, and novels such as John Irving's *Setting Free the Bears*; Nobel laureate Elfriede Jelinek has translated Thomas Pynchon's *Gravity's Rainbow* as well as dramas by Georges Feydeau and Oscar Wilde; and popular Russian mystery writer Boris Akunin has translated, among others, the works of Yukio Mishima and Kōbō Abe.

In all but the smallest domestic markets, professional translators, rather than novelists, dominate the field, but the extent to which fiction writers are involved in translation outside the United States suggests a deeper engagement with foreign literature abroad. This is reflected not only in how much more fiction in translation is available but also in the work of local writers. Ironically, since so much translation is from English, the works of novelists from the non-English-speaking nations are often colored by the American and British works with which they are so familiar. Here, too, influence is overwhelmingly in one direction.

WORLD LITERATURE IN THE UNITED STATES

Some contemporary works in translation can, of course, be found in bookstores throughout the United States. Since the end of World War II, books in translation have occasionally made or even topped a best-seller list—from the likes of Finnish author Mika Waltari's *The Egyptian* in the 1940s to Umberto Eco's *The Name of the Rose*—and many Nobel Prize winners (and crime writers) are widely published. Interest in translated fiction has come in waves over the past decades, although these have invariably focused on specific regions and styles. The Latin American "Boom" and its most popular manifestation, a form of magical realism, began in the 1960s and continued well into the 1980s. During the Cold War, dissident fiction from Eastern Europe and the Soviet Union was widely disseminated, and at the beginning of the twenty-first century, Scandinavian crime fiction was all the rage. After the terrorist attacks of September 2001 and the military engagement in Iraq, interest in Islam and the Arabic world has led to more fiction from that region being published.[8] Likewise, China's newfound economic might has led to Chinese fiction's making considerable inroads abroad, just as happened decades earlier with Japanese fiction. In addition, individual authors writing in foreign languages have earned both critical and popular acclaim, such as Michel Houellebecq, Haruki Murakami, W. G. Sebald, and Roberto Bolaño.

When publishers in the United States do seek out translated works, they often take their cues from elsewhere. Critical acclaim, literary prizes, and best-seller status—preferably in several different markets, rather than just the original local one—are prerequisites for most foreign fiction to be considered for the American market, especially by large commercial publishers. This herd mentality is widely practiced elsewhere as well, leading to a narrow, homogenous tier of international fiction that is widely available throughout the world and in many languages, whereas excellent works from less internationally celebrated authors can struggle to find the recognition and readers they deserve. Even though exceptional works do come into circulation in this way, too often it is the second-rate works—the earnest prize-winning novels and imitative local thrillers—that make the cut and disappoint both readers (with their mediocre quality) and publishers (with their low sales).

Fortunately, many smaller and more nimble publishers have been introducing a broader and more innovative range of foreign fiction to American audiences, but fewer resources and a tendency to concentrate on very narrow slices of international literature—as is the case for many university presses that specialize in fiction from specific countries and eras—have produced an eclectic though still impressive patchwork of foreign coverage.

The United States remains an influential literary nexus and a magnet to writers from around the world. Many authors from abroad have settled in the United States, permanently or temporarily, often taking positions at American universities. Ironically, what draws writers to the United States often keeps them at the margins, in comfortable but isolated niches removed from much of the domestic literary culture. The opportunities afforded by academia and the literary festival and conference circuit allow these authors a measure of success, as well as interaction with interested audiences, but too often they still barely register among the broader public. Even authors of the stature of Wole Soyinka, Chinua Achebe, and Ngũgĩ wa Thiong'o—arguably Africa's three greatest writers and all longtime American residents—remain relatively peripheral figures in the enormous American market. Those residing in the United States who still write in their foreign mother tongues, from French-writing African authors Emmanuel Dongala and Alain Mabanckou to the enormous number of Spanish-writing authors from Latin America and Spain, have even less impact, and many of their works remain unavailable in English translation. Only a few more adaptable writers, some of whom have switched languages and now also write in English (such as Aleksandar Hemon and Ha Jin), have managed to fit in and enjoy wider recognition and success.

Readers in the United States seem to prefer that in this nation of immigrants and assimilation, their authors become recognizably

Americanized beyond writing in English. Nostalgia for the old country is permissible, but America should be the reference point. The durable formula of combining ethnic background and American contexts has proved remarkably successful, and variations on the multigenerational, transnational historic saga are the most popular kind of vaguely foreign fiction—as long as they are strongly tied to present-day America: *The Joy Luck Club*, to name just one title out of thousands, is indicative of this phenomenon. The appeal of such works is understandable, and authors familiar with both foreign conditions and American sensibilities may indeed be best suited to introduce American audiences to other places and people and to bridge the cultural divides between them. Yet fiction by foreign authors that is not written specifically with American readers in mind can be far more revealing and certainly just as rewarding.

The presence in the United States of so many foreign authors—as well as publishers, magazines and websites, and organizations that foster and support international literature—has opened up many opportunities for interested readers. Too few readers take full advantage of the many available resources, but a well-informed readership—to which *The Complete Review Guide to Contemporary World Fiction* can, it is hoped, contribute—can find far more to select from than ever before.

A NOTE ON NAMES AND TITLES

Authors' Names

The transliteration (foreign scripts such as Arabic, Chinese, and Russian written in the Roman/Latin alphabet) of authors' names is still the cause of considerable confusion and can make it difficult to find information about them or their books. Names from many prominent languages are still not uniformly transliterated, and even when a single system of romanization has been adopted, older and regional variations linger on bookshelves, in catalogs, and on the Internet.

In some cases, the differences are insignificant, as in some of the diacritical fashions that publishers have followed, for example, publishing books under the names Kobo Abé and Kōbō Abe. When the differences are more fundamental, however, confusion reigns: Korean transliteration practice finds author Yi Ch'ongjun also still referred to as Lee Cheong-jun.

Chinese moved toward uniformity with the Wade-Giles system (Mao Tse-tung, Peking), which prevailed in translations from Chinese until 1979, superseded by the pinyin system (Mao Zedong, Beijing), which already had been used on mainland China for decades. The names of authors from the People's Republic of China are now uniformly written in pinyin. The names of Taiwanese authors, however, generally continue to be written in Wade-Giles, although pinyin was officially adopted there in 2009.

The great increase in translations from Arabic has also brought to the fore some of the issues with transliteration from that language. Aside from seemingly infinite spelling variations (even of a name that one would have thought would be standardized, such as Mohammed), the prefix al- (or el-) continues to sow confusion. Sometimes the prefix is integrated entirely into the surname (Rajaa Alsanea), but at other times it is not (Gamal al-Ghitani, Nawal El Saadawi). The Library of Congress and local libraries consistently disregard the prefix, shelving Alsanea's *Girls of Riyadh* under *S* (and cataloging her name as Rajā' 'Abd Allāh Ṣāni'), and local bookstores likely file it under *A*.

Different cultures' various usages of surnames create yet other complications. In East Asian languages, among others, surnames are cited first; *Mao* Zedong. The names of Japanese authors are almost always printed in Western form in English, with the surname last (Haruki *Murakami*). Chinese and Korean names are usually still printed with the surname coming first (*Gao* Xingjian, *Yi* Munyol), but increasingly frequently, publishers are placing surnames last (Young-ha *Kim*). The uniform adoption of placing surnames last is still a distant prospect and so is likely to continue to cause some confusion.

Similar questions of order arise with certain African authors: the Kenyan author who first published his books under his Christian name, James *Ngugi*, still uses the same surname but now publishes his work under the name *Ngũgĩ* wa Thiong'o.

Some cultures, like Burmese or Somali, do not have familial surnames in the Western sense that are passed down generations. Similarly, in Iceland, the name of the father (or occasionally the mother) is used along with the given name: *Arnaldur* Indriðason is the son of *Indriði* Guðmundur Þorsteinsson. (The most famous Icelandic author is an exception, having legally changed his name to *Halldór* Laxness from *Halldór* Guðjónsson.)

Spanish-language authors with their double surnames can also be confounding. Spanish custom uses first the paternal and then the maternal surname, with the paternal surname the one most commonly considered the official one, as in Gabriel *García Márquez*. Often, however, the maternal surname is dropped, and for a double given name, this can be confusing: it is Jorge Luis *Borges* (even though his full name is Jorge Francisco Isidoro Luis *Borges Acevedo*). Meanwhile, some authors have published under different variations of their names, with and without their maternal surname; for example, English translations have been published under both the names Leonardo *Padura* and Leonardo *Padura Fuentes*.

In this guide, the names under which translated titles were first published are used; in the case of particularly confusing alternate spellings, or the adoption of a later spelling that is now uniformly used, these are given as well.

Titles

Irritatingly often, publishers on both sides of the Atlantic (and beyond) are not in agreement regarding titles. American and British publishers occasionally differ on what title to use even for books originally written in English, and the practice of retitling a novel from one edition to the next—hardcover to paperback, for example—is not unheard of, especially in genre fiction. Publishers show even less restraint in regard to translated fiction. Understandably, the titles chosen for translations often do not correspond to the original, for any number of reasons, and many titles simply do not translate well.

For some of the classics, trying on a new title may seem like an exercise in futility, but at least it can help separate a new translation from the old one in the reader's mind, as in the case of Marcel Proust's *Remembrance of Things Past* (in C. K. Scott Moncrieff's classic translation) and the contemporary rendering, *In Search of Lost Time*. Still, even a more accurate rendering of a title rarely catches on: the title of Malcolm Pasley's 1992 translation, *The Transformation*, is much closer to Franz Kafka's *Die Verwandlung*, but in English the novella will surely always be known as *The Metamorphosis*.

Retranslations of more recent work generally reuse the same title, but British and American editions of the same translation far too frequently differ. Often the differences are so subtle as to seem nearly pointless, as when Per Olov Enquist's novel is presented as *The Visit of the Royal Physician* in Great Britain and as *The Royal Physician's Visit* in the United States. Occasionally they can seem almost ridiculous: Antonio Tabucchi's novel was published as *Pereira Declares* in the United States and *Declares Pereira* in Great Britain (and, fifteen years later, was reissued in Great Britain in 2010 as *Pereira Maintains*). In such cases, at least the different editions are recognizable on either side of the Atlantic; more often, though, the titles' similarities are tenuous (Michel Houellebecq's *Les particules élémentaires* is *The Elementary Particles* in the United States and *Atomised* in Great Britain) or nonexistent (Philippe Claudel's *Les âmes grises* became *Grey Souls* in Great Britain and *By a Slow River* in the United States).

Finally, the success of a movie version can lead to the rebranding of a book under the name under which the film was released. One of Pierre Boulle's books, originally published as *Monkey Planet*, is now sold as *Planet of the Apes*, and Vikas Swarup's novel, released as *Q & A*, is now published as *Slumdog Millionaire*.

In this guide, books are introduced with the titles under which they were first published, but later and alternative titles are provided as well.

A NOTE ON TRANSLATIONS

Translation enables us to read books that would otherwise remain inaccessible, but by its very nature, translation transforms a book, sometimes creating problems of which readers should be aware. Inferior translation—a translation that is simply bad—is the most obvious one and, unfortunately, not uncommon. Translators are often not paid very well, and not all are well qualified. Nonetheless, some publishers are willing to make do with untested but cheap labor, with unpredictable results. (A red flag to look out for is the translation copyright in the name of the publisher, rather than that of the translator, which indicates that the translation was a work for hire, thus giving the translator no rights regarding the presentation of the text.) Translations from most of the major languages into English by established translators can, for the most part, be relied on, but even the best ones are unlikely to be equally adept at handling several authors' differing styles. Occasionally, much or all of an author's work has one translator, as is the case with the English versions of the work of 2012 Nobel laureate Mo Yan, all of which were translated by Howard Goldblatt. This gives the English versions a consistency similar to that found in the originals. Too often, however, each book has a different translator. British translations are often imported unchanged by American publishers and include Anglicisms (and British spelling); conversely, American translations often sound too distinctly American for British readers. Approaches to translation also vary widely, from the strictly (and often woodenly) literal to the very free. Each language also poses unique problems, especially those whose grammar differs fundamentally from English grammar. Finally, translations frequently begin to seem dated even more quickly than do works written in English.

Many older works have been translated several times. Contemporary fiction is less frequently retranslated, and when it is, the new translation tends to displace the old. Usually, only fiction by famous—or suddenly famous—living authors is afforded the luxury of retranslation: Günter Grass's *The Tin Drum* was newly rendered into several languages for the fiftieth anniversary of its publication in 2009, and Orhan Pamuk's Nobel Prize led to a new translation of his novel *The Black Book* in 2006, only twelve years after it had first appeared in English. Imre Kertész's 2002 Nobel Prize also led to the retranslation of his two novels already available in English.

Shockingly, publishers occasionally still publish translations of foreign works from less common languages (such as the eastern European languages and Finnish) via a translation into a third language (usually French or German), which distances the final version even further from the original. Notable examples of such translations of translations are Polish author Stanisław Lem's *Solaris* (translated from the French translation), Hungarian writer Sándor Márai's *Embers* (translated from the German translation), and Romanian author Norman Manca's *Compulsory Happiness* (translated from the French translation).

In addition, translations are edited, and the English version is often cut. Surprisingly, many popular books, even those by acclaimed authors like Haruki Murakami, have been pared down in the English translation. Even a modern classic such as Uwe Johnson's admittedly massive *Anniversaries*, a four-volume work that is set mainly in New York City and is one of the most compelling accounts of the city during the late 1960s, was trimmed to half its size in translation. At least this was done with the author's cooperation; only now, several decades later, is an unabridged translation in the works.

More radical alterations are also not unheard of. The English translation of Albert Sánchez Piñol's *Cold Skin* omits an introductory section that reveals essential information about the protagonist, thereby fundamentally altering the book, and the entire setting of Frédéric Beigbeder's *£9.99* was transposed from France to England for the British edition, complete with changes in names and references, in a particularly brazen attempt to bring it closer to its new audience. Amy Yamada's novel published in English in 1994 as *Trash* is not even simply a translation of her 1991 novel of the same name. Rather, significant portions of the immensely popular Japanese original were cut, and much of her 1986 novella, *Jesse's Backbone*, was integrated into the text, creating a bizarre hybrid.

Despite the current popularity of the mystery and thriller genre, publishers also continue to present foreign series out of sequence. When new authors are introduced in translation, American and British publishers generally select the particular volume they believe will appeal most to English-speaking readers, and in the case of mystery series, this is rarely the first volume. If more work by the author is then deemed worth translating, publication may be haphazard, a major irritant when authors develop their characters across several books. As with most such editorial interference, publishers tend to withhold information from readers, and even when several books in a series are available, they may not indicate their proper order and/or any missing titles.

Finally, the translators' vital contribution to bringing foreign literature to English-speaking audiences is generally not adequately recognized and appreciated. My greatest regret in this guide, therefore, is not being able to include the names of the translators responsible for each of the works mentioned. Given the number of titles discussed here—many in multiple translations and several with multiple translators—it simply was not feasible.

NOTES

1. See appendix 1.
2. For an overview of literary publishing in China under Mao and during the post-Maoist transition, see Perry Link, *The Uses of Literature: Life in the Socialist Chinese Literary System* (Princeton, N.J.: Princeton University Press, 2000).
3. Rita Kothari, *Translating India*, rev. ed. (New Delhi: Foundation Books, 2006).
4. Andrew Baruch Wachtel, *Remaining Relevant After Communism: The Role of the Writer in Eastern Europe* (Chicago: University of Chicago Press, 2006).
5. Even so, in recent decades, translations from English have continued to dominate, consistently making up slightly more than 60 percent of all translated works in Europe. See Budapest Observatory, *Publishing Translations in Europe: Trends, 1990–2005*, Literature Across Frontiers (Aberystwyth: Mercator Institute for Media, Languages, and Culture, Aberystwyth University, 2011), http://portal.unesco.org/culture/en/files/41748/13390 726483Translation_trends_1990_2005_Dec_2010.pdf/Translation%2Btr ends%2B1990_2005_Dec%2B2010.pdf (accessed April 27, 2015).
6. While a growing amount of regional-language fiction translated into English is being published in India itself, the Translation Database at Three Percent (http://www.rochester.edu/College/translation/threepercent/index .php?s=database) records only a single work of fiction (a novel) published in the United States in 2013 that was translated from any of the languages (Hindi) native to the subcontinent.
7. In 2008, there were 275,232 traditionally published titles, and the number of "on-demand, short run and unclassified" titles more than doubled from the previous year's totals, to 285,394. See "On-Demand Printing Drove Title Output in '08," *Publishers Weekly*, May 25, 2009, 16.
8. Nevertheless, only 192 translations of novels translated from Arabic were published in Great Britain and Ireland between 1990 and 2010, a great improvement over the estimated mere 16 novels that were translated over the entire period from 1947 to 1967 but still an average of fewer than 10 a year. See Alexandra Büchler and Alice Guthrie, *Literary Translation from Arabic into English in the United Kingdom and Ireland, 1990–2010*, Literature Across Frontiers (Aberystwyth: Mercator Institute for Media, Languages, and Culture, Aberystwyth University, 2011),

https://lafpublications.files.wordpress.com/2011/04/laf-study-literary
-translation-from-arabic-into-english-in-the-uk-and-ireland-1990-2010
.pdf (accessed April 27, 2015). See also Salih J. Altoma, *Modern Arabic Literature in Translation: A Companion* (London: Saqi Books, 2005).

Europe

France, Belgium, and Switzerland

For more than a century, more literature has consistently been translated from French into English than from any other language. With **Honoré de Balzac** (1799–1850), **Victor Hugo** (1802–1885), **Alexandre Dumas**, père (1802–1870), **Gustave Flaubert** (1821–1880), and **Emile Zola** (1840–1902), as well as the science fiction pioneer **Jules Verne** (1828–1905), the French claimed many of the leading novelists of the nineteenth century. French authors have continued to play a significant and prominent role in the world republic of letters in the twentieth and twenty-first century, but in more recent times fewer individuals stand out, with only a handful of authors writing in French—such as **Marcel Proust** (1871–1922), **Albert Camus** (1913–1960), and crime writer **Georges Simenon** (1903–1989)—clearly establishing themselves in the highest tiers of the international pantheon.

Even with a continuing steady and strong flow of French fiction being translated into English, there have been lulls in interest in recent decades, as English-language readers tired of the *nouveau roman* and the perceived lack of emphasis on plot in French novels. The worthy but not widely read **Claude Simon** (1913–2005) and **Jean-Marie Gustave Le Clézio** (b. 1940), two of the last three French authors to win the Nobel Prize (in 1985 and 2008, respectively), have come to be seen as representative of far too much French fiction over the past decades, writing which has often been willfully experimental, passive, and stolid.

In some cases, the intellectual pretension of much modern French fiction has not translated well either, whether in the endless stream of introspective *autofictions* or in some of the belligerent novels of the controversial **Michel Houellebecq** (b. 1958). Nevertheless, the enormous amount of French fiction that continues to appear in English translation now has a far greater range, much of it exciting and innovative, than these generalizations suggest.

Forerunners

A number of authors whose works appeared in the earlier part of the twentieth century set many of the patterns that continue to dominate French fiction. If not quite protofeminist, the focus on women, often in surprising roles, in **Colette's** (1873–1954) work opened new vistas. A strong strain of very personal female writing in recent French literature has some of its roots in Colette's novels. **Louis-Ferdinand Céline** (1894–1961) is another, very different precursor of some of the autobiographical *autofiction* that remains popular, with the sustained radical style of his ellipsis-packed and slang-filled texts influencing many other authors. Céline's inspired ***Conversations with Professor Y*** (1955, English 1986), in which he attacks the literary establishment and defends and explains himself to a fictional interviewer (who finds himself completely out of his depth), is the best introduction to his methods and madness, both literary and political.

Marcel Aymé (1902–1967) is best known for his stories, which often have creative premises—most famously the character who is literally able to pass through walls—but he also wrote realist fiction and a variety of satires tending toward the gray and even the black.

Avoiding intellectual and literary-school labels, Aymé's works contain a distinctly French sort of populism. In his brief life, **Boris Vian** (1920–1959) was an accomplished musician, songwriter, and poet who also wrote fiction. He reveled in the absurd, with a comic touch and reliance on wordplay. As a member of the Collège de 'pataphysique, he was also, at least in spirit, a forerunner of the Oulipo, the group famous for writing that employs constraints. Vian's greatest success was *I Spit on Your Graves* (1946, English 1948), a pulp thriller that was originally published pseudonymously, claiming to be the translation of a work by "Vernon Sullivan," an African American author. Its sensational mix of racial issues and crime made it both a notorious and a best-selling novel.

Jean-Paul Sartre (1905–1980) is better known for his dramas, philosophical works, and massive studies of Gustave Flaubert and Jean Genet, but he also wrote several novels. *Nausea* (1938, English 1949), with its aimless, resigned, and self-absorbed narrator remains an immensely influential existential work.

Samuel Beckett's (1906–1989) earliest works of prose were written in English, including the collection of satirical stories *More Pricks Than Kicks* (1934) and the novel *Murphy* (1938). But his French trilogy in which the act of writing is central for the characters, *Molloy* (1951, English 1955), *Malone Dies* (1951, English 1956), and *The Unnamable* (1953, English 1958), would have secured his literary reputation even if he had not achieved greater fame as a dramatist. Even though these texts include sensational and shocking events, they are predominantly introspective and not plot driven in any traditional sense. In this trilogy, Beckett presents, with both intensity and humor, the struggle to capture experience in language.

The Old Guard

A number of French writers born in the earlier part of the twentieth century are still active or have been until very recently, though most have enjoyed only intermittent success in the English-speaking countries over the course of their long careers.

For a time, **Jean Dutourd** (1920–2011) enjoyed considerable and deserved success, beginning with his satire of profiteering, *The Best Butter* (published in Great Britain as *The Milky Way*; 1952, English 1955), or his more timeless novel of a man living with, as the title has it, *A Dog's Head* (1950, English 1951). In later works, such as *The Horrors of Love* (1963, English 1967), a novel almost entirely in dialogue about adultery and murder, and the artist tale *Pluche* (1967, English 1970), Dutourd uses his stories as platforms for discussion and the exposition of everything from philosophy and art to love. They are typical French novels of ideas, but with a greater emphasis on conveying the ideas along with entertaining plots. In the 1970s, Dutourd fell entirely and unjustly out of favor with English-language publishers and has since written dozens of works that have not been translated.

Michel Tournier (b. 1924) has had more consistent success abroad, especially with his works of fiction that adapt literary, historical, and biblical figures and stories, beginning with his own reworking of the *Robinson Crusoe* story, *Friday* (1967, English 1969). Among his most interesting juxtapositions is that of mass-murderer Gilles de Rais and Joan of Arc in *Gilles and Jeanne* (1983, English 1987). In *Eleazar, Exodus to the West* (1996, English 2002), he freely uses a biblical story as the underpinning for a nineteenth-century odyssey tale of the American West. His most resonant work is the symbol-laden novel set during World War II, *The Ogre* (published in Great Britain as *The Erl-King*; 1970, English 1972), with its fascinating, bizarre protagonist, Abel Tiffauges. Tournier uses both history and myth in this monstrous tale of innocence, culpability, and redemption. Tiffauges is a real-life fairy tale monster who, when he becomes a part of the Nazi machinery of terror, kidnaps boys to fill the ranks of the military, without being fully cognizant of his own culpability and the nature of the evil he is abetting.

Nouveau Roman

Even though the designation *nouveau roman* promises the new, few literary styles now seem as *passé*, as many of these works from the

KEEP IN MIND

- Greek-born **Albert Cohen** (1895–1981) lived in Switzerland most of his life and is best known for his massive comic epic of love and Jewish identity, *Belle du Seigneur* (1968, English 1995).
- **Albert Cossery** (1913–2008) was born in Egypt, and while he lived most of his life in Paris, all his novels are set in the Orient with which he was familiar from his youth. Languorous, stylish, and comic, his novels are delightful, polished entertainments (though certainly not politically correct).
- **Roger Grenier**'s (b. 1919) fiction includes his spare novella, *Another November* (1986, English 1998), the best example of his abilities and style, which distills lives and fates from his native Pau marked by World War II.
- Swiss author **Jacques Chessex**'s (1934–2009) slim novels based on shocking historical provincial incidents, *A Jew Must Die* (2009, English 2010) and *The Vampire of Ropraz* (2007, English 2008), are no less powerful for their brevity. Chessex also won the Prix Goncourt for *A Father's Love* (now published as *The Tyrant*; 1973, English 1975), a psychological study of a man who cannot escape the crushing influence of his overbearing father even after his father's death.
- A few representative novels by the influential intellectual **Philippe Sollers** (b. 1936) are available in translation, ranging from the writing exercise *The Park* (1961, English 1968) and the elliptical roman à clef, *Women* (1983, English 1990), to the meditations of a man involved in an art theft in *Watteau in Venice* (1991, English 1994).
- **Simone de Beauvoir** (1908–1986), who was married to Jean-Paul Sartre and is the influential author of works such as *The Second Sex* (1949, English 1952, 2009), also wrote several novels. Her Prix Goncourt–winning roman à clef, *The Mandarins* (1954, English 1956), is a revealing inside look at French intellectual life in the first decade after World War II.

1950s and 1960s have aged poorly. Many *nouveaux romans* offer tightly focused, introspective works that seem like a lengthy mulling over of the same thoughts, but they actually use a number of distinctive approaches and characteristics.

Nathalie Sarraute's (1900–1999) works are good examples of *nouveaux romans*. From her first collection of prose sketches, *Tropisms*

(1939, revised 1957, English 1967), Sarraute showed little interest in conventional storytelling, finding little need for plot or progressive action. Concentrating on inner lives and thoughts, her often anonymous characters are not entirely isolated, which keeps the books from being mere exercises in navel-gazing. Interaction with others is central, though it often is the failures or even the impossibility of mutual understanding and connection that are revealed.

Michel Butor (b. 1926) is the most experimental of the major exponents of the *nouveau roman*, though in more recent years he has moved away from writing what can be considered fiction. Several of his precisely structured novels are close records of a specific period, sometimes maddeningly so, as in the fascinating, sprawling *Degrees* (1960, English 1961), in which a character seeks to document reality perfectly. *A Change of Heart* (published in Great Britain as *Second Thoughts*; 1957, English 1958) is set entirely on the long train trip from Paris to Rome and is written in the second person. Both autobiographical and gothic, Butor's *Portrait of the Artist as a Young Ape* (1967, English 1995) is perhaps his strangest creation, but its quick and quirky oddness is the easiest introduction to a demanding author. The novel is described as "a caprice," in which the young protagonist is immersed in classical and mystical literature through a vast private library while also haunted by vivid dreams.

The most useful introduction to **Alain Robbe-Grillet**'s (1922–2008) fiction is his collection of critical pieces, *Towards a New Novel* (1963, English 1965, and as *For a New Novel*, 1966), since many of his novels are efforts to put theory into practice. Even though his texts are presented in an ostensibly neutral and detached manner and his descriptions may be painstakingly precise, and even though the individual pieces of his narratives seem clear, the larger picture is blurred. Chronology and memory are meant to be realistically depicted, conveyed with that same sense of vagueness and uncertainty with which they are often experienced. Robbe-Grillet's droning tone and use of repetition contrast with the thriller elements and often shocking pornographic content of his stories. Robbe-Grillet also wrote and directed several movies, and much of his fiction consequently has a cinematic quality.

Robbe-Grillet's technique works best in the suspenseful novel *The Voyeur* (1955, English 1958). In it, the traveling salesman Mathias visits an island, and it slowly becomes clear—to the extent anything in Robbe-Grillet's ambiguous narrative can—that he is responsible for the rape and murder of a young girl. Presenting multiple perspectives and versions of events, even the facts of the crime itself remain uncertain.

Much of Robbe-Grillet's later fiction wallows in pornographic excess, notably his Sadeian final novel, *A Sentimental Journey* (2007, English 2014). But his stylish *Repetition* (2001, English 2003) is an accessible and entertaining introduction to the author's work. Set in postwar Germany, it is a novel of ambiguity, repetition, and confused identities in which the central character witnesses what appears to be a murder, even though little is what it seems.

KEEP IN MIND

- Only the first two volumes of **Claude Ollier**'s (1922–2014) eight-novel *Le jeu d'enfant* cycle have been translated, which is surprising given the promising start of *The Mise-en-Scène* (1958, English 1988), set in North Africa with elements of a mystery and the perfectly handled uneasy uncertainty of the protagonist. Meanwhile, *Wert and the Life Without End* (2007, English 2011) is a novel of short fragments and impressions in which a soldier traumatized by war pieces together life and meaning.

- In his fiction, **Claude Simon**'s (1913–2005) layering of voice and text and his use of recurrent motifs often feel musically arranged; often, too, he withholds clear resolutions. Several of his novels deal with the past and especially the experience of war, the most notable among them *The Flanders Road* (1960, English 1961) and *The Georgics* (1981, English 1989). His short final piece, *The Trolley* (2001, English 2002), is the best entrée to the works of his late autobiographical period.

- **Robert Pinget**'s (1919–1997) works often display a lighter, even comic, touch. Many are concerned with the act of writing itself, and his later works, such as *The Enemy* (1987, English 1991), are increasingly fragmented texts.

The work of 2008 Nobel laureate, **Jean-Marie Gustave Le Clézio** (b. 1940), can be divided into two distinct phases, an experimental early one followed by a somewhat more conventional period, though stylistically his fiction is varied throughout. His work also is characterized by a concern with the costs of modernity and the loss of the primitive. From the loud dystopian capitalist visions and ecological disasters that figure in his early fiction, Le Clézio's work has become more nuanced and controlled while retaining a figurative richness. His first novel, *The Interrogation* (1963, English 1964), is still the best of his early work. The novel's protagonist is an aimless young man, Adam Pollo, who lives in the present with little concern for the past or the future. *The Interrogation* is a jumbled, fragmented character study in which Le Clézio lets Adam babble and philosophize, but its youthful energy and ambition excuse many of its weaknesses.

With *Desert* (1980, English 2009) and its juxtaposition of African nature and Western European industrial society, Le Clézio began a series of more approachable and readily appreciated works of fiction. Several later works, such as *Onitsha* (1991, English 1997), also are semiautobiographical, containing elements of the Mauritius-born and widely traveled author's family's life and history.

Le Clézio's Nobel Prize will likely lead to the translation of more of his works, including his most ambitious novel, the sweeping *Révolutions* (2003), into which he folds his familiar concerns and interests. *The Prospector* (1985, English 1993), a historical adventure tale, is a good starting point. In this novel, the Mauritian-born narrator, Alexis L'Etang, recounts both his obsession with the lost treasure of an "Unknown Corsair" in this idyllic Indian Ocean setting and the realities of the some of the ugliest battles of World War I, in which he fought.

Oulipo

The Ouvroir de littérature potentielle (Workshop for potential literature), widely referred to as Oulipo, was originally founded in 1960 as a co-commission of the Collège de 'pataphysique. Its members are dedicated to renewing literature by writing within a variety of constraints, often with a mathematical basis. The best-known examples of these are "N+7," in which every noun in a text is replaced by the seventh one after it in the dictionary, and the lipogram, in which the text is written without using a specified letter of the alphabet. Oulipians also continue to experiment with new and often elaborate constraints. As unlikely as it may seem, the results are often quite remarkable, with the constraints not as obvious and intrusive as might be expected. The highly entertaining encyclopedic guide, the *Oulipo Compendium* (1998, revised 2005), edited by Harry Mathews and Alastair Brotchie, is an invaluable companion piece for anyone interested in the movement.

Oulipo has foreign members, like Italo Calvino (1923–1985), Harry Mathews (b. 1930), and Oskar Pastior (1927–2006), but it has been dominated by authors writing in French. Founding member **Raymond Queneau** (1903–1976) has had the greatest influence beyond the group, and even before Oulipo, he experimented with some of the techniques the group embraced. Among Queneau's many fictional games, *Exercises in Style* (1947, English 1958) is particularly enjoyable and playful, retelling the same short and banal episode ninety-nine times, each in a different style. *Zazie* (now published as *Zazie in the Metro*; 1959, English 1960), Queneau's lively story of the Parisian adventures of a prepubescent but not entirely innocent girl, is his best known work. *The Flight of Icarus* (1968, English 1973), in which an author literally loses his character and sets off in search of him in a novel presented in the form of a play with little more than dialogue, is his most surprisingly delightful fiction.

Georges Perec (1936–1982) is the writer most closely associated with the Oulipo. His *e*-less novel, *La disparition* (1969)—rendered into English as *A Void* (1994) by Gilbert Adair (1944–2011)—is considered the prototypical Oulipian work. Surprisingly, this story full of disappearances—of vowels and characters, beginning with Anton Vowl (Voyl in the original)—is a convincing if somewhat scattershot work of fiction. The English version is necessarily a very loose translation but also thoroughly enjoyable. Perec also wrote a text to complement *La disparition* (or at least to put all those *es* to use), *Les revenentes* (1972), which contains no other vowels. Ian Monk (b. 1960), himself co-opted into the Oulipo (according to the official terminology) in 1998, translated this as *The Exeter Text* in the collection *Three by Perec* (1996).

Perec's œuvre is, however, considerably more varied, from his *Les choses* (now published as *Things: A Story of the Sixties*; 1965, English 1968), which is not nearly as reductive as the title might suggest, to his magnum opus and one of the great achievements of postwar French fiction, *Life A User's Manual* (1978, English 1987), in which the narrative is structured around puzzles and rules, offering a remarkable and truly multilayered reading experience. An apartment building is the novel's fundamental structure, with each chapter a snapshot of a part of the building and its inhabitants at the same single moment in time. Perec builds an intricate and interconnected work on this simple scaffolding. Almost all of Perec's work is worth reading, and his collection, *Species of Spaces and Other Pieces* (English 1997), is the best general introduction.

Jacques Roubaud (b. 1932) is among the few Oulipo authors regularly translated into English. His Hortense trilogy—*Our Beautiful Heroine* (1985, English 1987), *Hortense Is Abducted* (1987, English 1989), and *Hortense in Exile* (1990, English 1992)—is a light and amusing series, offering all sorts of Oulipian games and references and a bit of murder mystery. His *The Great Fire of London: A Story with Interpolations and Bifurcations* (1989, English 1991), a personal novel of memory, the creative act, and creative failure, also is worth seeking out. Roubaud is a mathematician, and the novel—the first in a series that continues with *The Loop* (1993, English 2009) and then *Mathématique* (1997, English 2012)—is the remnant of a grander literary project. A creative and artfully structured variation on fiction describing the creation of fiction, this constantly self-questioning and cross-referenced work also has a powerful emotional component, the death and memory of his wife.

Four works by **Hervé Le Tellier** (b. 1957) appeared in English in 2011 and are a fine cross section of Oulipian writing. They range from *Enough About Love* (2009), a novel about two married couples in which the constraints are hidden well enough to appear almost entirely conventional, to *The Sextine Chapel* (2005), which comes with its own explanatory diagram. Each of *The Sextine Chapel*'s very short chapters describes a coupling between two of the twenty-six characters (one for each letter of the alphabet), with each character hooking up with five different people over the course of the novel. Each chapter briefly describes the characters' (usually sexual) intercourse, as well as a shorter observation or thought that is not always obviously related to the act. The couplings have a symmetric design, which is shown in the diagram appended to the text, as well as several layers of Oulipian constraints, which readers are free to try to uncover or disregard.

Several of **Jacques Jouet**'s (b. 1947) works also are available in English, including the droll *Upstaged* (1997, English 2011), in which an unknown man referred to as "the Usurper" takes the place of an actor in the performance of a play for just its middle act, a premise allowing for both theatrical farce and political commentary. *Savage* (2001, English 2009) uses Paul Gauguin's life as a template in a brief work that examines what constitutes civilization, and *Mountain R* (1996, English 2004) offers three different perspectives on a monumental undertaking, the attempted (and then failed) construction of a nearly mile-high mountain.

Anne Garréta (b. 1962) was not co-opted into the Oulipo until 2000, but her first novel, *Sphinx* (1986, English 2015), is a remarkable example of constrained writing, as there is no indication anywhere in the text as to the gender of the narrator or the narrator's love interest. This is grammatically more challenging in the original French, but even in English the resulting genderless love story subtly but persistently forces readers to consider the gendered nature of everyday language. Because the protagonists could be either male or female, as well as homosexual or heterosexual, *Sphinx* also addresses basic assumptions about sexual roles and identity.

BEYOND THE OULIPO

- **Olivier Rolin**'s (b. 1947) *Hotel Crystal* (2004, English 2008), a sly little literary thriller set in the carefully described hotel rooms that the narrator visits around the world, owes much to the work of Georges Perec in both its presentation and its tone, while *Paper Tiger* (2002, English 2007) reconsiders the generation-defining year 1968.

- Like a modern-day Fernando Pessoa, **Antoine Volodine** (pseudonym, b. 1950) wraps and re-creates himself in layers of real and imagined identities in his often overlapping fiction—only a few available in translation—which is published under several different names. *Post Exoticism in 10 Lessons, Lesson 11* (1998, English 2015) is a good overview of the strange cosmos he has been constructing and the philosophy behind it. He continues to expand his own peculiar fictional universe in works that often shift between dream and reality. The lush, memory-invoking *Naming the Jungle* (1994, English 1996), set in Latin America, is an approachable introduction to his work, while *Minor Angels* (1999, English 2004) is a vivid postapocalyptic vision presented in short, distinct, bursts. Among his works published under his other pseudonyms available in English are *We Monks & Soldiers* (2008, English 2012; writing as Lutz Bassmann), and the trio of short works of fiction ostensibly written for children collected in *In the Time of the Blue Ball* (2002, 2003, English 2011; writing as Manuela Draeger).

- Philosopher **Sylvie Germain**'s (b. 1954) vivid, haunting fiction often has a touch of the mythic and supernatural.

- Egyptian-born **Edmond Jabès**'s (1912–1991) work offers a continuum of fiction, essay, and poetry. His meditative, questioning books grapple with the difficulties of writing and relating stories.

- **Maurice Blanchot** (1907–2003) is best known for his theoretical writing, but his compact works of fictions, culminating in the fragmented *Awaiting Oblivion* (1962, English 1997), are also of interest.

- **Hélène Cixous** (b. 1937) is another author notable for her theoretical writing, much—arguably too much—of which also informs her voluminous and varied fiction. Novels such as the lyrical, feminist *The Book of Promethea* (1983, English 1991) and the more political *Manna: For the Mandelstams for the Mandelas* (1988, English 1994), with its real-life characters, give a sense of her range.

- Bulgarian-born **Julia Kristeva**'s (b. 1941) cerebral thrillers such as *Possessions* (1996, English 1998) are influenced by her work in semiotics and psychology. (Kristeva also is married to Philippe Sollers.)

Autofiction

Although many authors weave autobiography into their fiction, the French sometimes seem to have taken that, and a concomitant self-absorption, to extremes. The term "autofiction" was coined only in the 1970s, when it was most widespread, but variations of it have continued. With their glorifying depictions of crime and baseness, **Jean Genet**'s (1910–1986) novels of the 1940s were early extreme examples of the genre. More recently, books about a woman's relationships with the men in her life have become a French staple; even **Marguerite Duras**'s (1914–1996) most popular works, such as *The Lover* (1984, English 1985), center on this dynamic. **Catherine Millet**'s (b. 1948) best-selling and very candid memoir, *The Sexual Life of Catherine M.* (2001, English 2002), simply dispensed with any fictional trappings but does not seem to have been sufficient to kill off the genre.

Annie Ernaux's (b. 1940) understated works focus on the intimate. Her œuvre consists almost entirely of works that blur the distinction between memoir and fiction, beginning with a novel, *Cleaned Out* (1974, English 1990), about a university student who has had an (illegal) abortion. Again and again in her works, Ernaux returns to her childhood and her parents' humble lives, creating an increasing sense of familiarity. A quarter century after *Cleaned Out*, Ernaux reconsidered that time of her life in *Happening* (1999, English 2001). Although each of her novels can stand on its own, they clearly are connected and, taken as a whole, the finest example of a large wave of introspective creative autobiographical writing in French.

Edouard Levé's (1965–2007) *Autoportrait* (2005, English 2012) is a self-portrait consisting only of a series of concisely expressed impressions and judgments, tallies and memories. This reduction of his life into what amounts to a list is surprisingly revealing and powerful. *Works* (2002, English 2014) is a similar compendium, in which Levé catalogs more than five hundred literary and artistic projects that he planned and imagined but never realized. In his novel *Suicide* (2008, English 2011), the narrator addresses a friend who had killed himself twenty years earlier, and it is difficult not to read a great deal more into this story, given that Levé killed himself shortly after completing the text.

If **Justine Lévy**'s (b. 1974) two autobiographical novels, *The Rendezvous* (1995, English 1997) and *Nothing Serious* (2004, English 2005), are of more interest than most, it is, in large part, because of some of their characters. *The Rendezvous* touches on the childhood and adolescence of the daughter of France's trendiest public intellectual, Bernard-Henri Lévy, and the woman to whom she lost her husband in *Nothing Serious* is reputedly Carla Bruni, who went on to become Mme. Nicolas Sarkozy, the first lady of France.

Creative Variations

Jean Echenoz's (b. 1947) work has always had a mischievous quality, starting with novels that seem to be detective and spy fiction but, instead of conforming to the genres' demands, twist them into the writer's own warped ends. In his novels based on real-life historical figures, such as *Ravel* (2006, English 2007), *Running* (2008, English 2009), about the long-distance running legend Emil Zátopek, and *Lightning* (2010, English 2011), about Nikola Tesla, Echenoz has a much more controlled style. Despite their simple, factual tone, these works have considerable emotional resonance.

Echenoz's finest book to date is the perfectly pitched *Piano* (2003, English 2004). It is the story of concert pianist Max Delmarc's life and then his afterlife, with two-thirds of the book describing his fate after his death. This absurd premise and Echenoz's wildly imagined inventions and plot twists produce an entirely unpredictable yet convincing and beautiful work of fiction.

Michel Houellebecq (b. 1958) has gained considerable international renown, largely on the basis of *The Elementary Particles* (published in Great Britain as *Atomised*; 1998, English 2000) and *Platform* (2001, English 2003). In his bleak fiction, his misanthropic alter egos long for human contact and company but are largely unable to make anything more than superficial connections (and have a great deal of inadequate sex). His unpleasant and often xenophobic protagonists are redeemed only by their frankness, and their relentless negativity is bearable only because Houellebecq creates generally intriguing stories about the banality of their lives. Houellebeccq's most outlandish scenario comes in *The Possibility of an Island* (2005, English 2005). This offers a futuristic vision of what the remnants of humanity may one day be like, as well as a story focused on the present-day Raëlian cult that is trying to transcend mortality through cloning, realizing an ideal world in which death and sex no longer are concerns.

The Elementary Particles was a cause célèbre in France for its damning indictment of modern French society, which Houellebecq depicts as an empty wasteland that has been "atomised" as people have lost themselves in individuality and seem incapable of forming meaningful bonds or ties. Houellebecq is relentless in his attack on a crumbling society—until the bizarre, uplifting conclusion that suggests a brighter future (of sorts). The topical premise of *Submission* (2015, English 2015) is a Muslim political party taking power in France in 2022 and beginning a thorough, successful process of Islamization. The narrator, François, is a typical discomfiting Houellebecqian protagonist. A university professor specializing in Joris-Karl Huysmans (1848–1907), he goes on a voyage of discovery as he considers what compromises to make in adjusting to this new society and finding his place in it.

Houellebecq's Prix Goncourt–winning novel about a successful photographer, Jed Martin, and the art world, *The Map and the Territory* (2010, English 2011), also contains dark edges and sharp satire but is considerably more mellow than his other work. Some of the humor comes at his own expense, as the real-life Houellebecq figures prominently as a character in the novel who befriends Martin. The author also brutally kills himself off, providing at least some of the requisite sensationalism that readers have come to expect in his novels.

KEEP IN MIND

- **Emmanuel Carrère**'s (b. 1957) fine fiction includes *The Mustache* (1986, English 1988), a small classic about the consequences of a small act, the protagonist's decision to shave off his mustache, that shakes the very foundations of his identity. His *Class Trip* (1995, English 1997) also is an agreeably sinister little novel.
- **Frédéric Beigbeder** (b. 1965) tackles sensational topics with verve. His spirited consumer culture critique–cum–advertising industry exposé, *£9.99* (2000, English 2002), was wittily retitled *Was £9.99, Now £6.99* for the paperback edition, but it lost something in a translation that transposed it, its characters, and its local color from France to England. Beigbeder's take on the collapse of the World Trade Center on September 11, *Windows on the World* (2003, English 2005), also was retouched in translation for American sensibilities but remains an impressive direct confrontation with those events.
- **Paule Constant** (b. 1944) offers historic exoticism in her darkly comic and critical colonial novels such as *Ouregano* (1980, English 2005), *The Governor's Daughter* (1994, English 1998), and *White Spirit* (1989, English 2006).

Singular Obsessions

Patrick Modiano's (b. 1945) varied, creative takes on the French occupation and its aftereffects, such as *Dora Bruder* (published in Great Britain as *The Search Warrant*; 1997, English 1999) and *Missing Person* (1978, English 1980), as well contemporary studies of memory and distance like *A Trace of Malice* (1984, English 1988), make for an interesting body of work. Mainly based on personal experience, especially from his youth, as well as often blurry memory, his fiction often has an overlap of incident and characters, yet each slim novel is distinctive. These are shadowy books full of uncertainty and, in their attempts at reconstructing and understanding the past, often have the feel of mystery fiction.

Much more of Modiano's work has become available in translation since he was named the 2014 Nobel laureate. *Night Rounds* (1969, English 1971, revised as *The Night Watch*, 2015) and *Ring Roads* (1972,

---

KEEP IN MIND

- **Éric Chevillard**'s (b. 1964) fiction leans toward the fantastical, even though the works often seem grounded in the naturalistic. Chevillard is more interested in postmodern playfulness than in plot in works ranging from **Palafox** (1990, English 2004), with its unusual eponymous creature that is the focus of the novel, to the piecemeal character-portrait in *The Crab Nebula* (1993, English 1997). Chevillard's amusing story of literary obsession, **Demolishing Nisard** (2006, English 2011), is a good introduction to his work.
- **Christian Oster**'s (b. 1949) self-absorbed men find their lives are often just out of their control, in works like his novels of loss *My Big Apartment* (1999, English 2002), *The Unforeseen* (2005, English 2007), and *In the Train* (2002, English 2010).
- **Christian Gailly**'s (1943–2013) spare and minimalist approach works well in the jazz-infused *An Evening at the Club* (2001, English 2003) and the creepy *Red Haze* (2000, English 2005).

English 1974, revised 2015), now published together with *La place de l'étoile* (1968, English 2015) as *The Occupation Trilogy*, and the collection of novels published as **Suspended Sentences** (English 2014), which includes *Afterimage* (1993), *Suspended Sentences* (1988), and *Flowers of Ruin* (1991, English 2014), are excellent entry points.

Lydie Salvayre's (b. 1948) remarkable fiction is often presented in the form of a monologue, a lone narrator's voice giving a lecture or making a confession. The presence of others may be acknowledged or even responded to, but Salvayre likes to remain in the head and voice of her protagonist. Her damaged or deluded characters range from the Pascal-reading former museum guide driven to murder in *The Power of Flies* (1995, English 2007) to a man with no clue but very set ideas about the art of conversation in *The Lecture* (1999, English 2005). Her satire of contemporary industrial management, *The Award* (1993, English 1997), is a rare superior workplace novel. The novel amounts to the transcript of an awards ceremony at which workers and managers are honored in front of their colleagues, the text alternating between the managers introducing the honorees and then the medal winners' speeches. Even as the expectations of worker loyalty and devotion veer into the absurd, Salvayre's straight-faced presentation sounds—hilariously—authentic.

Belgian author **Jean-Philippe Toussaint**'s (b. 1957) works center on male characters whose lives tend to be adrift, most notably in *The Bathroom* (1985, English 1990), in which the protagonist repeatedly finds himself tempted to withdraw from everyday life by living in his bathtub. Functional and often successful, these characters nevertheless are overwhelmed by the modern world and move along the path of least resistance in these wistful and charmingly screwball tales.

Younger Challengers

The Japanese-born Belgian diplomat's daughter **Amélie Nothomb** (b. 1967) is a veritable pop star in France, complete with trademark black outfit and striking headgear. An air of mystery is fostered by not only her unusual background but also her obsession with writing: she claims to complete four novels each year, only one of which she then selects for publication, with no intention of releasing the rest. As of 2014, she allegedly had finished more than eighty novels but had published only twenty-three.

The occasionally almost sketchy presentation of Nothomb's fiction might suggest that her work is flimsy, but it has considerable depth. A number of her books are autobiographical, including her widely acclaimed inside account of a year working as an office girl employed in mindless and useless tasks at a huge Japanese firm: *Fear and Trembling* (1999, English 2001). It is her novels of childhood and youth that are the most winsome. Although *The Character of Rain* (2000, English 2002) is a surprisingly convincing rendering of the infancy of a very peculiar child, *Loving Sabotage* (1993, English 2000) is her masterpiece. Taking place in the diplomatic compound of Beijing between 1972 and 1975, Nothomb's novel is both a disarming account of childish passions and conflicts and a revealing view of a China still mired in the Cultural Revolution. The exotic setting and the unsettling period in history obviously help supply an underlying tension, which Nothomb balances with the unreality of young Amélie's life in the isolated foreigners' ghetto, the San Li Tun quarter.

In France, **Florian Zeller**'s (b. 1979) well-known public persona clouds an appreciation of his fiction, but his clever novel of provocation, *The Fascination of Evil* (2004, English 2006), shows his promise as a writer. It is narrated by a young French author who travels to Cairo to appear at a book fair. His trip becomes a head-on confrontation with Islam, complicated by the opinionated, Houellebecq-like author who leads him on. Zeller shows himself to be particularly crafty in tying the story together with a clever final twist.

Muriel Barbery's (b. 1969) international best seller, *The Elegance of the Hedgehog* (2006, English 2008), is a subtler satire, though typically French in its fascination with class differences. Its quiet heroines—a well-read but underappreciated concierge and a preteen bent on suicide as a way to avoid winding up as stuck-up and hollow as the rest of her family—and the exotic stranger whose oriental wisdom opens new

---

KEEP IN MIND

- **Marie Darrieussecq**'s (b. 1969) fiction focuses on isolation and the personal, even in her debut novel, *Pig Tales* (1996, English 1997), a fairly heavy-handed political allegory in which the protagonist finds herself metamorphosing into a pig.
- **Didier van Cauwelaert** (b. 1960) addresses issues of identity and perception in his novel *One-Way* (1994, English 2003), in which a French boy is kidnapped as a child and a comedy of errors leads him to be treated as a Moroccan immigrant. *Out of My Head* (2003, English 2004; republished as a movie tie-in under the title *Unknown*) is a novel with a twist reminiscent of Richard Condon's *The Manchurian Candidate* (1959) when the main character, Martin Harris, is released from the hospital and suddenly cannot convince anyone, not even his wife, that he is who he says he is.
- **Benoît Duteurtre**'s (b. 1960) satires of modern life in France, such as *The Little Girl and the Cigarette* (2005, English 2007), are excessively broad but offer some amusement.

(*continued*)

KEEP IN MIND

- **Faïza Guène**'s (b. 1985) fiction is still unpolished, but her first book, describing immigrant and *banlieue* life, ***Kiffe Kiffe Tomorrow*** (published in Great Britain as *Just Like Tomorrow*; 2004, English 2006), offers good insight into what has become an explosive social situation in France.
- **Stéphane Audeguy** (b. 1965) has displayed a knack for novel twists on historical fiction. *The Theory of Clouds* (2005, English 2007) has an appealing framing device in presenting its stories of the meteorologically obsessed, while ***The Only Son*** (2006, English 2008) is a fictional memoir of Jean-Jacques Rousseau's older brother, a premise that allows for an amusing take on both the French history of the times and Rousseau's ideas.

vistas for them are appealingly presented, but the philosophical veneer on display is thin and does not withstand much scrutiny.

Foreigners

The French colonial legacy and the widespread use of the language around the world have produced a large body of French literature written by authors from other countries. Most of them are in the former French colonies, where French is often still an official language and widely used in the educational system. In addition, among authors choosing to write in a language not their own, French is second only to English, and in recent decades, an increasing number of authors have begun writing in French, including Chinese-born **Shan Sa** (b. 1972), Afghan-born **Atiq Rahimi** (b. 1962), and, most famously, **Milan Kundera** (b. 1929).

Russian-born **Andreï Makine** (b. 1957) settled in France in 1987. He is now heralded as a leading French writer, but he was able to get his first books published only by pretending the submitted manuscripts were translations of Russian originals. Much of his fiction centers on Soviet Russia and is written in a style reminiscent of early-twentieth-century Russian authors like Ivan Bunin.

Makine's fiction is very consistent, from the condensed novella of a man who hides behind another's identity, *Music of a Life* (published in Great Britain as *A Life's Music*; 2001, English 2002), to the autobiographical *Dreams of My Russian Summers* (published in Great Britain under its French title, *Le testament français*; 1995, English 1997). The continuing success of his work contrasts with the interest in works by authors writing in Russian about Soviet times, which since 1990 has almost completely dried up in the English-speaking world.

Much of Lebanese-born **Amin Maalouf**'s (b. 1949) fiction is historical, featuring figures from the poet Omar Khayyam in *Samarkand* (1988, English 1992) to Mani, the founder of what became known as Manichaeism, in *The Gardens of Light* (1991, English 1996). Maalouf's characters grapple with life in very unsettled times and places, and many of his novels, such as the biographical *Leo the African* (published in the United States as *Leo Africanus*; 1986, English 1988) and *Balthasar's Odyssey* (2000, English 2003), feature travelers seeking knowledge and engagement with the foreign. *The First Century After Beatrice* (1992, English 1994) is a different sort of fictional thought experiment. Set in the near future, it posits the discovery of a powder that makes it possible to ensure that all one's children will be male, and its widespread use predictably leads to catastrophe. Maalouf uses his science-fiction premise to present and criticize social and cultural norms in which males are valued much more than females and also warns of the political use and abuse of technological and scientific advances.

American-born **Jonathan Littell** (b. 1967) wrote his first novel, a bit of pulp science fiction, *Bad Voltage* (1989), in English and then stunned the French literary world with his second, the epic *The Kindly Ones* (2006, English 2009). An attempt to describe and explain the Nazi horror, written from the perspective of a man who worked at the heart of it and was present at many of the worst outrages, *The Kindly Ones* was a literary sensation, was awarded the Prix Goncourt, and became one of that year's best-selling titles. The massive novel, totaling nearly a thousand pages, divided critics. The scrupulous attention to historical detail is admirable, but Littell's

---

OTHER ESTABLISHED FRENCH AUTHORS

- **Pierre Péju**'s (b. 1946) training in philosophy comes to bear in his works. *The Girl from the Chartreuse* (2002, English 2005), with its lost characters, is both sentimental and touching, whereas *Clara's Tale* (2005, English 2007) is a more complex and very dark novel of the past.
- **Philippe Claudel**'s (b. 1962) novels *Grey Souls* (2003, English 2005, and as *By a Slow River*, 2006) and *Brodeck's Report* (published as *Brodeck* in the United States; 2007, English 2009) are haunting, dark tales of twentieth-century French village lives in the shadows of the two world wars.
- **Jean-Paul Dubois**'s (b. 1950) *Vie française* (published in Great Britain as *A French Life*; 2004, English 2007) is a decent survey of recent French history and society, as told in the story of one man's life.
- **Mathias Énard**'s (b. 1972) five-hundred-page stream-of-consciousness novel *Zone* (2008, English 2010) is a single-sentence tour de force in which the narrator, the French intelligence agent Francis Mirković, reflects on his life and contemporary European history. The topical novel *Street of Thieves* (2012, English 2014), narrated by a young Moroccan against the backdrop of contemporary turmoil in the Arab world, is more conventional in form.

---

narrator, Dr. Maximilien Aue, is not convincing. Aue's own depravity muddles Littell's message, and the book sinks under its own overwhelming weight.

Noir and Beyond: French Crime Fiction

A few French crime novelists besides Georges Simenon have had considerable international success, starting with **Maurice Leblanc** (1864–1941), the creator of Arsène Lupin, but the transition to English has not always been very successful. In many cases, only few works by significant crime novelists are even available in translation, beginning with **Jean-Patrick Manchette** (1942–1995), whose hard-edged and clipped tales are among the best of the darkest French noirs. Manchette's *Fatale* (1977, English 2011) is typical, escalating over barely a hundred pages into a bloodbath that upends the entire sleepy but corrupt social order of Bléville, the city on which the very fatale femme calling herself Aimée Joubert has her sights set. Even fewer of **Didier Daeninckx's** (b. 1949) politically oriented works of fiction are available in English, and the popular and fascinating works by Frédéric Dard (1921–2000), writing under the name **San-Antonio,** also never stood much of a chance in translation, with much of the creative wordplay and spirit of his novels too easily lost. **Thierry Jonquet's** (1954–2009) creepy mystery *Mygale* (published in Great Britain as *Tarantula* and, as the movie tie-in, *The Skin I Live In*; 1984, revised 1995, English 2002), his one novel available in English, keeps readers guessing about the exact identities of several of the characters and the fates others plan for them but neatly ties everything together in the end.

Other authors have fared better by at least appearing regularly in translation. **Tonino Benacquista's** (b. 1961) stand-alone novels are well-written entertainments that thrust the protagonists into murky and dangerous territory, from the art-world thriller *Framed* (1990, English 2006) to *Someone Else* (2001, English 2005), which describes the costs and consequences when two characters wager that they can transform themselves into completely new people. In *Badfellas* (published in the United States as *Malavita* and, as the movie tie-in, *The Family*; 2004, English 2010), American Mafia clan boss Giovanni Manzoni and his family are put in the witness protection program but cannot get settled in the French countryside because they cannot give up their Mafia habits.

Pascal Garnier's (1949–2010) chilling novels, a combination of Simenon and Manchette, shift suddenly from the calm to the shocking in their resolutions. **Jean-Claude Izzo** (1945–2000) describes both atmosphere and attitude in his grim and bloody *Marseilles* trilogy (1995–1998, English 2002–2007). **Fred Vargas's** (b. 1957) police procedurals featuring her Inspector Adamsberg are very leisurely. **Daniel Pennac's** (b. 1944) comic but socially very conscious amateur sleuthing adventures of the Malaussène family in Paris's Belleville district, are enjoyable lighter fare.

Popular Fiction

With isolated exceptions, such as Muriel Barbery's *The Elegance of the Hedgehog,* few of the books by even the most popular French authors have come close to best-selling status in the United States or Great Britain. Nevertheless, several of these works continue to be translated and are at least available in English.

Laurence Cossé's (b. 1950) novels often have sensational premises, including *A Corner of the Veil* (1996, English 1999), which centers on a document that proves the existence of God, and *An Accident in August* (2003, English 2011), the story of an eyewitness to Princess Diana's fatal car crash. **Anna Gavalda**'s (b. 1970) fiction is (just) a cut above generic chick lit, and **Marc Levy**'s (b. 1961) sappy fluff, beginning with *If Only It Were True* (now published as the movie tie-in *Just Like Heaven*; 2000, English 2000), is very light fiction but strikes some popular chords. **Jean-Christophe Rufin**'s (b. 1952) ambitious and exotic historical novels, ranging from *The Siege of Isfahan* (1998, English 2001) to *Brazil Red* (2001, English 2004), are packed with period detail and action, making decent adventure tales. Meanwhile, the prolific **Christian Jacq** (b. 1947) is a bona fide Egyptologist, which lends some authority to his numerous book series set in Pharaonic times.

Spain and Portugal

SPAIN

Miguel de Cervantes's (1547–1616) ***Don Quixote*** (1604/1615, most recently translated in English in 2003 and 2005) is widely considered the first novel of modern Western civilization and remains a cornerstone of contemporary fiction. Fiction flourished in the Spain of that time, with Cervantes just one of many prolific writers, but the mountain that is *Don Quixote* seems to have turned out to be as much a stumbling as a building block for subsequent Spanish authors.

Much of the twentieth century was a relatively barren time in Spain and Portugal while both countries endured increasingly sclerotic authoritarian rule. One individual in each country dominated the era: Francisco Franco in Spain, from 1939 to his death in 1975, and António de Oliveira Salazar in Portugal, where he was prime minister from 1932 until 1968. The prevailing conservatism in these countries extended to cultural matters as well, but once these men were out of power, the transition to democracy came relatively quickly, in 1974 with the Carnation Revolution in Portugal and with a new constitution in Spain in 1978. Further integration into the international community and greater economic growth followed after both countries joined the European Union in 1986. Portuguese and especially Spanish fiction have flourished in recent years under these more welcoming circumstances. Variations on popular historic fiction have been particularly successful, exemplified in **Arturo Pérez-Reverte**'s (b. 1951) works and **Carlos Ruiz Zafón**'s (b. 1964) international best seller *The Shadow of the Wind* (2001, English 2004), which have inspired a seemingly endless spate of imitators.

Among the most damaging and restrictive policies in Franco's Spain was the suppression of any language other than (Castilian) Spanish. Minority languages spoken in areas with distinctive cultural heritages, most notably Catalan, Galician, and Basque, were marginalized, even as their use became an expression of resistance to the regime. Since 1978, though, these languages have enjoyed official status. As a consequence, the literary output in all of them has increased substantially, though many regional writers continue to write in Spanish—or, as in the case of leading Basque author **Bernardo Atxaga** (b. 1951), collaborate on the Spanish translation of their own work.

Writing in Catalan

Catalan has what is roughly estimated to be 10 million speakers, mainly in Catalonia and the Balearic Islands (including Majorca and Ibiza). Catalan also is the official language of Andorra.

Mercè Rodoreda (1908–1983), who spent almost four decades in exile in France and Switzerland after the fall of Barcelona, is widely considered the greatest modern Catalan writer. While already modestly successful before leaving Spain in 1939, she wrote her greatest works abroad, including *The Pigeon Girl* (1962, English 1967, and as

The Time of the Doves, 1980, and *In Diamond Square*, 2013). Narrated by the humble, luckless, and ultimately desperate Natalia, *The Pigeon Girl* is a lyrical stream-of-consciousness narrative of a simple, typical life in the years up to and during the Spanish Civil War. A broader novel with multiple perspectives, *A Broken Mirror* (1974, English 2006) demonstrates Rodoreda's command of tone as she renders perfectly the various voices in a multigenerational family saga revolving around a wonderfully manipulative woman who becomes the family matriarch.

The slim collection *O'Clock* (1980, English 1986) is a fine introduction to the works by the very popular **Quim Monzó** (b. 1952). *O'Clock* consists of small stories in a realist vein that take an idea to an extreme, usually with a sudden twist or surprise, and told with a sense of humor. Quim's approach works even better in a more sustained work such as the novel *The Enormity of the Tragedy* (1989, English 2008). Despite the comic potential of the protagonist's affliction—a case of priapism (a permanent erection)—Monzó does not play it only for laughs. The character's condition is a decidedly mixed blessing and certainly too much for him handle. *The Enormity of the Tragedy*, too, has several darker edges, with an angry young stepdaughter with strong homicidal ambitions as a foil.

MORE CATALAN FICTION

- **Albert Sánchez Piñol's** (b. 1965) *Cold Skin* (2002, English 2005) and *Pandora in the Congo* (2005, English 2008) are interesting modern versions of the classical horror and adventure tales and the end of the age of exploration.
- **Jordi Coca's** (b. 1947) coming-of-age novel, *Under the Dust* (2001, English 2007), takes place in the early years of the Franco dictatorship.
- **Teresa Solana's** (b. 1962) amusing private-detective capers, *A Not So Perfect Crime* (2006, English 2008), *A Shortcut to Paradise* (2007, English 2011), and *The Sound of One Hand Killing* (2011, English 2013), are set in Barcelona's upper-class milieu.

Writing in Basque

The fewer than 1 million Basque speakers are concentrated in the Basque area of Spain and France.

In his realist novels like *The Lone Man* (1994, English 1996) and *The Lone Woman* (1995, English 1999), **Bernardo Atxaga** (b. 1951) addresses Basque separatism. The protagonists in both novels are former terrorists trying to move on with their lives. *The Lone Man*, set during the 1982 World Cup held in Spain, tells the story of a hotel owner harboring two wanted terrorists while also hosting the Polish national soccer team. The novel is a thriller and less introspective than *The Lone Woman*, which focuses on a protagonist trying to find her place in life again after several years in prison while her past continues to haunt her on all sides.

Atxaga's best-known work is the inventive *Obabakoak* (1988, English 1992). This book is more a loose collection of stories within stories (and the occasional essayistic digression) than a full-fledged novel. Despite centering on a Basque village, Obaba, and its colorful inhabitants, many of Atxaga's tales are not localized, his interest here being instead the universal possibilities of life and storytelling. Atxaga returns to Obaba in several other books, though never with the same ebullience as in *Obabakoak*. Of these, *The Accordionist's Son* (2003, English 2007), with its sweep of Basque history from the Spanish Civil War through the present is Atxaga's furthest-reaching attempt to register Basque conditions, including the rise and appeal of the militant separatist organization ETA. Although Atxaga eschews straightforward narrative in all his Obaba books—*Two Brothers* (1985, English 2001), for example, is largely narrated by various animals—this proves distracting in a historical chronicle like *The Accordionist's Son*.

Writing in Galician

The approximately 3 million speakers of Galician are concentrated in the province of Galicia, in the northwest corner of Spain. The language is more similar to Portuguese than to Spanish.

MORE GALICIAN FICTION

- **Xosé Luís Méndez Ferrín**'s (b. 1938) collection is entitled *Them and Other Stories* (English 1996).
- **Carlos Casares**'s (b. 1941) *Wounded Wind* (1967, English 2004) is a novel about Galician life under Franco.
- **Agustín Fernández Paz**'s (b. 1947) works such as the Lovecraftian horror novel *Winter Letters* (1995, English 2015).

Manuel Rivas (b. 1957) is the leading Galician author and is best known for *The Carpenter's Pencil* (1999, English 2001), which contrasts the lives of two very different men, both marked by the Spanish Civil War. The story of a Republican doctor and the man who haunts him as jailer but also acts as a sort of guardian angel, *The Carpenter's Pencil* presents two men in very different circumstances. The rough, uneducated Herbal wields more power but is forced into moral compromises. The pencil of the title is a constant reminder weighing on his conscience, retrieved after the execution of the artist who used it, a man whom Herbal shot to save him from a more painful death. Rivas's layered narrative can be confusing, but it is an affecting tale. *In the Wilderness* (1994, English 2003) has a fairy-tale feel, with characters reembodied as animals and a magical mix of the contemporary with the historical and mythical, though again Rivas's elaborate structure of overlapping yet separate stories is a denser read than might be expected of such a playful premise and setting.

Spanish Fiction Under Franco

The title figure in **Camilo José Cela**'s (b. 1916–2002) *Pascual Duarte's Family* (1942, English 1946, and as *The Family of Pascual Duarte*, 1964) is a criminal offering what amounts to both a confession and a defense, describing his poor circumstances and the violence of his life in a brutal, graphic story that is one of the highpoints of twentieth-century Spanish fiction. Its grim realism also set a tone found in much postwar Spanish fiction.

Although several important works are available in English, an astonishing amount of the work by 1989 Nobel laureate Cela still has not been translated, especially his more experimental fiction. An extraordinarily busy novel even by Cela's standards, *The Hive* (1951, English 1953) employs a vast number of characters to depict life in Madrid shortly after the end of the Spanish Civil War. This lively novel also is one of Cela's best, with many interlinking pieces, all taking place over only a few days, evoking the vibrancy of a society under a dictatorship. *Mazurka for Two Dead Men* (1983, English 1992) also is set during the civil war itself. Cela's contrapuntal presentation is used to good effect in this novel full of violence, death, and vengeance, which focuses on two deaths, years apart. *Christ Versus Arizona* (1989, English 2007) is a monologue without paragraph or sentence breaks, in which the narrator confesses his uncertainty in a story that seems to be a defense of the looseness of the oral narrative rather than any written record as a way of holding on to history. Its Wild West setting is far away from Cela's usual Spanish stories, but here again it is mainly about the telling. Similarly, his cryptic *Boxwood* (1999, English 2002) is a culmination of his experimental efforts.

Several of **Miguel Delibes**'s (1920–2010) realist novels center on a brief time of transition. In *The Path* (1950, English 1961), the young protagonist is about to leave behind village life to attend school in the city, while *Five Hours with Mario* (1966, English 1988) is essentially a widow's monologue about her deceased husband and their lives together. These novels of reflection and reminiscence, specifically of a certain idealized type of Spanish life, suggest the alternative world to the Francoist system. *The Wars of Our Ancestors* (1974, English 1992) transcribes a week-long dialogue between a doctor and a prisoner recounting his life and his almost accidental crimes of violence. The novel critiques the culture of *machismo,* honor, and violence carried down over generations in this fundamentally good character who does not fit into this kind of society, depicting the psychological and cultural impact of Spanish rural society on the individual.

Despite being a master of realist description, especially of the Spanish countryside, Delibes also wrote a great experimental allegory, *The Hedge* (1969, English 1983), a Kafkaesque tale whose original Spanish title, *Parábola del náufrago* (*Parable of a Shipwrecked Man*), is more

---

KEEP IN MIND

- **Carmen Martín Gaite**'s (1925–2000) evocative novels of memory and storytelling include *The Farewell Angel* (1994, English 1999), *Variable Cloud* (1992, English 1995), and the autobiographical *The Back Room* (1978, English 1983).
- **Juan Benet**'s (1927–1993) dense, dark flowing narratives of Spanish country life are *Return to Región* (1967, English 1985) and *A Meditation* (1969, English 1982).
- **Juan Marsé**'s (b. 1933) realist novels take place in Spain under Franco.
- **Esther Tusquets**'s (1936–2012) novels focus on the inner lives of women.

---

immediately revealing. The world presented here is dominated by a capitalist monolith in a supertotalitarian world. The novel's protagonist's role is that of an accountant who is permitted only to add (but not to subtract or multiply) abstract quantities. When he is no longer capable of functioning in the system, worn down by the dehumanizing nature of his job, he is sent to a retreat. There he becomes obsessed with a hedge, which Delibes uses as a rather obvious symbol. In many of his works, Delibes is concerned with technological development and the destruction of the natural world, and in *The Hedge* he creates a remarkable dystopia, abstract enough that it has aged well.

Beyond Franco

Juan Goytisolo (b. 1931) has spent most of his life outside Spain, in Paris and Morocco, but he has continued to write about his homeland. In these works, Goytisolo is sharply critical not only of the Franco regime but also of the conservatism of Spanish culture and the Catholic Church. With his idealization of Moorish culture and an unrepressed attitude toward sexuality, Goytisolo's sympathies throughout his work are always with the exiled and excluded.

Goytisolo's trilogy that begins with *Marks of Identity* (1966, English 1969) established him as a major author. Its Paris-based protagonist, the photographer Álvaro Mendiola, shares a biography with the author. Mendiola confronts what he sees as the failures of Spain, from its colonial past to its enfeebling present-day conservatism. Raised as a privileged child of a family that has benefited over the centuries from the exploitation he deplores, Mendiola also feels tremendous guilt. Goytisolo describes the stations of his life and moves his protagonist toward possible redemption. The novel is ultimately a challenge to an ingrained way of thinking that sees liberation in an unloosened language, reflected in Goytisolo's no longer strictly adhering to rules of grammar and punctuation, thereby allowing his words to flow freely.

The trilogy continues with *Count Julian* (1970, English 1974), which takes its title from the historical figure from Ceuta who aided the Moors in their invasion of Spain in 711, leading to the Islamic dominion over the Iberian Peninsula that lasted until the fifteenth century. The novel presents the reflective wanderings of an exile in Tangier. Though unnamed, he clearly is an extension of the Mendiola/Goytisolo figure in *Marks of Identity*. The meandering thoughts in this hypnotic narrative return repeatedly to detested Spain, as he vividly imagines its modern-day reconquest by the Moors. Despite being brutally critical of Spanish culture, *Count Julian* is also an homage, reflected in the many references in the text to and quotations from many Spanish writers. The concluding volume, *Juan the Landless* (1975, English 1977, revised 2009), is the least conventional in the trilogy. The novel is a loose collection of episodes and the protagonist's thoughts, opinions, and rants. Goytisolo's prose style drives much of his fiction, especially in *Juan the Landless* with its run-on (and cut-off) sentences and lack of capitalization at the beginning of his chapters. The novel ends memorably with the Spanish words collapsing into the phonetic and then mutating into the Arabic, a transformation that marks the abandonment of one culture and the embrace of another.

The compressed *Quarantine* (1991, English 1994) is a typical creative leap for Goytisolo, who is always willing to try a new or different approach and makes a great effort to match style and content. In the forty chapters of this novella, the narrator grapples with the death of a close friend as he accompanies the deceased on her forty-day journey through the underworld, providing a structure that is both Dantesque and true to Islamic tradition (which foresees such a period between death and eternity). *Quarantine* is a trance-like prose poem and a prayer for the dead that draws inspiration from and parallels to the first Persian Gulf War and the Spanish Civil War, as well as many artistic representations of death and the afterlife.

The Garden of Secrets (1997, English 2000) is divided into twenty-eight chapters, one for each letter of the Arabic alphabet. The novel centers on a reading circle of narrators trying to piece together a story about a poet who was a friend of Federico García Lorca and was arrested in 1936. With each narrator presenting a different part of the story in a different voice and style, *The Garden of Secrets* is a dazzling display of Goytisolo's talents. Though many of his works are clearly meant to be read aloud, in *The Garden of Secrets* he most obviously embraces the possibilities of shared storytelling.

Goytisolo often directly addresses (and attacks) history in his works, and *The Marx Family Saga* (1993, English 1996) may well be his most accomplished novel. Unusual for its non-Spanish focus, Goytisolo imagines that Karl Marx and his family have survived to the present day, now recognizing that Marx's ideas have failed and been abused over the years. Goytisolo is in complete command of his material here, and despite metafictional touches and the juggling of various stories, he presents a brilliant portrait of the failures of an ideology of which he fundamentally is convinced. A very funny novel, *The Marx Family Saga* is a modern classic that is by far the best literary response to the collapse of Communism in Eastern Europe.

Javier Marías's (b. 1951) novels usually have very little plot, but his polished and precise style, along with the compelling character development of his protagonists, exerts a strong fascination. Marías has built up a loosely connected collection of often self-referential works that constantly explore questions of identity. His stories are often based on actual autobiography, even though that, too, is partially fictional: Marías is one of the claimants to the throne of the semifictional Kingdom of Redonda, an uninhabited island in the Caribbean, and he has played that role to the hilt.

The Man of Feeling (1986, English 2003) displays the ease with which Marías can spin intertwined stories. Narrated by an opera singer, it tells of lonely existences adrift and reaching out to others but rarely able to connect. It is a relatively straightforward tale, the art here mainly in the telling, but also hints at some of the narrative games Marías uses in his later works.

In *Dark Back of Time* (1998, English 2001), a narrator named Javier Marías is the author of a novel, *All Souls*, set at the University of Oxford, who finds that after its publication the people on whom he had modeled his characters start to acquire the characteristics of their fictional counterparts. *Dark Back of Time* is a marvelous metafictional companion piece to the real Marías's *All Souls* (1989, English 1992), a novel that describes British academic life based on the author's own experiences. Marías brings an almost documentary approach to *Dark Back of Time*, complete with photographs, resulting in a very amusing novel of a flummoxed author and the blurred lines between fiction and reality (and cause and effect).

Many of Marías's works of fiction contain an abundance of literary and philosophical digressions. His trilogy *Your Face Tomorrow*, consisting of *Fever and Spear* (2002, English 2005), *Dance and Dream* (2004, English 2006), and *Poison, Shadow and Farewell* (2007, English 2009), is the work most representative of this tendency. Despite the promising premise of a narrator finding himself courted by and then in the employ of a branch of the British secret service, these works are largely uneventful. Even though he has a name here—or rather several variations of one—the narrator turns out to be that same unnamed protagonist from *All Souls*, but in this trilogy Marías goes beyond the involved games of *Dark Back of Time*. Moving in a world of incomplete knowledge and guesswork, in which his main functions are to observe and translate, the character has ample opportunity to reflect on the past, present, and future. Much of the trilogy has a rambling quality, as the tales loop around the small events described in the works, and Marías's style, with its long, winding sentences, accentuates a sense of unknowability while also lending the narrative a mesmerizing quality. An intellectual thriller without the easy satisfactions of secret missions brought to an end and all the questions answered, *Your Face Tomorrow* is a remarkable exploration of confronting a world of endless uncertainties.

Most of the examples of **Enrique Vila-Matas's** (b. 1948) extensive body of work available in English, including *Bartleby & Co.* (2000, English 2004), *Montano* (published in the United States as *Montano's Malady*; 2002, English 2007), and *Never Any End to Paris* (2003, English 2011), are writer-focused novels consisting of a small fictional foundation that serves mainly to support much larger essayistic ambitions. The narrator of *Bartleby & Co.* is a man who once aspired to be a writer but now dedicates himself to tracking those who, like Herman Melville's Bartleby, chose not to write or found they no longer could. A paean to not writing, Vila-Matas's effortless litany of citations and cross-references is a feast for book lovers, as is *Montano*, in which the protagonist is literally overwhelmed by the literary. He is hardly able to separate fact from fiction, identifies far too closely with the Swiss writer Robert Walser, and encounters Nobel laureate Imre Kertész, French writer Jean Echenoz, and other contemporary authors.

Vila-Matas's *Dublinesque* (2010, English 2012) is both an homage to Joyce's *Ulysses* and an elegy to the traditional world of literary publishing. Its protagonist, Samuel Riba, a retired publisher of the old school, finds himself adrift when he is no longer immersed in his business yet still sees nearly everything around him in literary terms.

KEEP IN MIND

- **Julián Ríos's** (b. 1941) fascinating, occasionally baffling, postmodernist works range from the massive footnote- and endnote-filled *Larva: A Midsummer Night's Babel* (1983, English 1990) and the similarly word-game-heavy *Poundemonium* (1986, English 1997) to the somewhat more accessible literary love letters of *Loves That Bind* (1995, English 1998) and the artist portrait *Monstruary* (1999, English 2001).
- **Antonio Muñoz Molina** (b. 1956) writes about uprooted lives and twentieth-century persecution in novels such as the collage-like *Sepharad* (2001, English 2003) and *In the Night of Time* (2009, English 2013), as well as his novella *In Her Absence* (2001, English 2006), a love story of an unlikely couple in which the man suddenly becomes convinced that, despite her appearance and

(continued)

KEEP IN MIND

actions being identical to his wife's, the woman he has returned home to is a simulacrum and not the woman he married.

- **Rafael Chirbes's** (1949–2015) work remains largely unavailable in English, despite the promise shown by his debut novel, *Mimoun* (1988, English 1992), describing the experiences of a Spanish teacher and would-be writer in Morocco. His novel *On the Edge* (2013, English 2016) is one of the major works of fiction about Spain during the recent financial crisis.
- **Javier Cercas's** (b. 1962) *Soldiers of Salamis* (2001, English 2004), *The Speed of Light* (2005, English 2006), and, his view of the failed 1981 military coup in Spain, *The Anatomy of a Moment* (2009, English 2011) are thought-provoking examinations of recent history and writing.

The Popular Explosion

There recently has been a remarkable explosion of popular historical fiction from Spain. **Arturo Pérez-Reverte** (b. 1951) led the charge with his globe-trotting historical thrillers, including a series featuring a soldier, Captain Alatriste, in seventeenth-century Europe. Pérez-Reverte's frequently humorous novels rarely tax readers with their skillfully used cultural or historical references. These novels are among the best of this sort of swashbuckling entertainment currently being produced. Pérez-Reverte's elaborate mystery *The Club Dumas* (published in Great Britian as *The Dumas Club*; 1993, English 1996) is typical in its knowledgeable presentation of a specific field—in this case, the world of used books and bibliophiles—but also rarely lets the action flag. **Carlos Ruiz Zafón's** (b. 1964) widely imitated international best seller, *The Shadow of the Wind* (2001, English 2004), stirs together a historical setting (Franco's Barcelona), bits of romance, a good deal of mystery, and, with its inspired "Cemetery of Forgotten Books," a strong bookish element as well. It is a good read but has spawned far too many books that follow his formula and take on the same tone.

Even pale imitations of *The Shadow of the Wind* are preferable to the many Spanish works that try to emulate Dan Brown's success with *The*

Da Vinci Code (2003). With the Catholic Church still a powerful entity, a rich artistic tradition, and recent experiences with fascism, monarchy, and democracy, Spain has proved to be particularly fertile ground for historical conspiracy fiction, even though many authors still go to the Vatican as conspiracy central. **Javier Sierra**'s (b. 1971) works, such as *The Lady in Blue* (1998, English 2007), are fairly typical, though even he felt he finally had to go full Da Vinci in *The Secret Supper* (2004, English 2006), in which the painting *The Last Supper* holds all the clues. Other titles that can be lumped together are **Matilde Asensi**'s (b. 1962) *The Last Cato* (2001, English 2005) and **Jorge Molist**'s (b. 1951) contemporary thriller of Knights Templar secrets, *The Ring* (2004, English 2008). One can only hope that this trend has bottomed out with **Juan Gómez-Jurado**'s (b. 1977) *God's Spy* (2006, English 2007), in which a serial killer is taking out cardinals in the Vatican.

Ildefonso Falcones's (b. 1959) Ken Follett–size epic, *Cathedral of the Sea* (2006, English 2008), set in the fourteenth century, cannot entirely ignore the church angle either but is at least a broader work of historical fiction that Falcones tries to make more than a far-fetched conspiracy story. While that offers some relief, Falcones's writing does not match his long-winded ambitions, producing a passable but unexceptional read.

Mysteries and Other Thrillers

Spain's recent history and the rapid changes during the post-Franco era are particularly well depicted in **Manuel Vázquez Montalbán**'s (1939–2003) novels featuring the famous detective and gourmet Pepe Carvalho. First introduced in the groundbreaking (but still untranslated) *Yo maté a Kennedy* (*I Killed Kennedy*, 1972), Carvalho is a CIA operative who worked as a bodyguard for John F. Kennedy and went on to become a Barcelona-based private investigator. Blending social and political criticism with hedonistic enjoyment and some metaphysics and set both in Spain and abroad, Vázquez Montalbán's Carvalho novels extend considerably beyond mere crime solving.

Writers like **Ray Loriga** (b. 1967), **Rafael Reig** (b. 1963), and **José Carlos Somoza** (b. 1959) have tried their hands at a variety of thrillers that frequently incorporate elements of science fiction. Loriga's *My Brother's Gun* (1995, English 1997) is a novel about a sharp, stylish, angry young man exploring how the media latch onto a crime, and the effect of the distorted coverage on those involved. The futuristic *Tokyo Doesn't Love Us Anymore* (1999, English 2003) comes disturbingly close to current realities, its narrator a salesman who deals drugs that allow either short- or long-term memory to be eroded. With the narrator himself in a trancelike state, the novel is a surreal journey of wishful forgetting and ugly realities in an odd mix of the hip and the well worn, too often reminiscent of the fictions of the likes of J. G. Ballard, William Burroughs, and Philip K. Dick.

Rafael Reig's *Blood on the Saddle* (2001, English 2005) and *A Pretty Face* (2004, English 2007) also are set in a slightly skewed reality. In both novels, Reig blends pulp crime fiction with science fiction tropes in a world where the Iberian Peninsula has been taken over by the United States. *A Pretty Face* is posthumously narrated by a murder victim, with the private eye Carlos Clot figuring in both. The roller-coaster twists and turns of these dense dystopian fictions can be confounding, but the sheer creativity of all this makes them worth a look.

José Carlos Somoza is harder to pin down. Some of his novels, such as the disappointing *Zig Zag* (2006, English 2007), are straight out of the Michael Crichton playbook, but others are more cleverly conceived. In *The Athenian Murders* (2000, English 2002), Somoza uses Greek philosophy in a murder mystery set in classical times. Whereas much of the text is presented as a record from those times, a translator (from the ancient Greek) of that account makes his presence felt in what turns out to be an inspired twist. For Somoza, it is all about the ideas, and *The Art of Murder* (2001, English 2004) also has some creative premises, including a new art craze, "hyperdramatic art," in which real people pose as the artworks. Somoza has some difficulty managing this novel of ideas and, as in *Zig Zag*, draws everything out far too long, but his thrillers are consistently among the most thought-provoking ones.

PORTUGAL

Eça de Queirós (1845–1900) is the leading Portuguese novelist in the grand European realist tradition, but otherwise Portuguese literature seems dominated by the offbeat. This small country was once the seat of an outsized empire, but much of its fiction is inward looking, a trait that has become more noticeable with the rise of a vibrant and largely independent postcolonial literature in Brazil and Lusophone Africa. Although many of the works by leading modern Portuguese authors can be considered experimental, they also rely on the familiar with an eye to renewal rather than just novelty that either explicitly or implicitly continues to draw on works by earlier masters. Most prominently, the classic national epic of Portugal in the age of discovery, **Luis Vaz de Camões**'s (1524–1580) *The Lusiads* (1572; many English translations), has reverberated through to modern times, most obviously in **António Lobo Antunes**'s (b. 1942) postcolonial echo, *The Return of the Caravels* (1988, English 2002), in which the contemporary world and the world of *The Lusiads* overlap.

The many-faced poet **Fernando Pessoa** (1888–1935) casts the longest shadow on Portuguese literature. Despite publishing very little during his life, Pessoa created dozens of false artistic identities for himself, including several fully realized heteronyms with their own distinctive personal histories, styles, and interests, and he seemed as obsessed with falsifying life as creating literature. The posthumous prose collection generally known as *The Book of Disquiet* and attributed to yet another heteronym, the bookkeeper Bernardo Soares, was published in four different English translations in 1991 alone. The 2001 Allen Lane edition (published as a Penguin Classics paperback in 2002) of Richard Zenith's translation is the most comprehensive version of Pessoa's work available in English. The work not only represents the synthesis of Pessoa's literary ambitions, but it also is a fundamental piece of twentieth-century literature that continues to be an important sourcebook and touchstone, as significant to Portuguese literature as Shakespeare is to English or Goethe to German. Even though later Portuguese authors have not gone to Pessoa's extremes of invention and falsification, he clearly inspired and influenced many of them, including Antunes, **Gonçalo M. Tavares** (b. 1970), and Nobel laureate **José Saramago** (1922–2010), who resurrected one of Pessoa's more famous heteronyms, Ricardo Reis (along with Pessoa himself), in *The Year of the Death of Ricardo Reis* (1984, English 1991).

José Saramago's (1922–2010) novels are often built on a striking premise like the mass affliction that strikes almost everyone in a city in *Blindness* (1995, English 1997), the Iberian Peninsula loosened from its European moorings and floating out to sea in *The Stone Raft* (1986, English 1994), or a proofreader's history-revising intrusion in a text in *The History of the Siege of Lisbon* (1989, English 1996). But readers are drawn into these scenarios by the fantastical elements and also by how Saramago presents the very mundane consequences. In *Death with Interruptions* (2005, English 2008), for example, death suddenly refuses to strike anyone within the confines of one country, but the realized dream of eternal life jeopardizes everything from the jobs of undertakers and life insurance salesmen to a church that promises a hereafter, as well as the state itself.

The Stone Raft, written around the time of the ascension of Portugal and Spain to what was then the European Economic Community (now the European Union), is an obvious political allegory, with Iberia cut off from Europe and adrift in the Atlantic. With a small cast of characters on their own pilgrimage at the center of the story, Saramago strikes a marvelous balance between the personal and the larger scale.

Saramago presents the consequences of his premises on society at large and especially national institutions, most obviously in the sly *Seeing* (2004, English 2006), a novel taking place several years later in the same country as *Blindness*. In what is taken to be an act of unconscionable subversion, a large majority of voters submit blank votes in the government's elections, a threat to the existing order that drives the state to increasingly desperate reactions, none of which moves an implacable electorate. These novels emerge from the Portuguese experience, but Saramago's abstractions take them considerably beyond it, making many of them seem like universal fables.

In several works, Saramago rewrites history or has his characters do so. *The Gospel According to Jesus Christ* (1991, English 1993) presents an alternative version of the Christ story, using the historical record but suggesting alternative motivations and details that give a whole new meaning to the foundations of Christianity. For better and worse, this is a religious work, and for all its literary merit, it is very much a theological thought exercise. *The History of the Siege of Lisbon* is a wonderful work of reinvention in which a proofreader inserts a single word into a work of history, altering it so that the record contradicts the traditional account and claims that the Crusaders had *not* come to the aid of the Portuguese at the siege of Lisbon. Even though the mistake is discovered, it cannot be entirely erased, and readers are alerted to it only by an errata slip. Among the unexpected consequences is how the proofreader deals with his mistake and offers an alternative Portuguese history based on this slightly different turn of events. The connection between reality and fiction, and the subjective nature of recording any history or telling any story—a recurring theme in Saramago's fiction—is especially pronounced in *The History of the Siege of Lisbon*.

Marked by long sentences and unbroken paragraphs, Saramago's work can be challenging, but for the most part, it is surprisingly approachable. Similarly, **António Lobo Antunes's** (b. 1942) fiction is often dense and, at first sight, considerably more daunting, but it is not inaccessible. The initial challenge is almost entirely visual: many of his novels are marked by paragraph breaks in the middle of a sentence, which is hard not to see as a typesetter's recurring slip and takes some getting used to.

In his portrayals, Antunes, a psychiatrist, strips his characters to their often very disturbed essence, often using multiple narrators and different perspectives in narratives that rarely unfold chronologically. These novels are not meant to be straightforward but curl back on themselves, are full of repetition, and mix the real and the surreal. With their visceral descriptions of an almost always ugly world, Antunes's work can seem bleak. Despite some humor, most of it is black, black stuff.

The colonial wars, which Antunes experienced firsthand as a military doctor in Angola, and the personal toll they took, figure prominently in his work. His early, more conventional novels, including *South of Nowhere* (1979, English 1983) and *Knowledge of Hell* (1980, English 2008), are searing confrontations with the war and the Portugal to which its protagonists return. Other novels are also built around Portuguese history and conditions but are more surreal in their presentation. *The Return of the Caravels* (1988, English 2002), a counterpart to Camões's *The Lusíads,* and *The Inquisitors' Manual* (1996, English 2003), Antunes's most obvious reckoning with the five decades of dictatorship in Portugal, are among the best in suggesting how much the past weighs on the present as he interweaves the two.

The remarkably talented **Gonçalo M. Tavares** (b. 1970) is the most promising contemporary Portuguese writer. His O Bairro (The Neighborhood) series consists to date of nearly a dozen short works inspired by literary figures, such as *Mister Brecht* (2004, English 2006) and *Mister Calvino* (2005, English 2007). The short stories and pieces in these works are reminiscent of Bertolt Brecht's *Stories of Mr. Keuner* (English 2001), with Tavares showing an astonishing range in his clever use of influence and reference. A larger selection of these works is now available collected as *The Neighborhood* (English 2012).

Each of the volumes of Tavares's O Reino (The Kingdom) quartet— *A Man: Klaus Klump* (2003, English 2014), *Joseph Walser's Machine* (2004, English 2012), *Jerusalem* (2004, English 2009), and *Learning to Pray in the Age of Technique* (2007, English 2011)—is a close study

KEEP IN MIND

- **Lídia Jorge**'s (b. 1946) *The Painter of Birds* (1998, English 2001) is about a woman whose identity is rooted in her complex relationship with her peripatetic father.
- **José Luis Peixoto**'s (b. 1974) *The Implacable Order of Things* (published in Great Britain as *Blank Gaze*; 2000, English 2008) is a gentle novel about rural Portuguese life.

of individuals; *Joseph Walser's Machine*, with its depiction of the title character as a cog in the machineries of modernity, is the standout.

The Portuguese islands of the Azores, farther from Lisbon than London, are small worlds of their own in the Atlantic, and Azorean-born **João de Melo**'s (b. 1949) *My World Is Not of This Kingdom* (1983, English 2003) is about these isolated specks of land. The town at the novel's center is a rotten place where evil—mainly in the form of the representatives of officialdom, the mayor and the priest—is only eventually surmounted. A story of excesses and abjectness, the colorful narrative creates a kaleidoscopic picture of an unusual world. Like the islands itself, it seems to float halfway between Latin American magical realism and continental neorealism.

Italy

Much of Italian fiction has been translated into English, but on the whole, Italian writers do not seem to have been able to establish themselves as firmly in the English-speaking world as have those from France, Germany, and Russia. Even the greatest prose classics, such as **Alessandro Manzoni**'s (1785–1873) *The Betrothed* (1827, English 1828 and numerous times since), are not widely read, and a prominent author like **Luigi Pirandello** (1867–1936) is best known for his plays while his worthwhile fiction is generally neglected. The range of novels, from the comic self-examination in **Italo Svevo**'s (1861–1928) *Confessions of Zeno* (1923, English 1930, and as *Zeno's Conscience*, 2001) to **Ignazio Silone**'s (1900–1978) anti-Fascist political works, *Fontamara* (1933, English 1934) and *Bread and Wine* (1937, English 1936), or **Cesare Pavese**'s (1908–1950) novels, may have led to the impression that Italian literature has little consistency.

Several of the writers born around World War I are those who have long dominated Italian fiction in English translation. **Giorgio**

Bassani (1916–2000) wrote mainly about Jewish life, especially under the Fascists, and his famous, haunting novel of doomed nobility and unrequited first love, *The Garden of the Finzi-Continis* (1962, English 1965, 1977), is representative of his work. Although **Primo Levi** (1919–1987) is best known for his nonfiction, his talents extended beyond that. His novel *If Not Now, When?* (1982, English 1985, 2015) explores partisan life in World War II, and the enjoyable *The Monkey's Wrench* (published in Great Britain as *The Wrench*; 1978, English 1986, 2015) is about a crane rigger who has worked all over the world sharing stories with a Levi-like narrator. The joy with which manual labor is presented here—in a novel in which the characters travel to Moscow—can make it seem downright Soviet, yet Levi's voices are convincing. While some of Levi's short stories deal with the Nazi-related subject matter for which his nonfiction is well known, some are very different in style and content.

Alberto Moravia's (1907–1990) work spanned much of the twentieth century, and he long was one of Italy's most prominent authors. His often sexually frank novels and their depiction of bourgeois life hold up well, but it is difficult to choose particular highlights in his large œuvre. Even though his characters do not always win readers' sympathies, Moravia's use of description and dialogue explain, if not excuse, their actions.

Moravia burst on the scene with *The Indifferent Ones* (1929, English 1932), employing a plain realism that was unusual for the time and foreshadowed much of his later fiction. Among his notable works are the adolescent tale and treatment of class, *Agostino* (1944, English 1947, 2014); *A Ghost at Noon* (now published as *Contempt*; 1954, English 1955), with its film industry background and marital tension; *Two Women* (1957, English 1958), a mother–daughter tale set during wartime; and *The Lie* (1965, English 1966), the diary of a writer frustrated in his attempts to capture the authentic in a work of fiction. Among his more outlandish works is *Two: A Phallic Novel* (published in Great Britain as *The Two of Us*; 1971, English 1972), in which the screenwriter, Federico, who has always been in the habit of talking to and arguing with his penis, continues his lively debate with his libidinal alter ego—and finds himself outmatched by his organ.

Natalia Ginzburg's (1916–1991) assured fiction creates a cumulative effect in which the initial sense of calm and control is eventually displaced by the very human emotions she describes. She is particularly skillful in presenting relationships and the female point of view in the novel *All Our Yesterdays* (1952, English 1956, originally *Dead Yesterdays* in Great Britain and *A Light for Fools* in the United States), set during World War II, as well as the epistolary *No Way* (published in Great Britian as *Dear Michael*; 1973, English 1974) and *The City and the House* (1984, English 1987), in which the letter form accentuates how every character is, in a way, an island.

Gesualdo Bufalino's (1920–1996) first novel, *The Plague-Sower* (1981, English 1988), was based on his experiences in a sanatorium where he was treated for tuberculosis at the end of World War II. The novel's fatalism and intense evocations of memory are found throughout much of his work. Death, and the understanding that it must be confronted as there is no escaping its finality, overshadows almost all of Bufalino's fiction, yet his novels are not gloomy. An adept writer, Bufalino often surprises with his subtle literary trickery. *Night's Lies* (published in the United States as *Lies of the Night*; 1988, English 1990), a novel in which each of four condemned men tells tales during the night before they are to be executed, is typical of Bufalino's deceptive narratives.

Many of the great **Italo Calvino**'s (1923–1985) works are fables, often fantastical. In *The Baron in the Trees* (1957, English 1959), a boy climbs up a tree and spends the rest of his life there, and in *The Cloven Viscount* (1952, English 1962), a seventeenth-century viscount's body is cut in half by a cannonball in battle, with the halves going on to lead separate lives until their actions bring them together again. Much of Calvino's work moves well into the realm of science fiction, especially the tales around the being called Qfwfq in collections like *Cosmicomics* (1965, English 1968), with its very broad humor. Other works are more ethereal, such as *Invisible Cities* (1972, English 1974), a collection of short, evocative pieces in which Marco Polo reports to Kublai Khan from cities in his vast empire. Though hardly typical of his work, it may be his most representative fiction. Calvino was also a member

of the Oulipo, which influenced much of his literary experimentation, most obviously and most enjoyably in *If on a Winter's Night a
Traveler* (1979, English 1981), a self-referential work of fiction full of
misdirection and several genre parodies, with the reader an active par-
ticipant in the unfolding experiences.

Just as Calvino's works transcend fantasy, **Leonardo Sciascia**'s
(1921–1989) are far more than simple mysteries. Sciascia's native Sicily
was the setting for most of his books, which often took on the Mafia, as
well as local political failures. An exception is his novel *The Council of
Egypt* (1963, English 1966), one of his best works, set in the time of the
French Revolution and dealing with history and falsification.

The early works of **Antonio Tabucchi** (1943–2012) are quasi mysteries, in which the author plays games with the reader, rarely ending
with a clear resolution. Tabucchi's interest is more philosophical than
the practical whodunit (or who is it, as identity is always a central issue
in his fiction). In *Indian Nocturne* (1984, English 1988), for example,

---

KEEP IN MIND

- One hundred very short and playfully metaphysical "novels" are collected in **Giorgio Manganelli**'s (1922–1990) *Centuria* (1979, English
  2005).
- **Giuseppe Tomasi di Lampedusa**'s (1896–1957) *The Leopard* (1958,
  English 1960) is a tale of late-nineteenth-century Sicily that became an
  international best seller and enjoys continued popularity.
- Despite the wordplay that is necessarily lost in translation, the mayhem
  of language and communication in **Carlo Emilio Gadda**'s (1893–1973)
  impressive fiction, *That Awful Mess on Via Merulana* (1957, English
  1965), makes for a novel that is more than a mere murder mystery.
- **Dino Buzzati**'s (1906–1972) *The Tartar Steppe* (1940, English 1952) is
  a classic about how life can simply pass by.
- **Tommaso Landolfi** (1908–1979) wrote creative and often gothic short
  stories.
- **Luigi Malerba**'s (1927–2008) fascinating, reality-questioning narratives are *The Serpent* (1965, English 1968) and *What Is This Buzzing,
  Do You Hear It Too?* (1968, English 1969).

a character travels to India looking for a missing friend, but the foreign and exotic locale dominates the short narrative. In *The Edge of the Horizon* (1986, English 1990), a morgue attendant is obsessed with learning the identity of a corpse, a "Carlo Nobodi."

Many of Tabucchi's books are set in Portugal, and he clearly feels a close affinity to that country's language and literature. Indeed, one of his finest novels is **Requiem: A Hallucination** (1991, English 1994), which he wrote in Portuguese (and which was translated into Italian by another writer). An homage to Portugal and especially Lisbon, as well as to the wonderful Fernando Pessoa (1888–1935), whose life and writing inform much of Tabucchi's work, *Requiem* is an appealing "hallucination" (as the subtitle has it). **Pereira Declares** (published in Great Britain first as *Declares Pereira* and now as *Pereira Maintains*; 1994, English 1995) also is set in Portugal, just before World War II but is a more realist work, with Tabucchi subtitling it *A True Account* (or, in the American edition, *A Testimony*). Pereira, the lead character, is in charge of a newspaper's cultural page but finds politics inescapable in Fascist Portugal. Tabucchi draws a sympathetic portrait of a man who is set in his ways and enjoys certain simple pleasures but ultimately finds himself morally obligated to take a stand. **The Missing Head of Damasceno Monteiro** (1997, English 1999), which takes place in contemporary Portugal, is about a journalist covering a sensational murder case, and while hardly a mystery thriller, its examination of media manipulation and conflicting interests, as well as a protagonist who would rather be writing a study of Elio Vittorini, produces an unusual but enjoyable read.

In novels such as **Inferences from a Sabre** (1984, English 1990) and *A Different Sea* (1991, English 1993), **Claudio Magris** (b. 1939) explores twentieth-century history, basing his stories and characters on historical facts and figures. His most ambitious work, **Blindly** (2005, English 2010), is presented in an almost musical counterpoint by an institutionalized man who appropriates the voices of other historical figures for his narrative. The layers of history in this novel range from a Danish seaman who travels from the frontiers of Australia to Iceland in the nineteenth century to the narrator's own experiences in Josip Tito's infamous Goli Otok gulag in Yugoslavia after World War II.

Umberto Eco's (b. 1932) medieval thriller, *The Name of the Rose* (1980, English 1983), was an international blockbuster and led to a still continuing parade of imitators. Of all the historical-intellectual mysteries published over the last forty years, few measure up to Eco's work. With its vivid and accessible presentation of scholarly life in medieval times and the satisfying mystery behind it, as well as Eco's sense of humor, *The Name of the Rose* remains exemplary. Eco has continued to use some of these same elements in his later fiction but has been unable to find a guise to utilize his scholarship as naturally and convincingly as he did in *The Name of the Rose*. Of his other works, *Foucault's Pendulum* (1988, English 1989) is the most successful, helped by the mystery and conspiracy in which the ideas are couched. *The Mysterious Flame of Queen Loana* (2004, English 2005) has an appealing premise, of an older man who wakes up with a peculiar case of amnesia: all his personal memories have been lost, but he remembers everything he has read. The story of his struggle to find what he has lost provides an interesting consideration of memory, meaning, and identity.

The works of Swiss Italian author **Fleur Jaeggy** (b. 1940) and the author writing under the pseudonym **Elena Ferrante** can be uncomfortably intense in their brutally honest descriptions of women's lives. Jaeggy's *SS Proleterka* (2001, English 2003) is a disturbing account of a daughter's attempt to come to terms with the distant man she knows as her father, while in the more successful *Sweet Days of Discipline* (1989, English 1991), the protagonist, largely abandoned by her family, recalls her days at boarding school. Both are very adult novels about being a teenager. Ferrante's protagonists are mature women who find that they have failed in some way as wives, daughters, or mothers and have not lived up to expectations (especially those of their own mothers). In *The Days of Abandonment* (2002, English 2005), a woman has to rebuild her life after her husband suddenly walks out on her and their two children. *The Lost Daughter* (2006, English 2008) is about a woman who has established her independence but finds it isolating. Like all of Ferrante's protagonists, her mother's expectations and inability to be supportive leave her incapable of being a good mother (or wife) herself, a failure with which she has accepted but still weighs on her. A psychologically astute and devastating quartet of books centered on the lives and relationship of two Neapolitan women, Elena, the narrator, and Lila—*My Brilliant Friend* (2011, English 2012), *The Story of a New Name* (2012, English 2013), *Those Who Leave and Those Who Stay* (2013, English 2014), and *The Story of the Lost Child* (2014, English 2015)—has received deserved critical and popular acclaim. This vivid and convincing saga of women's lives is a highpoint of recent European literature.

Among the oddest successes of recent years have been the works of the writing collective that now calls itself **Wu Ming**. Writing origi-

---

KEEP IN MIND

- The determinedly feminist and stylistically varied works of **Dacia Maraini** (b. 1936) range from the essentially documentary novel *Isolina* (1985, English 1993), based on a turn-of-the-century murder and trial, to the epistolary *Letters to Marina* (1981, English 1987).

- **Sandro Veronesi**'s (b. 1959) *The Force of the Past* (2000, English 2003) and *Quiet Chaos* (2005, English 2011) are novels in which the narrators deal with circumstances that lead them to intense introspection.

- **Susanna Tamaro**'s (b. 1957) tremendously popular *Follow Your Heart* (1994, English 1995) is an unavoidably sentimental and moving novel of an old woman writing to her granddaughter living in America.

- **Alessandro Baricco**'s (b. 1958) work extends to his own version of Homer's epic, *An Iliad* (2004, English 2006). His simply told tale, *Silk* (1996, English 1997), about a nineteenth-century silkworm merchant who travels to the then still very exotic Japan, and the charming linked novellas about portraiture, *Mr. Gwyn* (2011) and *Three Times at Dawn* (2012), published together in English in a single volume as *Mr. Gwyn* (2014), are his best work.

- **Andrea De Carlo**'s (b. 1952) fiction includes the film industry–focused road trip novel, *Yucatan* (1986, English 1990), and the story of the misadventures of four very urban professionals in the Umbrian countryside, *Windshift* (2004, English 2006).

- **Stefano Benni**'s (b. 1947) satirical novels include the science fiction novel *Terra!* (1983, English 1985) and *Margherita Dolce Vita* (2005, English 2006), with its depictions of an unusual but endearing family and the ominous outside threats it faces.

nally as **Luther Blissett**, their Q (1999, English 2004) is set in the sixteenth century and is a sort of intellectual-philosophical thriller of the Reformation, while *54* (2002, English 2006) has Cary Grant play a secret agent in a global romp. *Manituana* (2007, English 2009)—the first volume in a planned eighteenth-century triptych—is largely set in the Mohawk River Valley during the time of the American Revolution. Wu Ming's ambitiously political works are historical fiction that reflects contemporary conditions. The novels are long and detailed but creative.

Crime Fiction

Beside the work of Leonardo Sciascia, which is rarely found on the mystery shelves, Italian crime fiction has met with little success in the English-speaking world until recently. Even **Giorgio Scerbanenco** (1911–1969), after whom the leading Italian literary prize awarded for mysteries is named, made no inroads beyond the publication of *Duca and the Milan Murders* (1966, English 1970, and as *Betrayal* in Great Britain and *Traitors to All* in the United States, 2013). This was the second in his series of dark novels set in Milan and featuring Duca Lamberti. The son of a policeman, Lamberti became a doctor but lost his medical license and served a prison term for administering euthanasia. Scerbanenco's Milan is a contemporary microcosm, a fast-changing world full of moral ambiguities and social inequities, and the Philip Marlowe–like Lamberti, with his deeply ingrained sense of justice, repeatedly finds himself compelled to do what little he can to help those unable to help themselves. With *A Private Venus* (1966, English 2012), the first installment in the series is now finally also available, as eventually the entire quartet will be.

The writing team of **Carlo Fruttero** (1926–2012) and **Franco Lucentini** (1920–2002) fared best with American and British readers with their *The D. Case* (1989, English 1992), a variation on and resolution of Charles Dickens's unfinished novel *The Mystery of Edwin Drood*, but they also have written numerous other mysteries. The first novel on which they collaborated, *The Sunday Woman* (1972, English

1973), is a rich and witty portrait of Turin life and a fine example of the mystery genre.

Andrea Camilleri's (b. 1925) Montalbano books, which started with *The Shape of Water* (1994, English 2002), remains one of the most satisfying contemporary European mystery series. The books feature an appealingly idiosyncratic protagonist, his name a nod to Spanish author Manuel Vazquez Montalbán, and evoke both the flaws and the beauty of Sicily and Sicilian life (and cooking).

While his autobiographical account of life as *The Fugitive* (1994, English 2007) remains the most interesting introduction to his work (and the Italian legal system), **Massimo Carlotto** (b. 1956) also wrote a variety of good but bleak and brutal Italian noirs. **Carlo Lucarelli** (b. 1960) set much of his crime fiction in the present, but his De Luca books, taking place at the end of World War II, beginning with *Carte Blanche* (1990, English 2006), are the most successful. The novels are filled with moral ambiguity, and their stark feel and presentation fits the times and subject matter. **Gianrico Carofiglio** (b. 1961), a judge, has written a series of mysteries, starting with *Involuntary Witness* (2002, English 2005), that feature the lawyer Guido Guerrieri, who also gets involved in some sleuthing. Although Carofiglio's mysteries are not true courtroom dramas, legal procedure plays a larger role here than in most crime fiction, revealing the peculiarities of the Italian judicial system. *The Past Is a Foreign Country* (2004, English 2007), a stand-alone psychological thriller of youthful manipulation, temptation, and seduction, is not nearly as convincing as the less sensationalist Guerrieri books.

Addressing more profound questions about life and morality, **Niccolò Ammaniti**'s (b. 1966) novels transcend the simple thriller genre. All are hard-edged, and *I'm Not Scared* (2001, English 2003), presented from the point of view of a nine-year-old, is the most compelling. Later efforts like the more sensational *The Crossroads* (2006, English 2009) feel too forced.

Greece

The ancient Greek classics remain foundations of Western literature, but more recent Greek literature has had a far smaller reach. Greek poetry did flourish in the twentieth century: both **Giorgos Seferis** (1900–1971) and **Odysseas Elytis** (1911–1996) were awarded Nobel Prizes, and other major figures included the great **C. P. Cavafy** (1863–1933) and **Yannis Ritsos** (1909–1990). While the work of major Greek poets has consistently been translated, much less attention has been paid to Greek novelists. Especially in recent decades, little of the leading fiction published in Greece has been visible abroad. Many contemporary authors still can be judged by English-speaking audiences only on the basis of isolated translations.

Nikos Kazantzakis (1883–1957) is among the few modern Greek authors widely recognized and read abroad, and this cosmopolitan author even wrote some of his earliest works, including *Toda Raba* (1934, English 1964), in French rather than Greek. Although the film versions of *Zorba the Greek* (1946, English 1952, 2014) and *The Last*

Temptation of Christ (1955, English 1960) may be better known than the works on which they were based, these and Kazantzakis's other novels, including his story of the 1889 revolt against the Turks on Crete, **Freedom or Death** (1953, English 1956), are well worth revisiting. His ambitious verse epic *The Odyssey* (1938, English 1958), a sequel to Homer's work in which Odysseus embarks on further adventures that include the establishment of a utopian community, is particularly impressive.

Vassilis Vassilikos's (b. 1933) *Z* (1966, English 1968) is also better known in its film version, but the novel, based on an actual assassination, provides a vivid picture of the crudeness of Greek politics during that era. Much of Vassilikos's fiction is political, but he also strays into the surreal in works such as the very loosely tied together collection of stories, . . . *And Dreams Are Dreams* (English 1996). The inventive autobiographical *The Few Things I Know About Glafkos Thrassakis* (1978, English 2002), in which Vassilikos's fictional counterpart is reportedly finished off by cannibals, careens a bit out of control but serves as a good introduction to the author.

Poet **Aris Alexandrou**'s (1922–1978) only novel, *Mission Box* (1974, English 1996), is one of the most important Greek novels of recent decades but has barely registered among English-speaking readers. Set in 1949 at the end of the Greek civil war, it describes that conflict from the Communist perspective. Alexandrou's protagonist is the only survivor of an ill-fated mission to transport the box of the title—which symbolically turns out to be empty. Alexandrou's focus on language in conveying the revolutionary's struggles lift *Mission Box* far above the usual novel about political, ideological, and military clashes.

Margarita Karapanou (1946–2008) has an intense style and an often fragmentary presentation. In **Kassandra and the Wolf** (1974, English 1976), a young girl describes her early childhood in a quick rush of short and often disturbing episodes. *Rien ne vas plus* (1991, English 2009) describes an ill-fated marriage, offering two perspectives of events that allow for different interpretations of what actually went wrong.

KEEP IN MIND

- **Yoryis Yatromanolakis**'s (b. 1940) varied works range from *The Spiritual Meadow* (1974, English 2000), still written under the shadow of the ruling military junta in Greece, to *Eroticon* (1995, English 1999), a work of fiction presented ostensibly as a guidebook in the tradition of the *Kama Sutra*.
- **Amanda Michalopoulou**'s (b. 1966) works include a novel about two childhood friends, *Why I Killed My Best Friend* (2003, English 2014), and a collection of stories, *I'd Like* (2005, English 2008).
- **Eugenia Fakinou**'s (b. 1945) rich novel *The Seventh Garment* (1983, English 1992) offers several generations of female perspectives on Greek history.
- **Ioanna Karystiani**'s (b. 1952) *The Jasmine Isle* (1997, English 2006) is an intimate family story set on a beautiful island in the first half of the twentieth century, with women's lives in the foreground, as the men are largely absent at sea.
- **Menis Koumandareas**'s (1931–2014) small and slightly underdeveloped novella describes an affair between a young man and an older, married woman, *Koula* (1978, English 1991).

Two younger Greek authors seem poised for an international breakthrough. All the protagonists of **Alexis Stamatis**'s (b. 1960) novels are fugitives of sorts. Some are ostensibly on quests, such as the author who narrates *Bar Flaubert* (2000, English 2007), traveling across Europe searching for a mysterious writer he learns of while editing his father's autobiography, but they all are on journeys of self-discovery. The alcohol-steeped novel *The Seventh Elephant* (1998, English 2000) also sends its protagonist reeling across Europe, while in *American Fugue* (2006, English 2008) yet another writer travels abroad, this time to America, to participate in a writing program (much as Stamatis himself did, participating in the International Writing Program at the University of Iowa).

The characters in **Vangelis Hatziyannidis**'s (b. 1967) *Four Walls* (2000, English 2006) find themselves locked within their own four walls—sometimes by others, but as often of their own accord—in an off-kilter story that includes a sought-after recipe for making honey as a central element of the plot. *Stolen Time* (2004, English 2007) focuses on a two-week period in which a student agrees to be interviewed in a hotel by members of a sect. He is not the first or only one to go through this, but he discovers that it is not as harmless or simple a procedure as he originally thought, with consequences that go far beyond what he imagined.

Petros Markaris (b. 1937) is the one Greek mystery author who has had some success abroad. While his Inspector Costas Haritos mysteries can be a bit long-winded, the books' confident but easygoing style and the domestic and professional complications with which Haritos has to deal make for an exemplary national crime series, giving a better sense of contemporary Greek conditions than does the fiction of any other author whose books are available in English.

MATHEMATICAL FICTION

A number of Greek authors have dabbled in the odd subgenre of mathematical fiction.

Apostolos Doxiadis's (b. 1953) very approachable *Uncle Petros and Goldbach's Conjecture* (1992), translated into English and revised by the author in 2000, is a warm human portrait.

Tefcros Michaelides's (b. 1954) more mathematically demanding *Pythagorean Crimes* (2006, English 2008), set in the earlier part of the twentieth century, is a murder mystery in which notable mathematicians and artists of the time figure prominently.

Christos Papadimitriou's (b. 1949) "novel about computation," *Turing* (2003), was written in English and crams a lot of science into a fairly ambitious work of fiction, though at a rather basic level. Together with Apostolos Doxiadis, Papadimitriou also wrote the best-selling graphic novel, *Logicomix* (first published in Greek translation in 2008 and then in the original English in 2009), a comic book retelling of Bertrand Russell's life and search for truth.

FICTION BY GREEK EXPATRIATES

Several Greek authors living abroad have also produced significant works of fiction.

Vassilis Alexakis (b. 1943) writes mainly in French and deserves to be far better known than he is. His only work available in English, *Foreign Words* (2002, English 2006), explores language not only by having a protagonist who shares Alexakis's own Greek roots and French background but also by having him study the Central African language of Sango.

Panos Karnezis (b. 1967) moved to England in 1992, and all the acclaimed books he has written in English are set in Greece. From the descriptions of village life in his debut collection, *Little Infamies* (2002), to the large-scale novel about a Greek shipping tycoon, *The Birthday Party* (2007), Karnezis's fiction offers to English-speaking readers an accessible introduction to Greek life and culture of the past century.

Theodor Kallifatides (b. 1938) writes in Swedish and often about the Greek and emigrant experience. Only *Masters and Peasants* (1973, English 1977)—confusingly republished in a revised edition in 1990 as *Peasants and Masters*—is accessible in English. More recently, he has also jumped on the Scandinavian crime fiction bandwagon with his Inspector Vendel mysteries.

Germany, Austria, and Switzerland

French and Russian fiction dominated nineteenth-century Continental European literature, and German fiction came into its own at the beginning of the twentieth century. **Franz Kafka** (1883–1924) and **Thomas Mann** (1875–1955) remain among the most influential writers in Germany and beyond, their distinctive styles still attracting many imitators. **Hermann Hesse** (1877–1962) no longer enjoys quite the popularity he did a few decades ago, though his work has qualities beyond the introspective spiritual aspects that accounted for much of their original appeal. The works by authors who captured the era that ended with the collapse of Central Europe held together by the Hapsburg Empire, including **Stefan Zweig** (1881–1942) and **Joseph Roth** (1894–1939), have recently been revived in English translation. The most representative novels, **Robert Musil's** (1880–1942) unfinished epic, *The Man Without Qualities* (1930–1943, English 1953–1960, 1995), and **Hermann Broch's** (1886–1951) *The Sleepwalkers* (1930–1932, English 1932), are among the peaks of twentieth-century fiction. Other remarkable authors, as different as **Robert Walser** (1878–1956) and **Alfred Döblin** (1878–1957), also continue to be widely hailed.

Few of the best German writers stayed or survived in Germany after the rise of Nazism and through World War II. With the country then split into West and East Germany, its citizens having to come to terms with its recent terrible history and vast numbers of writers dead or dispersed abroad, German literature was slow in reestablishing itself after the war. The situation in Austria was similar, and even the neutral isolation that had spared Switzerland from the damage incurred elsewhere did not prove to be a great advantage in reviving a literary culture that continued to rely on the large readership found only in Germany.

THE FEDERAL REPUBLIC OF GERMANY

The pillars of German fiction after World War II, at least as seen abroad, are two of its Nobel laureates, **Heinrich Böll** (1917–1985) and **Günter Grass** (1927–2015). Böll's moral vision appealed to both East and West, and he was among the few writers who, during the Cold War, enjoyed great success in Eastern as well as Western Europe, his Catholic humanism independent and critical enough that it seems to have played better in the Soviet Union than in the United States. Despite the dozens of volumes of his work that were translated into English, his vision seems to have been quickly eclipsed and set aside with his death, his popularity soon dropping off. Heinrich Böll's novels do provide strong, morally compelling examples of twentieth-century German lives, especially in the family saga *Billiards at Half-Past Nine* (1959, English 1961) and *Group Portrait with Lady* (1971, English 1973). Some of his late work is even overtly political, especially *The Lost Honour of Katharina Blum* (1974, English 1975), which was inspired by the Baader-Meinhof terrorist group and presents a thinly veiled criticism of *Bild*, the influential German tabloid giant. The novel's alternative subtitle, *How Violence Develops and Where It Can Lead*, suggests that he saw little room for subtlety in these times.

Günter Grass's *The Tin Drum* (1959, English 1962, 2009) is a history of the first half of the twentieth century as recounted by the diminutive and obsessive madman Oskar Matzerath, who willed himself to stop growing when he was three. It is a vivid and coarse chronicle of the rise and fall of the Nazis and then the defeated nation. A landmark German novel, it is among the best of the postwar period and certainly the most important and, especially among foreign readers, overshadows much of Grass's other works.

The Tin Drum is the first volume in Grass's *Danzig* trilogy, which continues with the short *Cat and Mouse* (1961, English 1963) and then *Dog Years* (1963, English 1965), whose three narrators relate the experience of growing up in Danzig in the Nazi period and after. Neither has the striking immediacy of *The Tin Drum*, but they also are worth reading.

Although Grass's fiction deals extensively with political matters and large sweeps of history, it is his vividly drawn characters that make them particularly effective. *Local Anaesthetic* (1969, English 1970) is a curious take on the tumultuous years of student uprisings and protests in which a teacher and a student face the question of how to act in these times while undergoing a series of dental procedures to deal with the rottenness of their teeth and mouths, a convenient metaphor that Grass plays to the hilt.

The epic *The Flounder* (1977, English 1978) is dominated by women, its sections corresponding to the nine months of a pregnancy, each covering a different mythic or historic period and each having its own female cook. Here it is a talking fish that makes its way through history, while in *The Rat* (1986, English 1987) it is a representative rodent that figures prominently in an equally sweeping novel that also sees the return of Oskar Matzerath.

Most of the leading German-language authors of the postwar period participated in at least some of the meetings of the Gruppe 47 (Group 47), a loose but influential literary association formed in 1947 whose heyday lasted into the mid-1960s. Grass's tribute to this group, *The Meeting at Telgte* (1979, English 1981), may be less accessible to English-speaking readers than most of his other novels but is a fascinating "doubled" history. Set in 1647, its characters are the leading German authors of that time, fictionally brought together near the close of the Thirty Years' War, with Grass drawing clever parallels to the Group 47.

The extraordinary **Arno Schmidt** (1914–1979) was obsessed by literature. He was both a great writer and a great reader, and spent much time promoting lost masters. As well as translating works by James Fenimore Cooper, Edward Bulwer-Lytton, and Wilkie Collins (along with the occasional thriller and Stanislaus Joyce's two volumes of reminiscences of his brother James), Schmidt wrote exemplary and wonderfully imagined didactic dialogues for radio, introducing forgotten authors and works, selections of which have been collected in *Radio Dialogs I* (English 1999) and *Radio Dialogs II* (English 2003). Schmidt's own fiction is almost hyperliterary in its constant use of references, echoes, and allusions, yet he created a greater variety of truly original work than did any other German writer of his times. From relatively straightforward and realistic fiction set in the early postwar years to a number of futuristic and dystopian works, much of Schmidt's fiction is pointedly intellectual but also darkly humorous.

Schmidt also wrote several ambitious and experimental typescript novels, closer to hypertexts than conventional prose with their marginal and explanatory asides and typographical games. *Evening Edged in Gold* (1975, English 1980) is of particular interest, with its many autobiographical elements, while *The School for Atheists* (1972, English 2001), presented as a dense six-act drama, has been published in a wieldy format and is the best introduction to Schmidt's word (and typographical) play. Finally, the devoted John E. Woods, responsible for most of the translations of Schmidt's works into English, has now completed (but not yet published) his translation of Schmidt's magnum opus, the monumental *Zettel's Traum* (1970), a thirteen-hundred-page volume that weighs more than twenty pounds, in which a close analysis of the work of Edgar Allan Poe plays a major role.

Other authors are more approachable, and numerous individual German novels are easily preferred to any of Schmidt's, but the totality of his work, challenging though many parts of it are, is the most rewarding of that of any modern German author.

KEEP IN MIND

- **Wolfgang Koeppen**'s (1906–1996) trio of novels from the 1950s remain among the most significant in dealing with the early postwar years. *Pigeons on the Grass* (1951, English 1988), for instance, describes a single day in a large German city in those years.
- **Peter Weiss** (1916–1982) is best known for his drama, *Marat/Sade* (1964, English 1965), but his fiction is memorable as well, ranging from the experimental to the autobiographical to his greatest achievement, the trilogy *The Aesthetics of Resistance*, a work of political fiction of resistance in the Nazi era, of which only the first volume (1975, English 2005), has been translated into English.
- **Gert Hofmann**'s (1931–1993) fine, restrained novels include *The Film Explainer* (1991, English 1996) and *Lichtenberg and the Little Flower Girl* (1994, English 2004).

THE GERMAN DEMOCRATIC REPUBLIC

Uwe Johnson (1934–1984) was the leading writer who moved, in 1959, from East to West Germany. Several of his books were translated into English, and his epic work of the late 1960s, describing a year in the lives of a German woman and her daughter living in New York, the four-volume *Anniversaries* (1970–1983, English 1975–1987), has long been available only in a radically abridged translation. Fortunately, Damion Searls's complete translation is expected in 2017. *Anniversaries* is one of the great New York novels of recent decades, with its detailed portrait of the city in that era, but it also covers German history from its protagonist's birth in 1933 onward in retrospective scenes, culminating on a date on which readers know what awaits mother and daughter as they set out for Prague on the eve of the Soviet invasion that spelled the end of the Prague Spring.

Irmtraud Morgner's (1933–1990) *The Life and Adventures of Trobadora Beatrice as Chronicled by Her Minstrel Laura* (1974, English 2000) is one of the major works to come out of East Germany and certainly one of the most entertaining. The novel can best be described as work of feminist magical socialist realism. Its central character is a female troubadour who is awakened in the spring of 1968 from a slumber of more that eight hundred years in France. She then seeks to devote herself to her craft again, journeying to what she is told is "the promised land," the German Democratic Republic (GDR), to do so. The GDR turns out to be a disappointment regarding her hopes for female equality, but that does not keep her from pursuing her ambition. Its portrayal of contemporary East German life as well as its broader consideration of history and art from a female perspective is an enthralling achievement.

Christa Wolf (1929–2011) is one of the few East German authors whose work was also being published—and also enjoyed considerable success—in West Germany and who continued to be a significant figure in the unified Germany after 1990. Wolf's works range from her early novels of East German life, *The Divided Heaven* (1963, English 1965, and as *They Divided the Sky*, 2013) and *The Quest for Christa T.* (1968, English 1971), cleverly presented as quizzical rather than overtly critical; the autobiographical *A Model Childhood* (now published as *Patterns of Childhood*; 1976, English 1980) and *City of Angels* (2010, English 2013); her use of myth in *Cassandra* (1983, English 1984), consisting of "a novel and four essays"; and *Medea* (1996, English 1998). Typically, she poses questions rather than supplying answers, and while the vantage point is usually that of a woman, sister, or mother, she addresses everyday universals as well. Whether in first-person accounts such as *Accident* (1987, English 1989), set on a single day on which its narrator's thoughts center on her brother's brain surgery before she then learns of the Chernobyl disaster, or in reworking historical material, as in *No Place on Earth* (1979, English 1982), which imagines a meeting between the nineteenth-century writers (and later suicides) Heinrich von Kleist and Karoline von Günderrode, Wolf's works are both lyrical and provocative.

With a clear, unadorned style, **Christoph Hein** (b. 1944) unfolds his stories of (East) German lives to often powerful effect, most obviously so in his finest work, *The Distant Lover* (1982, English 1989), a chilling novel of self-imposed isolation and alienation in which a doctor tries to deal without emotion with the death of her lover, its narrator a product of a system in which emotional distance is a common mechanism for survival. In *Settlement* (2004, English 2008), five narrators recount the different segments of the central character's life, a harsh East German success story that continues past reunification. *Willenbrock* (2000, English

---

KEEP IN MIND

- **Ulrich Plenzdorf**'s (1934–2007) *The New Sufferings of Young W.* (1973, English 1979, and as *The New Sorrows of Young W.*, 2015), one of the most widely read and discussed books to come out of the GDR, is an insightful portrait of youth and East German conditions, shaped by two books with which its protagonist identifies: *The Catcher in the Rye* and Goethe's classic, *The Sorrows of Young Werther* (1774).
- **Thomas Brussig**'s (b. 1965) *Heroes Like Us* (1995, English 1997) is a moderately enjoyable comic novel in which the central figure plays an instrumental part in the fall of the Berlin Wall. The accounts of his life and escapades, as told to a reporter for the *New York Times*, is an amusing story of growing up in East Germany.
- **Uwe Tellkamp**'s (b. 1968) German Book Prize–winning *The Tower* (2008, English 2014) is an impressive broad epic portrait of East German life in the 1980s.

2003) shows the eponymous protagonist making the transition from East to the new Germany, facing a different set of challenges and opportunities that also bring frustration in a story of escalating small-scale violence.

Ingo Schulze (b. 1962) is one of the strongest talents to emerge from East Germany. His ambitious novel *New Lives* (2005, English 2008), which focuses on Germany's reunification, staggers under its own weight. Instead, the many individuals' overlapping stories in *Simple Stories* (1998, English 1999) is a more successful novel of East Germans facing the new Germany. Schulz's first work, *33 Moments of Happiness* (1995, English 1997), is a collection of sketches set in St. Petersburg when the Soviet Union collapsed. Presented in a variety of styles, the author occasionally seems to be experimenting with voices and approaches, although Schulze already has displayed considerable command of his material.

AFTER REUNIFICATION

All the changes that accompanied the reunification of the two Germanys in 1990 only slowly filtered into German fiction, especially outside the former GDR. The foremost figure of that decade, **W. G. Sebald** (1944–2001), was among the many whose work remained almost entirely untouched by reunification. His case is easy to understand as Sebald had long distanced himself from Germany, living and teaching in England, even though he still wrote in German. Several of Sebald's often elegiac texts address the German past, with the four-part *The Emigrants* (1992, English 1996) and *Austerlitz* (2001, English 2001) describing how the Nazi era shaped individual lives and fates. *Vertigo* (1990, English 1999) also delves deeper into history, presenting four episodes around well-known figures such as Stendhal and Kafka but, like all of Sebald's work, is also about the processing of memory. Sebald's own presence is a prominent one in most of these texts as he interacts with and responds to both the characters and the events. In many ways, these works do not seem to be fiction at all, least of all *The Rings of Saturn* (1995, English 1998), in which Sebald recounts a walking tour of Suffolk, offering digressions on whatever inspires him along the way. The flat style and the presentation are similar throughout these discursive works, which are further grounded in fact and reality by the photographs, newspaper clippings, and other images he invariably intersperses throughout his texts. These black-and-white images give the books a certain feeling of nostalgia, and much of Sebald's musing is melancholy, heightened by stories of exile and loss.

If Sebald's work can occasionally seem maddeningly rambling, most obviously in *The Rings of Saturn*, it is also rewarding. *Austerlitz* is closest to a conventional novel. With its focus on a single fate and the protagonist's search for identity and attempt to come to terms with an unknown past, it may be the most approachable of Sebald's works. While it bears all the hallmarks of a Sebald text, most notably in the form of a narrator recognizable as the author, these are more artfully employed here than elsewhere. Each of his other works, however, deserves attention as well.

Awarded the Nobel Prize in Literature in 2009, **Herta Müller** (b. 1953) began writing while she still was living in Romania, where she was born as part of the local German-speaking minority. Her short novel *The Passport* (1986, English 1989) describes everyday village life under the Ceauşescu regime, and the consequences of one of the characters, Windisch, applying for a passport in order to emigrate to West Germany. Although Müller did emigrate in 1987, she continued writing about the Romania she had grown up in. *The Land of Green Plums* (1994, English 1996) follows several university-aged Romanian youths with a background similar to Müller's who hope to find more freedom outside the provinces and in a more urban and intellectual environment, only to find that the dictatorial rule is just as oppressive there. The novel, in which several of the main characters die, is a dark indictment of the Ceauşescu regime, as is *The Appointment* (1997, English 2001), which focuses on a single character facing the authorities. Her Soviet concentration camp novel, *The Hunger Angel* (2009, English 2012), is closely based on the experiences of her friend, the writer and Oulipian Oskar Pastior (1927–2006). Müller's poetic use of language in often simple, short sentences, and her characters, numbed by their difficult situations from which there seems no escape, make for powerful if bleak works.

Gerhard Köpf (b. 1948) is an entirely different sort of writer from Sebald, as his ebullient novels of artistic creation and failure are both fun and often very clever. In *Papa's Suitcase* (1993, English 1995), a German bookseller goes on a wild chase for Ernest Hemingway's famous lost suitcase and the manuscripts it contained, a novel that is an homage to Hemingway even as it jokes at his expense. *There Is No Borges* (1991, English 1993) is an even more daring game with literary reputations and authorial identity, as an unsuccessful academic who has speculated that maybe Shakespeare was behind *Don Quixote* is receptive to the idea that perhaps even Jorge Luis Borges was merely an invention by Adolfo Bioy Casares. Köpf is also a professor, and this book has more theoretical digressions than any sort of story, but he is able to pull it off. Köpf's fictional biography of the great eighteenth-century artist Giovanni Battista Piranesi, *Piranesi's Dream* (1992, English 2000), is the tale of the ultimate frustrated artist, able to set his creations on paper but not to actually build them. Köpf's fantastical reimagining of Piranesi's life and ambitions makes this his most powerful work.

A judge and law professor, **Bernhard Schlink** (b. 1944) has always dealt with the complexities of guilt and morality in his fiction, beginning with a series of crime novels, but he achieved international recognition with *The Reader* (1995, English 1997). What begins as the narrator's account of his affair when he was in his teens with a woman two decades his senior becomes a novel of dealing with Nazi guilt when he meets her again years later and she is on trial for her role during the war. Even though she is not innocent, Schlink's twist on her culpability suggests a case where absolute judgments are too simplistic. The way that Schlink forces that conclusion with his far-fetched premise can, however, be off-putting. *Homecoming* (2006, English 2008) is another novel of dealing with the Nazi past, but this time the young protagonist is looking for his father and finds, of course, more than he bargained for. Schlink's style is straightforward, but his books are weighed down by their earnestness, too often seeming didactic and even contrived. With the lower expectations and greater freedoms of the genre, his mystery novels about the private detective Gerhard Self are, in some ways, more satisfying.

Much of **Jenny Erpenbeck's** (b. 1967) fiction engages with twentieth-century German history, with a focus on the small and individual scale rather than the large. *Visitation* (2008, English 2010) centers on a house in Brandenburg and tells the stories of a dozen characters who, over the decades, try to make their home there. The original German title—*Heimsuchung*, literally a "searching for home"—conveys the novel's theme even more clearly. *The End of Days* (2012, English 2014) is a novel of *what if?* and lost potential, imagining five different lives (and deaths) for its protagonist. Erpenbeck came of age in the GDR, but her novel of growing up in a totalitarian system, *The Book of Words* (2005, English, 2007), is set in an unnamed country more closely resembling a South American dictatorship. The young narrator is unable get a grip on the shifting, unstable reality around her, and even language cannot provide the hold she seeks.

Daniel Kehlmann (b. 1975) appeared on the international scene with *Measuring the World* (2005, English 2006), in which he contrasts and brings together two nineteenth-century German geniuses, explorer Alexander von Humboldt and mathematician Carl Gauss, each in his own way measuring the world. With these light and lively adventures of the mind and the real world,

---

KEEP IN MIND

- Several of publisher **Michael Krüger**'s (b. 1943) novels deal with writing and authenticity, including *Himmelfarb* (1993, English 1994), in which an academic's reputation rests on a single book that he did not write. *The End of the Novel* (1990, English 1992) is about an author essentially unwriting his novel, and *The Executor* (2005, English 2008) is about a literary executor's attempt to uphold an author's legacy, which proves considerably more complicated than anticipated.
- **Patrick Süskind**'s (b. 1949) one great success, *Perfume* (1985, English 1986), is the story of an eighteenth-century Frenchman with a perfect sense of smell (and no scent of his own).
- Born in Los Angeles, **Peter Stephan Jungk** (b. 1952) often uses American locales and lives in his novel, including *The Perfect American* (2001, English 2004), his fictional biography of Walt Disney (and the basis for an opera by Philip Glass), as well as *Crossing the Hudson* (2005, English 2009).
- *The Karnau Tapes* (1995, English 1997) by **Marcel Beyer** (b. 1965) is a documentary version of the final days in Hitler's bunker, told in part in the voice of Joseph Goebbels's eight-year-old daughter.
- Several novels by Austrian author **Thomas Glavinic** (b. 1972) have been translated into English, including his chess novel, *Carl Haffner's Love of the Draw* (1998, English 1999), and his version of the last-man-on-earth concept, *Night Work* (2006, English 2008).

Kehlmann offers two fine character portraits, allowing readers to complete the picture from his sketches, unlike much of the heavy German fiction that sometimes seems to consider each detail from every angle and does not tolerate any indeterminacy. *Me and Kaminski* (2003, English 2008) is a slighter novel, about a young art critic hoping to make his name with a biography of a famous painter but ill equipped to tackle the life of another when his own is such a mess.

AUSTRIA

Germans may generally be considered to be more severe, but the works of the best-known Austrian authors available in English make the

Austrians seem even less jolly. **Thomas Bernhard** (1931–1989) at least does display a wicked sense of humor in much of his fiction, but he, **Peter Handke** (b. 1942), and Nobel laureate **Elfriede Jelinek** (b. 1946) show a lot of angry intensity, tempered only by some melancholy, especially in Handke's later works.

Thomas Bernhard (1931–1989) is the master of the extended rant, his novels great riffs of misanthropy as he presents portraits of and encounters with various solitary lives. The central figures in his texts are often talented artists or otherwise intellectually gifted, living in some form of isolation, often deep in the Austrian countryside where conditions, and the locals, are in many respects still primitive. From his first novel, *Frost* (1963, English 2006), in which a medical intern is sent to observe a painter, to his last, *Extinction* (1986, English 1995), which recounts most of his fixations, Bernhard presents obsessive characters verging on madness. Death, illness—mental and physical—and suicide are common occurrences, along with an abundance of detail about each. Individuals are occasionally tolerable, society barely ever—and Austria itself is constantly berated and condemned. (Bernhard's animosity toward his homeland culminated in his testamentary decree proscribing any performance or publication of any of his work in Austria for the duration of the copyright; his heirs lifted the ban in 1998.)

Bernhard's works are often driven monologues, but they do not merely drone on. Instead, his almost musical use of rhythm and repetition makes them lively, even mesmerizing. He could be succinct, as in the 104 stories of *The Voice Imitator* (1979, English 1997), which makes a fine introduction. Bernhard's novella *Wittgenstein's Nephew* (1982, English 1986) is his most approachable work, based on his actual friendship with Paul Wittgenstein, the famous philosopher's nephew. Bernhard's tone in this work is just slightly softer here than usual as he deals with physical and mental decline, and death. Among his longer works, *Correction* (1975, English 1979), in which a Ludwig Wittgenstein-like figure has committed suicide, is one of the more compelling and impressive, but his entire œuvre can pull in readers with its almost maniacal intensity.

Peter Handke's (b. 1942) work shows greater variety, having gone through several stages. With its protagonist chasing all across the United States, *Short Letter, Long Farewell* (1972, English 1974) has many elements typical of his fiction, but its parodies of genres, from thriller to travelogue, are an appealingly off-beat variation on his themes. The superb and affecting *A Sorrow Beyond Dreams* (1972, English 1975), in which Handke tries to work through his mother's death, also explores the limits of writing. Indeed, the act of writing is one of his major preoccupations.

Handke's massive, digressive works such as the year-in-the-life novel *My Year in the No-Man's-Bay* (1994, English 1998) and *Crossing the Sierra de Gredos* (2002, English 2007), with their almost meditative calm, require more patience. Handke is unhurried, and his slow reflective loops over events and lives in these novels seem even more painstakingly precise than elsewhere, even as he eschews any strict realism. Even though Handke's descriptions are detailed and extensive, they remain something of a blur, as he is a master of impressions, not meticulous documentation.

Among his later works, a shorter novel like *On a Dark Night I Left My Silent House* (1996, English 2000) is a good starting point. A circular tale of storytelling, it is also a road trip novel through contemporary Europe. Plot is rarely central to Handke's novels—even though his works are full of incidents, piling up and occasionally building on one another—and his characters, who often remain unnamed, can seem frustratingly shadowy existences, regardless of how much one learns about and from them. Still, as *On a Dark Night I Left My Silent House* demonstrates, at his best this vagueness and seeming indecisiveness, combined with the constant probing and questioning by the characters (or author), can create a strong impression. At greater length, however, as in *Crossing the Sierra de Gredos*, this vagueness can become a very taxing read.

Elfriede Jelinek's (b. 1946) often lush (and harsh) and expansive and allusive prose does not translate as readily or well as either Bernhard's or Handke's, and whereas Bernhard's over-the-top misanthropy has a comic appeal, Jelinek's excoriations often do not rise beyond the ugly.

Although her work contains some humor, for the most part it is severe and judgmental. A deep-rooted hatred of many Austrian character failings as well as the country's sorry Nazi past marks Jelinek's work as much as it did Bernhard's, but her social and feminist criticism and class (self-) consciousness is steeped in a now outmoded Continental Marxism, and while British readers will at least be uneasily familiar with similar class distinctions, American readers will not be able to relate to much of this.

The tense family dynamics in *The Piano Teacher* (1983, English 1988), concerning a protagonist who has not lived up to her overbearing mother's expectations but still is closely bound to her, are typical of Jelinek's fiction of frustration. Here and elsewhere, Jelinek rarely presents anything resembling healthy sexual relations—yet another manifestation of the failures of this society. She deals with this most

---

AUSTRIAN PLAYWRIGHTS

In Austria, Bernhard, Handke, and Jelinek all are known as much for their works for theater as they are for their prose, and for several decades they were, in turn, among the most often performed contemporary dramatists on the world's major stages. It is striking, however, how little in their fiction, including conversations, resembles the quick give-and-take of dialogue common to drama. All three tend to embellish their prose. Handke took the focus away from the actual spoken word to extremes even on the stage, as in his play *The Hour We Knew Nothing of Each Other* (1992, English 1996), in which, despite the more than four hundred individual parts, not a single word is uttered.

KEEP IN MIND

- **Erich Hackl's** (b. 1954) slim, spare novellas concern small but terrible personal tragedies based on historic events. Examples are *Aurora's Motive* (1987, English 1989), *Farewell Sidonia* (1989, English 1991), and *The Wedding of Auschwitz* (2002, English 2009).
- **Christoph Ransmayr's** (b. 1954) lyrical allegory of Ovid's exile is entitled *The Last World* (1988, English 1991).

clearly in the particularly unpleasant *Lust* (1989, English 1992), with its portrait of dysfunctional—yet, for Jelinek, representative—family life. Her novels of postwar alienation, including *Wonderful, Wonderful Times* (1980, English 1990) and *Brassiere Factory* (1975, English 1988, and as *Women as Lovers*, 1994), also are bleak and disturbing but offer more engaging personal stories. *Die Kinder der Toten* (*Children of the Dead*; 1995, English forthcoming), which she considers her magnum opus, is another novel of brutal frankness, populated by the living dead, a graphic confrontation with history and mortality—or, rather, the refusal to accept and process either. More a tableau than a story that advances in anything resembling a linear form, it is a huge dose of everything Jelinek does and shows exactly what kind of a writer she is.

SWITZERLAND

Many of **Max Frisch**'s (1911–1991) fictions feel as though they were pieced together, as his interest seems to be more in the individual pieces than the bigger puzzle. Most of his novels do form a cohesive whole but also offer a sense of much that is absent, not so much that significant details have been left out but simply that totality is unfathomable and inconceivable.

The reflective nature of *Montauk* (1975, English 1976) rather than the American locale makes this slim volume a good introduction to Frisch. A personally revealing account of an aging man looking back on his life, it addresses many of the themes that run through Frisch's books, especially regarding relationships with women. His plainspoken approach makes this a particularly appealing book. *I'm Not Stiller* (1954, English 1958), from early in his career, is another story about being torn between women. Its protagonist, who fled Switzerland and is arrested upon his return, tries to convince everyone that he is truly someone else. Although his attempt at reinvention fails, it allows Frisch an amusing take on Swiss life in the 1950s in a novel that is surprisingly light for German fiction of that time, without ever appearing frivolous.

In Frisch's ***Homo Faber*** (1957, English 1959), the narrator is an engineer who would like to think the world is reducible to the purely technical—hence the title *Man the Maker*, the next step after *homo sapiens*. But when confronted with his inappropriate feelings for the woman he discovers is his daughter and facing mortality, he finds it is not as simple as that. In ***Man in the Holocene*** (1979, English 1980), in which the protagonist briefly finds himself essentially cut off from the rest of the world and becomes obsessed with the age of the dinosaurs, Frisch takes up similar themes, but in entirely new ways. Whereas the form of his early fiction is relatively conventional, *Man in the Holocene* is fragmentary, almost a scrapbook of the protagonist's short period of isolation. The text mirrors its character's uncertainty, with detailed descriptions alternating with discontinuities.

Peter Stamm's (b. 1963) *Agnes* (1998, English 2000) is a love story, but the narrator warns at the outset that it is a story that killed the woman for whom it is named. Despite their cool and detached and very direct style, Stamm's novels are not without passion, but in *Agnes*

KEEP IN MIND

- Though a leading Swiss writer, **Adolf Muschg**'s (b. 1934) work is difficult to find in translation. The most impressive of his works is ***The Light and the Key*** (1984, English 1989), which, despite its vampire protagonist, offers few bloodcurdling thrills. Instead, it is a discursive narrative focusing on aesthetics.
- **Pascal Mercier**'s (b. 1944) ***Night Train to Lisbon*** (2004, English 2008) is an elaborate novel of self-discovery and history in which a Swiss teacher of classics suddenly walks out on his job and routines in search of an elusive text and author. In ***Perlmann's Silence*** (1995, English 2011), the title character's act of plagiarism is the basis for a psychological and philosophical thriller that is also concerned with language itself.
- **Arno Camenisch**'s (b. 1978) novel ***The Alp*** (2009, English 2014), written in both German and Switzerland's fourth national language, Romansch, is the first in a rural Alpine trilogy.

as well as in *Unformed Landscape* (2001, English 2005), *On a Day Like This* (2006, English 2008), and *Seven Years* (2009, English 2011), the central figures have great difficulty overcoming their isolation, even when they turn to others. The protagonist (and mother) in *Unformed Landscape* has already been married twice, neither time particularly happily, and lives in a town in northernmost Norway set apart from the world. Daytime follows night only every six months there, but she has never known anything different, never having ventured south of the Arctic Circle. In *On a Day like This*, the protagonist is moved by fears of his own mortality to radically change his life, trying again, as it were, even as he refuses to hear the medical diagnosis that essentially decides his fate. Stamm never completely breaks through this iciness in any of his works, with *Agnes* still the best variation on these similar themes.

Genre Fiction

Although the German-speaking countries are not known for their crime fiction, two leading mystery authors are Swiss. **Friedrich Glauser's** (1896–1938) half dozen Sergeant Studer novels, most of which have only recently been translated into English, are definitely of a different place and time but for the most part are as enduring as Simenon's work. **Friedrich Dürrenmatt** (1921–1990) is better known for his plays, but his two Inspector Barlach novels, *The Judge and His Hangman* (1952, English 1954, 1955, 2006) and *The Quarry* (1953, English 1961, and as *Suspicion*, 2006), as well as his "Requiem for the Detective Novel," *The Pledge* (1958, English 1959, 2000), are creative examples of the genre, evil faced down, even though the resolutions are not tidy in the way expected for traditional mysteries. More recently, **Jakob Arjouni's** (1964–2013) novels featuring a German private detective of Turkish descent named Kayankaya are caustic but amusing views of the treatment of Germany's large immigrant community.

Both a lawyer and an author, **Ferdinand von Schirach's** (b. 1964) story collections, *Crime* (2009, English 2011) and *Guilt* (2010, English 2012), and his novel, *The Collini Case* (2011, English 2013), are based on professional and personal experiences.

THRILLERS

Phenomenally successful thriller writers such as the eminently readable **Johannes Mario Simmel** (1924–2009) and **Andreas Eschbach** (b. 1959), who also dabbles in science fiction, have barely registered in English, though older works by the very entertaining Simmel are worth seeking out.

Frank Schätzing's (b. 1957) ecological ocean thriller, *The Swarm* (2004, English 2006), and his novel about space exploration, *Limit* (2009, English 2013), are, if anything, too thorough and detailed.

DIRT PORN

With its young female narrator's graphic and intimate descriptions of how she revels in the unhygienic, **Charlotte Roche**'s (b. 1978) *Wetlands* (2008, English 2009) was a sensational best seller in Germany and attracted worldwide attention. The jaw-droppingly repellent dirt porn, with its infantile gross-out descriptions beyond the wildest imaginations of even booger-eating tweens, makes for an unappetizing read. Nonetheless, *Wetlands* is also a surprisingly tender work by a child of divorce that, oddly, has had a long shelf life.

Walter Moers (b. 1957) is known for his comics but has also written several works of fiction (that include many of his own illustrations). While the humor and wordplay in his elaborate adventure tales are rather basic and clearly aimed at younger audiences, adults can enjoy his novels set in the fictional Zamonia, such as *The 13½ Lives of Captain Bluebear* (1999, English 2000) and the wonderfully bookish *The City of Dreaming Books* (2004, English 2006).

Cornelia Funke's (b. 1958) works of fantasy, beginning with *Dragon Rider* (1997, English 2004), are more narrowly aimed at a young adult readership but are among the best in the genre, with the first two volumes of her *Inkworld* trilogy (2003–2007, English 2003–2008) particularly compelling explorations of the world of literary creation, even though the last installment, *Inkdeath* (2007, English 2008) is somewhat of a letdown.

Netherlands and Belgium

Before World War II, few Dutch or Flemish authors figured prominently in the world republic of letters. The versatile **Louis Couperus** (1863–1923), who reveled in the fin de siècle and was arguably more attuned to English and French than Dutch tastes, was deservedly popular abroad, but the few authors whose works have endured are an eclectic bunch. Arguably the great Dutch novel of the nineteenth century, **Multatuli**'s (Eduard Douwes Dekker, 1820–1887) *Max Havelaar* (1860, English 1927, 1967) is a playfully subversive and stylistically very modern work of fiction. While its criticism of Dutch colonialism (in what is now Indonesia) is powerful, it is Multatuli's literary experimentation that continues to impress, and its influence can still be found in recent Dutch fiction. Flemish author **Willem Elsschot**'s (1882–1960) works of fiction show a gentle humor, especially in describing working and business life, and have aged well. **Ferdinand Bordewijk**'s (1884–1965) father–son tale, *Character* (1938, English 1966), offers a grim and vivid picture of the times and local conditions.

Four authors, all prolific and with strong, colorful personalities, long dominated the local literary scene after World War II: **Willem Frederik Hermans** (1921–1995), **Harry Mulisch** (1927–2010), **Gerard Reve** (1923–2006), and **Hugo Claus** (1929–2008).

Reve's and, until recently, Hermans's works are underappreciated outside the Netherlands. Hermans's novels present moral and philosophical issues, often with an underhanded sense of humor. *The Darkroom of Damocles* (1958, English 1962, 2007), one of only two titles available in English, is a darkly ironic novel of deceptions and the failures of best intentions. The protagonist, Henri Osewoudt, is enlisted by Dorbeck, a man who could pass as his twin, in activities he is led to believe are in support of the Dutch resistance against the Nazis. Although Osewoudt means well, he is in far over his head. He sees Dorbeck, a man of action, as the person he could have been, but he eventually is unable to substantiate even Dorbeck's existence.

Although one of Gerard Reve's first books, the story collection *The Acrobat* (1956), was even written in English, it did nothing to launch his career. Only when he turned back to Dutch and his personal experiences, did Reve, a convert to Catholicism and a very public homosexual, find his milieu. Explicit for the times, his fiction is considerably less shocking now, but for the most part his mature work still seems too hot for British and American publishers to handle. Only his enjoyable novel of a day in the life of a very frustrated poet, *Parents Worry* (1988, English 1990), is available in English, although a translation of his 1947 debut and most popular work, *De Avonden* (*The Evenings*), is scheduled for 2016.

Harry Mulisch's (1927–2010) fiction is colored by a family background that exposed him to moral ambiguity and personal loss from a young age: his father was jailed for his wartime collaboration with the Nazis, and his Jewish mother lost most of her immediate family in the concentration camps. Mulisch's most famous work, *The Assault* (1982, English 1985), is one of many that deal with recent Dutch history and questions of morality. This five-part novel begins in 1945 with the murder of a Dutch collaborator, which leads to the separation of young Anton Steenwijk from his family, and then describes four later stages in Anton's life between 1952 and 1981. Revisiting the events of that fateful day, revealing new perspectives, and showing the lasting consequences, a complex picture of guilt and innocence emerges in a novel that explores coming to terms with a dark past.

Mulisch's magnum opus, *The Discovery of Heaven* (1992, English 1996), is ambitious from the start, a summing up of his life and interests. In it, God is set to break the covenant between heaven and earth and charges two angels with finding a human agent to retrieve the stone tablets on which the Ten Commandments are inscribed. The earthbound action centers on the two father figures of the chosen one, Max Delius and Onno Quist, who, despite their very different personalities, are close friends. A woman comes between them, and her child, Quinten, is the one charged with the heavenly mission. The best parts of *The Discovery of Heaven* are the relationships between the two men and with the woman, when the supernatural elements are not in play. With its dramatic conclusion, the novel defies easy categorization, but its treatment of philosophical and theological issues certainly qualifies it as an intellectual thriller. It is Mulisch's masterpiece and one of the great European novels of the postwar era.

Mulisch's modern "golem" story, *The Procedure* (1998, English 2001), is a fascinating creation tale, setting scientific, human, and artistic creation side by side. A novel of ideas, it is the most artfully constructed of his works. In *Siegfried* (2001, English 2003), the narrator is a Dutch author who in many ways resembles Mulisch and who also has long been preoccupied with the phenomenon of Nazism and its consequences. The author has decided that perhaps the only way to grasp the figure of Hitler is through fiction, and on a visit to Vienna he is supplied with the perfect material for such a hypothetical novel, the possibility that Hitler had a son. Mulisch complicates his tale by blurring the lines between fact and fiction, and this short novel feels almost too compressed to hold everything that he has to say but still is a powerful and disturbing work.

Flemish author **Hugo Claus** (1929–2008) was a highly regarded poet and also wrote for the stage and film, but he is best known for his great novel *The Sorrow of Belgium* (1983, English 1990). With its protagonist, Louis Seynaeve, the same age as Claus, this coming-of-age novel set during World War II describes a Flanders where many are complicit in and amenable to the Nazi presence, producing an unsettling portrait of the place and times. *The Duck Hunt* (1950, English 1955, and as *Sister of Earth*, 1966) is also a story of adolescence, influenced by William Faulkner. Of Claus's other novels available in translation, *Desire* (1978, English 1997) is the most interesting. Describing a group of drinking buddies from a local tavern who set out for America and Las Vegas, it is a brutal little morality play.

Among contemporary Dutch authors, only **Cees Nooteboom** (b. 1933) rivals Mulisch in terms of international recognition, and his literary fiction, generally less closely tied to Dutch specifics (except, ironically, when addressing questions of language), has an even more obvious transnational appeal. His novels tend to be puzzles, playfully constructed like some of the works of Italo Calvino and Jorge Luis Borges, and self-referentially philosophical in the manner of Milan Kundera. Almost always rewarding what limited perseverance his fiction requires, little of it is annoyingly bewildering. Several of Nooteboom's novellas even feature writers and center on storytelling. In both *A Song of Truth and Semblance* (1981, English 1984) and *In the Dutch Mountains* (1984, English 1987), the relationship between creators and their unfolding creations is central, while in *The Knight Has Died* (1963, English 1990), a man tries to complete a novel left unfinished by a friend of his who died.

In *Rituals* (1980, English 1983) and *The Following Story* (1991, English 1994)—two of Nootcboom's finest novels—as well as *Lost Paradise* (2004, English 2007), Nooteboom leaves his characters unrooted, moving them in time and place. The beautifully wrought *Rituals* is a three-part novella of encounters during the life of its protagonist, Inni. A father and son he meets, decades apart, try to impose different sorts of extreme order on their lives, looking for meaning in rituals. Inni also is searching for a foothold, and it is his more aimless drifting that proves more viable.

Both of David Colmer's translations of two of **Gerbrand Bakker's** (b. 1962) novels have won major English-language literary prizes. *The*

Twin (2006, English 2008) won the 2010 International IMPAC Dublin Literary Award, and *The Detour* (published in the United States as *Ten White Geese*; 2010, English 2012) won the 2013 Independent Foreign Fiction Prize. These concentrated atmospheric meditations, with their isolated figures and sense of mystery, are fine, thoughtful works of fiction.

The most promising younger Dutch talent is the prolific **Arnon Grunberg** (b. 1971), who has written several very entertaining novels about young men trying to find themselves, most notably *Silent Extras* (1997, English 2000) and *The Story of My Baldness* (published under the pseudonym Marek van der Jagt; 2000, English 2004). These are funny novels of halfhearted ambition, with the characters having grand plans but their will to follow through always ebbing quickly away. Grunberg's most ambitious variation on the theme, *The Jewish Messiah* (2004, English 2008), is about a Swiss youth whose misguided empathy for the Jewish people leads him to become a Hitlerian messiah (and eventually the leader of Israel). This novel offers some promising satire but goes off the rails when Grunberg seems to lose patience with developing his idea and hurries through the later parts. He does not seem to know what to do with a protagonist who actually succeeds.

Grunberg's finest novel to date is the heartbreaking *Tirza* (2006, English 2013), a painstakingly detailed depiction of a man slowly coming entirely unglued. The main character, Jörgen Hofmeester, has been abandoned by his wife and put out to pasture at work, and the sole remaining light of his life is his daughter, Tirza, who is now on the cusp of adulthood. The well-meaning but hapless Hofmeester clearly has difficulty letting go, but Grunberg only slowly reveals how truly desperate he has become.

Flemish author **Paul Verhaeghen**'s (b. 1965) almost ridiculously ambitious *Omega Minor* (2004, English 2007) is among the region's most impressive individual recent works that are available in English. Among much else, it covers the Jewish experience in the Third Reich, the Manhattan Project, and the building of the Berlin Wall. It is about the telling and the making of history amid personal guilt and innocence. Verhaeghen takes his time in unfolding his large tapestry, but it turns out to be a superior thriller as well—complete with a rather too sensational denouement. As the rare book that can pass as both a pulp airport novel and literary fiction, it is not entirely successful but does deliver an extraordinary bang for its buck.

KEEP IN MIND

- **Tim Krabbé** (b. 1943) is best known for the film adaptations of his creepy novel *The Vanishing* (1984, English 1993), although the 1993 Hollywood remake retreated from his horrific ending. His other short psychological thrillers, *Delay* (1994, English 2005) and *The Cave* (1997, English 2000), also have implausible elements, but in each the pieces come together in enjoyably unsettling conclusions.
- **Marcel Möring**'s (b. 1957) novels entail memory, history, and Jewish identity, especially *The Great Longing* (1992, English 1995), which deals with the family-shattering early loss of one's parents.
- **Leon de Winter**'s (b. 1954) very entertaining *Hoffman's Hunger* (1990, English 1995), a novel that is everything from a spy caper to a portrait of a man overwhelmed by too many hungers, is among the few of his consistently enjoyable and wide-ranging, John Irving–like works available in English.
- **Herman Koch** (b. 1953) specializes in well-turned dark comic morality tales, and with its outrageous twists, the best-selling *The Dinner* (2009, English 2012) is the best of these.
- **Connie Palmen**'s (b. 1955) novels of relationships are worth reading.
- **Hella S. Haasse**'s (1918–2011) well-regarded historical novels are worth reading as well.
- **Margriet de Moor**'s (b. 1941) clever—if perhaps overly impassioned—crowd-pleasers merit attention.

Scandinavia

Maybe it is the long winter nights and the cold, but a slightly gloomy pall seems to hang over the fiction from the Scandinavian countries, reinforced by the works of some of the region's best-known artists: Ingmar Bergman's black-and-white films, Edvard Munch's paintings of *The Scream*, and plays and novels by writers such as **Henrik Ibsen** (1828–1906), **August Strindberg** (1849–1912), and **Knut Hamsun** (1859–1952). Even now, with a wave of crime fiction from the region appearing in translation, the focus is, as the genre demands, on the bleak and darker side of life.

Despite their small populations—Sweden is the giant of the region but has only around 9 million inhabitants, and Iceland's population is just over 300,000—each of the Nordic countries has a strong reading and publishing culture, supporting a great variety of fiction. In many respects, it is also a shared literary culture: even though these are distinct nations, their overlapping histories and continued close regional cooperation in many areas, as well as widespread linguistic similarities, has produced a reading and writing community that extends through-out the region.

Nordic Crime Fiction

In recent years, the worldwide interest in Scandinavian mysteries and thrillers has led to an astonishing amount of genre fiction flooding the market. In quantity and variety, this regional boom is comparable to that of Latin American magic realism in the wake of Gabriel García Márquez's *One Hundred Years of Solitude* (1967, English 1970) and then fiction by English-speaking authors originally from India after Salman Rushdie's *Midnight's Children* (1981). While the ten books of the Martin Beck series by the Swedish wife-and-husband team of **Maj Sjöwall** (b. 1935) and **Per Wahlöö** (1926–1975) are among the lasting milestones of recent Scandinavian fiction, they were relatively isolated. Now that has changed, led by Swedish author **Henning Mankell** (1948–2015), specifically his Kurt Wallander series, which began with *Faceless Killers* (1991, English 1997). While the low national rates of violent crime in these countries make them unlikely settings for crime fiction, the very rarity of murder may be a contributing factor to the success of these books, with their greater emphasis on psychological and social insight. The remoteness of these countries and their strong national identities, even as they find themselves increasingly closely tied to the global economy, has also created a juxtaposition that authors have effectively exploited.

Henning Mankell was the leader of the new Scandinavian wave, and the figure of Wallander is a particularly successful creation. In Mankell's books, as in those by Sjöwall and Wahlöö, social observation and commentary are prominent but not so obtrusive as to weigh down the thrillers themselves, a balance that many Scandinavian crime writers have found. Of the rapidly expanding list of mystery authors whose work is available in English, the most notable are Norwegians **Jo Nesbø** (b. 1960) and **Karin Fossum** (b. 1954), Swede **Kjell Eriksson** (b. 1953), Dane **Jussi Adler-Olsen** (b. 1950), and Icelander **Arnaldur Indriðason** (b. 1961). Swedish author **Stieg Larsson**'s (1954–2004) posthumously published *Millennium* trilogy—*The Girl with the Dragon Tattoo* (2005, English 2008), *The Girl Who Played with Fire* (2006, English 2009), and *The Girl Who Kicked the Hornet's Nest* (2007, English 2010)—is a more ambitious work, and it has been spectacularly successful.

DENMARK

Denmark's three Nobel laureates—**Henrik Pontoppidan** (1857–1943) and **Karl Gjellerup** (1857–1919), who shared the prize in 1917, and **Johannes V. Jensen** (1873–1950), who won it in 1944—hardly figure any longer in English translation. **Martin Andersen Nexø's** (1869–1954) four-volume *Pelle the Conqueror* (1906–1910, English 1913–1916) resurfaced as the basis for an Academy Award–winning film in 1988, but the only older Danish writers who are still widely read are **Hans Christian Andersen** (1805–1875) and **Karen Blixen** (writing also as Isak Dinesen and mainly in English, 1885–1962).

The internationally best-known Danish literary figure of recent times is **Peter Høeg** (b. 1957), whose *Smilla's Sense of Snow* (published in Great Britain as *Miss Smilla's Feeling for Snow*; 1992, English 1993) was a global success. Høeg presents a strong but flawed protagonist and bleak settings in this stirring thriller that encompasses everything from postcolonial and minority concerns to biological threats. Its otherness extends even to an ambiguous ending, but despite not offering the usual satisfaction of a rounded-off story, Høeg's book is consistently compelling. His penchant for the quirky and outsiders, characters with special qualities who are looking for escape or on the run—whether circus folk, as in *The Quiet Girl* (2006, English 2008); animals, as in *The Woman and the Ape* (1996, English 1996); or children, as in *Borderliners* (1993, English 1994)—can seem a bit forced. His first book, *The History of Danish Dreams* (1988, English 1995), tries to tell too many stories but has some appeal as a multigenerational picture of the times. Høeg's later works are more controlled, if not necessarily much more restrained.

Much of **Henrik Stangerup**'s (1937–1998) fiction is even more directly colored by politics and philosophy than Høeg's. A social-critical work like ***The Man Who Wanted to Be Guilty*** (1973, English 1982), a dystopian vision rooted in the Danish experience, may no longer translate quite as well as his historically based novels, but even these have a dense and often brooding intensity. Stangerup often uses foreign settings, sending his characters to Continental Europe, as in ***The Seducer*** (1985, English 1990) and ***Brother Jacob*** (1991, English 1993), or even Brazil, as in ***The Road to Lagoa Santa*** (1981, English 1984). But even in the most exotic or cosmopolitan locales, the characters, often based on historical figures, remain almost comically Scandinavian. The original Danish title of *The Seducer* is *It Is Hard to Die in Dieppe*, which is the subtitle of the English-language edition. It traces the life of the now obscure nineteenth-century literary critic Peder Ludvig Møller in a long tradition of tales of talented but failed writers and offers fascinating insights into the Danish literary culture of that era.

Some of the most interesting recent Danish works are short and precise. **Solvej Balle**'s (b. 1962) loosely connected collection of stories, *According to the Law* (1993, English 1996), is presented—slightly differently than in the Danish original, which is a more unified text—as "four accounts of mankind." These short philosophical forays are intriguing, artful fictions in which each of the four main characters is searching for absoluteness, often with creative abandon. **Peter Adolphsen**'s (b. 1972) work also is minimalist, yet in ***Machine*** (2006, English 2008) and ***Brummstein*** (2003, English 2011), he reflects on nothing less than all of history and even prehistory. Even though he also focuses on individuals' lives and fates, the contrast with the immensity of time and nature is striking in these unusual works. *Machine* takes a drop of oil across millions of years, from its origins as the heart of a prehistoric horse through its transformation into oil, gasoline, and then the exhaust fumes of a car. It is the fatal effect of the particles of that cancer-causing exhaust on which the novella turns, and Adolphsen's description of the complexity—and arbitrariness—of cause and effect is poignant.

LITERATURE OF THE FAROE ISLANDS

Even the small Faroe Islands (population ca. 50,000) has supported some authors, writing in Danish or Faroese.

Heðin Brú's (1901–1987) novel of Faroese life, *The Old Man and His Sons* (1940, English 1970), remains the best introduction to the Faroes.

Gunnar Hoydal's (b. 1941) *Under Southern Stars* (1992, English 2003) is the most interesting recent work available in English, contrasting the experiences of a diplomat's family in Latin America with that in their native Faroes.

KEEP IN MIND

- **Morten Ramsland**'s (b. 1971) *Doghead* (2005, English 2007) is a rowdy, big family novel about three generations.
- **Christian Jungersen**'s (b. 1962) *The Exception* (2004, English 2006) sets small-scale group- and workplace-dynamics against a backdrop of genocide, with some very visible cracks in the veneer of Scandinavian calm and idealism.
- **Naja Marie Aidt**'s (b. 1963) dark collection of stories, *Baboon* (2006, English 2014), and her novel *Rock, Paper, Scissors* (2012, English 2015) introduce a major talent to English-speaking readers.
- **Jens Christian Grøndahl** (b. 1959) wrote meditative and personal novels in which his protagonists have to face a sudden change in a domestic world that seems comfortably settled.
- **Villy Sørensen** (1929–2001) is known for short stories in collections like *Tutelary Tales* (1964, English 1988), as well as his variation on classical myth, *The Downfall of the Gods* (1982, English 1989).
- **Carsten Jensen**'s (b. 1952) *We, the Drowned* (2006, English 2010) chronicles the adventures of the seafaring inhabitants of the small community of Marstal, from the mid-nineteenth century through the end of World War II.

FINLAND

In several respects, Finland is the odd man out among the Scandinavian countries, particularly because of the Finnish language, which bears no resemblance to those of the other Scandinavian countries. Its linguistic isolation has also meant that relatively little Finnish literature has been translated into English, though ironically one of the most successful foreign novels ever published in the United States was written in Finnish, **Mika Waltari**'s (1908–1979) best-selling historical fiction, *The Egyptian* (1945, English 1949).

Aleksis Kivi's (1834–1872) *Seven Brothers* (1870, English 1929, 1991) is the one Finnish classic that still holds interest today. Its comically exaggerated presentation of many national characteristics, from a very stubborn and occasionally hapless self-sufficiency and individuality to a specific sort of dry humor, continue to be found in Finnish fiction.

The prolific **Arto Paasilinna** (b. 1942) has achieved the greatest international success with his creative and comic novels. Despite being widely translated into many languages, only a very limited amount of his work is available in English. *The Year of the Hare* (1975, English 1996) and *The Howling Miller* (1981, English 2007) are representative earlier works that show his talents and humor, featuring self-reliant protagonists who, naturally (and comically), have their clashes and confrontations with society at large. Paasilinna is very good at presenting their stubborn independent streaks, and he always sides with the sensible, nature-loving, quick-thinking loners over the meddling, stifling bureaucracy of government and the big city. The majority of Paasilinna's novels could be called variations on these same themes, but with enough diversity to offer enjoyable light entertainment.

Among the most successful and accessible recent translations from the Finnish is **Johanna Sinisalo**'s (b. 1958) charming *Not Before Sundown* (published in the United States as *Troll*; 2000, English 2003). Set in a contemporary Finland where trolls do exist (but are very rarely seen), the chapters alternate between a straightforward narrative, centered on a man who takes in a troll, and a variety of background

---

KEEP IN MIND

- **Sofi Oksanen**'s (b. 1977) popular and acclaimed novels *Purge* (2008, English 2010) and *When the Doves Disappeared* (2012, English 2015) trace Estonia's tumultuous history from the 1940s through the 1990s under both Nazi and Soviet rule.
- **Leena Krohn**'s (b. 1947) unsettling story of a stranger in a strange land, *Tainaron* (1985, English 2004), is typical of her fantastical fiction. Krohn's *Collected Fiction* (English 2015) is a representative selection of her remarkable work.
- **Anita Konkka** (b. 1941) is the author of *A Fool's Paradise* (1978, English 2006).
- **Väinö Linna**'s (1920–1992) novel of the Finnish civil war, *The Unknown Soldier* (1954, English 1957, and as *Unknown Soldiers,* 2015), still casts a shadow over fiction dealing with Finnish history and has an easy claim to being the greatest novel about that period.

---

information from books and newspapers about the species. Sinisalo's not-very-far removed alternate reality balances comedy, poignancy, and a good story—and the troll is hard to resist.

Finland also is home to a small but significant Swedish-speaking minority, which includes several notable authors. Although **Tove Jansson** (1914–2001) is best known for her Moomin comics, she also wrote fiction. Her short autobiographical novels, *The Summer Book* (1972, English 1974) and *Fair Play* (1989, English 2007), are models of restraint, about the simple and everyday whose imagery and small episodes linger on. The psychological drama that unfolds in *The True Deceiver* (1982, English 2009) is also presented in an understated, almost simple, style. In this novel, a young woman, Katri Kling, wants to insinuate herself and the only person she cares for, her brother, in the life—and house—of a local artist but finds that the means to her ends are, in part, beyond her.

Several of **Bo Carpelan**'s (1926–2011) books have been translated, of which his novel *Axel* (1986, English 1991) is the most important. Presented largely in the form of a fictional diary, Carpelan here reimagines the life of his great-uncle Axel Carpelan and his relationship with

KEEP IN MIND

- **Monika Fagerholm** (b. 1961) wrote the novels *The American Girl* (2004, English 2010) and its sequel, *The Glitter Scene* (2009, English 2011).

the composer Jean Sibelius. The novel is effective both as biography and, in evoking a close friendship and describing the role of music in these characters' lives, as a work of fiction.

ICELAND

Even though there are only around 300,000 speakers of Icelandic, almost all concentrated on the geographically remote island, the Icelandic literary culture is thriving, and a considerable amount of its fiction is available in English translation.

With a literary tradition going back to the Old Norse *eddas*, it is the 1955 Nobel laureate **Halldór Laxness** (1902–1998) who is the best introduction to contemporary Icelandic literature. He published his first book at seventeen, and after traveling widely through Europe and spending several years in the United States, he settled in his native Iceland. Although he drifted away from the Catholicism he had embraced as a young man and turned instead to socialism, religion (and religious figures) continued to play a role in many of his novels.

Among Halldór's major works available in English are several grand sagas of the nation and its people. *Independent People* (1934–1935, English 1945) is a story about trying to live off the land in the early twentieth century. *World Light* (1937–1940, English 1969) is the anti-romantic tale of a deluded young poet, destined not to achieve the fame of which he is so certain. Even though much of Halldór 's fiction is set solely in Iceland, in several novels his protagonists compare island life with that abroad, notably in *Paradise Reclaimed* (1960, English 1962), in which a farmer weighs the opportunities offered by Mormonism and abroad, in Utah, against those back home.

THE BJÖRK CONNECTION

Several prominent authors have a connection to Iceland's best-known recent cultural exports, singer-actress Björk and her band, The Sugarcubes.

The poet **Sjón** (b. 1962) wrote the lyrics to some of her songs (and was nominated for an Academy Award for "I've Seen It All"), and his short novel *The Blue Fox* (2004, English 2008) is a delicate piece set in the late nineteenth century that uses rough nature in a contrast to the more ethereal.

Bragi Ólafsson (b. 1962), The Sugarcubes' bassist, has written several novels, the first translated as *The Pets* (2001, English 2008). It is narrated by a protagonist who hides under his bed for most of the novel in order to avoid a confrontation.

KEEP IN MIND

- **Einar Kárason**'s (b. 1955) *Devil's Island* (1983, English 2000) describes Iceland's transformation after World War II, focusing on the effect of the British and then the American military presence on the local population.
- **Ólafur Gunnarsson**'s (b. 1948) broad societal panoramas include *Trolls' Cathedral* (1992, English 1997) and *Potter's Field* (1996, English 2000).
- **Hallgrímur Helgason**'s (b. 1959) *101 Reykjavík* (1996, English 2002) is an agreeably laid-back slacker perspective of contemporary Iceland, and his *The Hitman's Guide to Housecleaning* (2012, Icelandic 2008) was originally written in English but was first published in Icelandic.

Among Halldór's other (and shorter) novels, the more overtly political *The Atom Station* (1948, English 1961) is still of interest and not nearly as dated as one might imagine, given the subject matter. The comic *Christianity at the Glacier* (1968, English 1972, revised as *Under the Glacier*, 1999) mixes local religion and mythology in an entertaining story about an emissary sent by the bishop of Iceland to look into the activities of a pastor in a distant corner of the country.

The emissary is sent as an observer, not an investigator, instructed simply to record conversations and document what he finds. He even identifies himself simply as EmBi, the emissary of the bishop, rather than by name. The local customs in the distant outpost prove far stranger than he expected, however, and he finds his uninvolved objectivity hard to maintain.

Einar Már Guðmundsson's (b. 1954) modern, urban fiction is informed by poetry and international influences and shows considerable experimental range. The poetic hodgepodge in the rapid succession of short chapters of *Epilogue of the Raindrops* (1982, English 1994) is stylistically interesting, but Einar's better-grounded chronicle of a character losing his grip on reality in *Angels of the Universe* (1993, English 1995), taking place during the 1960s, is the more convincing work.

NORWAY

Norway has long had a rich literary tradition and with **Dag Solstad** (b. 1941), **Per Petterson** (b. 1952), **Jan Kjærstad** (b. 1953), **Lars Saabye Christensen** (b. 1953), **Jon Fosse** (b. 1959), and **Karl Ove Knausgaard** (b. 1968) boasts some of Europe's leading contemporary writers.

Nobel Prize winners **Knut Hamsun** (1859–1952) and **Sigrid Undset** (1882–1949) remain the most popular modern Norwegian authors. Even though Hamsun became a Nazi sympathizer (going so far as to give his Nobel Prize medal to German propaganda minister Joseph Goebbels), the breadth and depth of Hamsun's output have sustained his literary reputation and much of his work, beginning with the classic starving-artist novel, *Hunger* (1890, English 1899, 1967, 1996), as well as those novels describing Norwegian country life. Undset is best known for her historical works set in the Middle Ages, especially *Kristin Lavransdatter* (1920–1922, English 1923–1927, 1997–2000). Less well known, **Sigurd Hoel**'s (1890–1960) novels offer good snapshots of Norway in the first half of the twentieth century, with *Sinners in Summertime* (1927, English 1930) an interesting glimpse of the 1920s and *Meeting at the Milestone* (1947, English 1951, 2002) an early attempt to describe Norway under German occupation during World War II.

Jens Bjørneboe's (1920–1976) soft-porn novel, *Without a Stitch* (1966, English 1969), was the first of his works to be translated into English, on the heels of the 1968 Danish film version and at a time when Scandinavia was seen as a center of sexual freedom. A rapid change in sexual mores and literary permissiveness have now made it little more than an amusingly dated curiosity, but Bjørneboe's other works are still worth seeking out. His audacious *History of Bestiality* trilogy—*Moment of Freedom* (1966, English 1975), *Powderhouse* (1969, English 2000), and *The Silence* (1973, English 2000)—is a dark but powerful consideration of what the world has come to, a creative philosophical indictment of Europe and European culture that is strongly influenced by the 1960s disillusionment with postwar society and reconstruction.

Several of **Lars Saabye Christensen**'s (b. 1953) works are built on a fateful twist for the main character and then describe how he deals with it. In *The Joker* (1986, English 1991), the protagonist reads his obituary in the newspaper; the title character in *Herman* (1988, English 1992) is a young boy who goes bald; and in *The Model* (2005, English 2007), a painter's midlife crisis is exacerbated to near hysteria when he learns he will lose his eyesight. Each of these works has some appeal, but Christensen fares better when he tackles larger subjects. In his longer novels that present life stories of growing up in Norway, such as *Beatles* (1984, English 2009) and *The Half Brother* (2001, English 2003), he allows his stories to unfold more slowly, building up his characters and providing enough background to make them more compelling.

Jan Kjærstad's (b. 1953) massive *Wergeland* trilogy—*The Seducer* (1993, English 2003), *The Conqueror* (1996, English 2007), and *The Discoverer* (1999, English 2009)—as well as **Dag Solstad**'s (b. 1941) slim *Shyness and Dignity* (1994, English 2006) are among the highpoints of recent Scandinavian fiction. Each focuses on the life of an individual: Kjærstad's trilogy is an examination and constant reexamination of media celebrity Jonas Wergeland's life. Solstad's novel centers on one decisive day in the life of a teacher. Firmly anchored in culture—modern culture, specifically television in Wergeland's case and literature in schoolteacher Elias Rukla's case—these novels are detailed portraits of Norwegian society as refracted through the experiences, small and large, of these two well-drawn figures.

Each new book that appears in translation has solidified **Per Petterson**'s (b. 1952) reputation, and he may well be Norway's leading contemporary author. Family and personal history play a role in all his works. *In the Wake* (2000, English 2002) is the most personal of his novels, in which Petterson deals with the tragic death of his parents and two of his brothers in a horrific ferry accident. Two novels that also look back to the time of World War II, *To Siberia* (1996, English 1998) and *Out Stealing Horses* (2003, English 2005), are less grim, but here too Petterson does not shy away from hard reality with his spare, evocative prose and sure hand in unfolding his tales.

In **Karl Ove Knausgaard**'s (b. 1968) *A Time to Every Purpose Under Heaven* (published in the United States as *A Time for Everything*; 2004, English 2008), young Antinous Bellori encounters actual angels in the sixteenth century and then devotes his life to studying them, the novel becoming both a commentary on and a reimagining of many biblical stories. Far more ambitious is Knausgaard's mammoth six-volume *Min Kamp* (2009–2011), the first volume of which was published as *My Struggle* in the United States and *A Death in the Family* in Great Britain in 2012. This first-person account is closely (and, in his native Norway, very controversially) based on the life of the author and his family, with the defining event in the first volume the death of the narrator's father. Knausgaard describes specific episodes and memories from his life—mainly his youth—in great detail, and part of his struggle here is in trying to figure out where to fit the pieces of his life. Proustian in its attention to detail and emotional resonance, *My Struggle* might even be compared with *In Search of Lost Time*.

KEEP IN MIND

- The great **Tarjei Vesaas**'s (1897–1970) fiction, most notably the haunting *The Ice Palace* (1963, English 1966), is written in simple, straightforward prose.
- **Jon Fosse** (b. 1959) is Norway's leading dramatist, but he has also published many works of prose and poetry. The novel *Melancholy* (1995, English 2006) centers on real-life Norwegian landscape painter Lars Hertervig (1830–1902) and his nervous breakdown, while in *Melancholy II* (1996, English 2014), set shortly after the painter's death, his surviving sister provides an alternate perspective on the artist's life.
- **Linn Ullmann**'s (b. 1966) novels are marked by the gloom that hangs over them as death is anticipated, as in her novella dealing with euthanasia, *Grace* (2002, English 2005), or contemplated, as in *Stella Descending* (2001, English 2003).
- **Jostein Gaarder**'s (b. 1952) phenomenally successful novel-account of the history of philosophy, *Sophie's World* (1991, English 1994), is targeted to teenagers, being transparently pedagogic yet artful enough for them to find it captivating.
- **Roy Jacobsen** (b. 1954) wrote a stirring account of one man's stand against the Soviets on the Finnish front in 1939, *The Burnt-Out Town of Miracles* (2005, English 2007), as well as *The New Water* (1987, English 1997).
- **Knut Faldbakken**'s (b. 1941) works focus on personal, particularly sexual, issues. They begin to seem dated and limited, though, when compared with the not yet translated energetic novels straight out of—while also highly critical of—contemporary pop and consumer culture written by his son **Matias Faldbakken** (b. 1973; writing as Abo Rasul), such as *The Cocka Hola Company* (2001).
- **Kjartan Fløgstad**'s (b. 1944) *Dollar Road* (1977, English 1989), a far-reaching fictional survey, chronicles four decades of changing Norwegian life through the 1970s.

SWEDEN

Currently, the dominant representatives of contemporary Swedish literary fiction in translation are still from the generation born in the mid-1930s, writers like **Per Olov Enquist** (b. 1934) and **Lars Gustafsson** (b. 1936). Swedish writers have also consistently been at the forefront of the Scandinavian crime fiction boom, beginning with the books by the Sjöwall–Wahlöö team and more recently with the work of **Kerstin Ekman** (b. 1933) and of Henning Mankell, and Stieg Larsson's *Millennium* trilogy.

The fiction of some earlier established Swedish authors is still available and read in English translation, most notably that by **Selma Lagerlöf** (1858–1940) and **Hjalmar Söderberg** (1869–1941). **August Strindberg** (1849–1912) could be included as well, though his plays tend to take precedence over his fiction. Then the end of World War II marked a new starting point. Although **Pär Lagerkvist** (1891–1974) already was an important figure, his chilling book of evil and hatred, *The Dwarf* (1944, English 1945), solidified his international fame. His later works, such as *Barabbas* (1950, English 1951) and *The Sibyl* (1956, English 1958), often creatively treat religious subjects and themes and also deservedly remain popular.

One of the few of **P. C. Jersild**'s (b. 1935) novels available in translation is the postapocalyptic *After the Flood* (1982, English 1986), set in a world devastated by a nuclear conflagration, albeit much of his work also displays a light and humorous side. The most imaginative efforts, including his first great success, the Italo Calvino–inspired bird's-eye romp through part of history, *Calvinols resa genom världen* (1965), and *Holgerssons* (1991), in which Jersild resurrects and appropriates Selma Lagerlöf's Nils Holgersson, have not yet been translated. Jersild's creative approach to social criticism is on display in *A Living Soul* (1980, English 1988), which is narrated by a disembodied human brain. *Children's Island* (1976, English 1986) is the story of a boy who wants to find the answers to life's pressing questions before he is overwhelmed by puberty and adulthood, which is strongly colored by its setting and time, the Stockholm of the mid-1970s. It is the most obviously appealing of Jersild's works.

Several of **Torgny Lindgren**'s (b. 1938) works of fiction are explicitly religious, like his elaboration of the biblical story in **Bathsheba** (1984, English 1988), but even those that are not have a moral gravity. **Light** (1988, English 1992), yet another Scandinavian novel that centers on an isolated community in a world that has collapsed, is an examination of trying to determine right and wrong. Simply told, Lindgren's story of two long estranged brothers, **Sweetness** (1995, English 2000), is one of his greatest successes, and **Hash** (2002, English 2004)—referring to an elaborate dish, not the drug—narrated by a 107-year-old former newspaper reporter, has a lot of quirky charm.

Per Olov Enquist (b. 1934) is one of Sweden's most often translated authors, and his work (which includes several strong dramas) is among the most consistent and provocative. *The Legionnaires* (1968, English 1973), which investigates the controversial repatriation of 167 soldiers from the Baltic states who served in the German army during World War II but surrendered to the Swedish authorities (and wanted at all costs to avoid being returned to what by then was part of the Soviet Union), is the most straightforwardly documentary of Enquist's novels.

Enquist bases much of his fiction on historical fact, with many of recent works relying primarily on historical figures, both famous and obscure. *The Royal Physician's Visit* (published in Great Britain as *The Visit of the Royal Physician*; 1999, English 2001) centers on Danish King Christian VII and his personal physician, Johann Friedrich Struensee. The king is a frail but willful puppet, supposedly all-powerful yet beaten into submission as a child and then manipulated by the politicians at court. Struensee, hired as the king's personal physician, cannot help but take advantage of the situation in which he finds himself. He merely wants to do good, and the king—preoccupied with himself and indifferent to policy and politics—willingly becomes an instrument for him to test his enlightened philosophy. The experiment, however, proves too bold for others in power, and Struensee's efforts go for naught, a small, false start toward enlightened government snuffed out before it could take hold.

The Book About Blanche and Marie (2004, English 2006) is about Blanche Wittmann—a famous hysteria patient of Jean-Martin Charcot—and Marie Curie, in whose laboratory Blanche eventually works. Invented biography, literary interpretation, and speculative digressions all can be found in this unusual and colorful narrative tour de force. *Captain Nemo's Library* (1991, English 1992) is the only one of Enquist's novels available in English that is not based on history. Instead, this is a personal and domestic tale of two boys who were switched at birth and then, when the mistake was discovered, switched back again at age six, leaving each, completely displaced, with his biological family..

Lars Gustafsson (b. 1936) is the other major Swedish author whose works are widely available in English, most of which are more accessible than Enquist's or Lindgren's fiction. Several of the longtime University of Texas, Austin, professor's novels are set in Texas, beginning with the amusing and typically philosophically playful *The Tennis Players* (1977, English 1983). Not all of Gustafsson's Texas novels have been translated, but *The Tale of a Dog* (1993, English 1998) has, and even though the narrator is not quite believable as that of the Texas judge he is meant to be, this story of a Paul de Man–like professor's murder is a satisfying display of Gustafsson's moral and philosophical interests and literary abilities. Gustafsson's most formally complex (and longest) novel, the three-part *Bernard Foy's Third Castling* (1986, English 1988), begins as a thriller, but its clever, self-reflexive structure continually offers new perspectives and surprises.

Among Gustafsson's strongest works is *The Death of a Beekeeper* (1978, English 1981), presented in the form of the notes left behind by a man suffering from cancer who had resigned himself to his death. The former teacher, also named Lars, shares Gustafsson's birth date, as does one of the central characters in *Funeral Music for Freemasons* (1983, English 1987), which follows the lives and different fates of three friends. Indeed, in some of his novels Gustafsson himself is a presence, and the title of one of them, *Herr Gustafsson själv* (1971), not yet available in English, even translates as *Mr. Gustafsson Himself.* The most entertaining of these variations of the author playing a part is the fantastical *Sigismund* (1976, English 1985), set in contemporary Germany but ranging across past and future in dream and reality.

CONTROVERSIAL SWEDISH NOBEL PRIZE WINNERS

Although **Harry Martinson** (1904–1978) and **Eyvind Johnson** (1900–1976) shared the 1974 Nobel Prize, it seems that winning the prize did nothing to enhance their reputations or spur interest in their work. Given that the Swedish Academy chose to honor two of its own over Saul Bellow, Graham Greene, and Vladimir Nabokov, some skepticism was perhaps in order, but works by both authors had appeared in English long before they received the prizes and still offer some interest. The best known of these, Martinson's *Aniara* (1956, English 1963, 1991), is a worthwhile curiosity. A rare example of not one but two genres widely underrepresented in translation, *Aniara* is both an epic poem and a work of science fiction. Martinson's existential focus makes it easier to overlook the dated aspects of this novel-in-verse, and it is considerably better than the typical apocalyptic works of that atom-testing age.

KEEP IN MIND

- **Stig Dagerman** (1923–1954) was the star of postwar Swedish literature, bursting on the scene with a book about those dark times, *The Snake* (1945, English 1995), a collection of stories about confronting fear, most of which takes place in an army barracks. A sense of menace and violence helps, but most of Dagerman's work is still that of a very young writer. Unfortunately, he quickly burned out and committed suicide.
- **Kerstin Ekman** (b. 1933) bridges the divide between literary and genre fiction with books ranging from the crime novel *Blackwater* (1993, English 1996) to *The Forest of Hours* (1988, English 1998), a troll story covering five centuries.
- **Mikael Niemi**'s (b. 1959) *Popular Music from Vittula* (2000, English 2003) is a ribald tale of growing up in the far north of Sweden.

Baltic States

In recent centuries, the small Baltic states have only enjoyed brief periods of independence: for about two decades between the two world wars and since the collapse of the Soviet Union. Until recently, aside from a few anthologies, very little fiction from the region had been translated into English, from either the Soviet period or afterward.

ESTONIA

Estonia is the smallest of the Baltic nations, but its fiction is the best represented in English, and **Jaan Kross** (1920–2007) is the region's best-known author. His collection *The Conspiracy and Other Stories* (1988, English 1995) deals with hardships during World War II caused by both the Germans and the Soviets. *Treading Air* (1998, English 2003) is Kross's one translated novel covering modern Estonian history. It is the story of an Estonian more or less of Kross's generation, first describing his comfortable and promising youth and then how his future is crushed by the forces of history, the protagonist remaining in Estonia as the Soviet grip on the nation takes hold and having to work in more or less menial jobs. Kross offers a good though occasionally plodding portrait of the nation and what it has endured, but it is his more creative historical novels written during Soviet times that so far have secured his reputation abroad. Both *The Czar's Madman* (1978, English 1992) and *Professor Martens' Departure* (1984, English 1994) are reflections on freedom, conviction, and action. Though set in czarist times, they also are commentaries on Soviet rule in Estonia.

Mati Unt's (1944–2005) *Things in the Night* (1990, English 2005) is a literally electrically charged novel. His *Diary of a Blood Donor* (1990, English 2008) uses *Dracula* as a foundation, with characters whose names echo those in Bram Stoker's vampire classic. Both are allegories of the late Communist age, with Estonian nationalism rumbling under the Soviet yoke. Plot is secondary and constantly shifts the ground under the reader, mixing personal, political, and mythical. Unt's more approachable documentary novel, *Brecht at Night* (1997, English 2009), describing Bertolt Brecht's time in Finland in 1940, is a character study of the complicated, sly, and pampered author into which Unt also weaves the story of Estonia during this period of Soviet expansion into the Baltic states.

Tõnu Õnnepalu's (b. 1962) short *Border State* (1993, English 2000), a confession of sorts, is yet another novel of a foray into the wide

---

KEEP IN MIND

- **Jaan Kaplinski**'s (b. 1941) autobiographical *The Same River* (2007, English 2009), set in the 1960s, is the first work of fiction by this major poet available in English.
- **Enn Vetemaa** (b. 1936) made only a barely noticed appearance in English, but his *Three Small Novels* (English 1977), published by Moscow's Progress Publishers, rates a second look.
- **Andrus Kivirähk**'s (b. 1970) *The Man Who Spoke Snakish* (2007, English 2015) is a fantasy novel that is an allegory of ancient traditions and changing times.

open West from the previously isolated East as the overwhelmed narrator describes going to Amsterdam and Paris and the crime he committed there. The more substantial *Radio* (2002, English 2014) is a closer exploration of Estonia, its narrator returning to his homeland after a decade in Paris but still finding himself on a journey of self-discovery. A significant aspect of both novels is the narrator's homosexuality and his efforts to come to terms with it.

LATVIA

Very little Latvian literature has been made available in English, even after the country regained its independence. Despite spending decades in exile in the United States, the works of the prolific **Anšlavs Eglītis** (1906–1993) are essentially unknown there, and almost none have been translated. **Alberts Bels** (b. 1938) has fared somewhat better, at least in regard to his earlier works. The 1980 volume that includes both *The Voice of the Herald* (1973) and *The Investigator* (1967) is a Soviet-era Progress Publishers production, but at least *The Cage* (1972, English 1990) was published in Great Britain. Both *The Investigator* and *The Cage* use some of the devices of the traditional mystery novel, but Bels clearly is addressing Soviet conditions, especially in the very obvious allegory of *The Cage*, in which the protagonist finds himself literally caged.

The first novel from independent Latvia to appear in English is by the talented **Inga Ābele** (b. 1972). Her decade-spanning *High Tide* (2008, English 2013) is a formally creative narrative that essentially unfolds backward.

LITHUANIA

The one Lithuanian work of fiction to find a wider international readership is **Icchokas Meras's** (1934–2014) *Stalemate* (1963, English 1980), a novel about the Vilnius ghetto during the Nazi occupation. It both evocatively portrays ghetto life and creates considerable tension with the obscenely high-stakes chess game that runs through it between the Nazi commandant Schoger, who oversees the ghetto with an iron hand, and a teenage prodigy. Despite this novel's international success, none of Meras's other works has been translated.

Ričardas Gavelis's (1950–2002) *Vilnius Poker* (1989, English 2009) is one of the last big books describing the absurdities of the Soviet system. It is a groundbreaking work of Lithuanian literature, the great city-novel of Vilnius in the Soviet era. It is a harsh, almost reckless portrait of an overwhelmed and paranoid people and city, with an ugly omnipresent outside force determined to abase it further—symbolic of forces like the KGB but also simply the population's broken spirit and what the citizens have become. This fragmented novel has several perspectives, each narrator barely able to see anything beyond the present, all of their hopes more or less abandoned.

WAIT FOR IT

- **Jurga Ivanauskaitė** (1961–2007) was the leading younger author in Lithuania, whose novels are creative takes on local conditions as well as numerous Tibet-inspired works. None of her fiction is available yet in English.

Eastern Europe I

After the collapse of Communism, Czechoslovakia, Hungary, and Poland made the transition to free-market democracies more smoothly than did most of the other former Soviet-bloc nations. Here, too, the domestic literary marketplace was completely overturned as well. For four decades, the state's control of publishing, from editorial decisions to the size of print runs, had been pervasive, albeit also affording writers who worked within the system considerable security. Books were inexpensive, and a literary culture was actively (if very circumspectly) fostered. Then with the collapse of the Communist regimes, many restrictions (and much support) fell away. Publishers flooded the market with previously unavailable work, and foreign popular fiction easily crowded out domestic efforts, leading to what was widely seen as both a dumbing-down and a selling-out of literature.

During this sudden transition, many writers, especially those with audiences in the West, also lost their subject matter. Overnight, dissident fiction was passé. Writers from the German Democratic Republic had it the easiest, as they were readily integrated into a large, existing market and generally adapted to the new conditions quickly. In the linguistically isolated Eastern European countries, though, authors had a more difficult time. Even in the best of times, relatively little fiction was translated into English from east European languages, and without the frisson of the forbidden, the interest of English-language publishers and readers in contemporary eastern European fiction plummeted. But with some carryover from Communist times, and a few distinctive new voices attracting attention, the situation in the Czech Republic, Slovakia, Hungary, and Poland is not as dismal as

CRIME FICTION IN EASTERN EUROPE

It was nearly impossible to write or publish realistic contemporary crime fiction under the totalitarian regimes, since such books might suggest failures or shortcomings of the system. Consequently, the crimes presented in the fiction of the Soviet-dominated era usually were those considered to be against the state, rather than against individuals, the guilty party inevitably (indeed, by definition) the class enemy—or a foreign agent. Nevertheless, mystery novels in the classic English tradition (and often with an English setting), such as Hungarian **Jenő Rejtő**'s (1905–1943)—writing as P. Howard—were immensely popular during Communist times.

Czech author **Josef Škvorecký**'s (1924–2012) Lieutenant Boruvka is the most interesting detective figure to come out of Communist Eastern Europe, with Škvorecký creating the character while still in Czechoslovakia and continuing to use him in his fiction after he moved abroad in 1969. Boruvka eventually also resettled, as did his creator, in Canada. Though not his best work, the Boruvka stories and novels are among the few describing actual criminal police work in a Communist country.

Even after the Communist era, little crime fiction from the region has been translated. Polish author **Marek Krajewski**'s (b. 1966) novels, beginning with *Death in Breslau* (1999, English 2008), were among the first to gain a wider audience, but they do not deal with contemporary conditions and instead take place, as does Czech author **Pavel Kohout**'s (b. 1928) *The Widow Killer* (1995, English 1998), around the time of the Third Reich.

in other formerly Soviet-dominated areas (Ukraine, southeast Europe, and the Central Asian states). Even so, English-speaking readers still have access to only a very small selection of fiction from the region.

CZECHOSLOVAKIA

Even though **Jaroslav Hašek**'s (1883–1923) *The Good Soldier Schweik* (1921–1923, English 1930, 1973) and several works of fiction by **Karel Čapek** (1890–1938), who is best known for coining the word "robot" in his play ***R.U.R.*** (1920, English 1923, 1990), remain in print and circulation in English, the two best-known Czech writers of the twentieth century turned to other languages for some or all of their work. The iconic **Franz Kafka** (1883–1924) wrote in German, and **Milan Kundera** (b. 1929), the most acclaimed Czech postwar novelist, eventually turned to writing in French after moving to France in 1975 and being stripped of his Czechoslovak citizenship. Both are known for the precision of their expression, and Kundera also takes great pains to ensure the final editions and translations of his work are definitive; his first novel, *The Joke* (1967), went through five English translations between 1969 and 1992.

Most of Kundera's books have been novels of ideas, and his penchant for essayistic asides has grown more pronounced over the decades. With its four different narrators and mix of humor and politics (a character's future is ruined by a politically incorrect joke he writes on a postcard), the polyphonic *The Joke* is already a typical Kundera novel. Several more also deal with Czech conditions, combining his literary and philosophical musings with stories grounded in the political minefield of living in Czechoslovakia in those years, especially in regard to the brief and quickly extinguished hope of the Prague Spring in 1968. The loosely connected narratives of ***The Book of Laughter and Forgetting*** (1978, English 1980, 1996), in which the author appears as himself repeatedly stepping forward to comment and digress, and ***The Unbearable Lightness of Being*** (1984, English 1984), set in 1968 Prague, are the most successful of these works.

Immortality (1990, English 1991), though written in Czech, is set in France and is Kundera's most metafictional work, with Kundera himself present as the narrator and going so far as to offer conversations between Goethe and Hemingway in the afterlife. The whole novel unfolds around a simple gesture, which Kundera uses as a starting point for his digressions on everything from the form of the novel to death. Beginning with *Slowness* (1995, English 1996), Kundera's novels have been written in French, and although somewhat more focused on story than is the digressive *Immortality*, these works continue in the same vein to varying degrees, making up a slightly lesser part of his impressive œuvre.

Bohumil Hrabal (1914–1997) is venerated by Central European writers (and readers), including Kundera, although he is unaccountably far less known in English translation. *A Close Watch on the Trains* (now published as *Closely Watched Trains*; 1965, English 1968), set at the end of World War II, with its varied cast of mainly small-town characters, provides a healthy dose of sex and, with its both humorous and melancholy feel, is a good example of his work. Despite being a prolific story writer, Hrabal's finest works are two novels. *I Served the King of England* (1971, English 1989) is a rise-and-fall story, the narrator beginning as a lowly busboy who, after World War II, briefly runs his own hotel and makes millions, only to lose it all after the Communist takeover. The aging narrator of *Too Loud a Solitude* (1977, English 1991) has long worked in a wastepaper-recycling plant. Over the years he has steadily taken forbidden books consigned to be destroyed and has educated himself by reading them. As he tells his story, his spirit has been crushed by modern ways and indifference, as also symbolized by the new and impersonal recycling plant, which has made obsolete the one at which he has worked his entire life.

Although **Pavel Kohout** (b. 1928) is best known as a dramatist, some of his black satires of life under Communism had wonderful premises and deserve better than the obscurity into which their English versions have fallen. In *White Book* (1970, English 1977), the protagonist learns through sheer willpower how to defy the laws of gravity and thus is able to walk on ceilings, an ability the state cannot condone and forcefully opposes. In the very dark novel *The Hangwoman* (1978, English 1981), a girl's only opportunity for an education is at a school that would train her to become the world's first female executioner. *I Am Snowing* (1993, English 1994) is one of the first translated novels examining the transition from Communism, dealing mainly with the question of collaboration under the old regime but also touching on the Nazi period. It is a surprisingly bleak novel, as the yoke of the Communist era still hangs heavily on its characters, and instead of seizing the opportunities the new circumstances should offer, the protagonist Petra sees only uncertainty.

The Holocaust has been central to almost all of **Arnošt Lustig**'s (1926–2011) fiction, most of which is set around the time of World War II. Along with Aharon Appelfeld and Imre Kertész, Lustig's straightforward depictions of harsh realities make him the leading exponent of the literature examining those events and their human toll.

Much of **Ivan Klíma**'s (b. 1931) work uses autobiographical elements. His most appealing works are the collection of stories of artists and intellectuals that opposed the Communist system and the jobs that they took just in order to survive, which includes *My Golden Trades* (1990, English 1992) and the novel *Love and Garbage* (1987, English 1990), in which the narrator becomes a street sweeper. *Judge on Trial* (1979, English 1991) is a much broader examination of the moral and ethical issues that arise under totalitarian regimes. The personal and moral compromises that the protagonist, Adam Kindl, must make are the same as those many Czechoslovak citizens faced, but his position in the justice system makes these compromises even more consequential. An obvious attempt to write a summary of an era and a nation, with echoes of and homages to other Czech literary greats, *Judge on Trial* is, in parts, too forced and drawn out but is still a fine novel.

Klíma has continued to write and publish after the collapse of Communism. With its protagonist a (religious) minister, *The Ultimate Intimacy* (1996, English 1997) only peripherally touches on the political changes after 1990, whereas *No Saints or Angels* (1999, English 2001), narrated by a woman whose husband has left her and who is struggling to raise her teenage daughter, is a more complete work of contemporary Czech life.

KEEP IN MIND

- **Josef Škvorecký's** (1924–2012) *The Engineer of Human Souls* (1977, English 1984), contrasting life in Communist Czechoslovakia with that in exile in Canada, is a central text in his output. From his *Dvorak in Love* (1984, English 1986), describing the Czech composer's visits to the United States in the late nineteenth century, and *The Bride of Texas* (1992, English 1996), about the American Civil War, to murder mysteries, he has produced several variations on his Czechoslovak themes.
- **Ludvík Vaculík's** (1926–2015) novels include *The Axe* (1966, English 1973), with its portrayal of disillusionment with Communism in Czechoslovakia, and the more surreal *The Guinea Pigs* (1973, English 1973).
- **Vladimír Páral's** (b. 1932) comic and entertaining depictions of everyday life, *Catapult* (1967, English 1993), *The Four Sonyas* (1971, English 1993), and *Lovers and Murderers* (1969, English 2002), are not always obviously political.
- **Jiří Gruša's** (1938–2011) life story in *The Questionnaire* (1978, English 1982) is a clever exposition.

CZECH REPUBLIC

On January 1, 1993, Czechoslovakia was split into the Czech Republic and Slovakia, a division that has not been treated extensively in the post-Communist literature in translation. As is also true regarding much of the fiction from elsewhere in eastern Europe, the familiar authors still dominate what little is available in English from either state, with few new authors breaking through as of yet.

Among the few who have is **Jáchym Topol** (b. 1962), whose voice is definitely that of a new generation. Topol's exuberant *City Sister Silver* (1994, English 2000) is set during the tumultuous Czech transition from a Communist state to a free-market democracy. Lauded for its use of language in the original, which is full of colloquialisms, slang, neologisms, and idiosyncratic spelling, the translation at least conveys a sense of much of what the author was trying to do in his freewheel-

KEEP IN MIND

- **Patrik Ouředník** (b. 1957), a resident of France since the mid-1980s, is interested in abstract literary and linguistic experimentation, as demonstrated in his *Europeana: A Brief History of the Twentieth Century* (2001, English 2005), as well as in *Case Closed* (2006, English 2010), which is ostensibly a mystery but in which the crimes and police investigation also allow Ouředník to offer an amusing critical look at the Czech character over recent decades.

ing novel. The narrator, Potok, leads the reader in an impressionistic, multilayered narrative through Czechoslovakia's unrestrained first years after Communism. The plot can be difficult to follow, but Potok's adventures take him far and wide through those anything-goes years and suggest just how tumultuous they were.

More popular, and more approachable is the fiction of **Michal Viewegh** (b. 1962), though astonishingly only his *Bringing Up Girls in Bohemia* (1994, English 1997) has been translated to date. It is one of the more enjoyable novels situated in rapidly changing eastern Europe, and the novel's heroine, the flighty Beata, is an ideal character to skim across all aspects of the new society, despite meeting an unhappy end.

SLOVAKIA

Foreign readers may still hardly differentiate between Czech and Slovak literature, especially considering how little explicitly Slovak fiction is available. **Martin M. Šimečka's** (b. 1957) powerful *The Year of the Frog* (1990, English 1993) is a work about the Communist Czechoslovakian state and its abuses. Its protagonist is a young man prevented from going to university because his dissident father is in prison, so he takes a series of jobs that do not require any qualifications. However worthy, Šimečka's novel seemed almost immediately to be eclipsed by events. **Peter Pišt'anek's** (1960–2015) trilogy begins with *Rivers of Babylon* (1991, English 2007), which tackles the rapidly changing Slovakian scene. In this satire, the country bumpkin Rácz avails himself of all the opportunities that the changing political systems present as he moves up quickly in this new world, in one of the grander comic epics of recent times. The second volume of the trilogy, *The Wooden Village* (1994, English 2008), is similarly inventive, and the last volume, *The End of Freddy* (1999, English 2008), is a more adventurous mix of airport thriller, adventure story, and satire.

HUNGARY

Communist rule not only affected active writers but also determined the fate of previously published work. The work of many of the leading local writers from the first half of the twentieth century had been prohibited or ignored, so after the fall of Communism, interest in these writers has been renewed, especially in Hungary and Romania. In the Hungarian case, this interest has extended abroad, with new editions and translations of many of these authors. The tragic story of **Sándor Márai** (1900–1989), who spent some forty years in obscurity in American exile before committing suicide, just before achieving an international breakthrough, is the best known. **Miklós Bánffy**'s (1874–1950) epic Transylvanian trilogy (1934–1940, English 1999–2001), the creative fiction of **Gyula Krúdy** (1878–1933) and **Dezső Kosztolányi** (1885–1936), and the deceptively light and playful novels of **Antal Szerb** (1901–1945) also have now reached larger audiences abroad.

Despite this renaissance of early-twentieth-century Hungarian literature, the path to the English-speaking market has rarely been smooth for Hungarian fiction. Even after becoming a surprise modern-day best seller in several European countries, Márai's *Embers* (1942, English 2001) shockingly was published in a second-hand translation, from the German translation rather than the original Hungarian. And only after he had been awarded the 2002 Nobel Prize did **Imre Kertész** (b. 1929) begin to receive greater attention in the English-speaking world.

Some of the books by the popular author **Magda Szabó** (1917–2007) appeared in English in the 1960s, most notably the novel *Night* *of the Pig-Killing* (1960, English 1965), but she really established herself among English-speaking readers only with the second translation of *The Door* (1987, English 1994, 2005). This story of the relationship between a writer and her aging and very independent housekeeper is a profound and, from its opening sentences, striking work. Its unusual success the second time around, barely a decade after it was first translated (when it inexplicably attracted little attention), demonstrates the roles of luck, timing, circumstances, and the commitment and capacity of publishers in the fate of a book.

Two of **Imre Kertész's** (b. 1929) novels were available in English before he received the Nobel Prize; these, too, were then released in new translations: *Fateless* (1975, English 1992, and as *Fatelessness*, 2004) and *Kaddish for a Child Not Born* (1990, English 1997, and as *Kaddish for an Unborn Child*, 2004). Much of Kertész's œuvre is interconnected, consisting of autobiographical books about the Holocaust and about writing about the Holocaust. Although there are earlier works, *Fatelessness* is the obvious starting point for his fiction. His experiences in Budapest and then the Nazi concentration camps during World War II, as well as the difficulty of returning home after the war, are the basis for almost all his later novels. In *Kaddish for an Unborn Child*, as also in *Liquidation* (2003, English 2004) and *Fiasco* (1988, English 2011), Kertész describes the difficulties of dealing with those experiences, and especially of writing about them. While best understood and appreciated in the context of his entire output, each of these variations on his themes is compelling.

Much of **George (György) Konrád's** (b. 1933) fiction is autobiographical as well, including his first novel, the harrowing *The Case Worker* (1969, English 1974), based on his own experiences as a social worker. It is unusual in that its unvarnished look at bureaucracy and its failures does not specifically target or blame ideology. In Konrád's *The City Builder* (1975, English 1977), which uses urban planning as a metaphor for the planned society, the protagonist is worn down over the years, from being an architect with grand plans to becoming a cog in the totalitarian machine. In *The Loser* (1982), published in English long before it could appear in Hungarian, the protagonist, who is a patient in a mental institution, tries to escape his personal failures and ambitions and the insanity of the outside world.

Celestial Harmonies (2000, English 2004), **Péter Esterházy's** (b. 1950) splintered novel about his father and his family, spans much of Hungarian history and is one of the most important texts to appear in Hungary in recent times. It is not in any way a straightforward narrative, however, and is as much concerned with language and memory as it is with history but rewards the effort needed to understand it. Unfortunately, it is only half the story, for after writing it, Esterházy discovered that his father had, in fact, been a longtime informer to the secret police, which led him to write a "revised edition," a sequel incorporating the newly revealed information. Published in 2002 as *Javított kiadás*, this necessary supplement to *Celestial Harmonies* has not yet been translated into English.

Esterházy's most experimental fiction, such as the nearly two-hundred-page *Függő* (1981), written as a single sentence, has not been translated, but several somewhat more accessible works have been. In *Helping Verbs of the Heart* (1985, English 1991), Esterházy deals with his mother's death. *A Little Hungarian Pornography* (1984, English 1995), appropriately laden with sex, is another collection of fragments that serves as a good introduction to the author. His homage, *The Book of Hrabal* (1990, English 1994), is a dense work with multiple perspectives but does offer Western readers more reference points, from Bohumil Hrabal to Charlie Parker.

Péter Nádas's (b. 1942) childhood novel, *The End of a Family Story* (1977, English 1998), recalls 1950s Hungary and family history, but his *A Book of Memories* (1986, English 1997) is his greatest achievement. With its book-within-a-book, multiple perspectives, and evocations of sensuality and yearning, this partially autobiographical meditation on memory and creativity is written in the tradition of books by Marcel Proust and Robert Musil. At well over a thousand pages, the loosely structured *Parallel Stories* (2005, English 2011) is an even more massive novel of twentieth-century Central European life and history. Dominated by two families, one Hungarian and one

German, and accounts of two specific eras—the early 1960s, and the time around the fall of the Berlin Wall—Nádas's work weaves in many parallel (and perpendicular) stories, though much is left frustratingly open-ended.

László Krasznahorkai (b. 1954) has slowly crept into the consciousness of readers in the English-speaking world via the cult favorite Béla Tarr's film versions of his work, including *Satantango* (1985, English 2012) and *The Melancholy of Resistance* (1989, English 1998). Krasznahorkai's puzzling narratives are not easily disentangled, with their long sentences, dense and detailed precision, and single-paragraph chapters demanding concentration, but the sense of unease he creates in his depictions of societal instability are remarkable. *The Melancholy of Resistance*, all sinister gloom, is set in a small Hungarian town, on which a traveling circus, complete with the world's largest stuffed whale, has descended. In *War and War* (1999, English 2006), an archivist transports an ancient manuscript to New York and plans to upload it on the Internet in order to preserve it before committing suicide. The story in the manuscript, another journey tale, unfolds side by side with the protagonist's. The chapters of Krasznahorkai's novel *Seiobo There Below* (2008, English 2013) are connected by their themes of beauty and art rather than plot or story. It is the first of Krasznahorkai's works appearing in English that also fully exhibits his fascination with Japan and Japanese culture.

Romania has sizable German- and Hungarian-speaking minorities, each of which has an impressive literary tradition. Both the rising stars **Attila Bartis** (b. 1968) and **György Dragomán** (b. 1973) were born in Romania before eventually moving to Hungary. Bartis's dark but dynamic *Tranquillity* (2001, English 2008) is an account of a nightmarish mother–son relationship during the slow collapse of the Communist system in Hungary. In **György Dragomán**'s (b. 1973) widely acclaimed *The White King* (2005, English 2007), an eleven-year-old boy talks about growing up in a totalitarian regime resembling that of Ceauşescu's Romania.

KEEP IN MIND

- **György Dalos**'s (b. 1943) translated novels range from futuristic satire to fictionalized autobiography. As a sequel to George Orwell's *1984* (1949) and with its setting in England, the timely *1985* (1982, English 1983), in which Dalos kills off Big Brother, may be easier than most East European satires for Western readers to relate to. *The Guest from the Future* (1996, English 1998) is a creative historical fiction about the relationship between Anna Akhmatova and Isaiah Berlin.

POLAND

Several Czech poets found international acclaim after World War II, notably the 1984 Nobel laureate **Jaroslav Seifert** (1901–1986) and the brilliant **Miroslav Holub** (1923–1998), but it is Poland, with its two Nobel laureates—**Czesław Miłosz** (1911–2004) in 1980 and **Wisława Szymborska** (1923–2012) in 1996—as well as **Tadeusz Różewicz** (1921–2014) and **Zbigniew Herbert** (1924–1998) that might well look to outsiders as a nation where all the leading authors have devoted themselves to poetry, at least in recent decades.

The works of the great Polish novelists of the late nineteenth and early twentieth centuries, including those by Nobel winners **Henryk Sienkiewicz** (1846–1916) and **Władysław Reymont** (1867–1925), now are largely out of fashion in the West. Although Sienkiewicz's best-known work, *Quo Vadis* (1895, English 1896), lingers, his other historical novels and works such as Reymont's four-season epic *The Peasants* (1902–1909, English 1924–1925) and **Bolesław Prus**'s (1847–1912) grand *The Doll* (1890, English 1972, revised 1996) barely register any longer. In contrast, the groundbreaking and still strikingly modern novels of the interwar period, **Stanisław Ignacy Witkiewicz**'s (1885–1939) dark, utopian *Insatiability* (1930, English 1977, revised 1996) and **Witold Gombrowicz**'s (1904–1969) playfully existential *Ferdydurke* (1937, English 1961, 2000), as well as the fiction of **Bruno Schulz** (1892–1942) stand almost in isolation in Polish literature. World War

II and then the Communist takeover made it difficult for Polish writers to build on these works.

Even the major novelist of the postwar period, **Stanisław Lem** (1921–2006), is set apart from the rest of contemporary Polish literature, unfairly marginalized as a science fiction author. While some of his work can be considered straightforward science fiction, Lem goes far beyond plot- and gadget-driven fiction with his philosophical and futuristic speculation, and among his most successful works are a variety of metafictions, beginning with *A Perfect Vacuum* (1971, English 1979), which consists of book reviews of imaginary books. Even at its most comic, his fiction builds philosophically intriguing thought-experiments on its creative premises. *Solaris* (1961, English 1970), a novel that is truly other-worldly—and was filmed twice, by Andrei Tarkovsky (1972) and Steven Soderbergh (2002)—in which space travelers encounter a planet-spanning entity that is an intelligent life-form but remains beyond their comprehension, as well as various and often comical works featuring space traveler Ijon Tichy, are consistently entertaining.

The arc of **Tadeusz Konwicki's** (1926–2015) work covers the years from the end of World War II through the fall of Communism in Poland. In the existential *A Dreambook for Our Time* (1963, English 1969), the main character is still haunted by the war even years later. The devastatingly critical *The Polish Complex* (1979, English 1982) and *A Minor Apocalypse* (1979, English 1983) manage also to be deeply personal documents about individual fates within the oppressive system. Like Russian author Vladimir Sorokin's (b. 1955) Soviet classic *The Queue* (1985, English 1988), *The Polish Complex* is told entirely by people waiting in a long line: it is the day before Christmas, and the narrator, named Tadeusz Konwicki, stands in line in front of a jewelry store. In its digressions, *The Polish Complex* reveals the conditions and circumstances of various people in that time.

Most of **Andrzej Szczypiorski's** (1924–2000) far more traditional works are concerned with aspects of the German and Jewish questions, especially in his novel of occupied Warsaw, *The Beautiful*

Mrs. Seidenman (1986, English 1990). *Self-Portrait with Woman* (1994, English 1995), a novel framed as an attempt to consider the post-Communist transition, is a broader but also more personal document. In the novel, the central character, Kamil, lets the loves of his life pass in review as the most appropriate means of summing up what he has lived through. More attuned to the international literary marketplace, Szczypiorski's is easily among the most approachable recent Polish fiction but is far more conventional, too.

Paweł Huelle's (b. 1957) *Who Was David Weiser?* (1987, English 1991), a retrospective look at the disappearance of a Jewish boy in 1957 Gdansk, with elements of magical realism, was an auspicious if uneven debut. Huelle's later novels have become increasingly looser and digressive, with a good deal of what amounts to milling around, though built on appealing premises. *Castorp* (2004, English 2007) imagines the Gdansk (Danzig) university years of Hans Castorp from Thomas Mann's *The Magic Mountain*, in an entertaining literary usurpation that is his most broadly appealing novel to date. *Mercedes Benz* (2001, English 2004) is yet another tribute—though very different from Péter Esterházy's *The Book of Hrabal*—to Bohumil Hrabal, a family history focusing on the cars they have owned that makes for a particularly creative examination of the past few decades of Polish history. *The Last Supper* (2007, English 2008) follows a number of characters who have been asked to pose for a picture for a contemporary version of Leonardo da Vinci's *The Last Supper* in a more scattershot depiction of modern Polish society.

Slightly unusual slices of common lives are found in **Jerzy Pilch**'s (b. 1952) genial entertainments *His Current Woman* (1995, English 2002), with its hapless narrator, and the alcoholic tale *The Mighty Angel* (2001, English 2009), with its even sorrier characters. **Olga Tokarczuk**'s (b. 1962) small-town portraits *House of Day, House of Night* (1998, English 2003) and the more ambitious *Primeval and Other Times* (1996, English 2010)—set in a place called Primeval—are about daily life during the twentieth century that also has mythical, timeless qualities.

A third leading author of that generation and these times is **Andrzej Stasiuk** (b. 1960), whose novels convey a post-Communist desperation as the economic transformation of Poland wreaks havoc on so many lives, whether in a small town, as in *Tales of Galicia* (1995, English 2003), or in Warsaw, as in *Nine* (1999, English 2007). *White Raven* (1995, English 2001), in which the characters attempt to at least briefly escape the changes that have overwhelmed them, is a good if slightly underdeveloped introduction to the author's works.

Magdalena Tulli's (b. 1955) works of fiction, such as *Dreams and Stones* (1995, English 2004), *Flaw* (2006, English 2007), and *Moving Parts* (2003, English 2005), with its narrator chasing down his characters and story, are completely different, poetic meditations that go beyond the Kafkaesque in their sparse plots. Tulli's unusual perspectives give all her writing and descriptions a surreal quality, and even *Flaw*, the story of a city square and the nearby inhabitants' lives, with the local order increasingly upset by refugees coming and camping out there, is not straightforward.

OTHER POLISH WRITERS

The works of other leading Polish authors are more difficult to classify.

Despite its embellishments, **Ryszard Kapuściński**'s (1932–2004) travel writing is among the most creative nonfiction of recent years and has made him one of the most popular Polish authors abroad. His vastly entertaining portrait of the end of Ethiopian Haile Selassie's reign, *The Emperor* (1978, English 1983), and *The Soccer War* (1979, English 1990) will always be widely read.

Stanisław Lec (1909–1966) is an author who remains to be rediscovered, with only a few collections of his classical aphorisms, *Unkempt Thoughts* (English 1962) and *More Unkempt Thoughts* (English 1968), having made it into English thus far.

KEEP IN MIND

- **Wiesław Myśliwski**'s (b. 1932) *Stone Upon Stone* (1999, English 2011) and *A Treatise on Shelling Beans* (2006, English 2013) are entertaining tours leading readers through twentieth-century Poland and the many changes it has undergone.
- **Jerzy Andrzejewski**'s (1909–1983) *Ashes and Diamonds* (1948, English 1962) is the most immediate novel of the postwar transition to Communism in Poland, and even though some aspects of it may now appear naive, it captures well the spirit of the time. Later works by Andrzejewski make an interesting progression of disillusionment with a system he once fervently admired.
- **Kazimierz Brandys** (1916–2000) went into exile in 1981, and his non-fiction is of particular documentary interest, but he also wrote several fine novels, including *Rondo* (1982, English 1989), dealing with the German occupation, and *A Question of Reality* (1977, English 1980).
- Untamed **Marek Hłasko** (1934–1969) was the best-known writer of the counterculture to establish himself in Poland. His fiction, including the novels *The Eighth Day of the Week* (1957, English 1958), about a young couple looking for a private place to be intimate, and *Killing the Second Dog* (1965, English 1990), about two Poles in 1960s Israel, is unlike almost anything else written in Polish at that time.
- **Stefan Chwin**'s (b. 1949) *Death in Danzig* (1995, English 2004), **Piotr Szewc**'s (b. 1961) *Annihilation* (1987, English 1999), and **Marek Bieńczyk**'s (b. 1956) *Tworki* (1999, English 2008) all are powerful novels set during World War II and are the only titles available in English by these authors.

Eastern Europe II

ALBANIA

Under the rule of Enver Hoxha from the end of World War II until his death in 1985, Albania was the most isolated nation in Europe, a totalitarian state essentially cut off from the rest of the world. Even its closest allies, the Soviet Union and then China, began to distance themselves when they began to liberalize after the deaths of Stalin and Mao. Perhaps not surprisingly, in Albania there was less emphasis on fostering the arts than in many Communist nations, but stricter adherence to socialist realism. Even in the post-Communist era, Albania supports only a relatively small literary scene.

Some officially sanctioned literature was occasionally made available in translation by the Albanian authorities before 1990, such as some of the works by **Dritëro Agolli** (b. 1931), who, as the longtime head of the national Writers' Union, was the regime's standard-bearer, but he

seems to have been able to move beyond the ideological limitations
Albania imposed after its fall. The dominant figure of modern Albanian literature has long been **Ismail Kadare** (b. 1936). (Note, however,
that the majority of the English versions of Kadare's books have been
translated from the French translations, not from the original Albanian.) Kadare's international success and renown presumably allowed
him more freedom in what he wrote than was afforded to most other
writers, but this did not prevent some of his work from being banned.
Most of his criticism of Albanian conditions in his carefully conceived
fiction is veiled, with much of his writing allegorical and set long in
the past.

Kadare uses historical events simply as a starting point in many of
his novels, ranging from Pharaoh Cheops's grand project in *The Pyr-*
amid (1992, English 1996) to minor episodes like a research trip to
Albania by two scholars in the 1930s seeking to unravel the enigma of
Homer's oral epics in *The File on H.* (1980, English 1998). At his most
creative, Kadare offers free fantasies such as *The Palace of Dreams*
(1980, English 1993), which describes an Ottoman state with a bureaucracy for handling all its citizens' dreams. This is also one of his novels
that was banned in Albania shortly after its publication. In the novel,
the protagonist, Mark-Alem, who comes from an illustrious family,
begins work in the Tabir Sarrail, the government institution that is the
"Palace of Dreams." Dreams are collected, sorted, and analyzed here,
ostensibly to root out crimes or conspiracies, and as Mark-Alem rises
through the ranks in the mysterious organization, he finds just how far
the state's reach extends.

Living in exile in France since 1990, Kadare has since written
more directly about Albania, most notably in *The Successor* (2003,
English 2005), based on the actual mysterious 1981 death of the designated successor to Hoxha, Mehmet Shehu, and *Spring Flowers,*
Spring Frost (2000, English 2002), which considers more recent
changes in Albania. While the death at the heart of *The Successor*
first is officially described as a suicide, in fact, it is unclear whether
the successor took his own life or was murdered. Kadare revisits

the case from a variety of perspectives (including, ultimately, the Successor's own, from beyond the grave), making for a chilling and disturbing portrait of an isolated totalitarian society dominated by uncertainty.

From the Greek government's zealous opposition to the name of the Republic of Macedonia to Serbian claims on Kosovo, territorial and ethnic issues remain extremely sensitive in this volatile region, and divergent historical claims are a constant source of antagonism. Kadare has been criticized for the strident nationalism evident in some of his works, notably *The File on H.* and some of the other fiction from the Hoxha years, but foreign readers may well find that it offers an authentic Balkan feel. While this nationalism cannot be entirely disregarded or excused, it should not be allowed to blot out the entirety of his work.

The Loser (1992, English 2007) is currently the only one of **Fatos Kongoli**'s (b. 1944) novels available in English translation. It is a remarkable though bleak account of one man's life, symptomatic of a whole nation crushed by totalitarianism. Already extensively translated into other languages, more of the talented Kongoli's work should also soon become available in English.

CONTEMPORARY ALBANIAN FICTION

The anthology *Balkan Beauty, Balkan Blood* (English 2006), edited by Robert Elsie, is the best overall introduction to contemporary Albanian fiction. The fourteen stories include a few published before the end of the Hoxha regime, including **Dritëro Agolli**'s "The Appassionata," which describes the consequences of personal desires and ambitions in this tightly controlled state. Three stories are by **Ylljet Aliçka** (b. 1951), of which "The Slogans in Stone," about a schoolteacher sent to a remote region to tend to what amounts to a garden of slogans set in stones, stands out; it is also the basis for the film *Slogans* (2001), directed by Gjergj Xhuvani.

BULGARIA

Ivan Vazov's (1850–1921) classic *Under the Yoke* (1893, English 1894, 1955, 2004) revolves around the 1876 uprising against the Ottomans, who then still ruled much of the Balkans. This remains Bulgaria's foremost national novel, and only very little Bulgarian fiction has been translated into English since then.

Angel Wagenstein (b. 1922) is better known abroad as a screenwriter, and even though it is a bit old-fashioned, his *Farewell, Shanghai* (2004, English 2007) is a spirited saga of the lives of Europeans who fled the Nazis and sought refuge in Shanghai before and during World War II. Wagenstein's stories are crowded and fast moving, as is also *Isaac's Torah* (2000, English 2008), which describes the life of an Eastern European Jew, beginning with his youth in a town that was then still part of the Austro-Hungarian Empire but in turn becomes part of Poland, Nazi Germany, and the Soviet Union. A saga of the century that leads Isaac through the world wars and both Nazi and Soviet concentration camps, it is a story of the Eastern European Jewish experience, told with a great deal of humor.

Whereas Wagenstein is an author of the old school, focusing on Jewish experiences with an emphasis on telling compelling stories, **Georgi Gospodinov**'s (b. 1968) works are more contemporary in both form and content. *And Other Stories* (2001, English 2007) is a small collection of very short stories in which Gospodinov toys with a variety of ideas, using inventive premises and getting straight to their point. In "Peonies and Forget-Me-Nots," only three pages long, he has two strangers, a man and a woman waiting at the airport, invent memories of a lifetime together, both the past and the future. It is a beautiful little piece that captures both the impossibility and the realization of true love.

Gospodinov's *Natural Novel* (1999, English 2005) is a more extended postmodern game, a domestic story—the narrator's marriage is collapsing—that is full of digressions and observations. The narrator is also a writer, and his personal crisis extends to his work, making the

KEEP IN MIND

- **Vladislav Todorov**'s (b. 1956) pulp noir *Zift* (2006, English 2010) is set in the early 1960s, when its narrator, known as "Moth," emerges from prison into the socialist reality of that time after serving two decades for a crime he did not commit.
- **Alek Popov**'s (b. 1966) comic novel *Mission London* (2001, English 2014) describes the misadventures of the newly arrived Bulgarian ambassador in London.

novel a meditation on writing as well. *The Physics of Sorrow* (2011, English 2015) is even more overtly autobiographical. In this ambitious novel, Gospodinov deftly merges personal experience, Bulgarian history, and the Greek legend of the Minotaur and his labyrinth.

ROMANIA

The Romanian writers who are the most widely recognized and influential abroad are also those who left the country and wrote in French and German: playwright **Eugene Ionesco** (1909–1994), **E. M. Cioran** (1911–1995), and poet **Paul Celan** (1920–1970). **Mircea Eliade** (1907–1986) also settled abroad, and though best known as a scholar of religion and mythology, he wrote several novels as well, continuing intermittently to write fiction in Romanian while abroad. The layered mysteries of *The Old Man and the Bureaucrats* (1968, English 1979) are an intriguing take on totalitarian Romania, and *Youth Without Youth* (1979, English 1988) is a rather odd novel of ideas (complete with Nazi conspiracy), in which an old man is rejuvenated by a lightning strike. Eliade's most successful novel is *The Forbidden Forest* (English 1978), first published in French in 1955, in which he uses symbolism and mythology to chronicle the struggles of his protagonist in a Romania and Europe that are collapsing with the approach and then the explosion of World War II.

Among the earliest of Eliade's works is the autobiographical ***Bengal Nights*** (1933, English 1993), describing an affair he had with a young woman while living in India. Remarkably, the woman, the Bengali author Maitreyi Devi (1914–1990), came across the novel decades later and, after meeting Eliade again at the University of Chicago in 1973, wrote her own fictionalized version of their relationship, ***It Does Not Die*** (1974, English 1976). The two novels offer fascinating contrasting accounts, as does the local reception of each, with Maitreyi making Eliade promise that no English translation of his novel would appear before her death, thus making her version the only one with which Indian readers were familiar for two decades, much as Romanian readers had long known only Eliade's.

Foreign influence and experience also are evident in the work of **Gellu Naum** (1915–2001), one of several Romanian authors of the prewar avant-garde who adopted surrealism. ***My Tired Father*** (1972, English 1999) is a collage of prose fragments, more poem than autobiographical narrative, and the novel ***Zenobia*** (1985, English 1995) is a full-length work of fiction that constantly challenges the reader with its dreamlike evocations and shifting realities. The protagonist—the author himself, using his own name—invents and uses this Zenobia as a love object in a book that seems to move in and out of his control.

Although **Norman Manea** (b. 1936) published extensively in Romania, his work was censored. He went into exile in 1986. Manea's novel ***The Black Envelope*** (1986, English 1995) is ambitious in its presentation, and the description of its disgraced protagonist's quests, based on his investigation of his father's death decades earlier, make for a sharp picture of 1980s Romania. His novel of exile, ***The Lair*** (2009, English 2012), presents intellectual life both under the Ceaușescu regime and in American exile, to which his characters adapt very differently. One of the figures is a thinly disguised stand-in for Mircea Eliade. The novel circles repeatedly back over events and episodes, with history—both personal and national—continuing to weigh on the characters, making it difficult for them to move on.

Manea's collection of stories, ***October, Eight O'Clock*** (1981, English 1992), with its tales of youth in wartime and then of the totalitarian state that arose in the postwar years, and the four longer works in *Compulsory Happiness* (1989, English 1993) are more focused, offering examples of both the burden of having survived in a concentration camp and the absurdities of life in totalitarian Romania.

Filip Florian's (b. 1968) *Little Fingers* (2005, English 2009) and *The Days of the King* (2008, English 2011) are among the rare recent novels to come out of Romania. In *Little Fingers*, the discovery of a mass grave during an archaeological dig sets the action in motion. The remains are said to be hundreds of years old, but the locals believe they are more recent. This premise is less the foundation of a mystery to be solved than an opportunity for Florian to allow a number of voices and stories to unfold. *The Days of the King* is lighter, set in Bucharest during the second half of the nineteenth century. In the novel, a German dentist, Joseph Strauss, comes to the city—which he had never even heard of before—and sees its transformation into a cultured European capital.

Leading contemporary Romanian author **Mircea Cărtărescu**'s (b. 1956) *Nostalgia* (1989, English 1995) is a story collection called a novel and is yet another Romanian work of fiction with a very surreal feel to it, grounded in Bucharest in the 1980s. Cărtărescu's major work, his *Blinding* trilogy (1996–2007, English, first volume, 2013), takes place

---

WRITERS FROM ROMANIA'S GERMAN- AND HUNGARIAN-SPEAKING COMMUNITIES

Romania was part of the Austro-Hungarian Empire and still has large German- and Hungarian-speaking communities, from which a number of writers have emerged. **Herta Müller** (b. 1953), the 2009 Nobel laureate, and her then husband, **Richard Wagner** (b. 1952), left Romania in 1987, and both have established themselves as leading German authors. Both **Attila Bartis** (b. 1968) and **György Dragomán** (b. 1973) are now up-and-coming authors living in Hungary. Among their books available in English, Müller's *The Land of Green Plums* (1994, English 1996), Wagner's *Exit* (1988, English 1990), and Dragomán's *The White King* (2005, English 2007) offer good portraits of life in Communist Romania.

KEEP IN MIND

- **D. R. Popescu**'s (b. 1935) *The Royal Hunt* (1973, English 1985) is a harsh allegory of Romanian conditions in the 1950s, which, like the fiction of Eliade and Naum, moves far beyond simple realism.
- **Dumitru Tsepeneag**'s (b. 1937) works have roots in the avant-garde tradition. Examples are *Pigeon Post* (1989, English 2008), which explores writing a book that the longtime French exile wrote in French (and first published under the pseudonym Ed Pastenague), and his book of variations, *Vain Art of the Fugue* (1991, English 2007).

---

in the Communist Romania where Cărtărescu grew up, but he transcends and transforms it into a literarily ambitious work that extends into the surreal.

YUGOSLAVIA

For some decades, Yugoslavia may have been a unified state, but it was always multilingual. In the wake of its collapse, the linguistic divisions have been accentuated, with Serbo-Croatian now more emphatically divided into Serbian, Croatian, and Bosnian. But even in the Yugoslavian period, other, quite different, languages also had significant numbers of speakers, notably Slovenian, Albanian, and Macedonian. Serbo-Croatian, however, dominated what was known abroad as Yugoslavian literature.

Croatian author **Miroslav Krleža**'s (1893–1981) novels of the period between the wars describe the collapse of the Austro-Hungarian empire, from the existential questioning of the painter-protagonist who returns to his hometown after spending years abroad in *The Return of Philip Latinovicz* (1932, English 1959) to a lawyer's futile struggle against the widespread corruption of the society around him that leaves him, as the title of the novel explains, *On the Edge of Reason* (1938, English 1976). *The Banquet in Blitva* (1938/1962, English 2004) is an intense and all-too-plausible political farce pitting the fictional Baltic nations of Blitva and Blatvia against each other. Unfortunately, the English translation does not include the last of the original three volumes, and none of Krleža's multivolume *Zastave* (1967/1976), set in Croatia between 1912 and 1922, is yet available in English.

Nobel laureate **Ivo Andrić** (1892–1975) is best known for the works he wrote during World War II, as well as *The Bridge on the Drina* (1945, English 1959), a historical novel spanning several centuries and built on stories centered on the famous bridge. Both of **Meša Selimović**'s (1910–1982) novels, ***Death and the Dervish*** (1966, English 1996) and ***The Fortress*** (1970, English 1999), are set in historic Sarajevo. In *Death and the Dervish*, a Sufi dervish tries, in a sustained nightmare of frustration, to save his brother from a death sentence for a crime that is never specified. *The Fortress* is not quite as dark, describing Selimović's moral protagonist's struggles in a largely immoral world in which the individual is nearly crushed by the government's overwhelming forces that do not have to answer to its citizens and that lead by poor example.

Though not a full-fledged exile—he frequently returned to Yugoslavia—**Danilo Kiš** (1935–1989) spent much of his life in France. His writing evolved from book to book, showing a variety of influences from James Joyce through Vladimir Nabokov and Jorge Luis Borges. His work set around World War II, including the powerfully understated novel of a childhood experience of the war, ***Garden, Ashes*** (1965, English 1975), as well as ***Hourglass*** (1972, English 1990), is based on his and his family's experiences. The father in *Garden, Ashes* is the central figure in *Hourglass*, though identified only by his initials, E. S., until he signs his name, Eduard, in a concluding letter. Much of this complex fiction, a study of the impossibility of trying to fully understand another person, is presented in the form of an interrogation. Among Kiš's later fiction is the more overtly political *A Tomb for Boris Davidovich* (1976, English 1978), a collection of portraits of revolutionaries and their fates that uses much factual and documentary material to indict Stalinism.

Borislav Pekić's (1930–1992) major works are characterized by the author's tremendous range. ***The Time of Miracles*** (1965, English

1976) is a radical revision of the life of Jesus, particularly the miracles he performed, and his death—with Simon of Cyrene crucified in his stead. The tragic-comic novel *The Houses of Belgrade* (now published as *Houses*; 1970, English 1978) connects the city's history with a protagonist who has spent decades sequestered in his home before venturing out into the Belgrade of 1968. The epistolary novel *How to Quiet a Vampire* (1977, English 2004) is about personal demons, not actual vampires, but is no less gripping for that. It tells the story of Konrad Rutkowski, a professor who was once an SS and Gestapo officer who is traveling to a Mediterranean resort town for a vacation twenty years after the end of the war and confronts his Nazi past there. A philosophical exploration of Nazism and personal responsibility dressed up to feel almost scholarly, this is nevertheless also a compelling personal story.

Milorad Pavić (1929–2009) experimented with a variety of nonlinear and interactive fiction throughout his career. His encyclopedic cross-referencing *Dictionary of the Khazars* (1984, English 1988) is the most successful of these works, but the formal experiments of novels that allow for different readings, such as *Landscape Painted with Tea* (1988, English 1990), which is presented as a sort of crossword puzzle, and the "Tarot novel" *Last Love in Constantinople* (1994, English 1998), in which the reader may read the different chapters in the order designated by laying out a pack of tarot cards, are interesting examples of the possibilities of hypertexts. Several of these books are also published in separate "male" and "female" versions, though the textual differences between them are, in fact, minimal. Pavić's attention to narrative and story and his ability to craft his puzzles on these solid foundations make these works more appealing than most such fiction.

After 1991

The protracted dissolution of Yugoslavia began in 1991, when Slovenia and Croatia, and then Macedonia, declared their independence. Several of the region's most prominent authors have emigrated since then, notably **David Albahari** (b. 1948), **Dubravka Ugrešić** (b. 1949), and **Slavenka Drakulić** (b. 1949). Especially in the heart of the former

Yugoslavia, the extended conflict among ethnic, linguistic, and religious groups has strongly colored much of the recent fiction by the writers still living there.

Dubravka Ugrešić and Drakulić have also written a considerable amount of nonfiction, often based on their own experiences and observations, and much of Ugrešić's fiction is only a small step removed from this. Her *Fording the Stream of Consciousness* (1988, English 1991), a novel about the international community of writers, written and set in a time when there still was a divide between East and West, is a good point of reference, and her later works then consider the changing circumstances in Europe. Both *The Museum of Unconditional Surrender* (1996, English 1998) and *The Ministry of Pain* (2004, English 2005) examine the experiences of the East European exile. Ugrešić describes in *The Museum of Unconditional Surrender*, while also mixing in essayistic digressions, the work of artists like Ilya Kabakov who are trying to hold on to the past or to re-create it She presents modern rootlessness and the loss of home and identity in different combinations, using examples of exiles adjusting to and hiding behind layers of identity.

Words Are Something Else (English 2003) includes selections from five of David Albahari's collections of stories. All were written before he moved to Canada and first were published between 1973 and 1993. It is a very good introduction to this writer, with several of the pieces dealing with his family and his relationship with them, as well as short examples of his narrative techniques. A more sustained effort about dealing with his father's death, as well as the difficulties of writing about it (or, indeed, anything) can be found in the short but dense *Tsing* (1988, English 1997). *Bait* (1996, English 2001) explores memory in the context of a parent's death. *Snow Man* (1995, English 2005), despite its potentially off-putting presentation as a single unbroken paragraph, is a darkly comic novel of the frustrations of exile, writing, and academia. Besides the story collections, *Götz and Meyer* (1998, English 2004) is Albahari's most approachable work. It is a disturbing examination of the routine of mass murder under the Nazis. Its eponymous protagonists are mere cogs in the killing machinery but, as Albahari insists, share in the responsibility.

KEEP IN MIND

- Among the works from the region deal directly with the Yugosla-vian civil wars of the 1990s are **Nenad Veličković's** (b. 1962) *Lodgers* (1995, English 2005), a teenager's account of Sarajevo under siege, and **Miljenko Jergović's** (b. 1966) celebrated collection of stories, *Sarajevo Marlboro* (1994, English 2004).
- **Zoran Živković** (b. 1948) is the author of ambitious science fiction, especially the complicated novel *The Fourth Circle* (1993, English 2004) and the bookish crime novel *The Last Book* (2007, English 2008).
- **Zoran Ferić's** (b. 1961) novel *The Death of the Little Match Girl* (2002, English 2007) takes place in 1992 and is a microcosm of Yugo-slavia's transitional period.
- **Muharem Bazdulj's** (b. 1977) entertaining collection *The Second Book* (2000, English 2005) contains many stories based on historical figures, from Nietzsche to William and Henry James to an Egyptian pharaoh.

SLOVENIA

Slovenia broke free of Yugoslavia relatively easily and, with its border and close ties to Austria and Italy, was also readily integrated into the Europe Union in 2004. Only a few works of fiction from there have been translated, however. **Boris Pahor** (b. 1913) is the best-known Slovene author of the twentieth century. Born in Trieste when it was still part of the Austro-Hungarian Empire, he has spent most of his life in Italy, but his 1967 memoir about his experiences in several Nazi concentration camps, *Pilgrim Among the Shadows* (now published as *Necropolis*; English 1995), is his only work available in translation.

Drago Jančar's (b. 1948) *Northern Lights* (1984, English 2001) sends its protagonist to the city of Maribor in the tense, unreal time of 1938 in an evocative novel of the prewar period. *Mocking Desire* (1993, English 1998) has a visiting Slovenian author, Gregor Gradnik, teaching creative writing in New Orleans, thereby allowing for both a novel of clashing cultures and meditations on literature and melan-choly, with Robert Burton's seventeenth-century classic, *The Anatomy of Melancholy*, as a guiding text for its protagonist.

KEEP IN MIND

• **Andrej Blatnik**'s (b. 1963) short books of stories include *Skinswaps* (1990, English 1998) and *You Do Understand* (2009, English 2010).

Some of **Miha Mazzini**'s (b. 1961) entertaining works are readily accessible in English, including *The King of the Rattling Spirits* (2001, English 2004), a coming-of-age novel set in the Yugoslavia of the 1970s. *The Cartier Project* (1987, English 2004), reportedly one of the best-selling Slovene books ever, is an amusing look at the country in decline in the 1980s. The narrator, Egon, has learned the tricks of getting by but manages little else in the dank and dreary world he inhabits. His one indulgence is perfume, specifically the foreign, decadent luxury of the brand called Cartier, and one of the novel's plotlines involves his efforts to get more of it. Less tied to locale, Mazzini's *Guarding Hanna* (2000, English 2002) is about a disfigured mob enforcer who spent little of his adult life in proximity to other but was forced to protect a witness in close quarters for a week. Mazzini has fun with this premise, as Hanna also becomes the narrator's protector by showing him the ways of the world from which he has been isolated.

MACEDONIA

Goce Smilevski's (b. 1975) novel *Conversation with Spinoza* (2002, English 2006) is hardly a regional work but stands out among the little recent Macedonian fiction available in translation. Biographical and, not surprisingly, philosophical, it is essentially a reflection both of and on Spinoza's life and philosophy. By directly addressing both the reader and Spinoza in parts of the novel, Smilevski also creates an unusual sense of immediacy.

Smilevski's *Freud's Sister* (2007, revised 2010, English 2012) is a lesser work but has attracted much more interest and has been widely translated. Its subject matter is sensational: four of Sigmund Freud's sisters died in Nazi concentration camps, and the novel's central question is why Freud failed to ensure that they, too, could escape Nazi-occupied Austria, as he managed to do so with his family. The novel is narrated by one of those sisters, Adolfina (Esther Adolfine), about whom very little is known. This allows Smilevski considerable liberties, but the novel's ambitions—among other things, it is a portrait of an epoch (painter Gustav Klimt's sister is a close friend of Adolfina's), a commentary on how mental illness was regarded and treated in those times, as well as an attempt to fathom Freud's horrible final betrayal—pull it in different directions. Already revised in the original and further edited in its English translation, *Freud's Sister* feels almost too polished. With his story also based so closely on a devastating historical fact—Freud's apparent abandonment of his sisters—Smilevski also makes the very dubious choice of sending Adolfina to her death in the gas chambers with her sisters, though in fact she was not included on the transports from Theresienstadt, where they were originally interned, perishing there instead.

Russia, Soviet Union, and Central Asia

RUSSIA

The late nineteenth century may have been the heyday of Russian literature, with the novels of **Fyodor Dostoyevsky** (1821–1881) and **Leo Tolstoy** (1828–1910) and the short stories of **Anton Chekhov** (1860–1904) on any short list of literary classics of the modern era. But even during the long Soviet period (1917–1991), a considerable amount of remarkable work was written. Dissident voices, in particular, attracted attention in the West, but since the collapse of the Soviet Union, few contemporary Russian authors besides **Boris Akunin** (b. 1956), with his historical detective fiction, and **Victor Pelevin** (b. 1962) are widely published or read abroad.

Along with the poets of the early Soviet period, fiction by authors such as **Isaac Babel** (1894–1940), **Andrey Platonov** (1899–1951), and **Mikhail Bulgakov** (1891–1940) have proved lasting, and even though the work of **Maxim Gorky** (1868–1936) has not remained as popular in the United States, it was very influential in the developing world. Under Joseph Stalin, the mandated socialist realism was briefly taken to extremes, but the cultural thaw after his death in 1953 resulted in somewhat more permissiveness by the authorities. Nevertheless, aside from **Aleksandr Solzhenitsyn**'s (1918–2008) *One Day in the Life of Ivan Denisovich* (1962, numerous English translations, most recently the authorized version in 1990), most of the great Soviet novels of the next few decades were first published abroad, beginning with **Boris Pasternak**'s (1890–1960) *Doctor Zhivago* (1957, English 1958, 2010).

Mostly because of political conditions, many Russian writers left the country after the 1917 October Revolution. Among those who left at the Soviet takeover was Nobel laureate **Ivan Bunin** (1870–1953), who continued to write about his homeland while in exile. The young **Vladimir Nabokov** (1899–1977) first achieved success with his Russian works, written mainly in Berlin, before emigrating to the United States and switching to English. Beginning in the 1960s, a wave of dissident authors moved abroad, almost all continuing to write in Russian. More recently, a new generation of Russian-born but English-writing authors have established themselves in the United States. While **Gary Shteyngart** (b. 1972) left the Soviet Union as a child, **Olga Grushin** (b. 1971), **Anya Ulinich** (b. 1973), **Lara Vapnyar** (b. 1971), and **Ekaterina Sedia** (b. 1970) are among those writers who came to America during the collapse of the Soviet Union.

While much of the officially sanctioned fiction published in the Soviet Union was hopelessly idealistic, depicting the great promise of a workers' state, an astonishing percentage of dissident Soviet and then Russian novels—or at least of those translated into English—are dystopian fantasies of the Russian future. Beginning with **Yevgeny Zamyatin**'s (1884–1937) *We* (1920/1921, numerous English translations), the nightmarish potential of totalitarianism has been a popular subject. By the 1970s, many of these dystopias referred explicitly to Soviet institutions and were set in some form of the Soviet empire. This trend of fiction involving very dark futuristic visions of what Russia might become has continued almost unabated.

SOVIET RUSSIA

Much of the finest Soviet literature was suppressed and could not readily be published either domestically or abroad, leading to a lag between when it was written and when it became available. Novels such as Andrey Platonov's dark satirical tale of early collectivization, *The Foundation Pit* (English 1973, 1975, 1996), did not appear in Russian for more than three decades after it was written, and even then, only abroad. **Vasily Grossman**'s (1905–1964) magnum opus of World War II, *Life and Fate* (English 1985), was first published posthumously in 1980. These and other works continue to complete the picture of the Soviet era, but because many became accessible to readers in Russia itself only with the collapse of the Communist state, they are an odd literary discontinuity. Similarly, the *samizdat* and dissident literature that was most familiar to Western audiences was generally not widely circulated inside Russia itself. From the 1960s onward, much of the sizable unofficial literature was published abroad and in translation but not in Russia itself (beyond the limited circulation of *samizdat*). The officially sanctioned local literature published in the Soviet Union was (and remains) little known abroad.

Few authors were able to reach readers both inside and outside the Soviet Union. The authorities tolerated little that could be considered critical, while foreign publishers showed little interest in the domestically sanctioned and popular Russian fare of the times. Writers like **Alexander Solzhenitsyn** (1918–2008) were rendered voiceless in Russia, at best able to publish abroad or to go—or be forced—into exile. After he was awarded the 1970 Nobel Prize in Literature and several of his texts that could not appear in the Soviet Union were published abroad, Solzhenitsyn was expatriated in 1974.

Solzhenitsyn's forceful narratives of the 1960s include *One Day in the Life of Ivan Denisovich, The First Circle* (1968, English 1968, two translations), and *Cancer Ward* (1968, English 1968/1969, and as *The Cancer Ward*, 1968) and center on protagonists who are imprisoned or otherwise isolated and marginalized. These works' initial success was

---

KEEP IN MIND

- Alexander Zinoviev's (1922–2006) massive satire is entitled *The Yawning Heights* (1976, English 1979).
- The title of **Venedikt Erofeev's** (1938–1990) alcohol-steeped and darkly comic novel is *Moscow to the End of the Line* (1973, English 1980, and as *Moscow Circles*, 1981, and *Moscow Stations*, 1997).
- The fiction of **Yuri Trifonov** (1925–1981) is a rare example of work by a widely translated Soviet author who also was successful inside the system.

---

due in part to how they validated Western conceptions of the Soviet system and its abuses, but Solzhenitsyn's accounts of these individuals' struggles also have true literary merit. The huge amount of his later writing makes these works even more daunting, and they are of greater documentary than obvious literary interest. *The Gulag Archipelago, 1918–1956* trilogy (1973, English 1974–1979) is subtitled *An Experiment in Literary Investigation*. *The Red Wheel* cycle, beginning with *August 1914* (1971, revised 1983, English 1972, 1989), is a large-scale and very detailed idiosyncratic take on early-twentieth-century Russian history. They remain essential but not easy reading for anyone interested in these periods and events.

From the Soviet Union to the New Russia

The satirical fiction of **Vladimir Voinovich** (b. 1932) continues in the Russian tradition from **Nikolai Gogol's** (1809–1852) czarist-era works through the classic novels by **Ilya Ilf** (1897–1937) and **Evgeny Petrov** (1903–1942). In his comedy of errors, *The Life and Extraordinary Adventures of Private Ivan Chonkin* (1975, English 1977), and its sequel, *Pretender to the Throne* (1979, English 1981), Voinovich upends many Soviet expectations. The mere concept of a World War II version of Jaroslav Hašek's good soldier Švejk subverted the traditional glorification of war heroes, and Chonkin's tragicomic misadventures mock many aspects of the Soviet system. Voinovich emigrated in 1980, but the target of his satire continued to be the Soviet Union, in both the dystopian *Moscow 2042* (1987, English 1987), in which he imagines Soviet-style Communism realizing its full and final dreadful potential, and *Monumental Propaganda* (2000, English 2004), whose characters try to deal with the post-Soviet transition in a sleepy Russian town. Coming at the end of an era that many were glad to see gone, *The Fur Hat* (1988, English 1989), Voinovich's tale of the literary hierarchy in the Soviet Union and in the official Writers' Union, may seem passé, but this melancholy comic tale of a successful but mediocre career literati is still enjoyable.

Andrei Bitov's (b. 1937) allusive homage to Russian literature, *Pushkin House* (1978, English 1987), is a much heavier work. With sections of it taking their titles from classic Russian novels and the author frequently commenting on the narrative as it progresses, the novel is a very literary (and literarily referential) work that twists itself into some postmodern knots. Nonetheless, it is a welcome change from the relatively blunt satire or grim realism that often seem to be the only two options in the Soviet writing published in the West. *The Symmetry Teacher* (2008, English 2014), presented as a translation (of sorts) of an older, apparently lost, text, plays similar literary games as Bitov again pays homage to his literary forebears and the art of storytelling.

The two novellas by **Vladimir Makanin** (b. 1937) collected in *Escape Hatch* (1991, English 1996), both written as the Soviet Union was collapsing, are dystopian fantasies far from the hopeful works one might have expected at that time. In the title piece, the protagonist—Klyucharyov, a Makanin stand-in who appears in several of his works—lives in a world that is decaying and becoming increasingly dangerous, but through an escape hatch, he also gains access to a subterranean haven with all the trappings of civilized and cultured life. The underground alternative seems to be the better world, yet inevitable doom also seems to hang in the air there. As passage between the worlds becomes more difficult, Klyucharyov must choose between them. In *The Long Road Ahead*, a utopian society of the future turns out to be living a lie, as it turns out that the food the people consume is not synthetically processed but is still the product of old-fashioned

---

KEEP IN MIND

- **Yuri Druzhnikov**'s (1933–2008) classic novel of the 1960s is *Angels on the Head of a Pin* (1989, English 2002).
- **Mark Kharitonov**'s (b. 1937) *Lines of Fate* (1992, English 1996) uses the device of a scholar piecing together a writer's life—and, with it, a picture of Soviet history—from his very fragmentary works.
- **Yuri Rytkheu**'s (1930–2008) fiction takes place on the far eastern Siberian region of Chukotka.

---

animal slaughter and butchery. When the main character makes this discovery, he finds himself in limbo, unwilling to return to society with this ugly knowledge. Makanin evokes a sense of menace in both novellas, and the blend of the surreal and real is particularly effective. By comparison, ***Baize-Covered Table with Decanter*** (1993, English 1995) feels like a step back, as yet another novel revolving almost entirely around an interrogation. Although Makanin creatively catalogs the horrors and psychological games involved, played out in the narrator's mind, it is hard not to feel that we have been through all this before.

The New Russia

Vladimir Sorokin (b. 1955) briefly popped up in the West with *The Queue* (1985, English 1988), his miniature of Soviet society. With only the words of those waiting in line to make some sort of purchase, dialogue without any narrative embellishment, the novel is a charming and rich depiction of queuing—a familiar Communist-era institution with its own rules and customs, in which just the possibility of obtaining *something*, even without knowing what it was, was enough to make people line up. When Sorokin finally resurfaced in translation two decades later, with *Ice* (2002, English 2007), he seemed like an entirely different author. *Ice* tells the story of a bizarre cult and the search for the chosen few, which is expanded in ***Bro*** (2004) and ***23,000*** (2005), published together with *Ice* as the middle volume as the ***Ice Trilogy*** (English 2011). At times, the trilogy can be a frustrating grab bag that mixes allegory and thriller but, in its scope and reach, is often compelling. Sorokin is one of the leading, most controversial, and prolific Russian authors, and more of his work will inevitably be made available in English, most of it along the lines of the often brutal but imaginative *Ice Trilogy*, or ***A Day in the Life of an Oprichnik*** (2006, English 2011), yet another Russian dystopia, set in 2027, in which the country returns not only to Soviet ways but also to much earlier czarist institutions.

Victor Pelevin (b. 1962) is the most original popular voice to come out of Russia. His everyday premises and situations tend toward the absurdist, and with characters that inhabit different time frames or that acquire different corporeal forms—humans that are also insects, or were-foxes (as opposed to werewolves) that take on a human appearance—he sometimes founders in his excesses, especially when he indulges in philosophical and metaphysical speculation. At least parts of his work can delight with their mind-boggling invention, but Pelevin is at his best in more narrowly focused works such as ***Omon Ra*** (1992, English 1994). The young narrator of this novel sees his dream of becoming a cosmonaut fulfilled, only to find that the entire Soviet space program is a vast Potemkin village. A clever satire of both the space program and the larger Soviet political system, it is also one of Pelevin's more controlled efforts. ***Babylon*** (published in the United States as *Homo Zapiens*; 1999, English 2000) skewers Russia's rapid decline into a society dominated by consumerism and widespread media manipulation and is one of the more amusing pictures of contemporary Russia.

A more ambitious work such as ***The Clay Machine-Gun*** (published in the United States as *Buddha's Little Finger*; 1996, English 1999) is bound to impress with its creative daring, but Pelevin also makes it easy for himself by resorting to mental instability and dream scenes. In this novel and elsewhere, the surrealism of his fiction eventually feels forced. Similarly, the overcomplicated premises of a novel like ***The Sacred Book of the Werewolf*** (2005, English 2008) become a tiresome distraction. The fantastic handiwork of ***The Life of Insects*** (1993, English 1996), with its half-human, half-insect world, presenting both a familiar (Russian) and a very strange reality, or the alternate virtual-reality labyrinth he conceives for his modern retelling of the legend of Theseus and the Minotaur in his chat-room dialogue novel, *The Helmet of Horror* (2005, English 2006), are admirable, but his work rarely manages to be entirely satisfying.

Tatyana Tolstaya's (b. 1951) *The Slynx* (2001, English 2003) presents yet another Russian dystopia, describing the very primitive conditions some two hundred years after nuclear catastrophe has struck. In *The Slynx*, books are reserved for the rulers, and as in Soviet times, literature is regarded as dangerous. Tolstaya uses these conditions to connect this dystopic world to our familiar one. Despite being vividly imagined, too much of *The Slynx* resembles familiar futuristic fictions. Tolstaya strains to outdo her predecessors in Hieronymus Bosch–like hellish visions but too often loses her focus on the narrative itself.

Prize-winning author **Mikhail Shishkin** (b. 1961) is one of the leading writers in post–Soviet Russia and has begun to make a great impression abroad as well. Much of *Maidenhair* (2005, English 2012), the first of his works to be translated into English, consists of the back and forth of dialogue as a Swiss official questions asylum seekers from the former Soviet Union, but the novel also has several different planes. The interpreter who translates from the Russian is both a conduit and narrator as well as the central figure in the novel. Among the projects on which he once worked was a biography of a Russian singer, and along with some of his own memories, the novel contains extensive excerpts from his working material, such as the singer's diaries, which she began nearly a hundred years earlier. Tying in even myth and ancient history, Shishkin constructs an unusual epic in which he reflects on Russian history, the telling of stories—personal and historic—and human relationships.

Shishkin's *The Light and the Dark* (2010, English 2013) is an unusual epistolary novel, the exchange of letters between separated lovers that begins during the Chinese Boxer Rebellion. A tale of lost and impossible love, the chapters alternate between his and her letters in two diverging time lines. Facing an increasingly unbridgeable divide, they ultimately are writing for themselves, not for each other, in a novel that again suggests the power and importance of writing itself.

KEEP IN MIND

- **Ludmilla Petrushevskaya's** (b. 1938) novel of a family in crisis, in a country in crisis, is entitled *The Time: Night* (1992, English 2000). Her collections of short stories are particularly worth seeking out.
- **Vladimir Sharov's** (b. 1952) remarkable *Before and During* (1993, English 2014) is the first of his works available in English.
- **Dmitry Bykov's** (b. 1967) *Living Souls* (2006, English 2010) is a darkly comic dystopian vision of a future Russia and civil war.
- **Ludmila Ulitskaya's** (b. 1943) fiction is worth a look.

Genre Fiction

As in all the Communist nations, little domestic crime and mystery fiction was published during Soviet times. Even though theft and murder could not be entirely ignored, they had to be situated within the prevailing ideological framework. Accordingly, domestic private-eye and detective novels never had a chance, and the formula for procedurals almost always relied on subversive foreign agents being thwarted. However, post–Soviet (and crime-ridden) Russia has seen an explosion of the mystery and thriller genre, although leading authors such as **Darya Dontsova** (b. 1952) and **Alexandra Marinina** (b. 1957) have not been translated.

Among the few crime writers to find a wider readership abroad is the prolific and talented **Boris Akunin** (b. 1956), whose novels are set in prerevolutionary Russia. Akunin's series of historical mysteries featuring Erast Fandorin offers both local color and clever literary play. Each volume is based on a specific kind of mystery novel, beginning with the conspiracy tale *The Winter Queen* (1998, English 2003). Balancing irony and respect for the genre, Akunin's novels are those of a clever, well-read craftsman and are fine examples of what can be done within the framework of the crime novel. The second series is closer to the classic Russian literary tradition. set in the nineteenth century. It begins with *Sister Pelagia and the White Bulldog* (1999, English 2007), in which a nun does the investigating.

Science fiction fared somewhat better than crime novels in Soviet times, led by the **Strugatsky** brothers, **Arkady** (1925–1991) and **Boris** (1933–2012). Their stories offer considerably more than mere escapism and stand up well for works in a genre that can quickly become dated. *Hard to Be God* (1964, English 1973, 2014) is a fine novel in which historians from an advanced civilization travel to a more backward planet where inhabitants are suffering under an increasingly totalitarian regime. One of the historians feels compelled to intervene, raising a number of ethical questions. Andrei Tarkovsky's classic film *Stalker* is based on the Strugatskys' most famous work, *Roadside Picnic* (1972, English 1977, 2012). In that story, aliens' detritus is found at various spots on the earth, and even though it appears to be simply the garbage they left behind, it is far more advanced than human technology. These artifacts can be incredibly useful—an apparently endless power supply, for example—but many are also entirely beyond the grasp of human understanding.

Sergei Lukyanenko (b. 1968) is currently immensely popular in Russia, and his elaborate fantasy series that begins with *The Night Watch* (also published as *Night Watch*; 1998, English 2006) became the basis of several trashy Russian blockbuster movies. Lukyanenko's supernatural otherworld, an elaborately imagined reality of so-called Others who exist not only in this world but on another plane as well, has some appeal, especially in the alternate version of contemporary Moscow in which the series starts, but despite their immoderation his novels still rarely go beyond the genre's limitations.

BELARUS

Despite his differences with the Soviet regime, the most highly regarded and popular Belarusan author, **Vasil Bykov** (1924–2003), remained in the Soviet Union until its collapse. Only in 1998 did he emigrate from his homeland, a sign of how badly conditions in Belarus had deteriorated in the post-Soviet era under Alexander Lukashenko.

Not surprisingly, little fiction of note has emerged recently from this totalitarian outlier of Europe.

Bykov is best known for his realistic wartime novels. In contrast to much war fiction, especially in Soviet literature, his works do not simply glorify the actions and achievements of those involved in the conflict but instead present a more nuanced picture of combat and wartime, taking into account the moral complexities of war. Several of these books have been translated into English, though generally from the Russian versions rather than the Belarusan originals. *Sign of Misfortune* (1982, English 1990), on the dreadful life of a Belarusan farming couple during the German occupation in World War II, is a bleak but good example of his work and this genre.

Victor Martinovich's (b. 1977) *Paranoia* (2010, English 2013) never mentions the author's native Belarus, but the totalitarian state that is so convincingly depicted in the novel closely resembles it. It is no surprise, then, to learn that the book was removed from local bookstores only a few days after its publication.

UKRAINE

Even before the Orange Revolution, which started in the fall of 2004, Ukraine had a burgeoning literary scene, though little of it is apparent in English translation yet.

Yuri Andrukhovych (b. 1960) is the most visible representative of the new Ukrainian wave. In autobiographical works like *The Moscoviad* (1993, English 2008), about his time studying at the Gorky Institute, Moscow's famous writers' school, and the untranslated *Taiemnytsia* (2007), Andrukhovych depicts the Soviet period in its last days. Poetic excess, in both word and deed, often fueled by alcohol, as well as mind-altered states and uncertain realities figure prominently in much of his work, especially in the fantastical *Recreations* (1992, English 1998) and *Perverzion* (1993, English 2005). Andrukhovych's dense body of work, with its references to the larger contemporary

Ukrainian literary scene and his own experiences, is best appreciated together rather than separately, but each volume also can be enjoyed on its own.

Even though Ukrainian-writing authors have begun to enjoy considerable success abroad, the best-known contemporary Ukrainian author, **Andrey Kurkov** (b. 1961), writes in Russian. Several of his novels are among the most likable entertainments written in that language in recent years. *Death and the Penguin* (1996, English 2001) is set after the fall of Communism, its protagonist a writer who has adopted a penguin from the local zoo that was not able to provide for the upkeep of the animals any longer and who now makes a living writing obituaries that turn out to be uncomfortably prescient. Their adventures continue in *Penguin Lost* (2002, English 2004), and both books provide a poignantly amusing view of the first years of the newly independent Ukraine. *A Matter of Death and Life* (1996, English 2005), in which a man arranges for a hit man to assassinate him but then changes his mind, is also a morbidly funny take on Ukrainian conditions in the mid-1990s.

Oksana Zabuzhko's (b. 1960) *Field Work in Ukrainian Sex* (1996, English 2011) features a Ukrainian protagonist who is a guest lecturer at an American university and is looking back on a destructive affair. While much here is familiar, Zabuzhko's voice and some of the exotic elements suggest a promising talent. The far more ambitious *The Museum of Abandoned Secrets* (2009, English 2012) is a reckoning with contemporary Ukrainian history and conditions from a feminist perspective, in a complex saga that combines realism and mythical elements.

KEEP IN MIND

- **Volodymyr Dibrova**'s (b. 1951) *Peltse* (1984) and *Pentameron* (1993) are comic absurdist novellas still set in the Soviet period. They were published in one volume in English in 1996.

MOLDOVA

Tucked between Ukraine and Romania, the former Moldavian Soviet Socialist Republic became independent Moldova in 1991. The official national language is Romanian (though it continues to also be called Moldovan, as the Soviets insisted), but almost no fiction from the area has been translated into English. Russian-writing **Vladimir Lorchenkov**'s (b. 1979) *The Good Life Elsewhere* (2008, English 2014), a darkly comic tale of Moldovans seeking a better life abroad, follows in the tradition of Soviet-style satire with its absurdist features but also provides an entertaining portrait of the poorest country in Europe.

THE CAUCASUS

The Caucasus—the area between the Black Sea and the Caspian that includes the former Soviet states of Armenia, Azerbaijan, Chechnya, and Georgia—has a rich literary tradition, though little fiction from the area has been translated into English.

Several works by **Otar Chiladze** (1933–2009), the leading Georgian writer to emerge in the Soviet Union, have been translated, notably his popular first novel, *A Man Was Going Down the Road* (1972, English 2012). This is a broad epic about Georgia, especially under Russian rule, that builds on the story of Jason and the Golden Fleece. Other recent fiction from post–Soviet Georgia includes novels such as *Journey to Karabakh* (1992, English 2014) by **Aka Morchiladze** (b. 1966) and *Adibas* (2009, English 2014) by **Zaza Burchuladze** (b. 1973)

Abkhazian author **Fazil Iskander**'s (b. 1929) most impressive work is the collection of connected stories centering on an imaginary Abkhazian village. Although Iskander began writing the stories, which were published in *Sandro of Chegem* (English 1983) and *The Gospel According to Chegem* (English 1984), in the 1970s, the complete collection was not published in the original Russian until 1989. The stories' narrator recounts the adventures of his Uncle Sandro from the early nineteenth century to Stalinist times and contains an enormous cast of characters, with appearances from various historical figures, including Stalin himself. Iskander's work has plenty of humor, is vividly imagined, and full of creative storytelling.

CENTRAL ASIA

During the Soviet era, there was some effort to encourage regional literature, though much of it was written in Russian. But after the collapse of the Soviet Union, very little new fiction has come out of many of these areas, especially Central Asia, which is still dominated by totalitarian regimes.

Chingiz Aitmatov (1928–2008) was one of the most important writers from what is now Kyrgyzstan. His most ambitious novel, *The Day Lasts More Than a Hundred Years* (1981, English 1983), offers an evocative depiction of Kazakh life under Soviet rule. The novel tells the story of an old man traveling to try to give his friend a proper burial. But an odd science fiction story line involving an American and a Soviet cosmonaut surreptitiously making contact with intelligent aliens is less than ideally integrated into the book. Despite the story's consequences for the central character's mission and its effective critique of Cold War politics, it makes for a very strange fit. *The White Ship* (1970, English 1972) ends darkly, with its young protagonist, just a boy, committing suicide, but Aitmatov's novella compellingly contrasts a very environmentally conscious Central Asian tradition with a harsher Soviet reality.

Russian-born **Yury Dombrovsky** (1909–1978) was exiled to Kazakhstan in the 1930s and wrote wonderful autobiographical novels inspired by his experiences there. *The Keeper of Antiquities* (1964, English 1969) and Dombrovsky's magnum opus, *The Faculty of Useless Knowledge* (1978, English 1995), both featuring an archaeologist named Zybin, are set in Kazakhstan during the Stalinist terror. Dombrovsky expertly uses the locale to accentuate the absurdities of the Soviet system in which the young archaeologist finds himself a pawn in a show trial, and his historical expertise helps paint a rich picture of the area. The setting—and Dombrovsky's sense of humor—give *The Faculty of Useless Knowledge* a feel very different from that of the other fiction covering the same period but set in Moscow or from the later Gulag fiction.

Andrei Volos (b. 1955) was born and raised in Tajikistan but left after the collapse of the Soviet Union. In *Hurramabad* (2000, English 2001), he describes the fate of several ethnic Russians with strong ties to Tajikistan who are ultimately robbed of their last illusions, their hopes of being able to continue living in their homeland as before, which are dashed as the pent-up resentment against all Russians boiled over in Tajikistan in the early 1990s. The English edition of the novel, which contains only half the original stories, graphically documents the country's resurgent nationalism and tribalism as well as everyday life as Tajikistan made its very rough transition to becoming an independent nation-state in the 1990s.

Hamid Ismailov (b. 1954), an Uzbek author born in Kyrgyzstan, has lived in exile in Britain since the 1990s; his work is still banned in Uzbekistan. Several of his novels have been translated from Russian, notably *The Railway* (1997, English 2006), set in Gilas, a fictional town and crossroad, and *The Dead Lake* (2011, English 2014), a novel about the fallout of the Soviets' nuclear tests on the steppes of Kazakhstan. The novel of most immediate interest to American audiences is Ismailov's *A Poet and Bin-Laden* (2005, English 2012), which chronicles the radicalization of an Uzbek poet, Belgi, in the wake of the attacks on September 11.

MONGOLIA

Despite being forced to adopt a Mongolian name, **Galsan Tschinag** (b. 1943) is in fact Tuvan—and, having studied in Leipzig, writes mainly in German. His novel *The Blue Sky* (1994, English 2006)—the first in an autobiographical cycle—is the first of his books to be translated into English, and it offers a good, if incomplete, introduction to his work. Describing his boyhood during a time when Soviet collectivization threatened traditionally nomadic Tuvan life, Tschinag impresses with his ability to convey this harsh natural world and the relationship of the characters to it.

G. Mend-Ooyo's (b. 1952) poetic *Golden Hill* (1999, English 2007), another autobiographical work steeped in the Mongolian countryside and lore, is the rare work of fiction actually translated from Mongolian. Difficult to place in any familiar literary tradition, its appeal is largely as a piece of exotica.

United Kingdom and Ireland

British fiction has always had great variety, even though much of it is Anglo-centric, usually English. Even when the colonial experience provided new perspectives, works such as **E. M. Forster's** (1879–1970) *A Passage to India* (1924), **George Orwell's** (1903–1950) *Burmese Days* (1934), and Anglo-Irish author **Joyce Cary's** (1888–1957) *Mister Johnson* (1939) remained distinctly English at their hearts. In recent decades, however, the British retreat from colonial governance has invigorated writing throughout the Commonwealth, and British writing as a whole has become much less insular. Even though the colonial heritage is only slowly being shaken off, contemporary British authors have been able to look abroad with much less of that baggage than previous generations had. Meanwhile, first- and second-generation British immigrants such as **V. S. Naipaul** (b. 1932) and **Zadie Smith** (b. 1975) have become major contributors to what has become a much more fluid exchange with the world at large. Traditionally popular British fiction, from mysteries to social novels with their peculiarly English preoccupation with class, as well as newer genre variations, such as the chick lit wave that came in the wake of **Helen Fielding**'s (b. 1958) ***Bridget Jones's Diary*** (1996), also enjoy great success both in Britain and abroad.

The political devolution of Wales and Scotland in the late 1990s has been part of a greater independence movement that has also seen vastly increased support for and interest in local literature. While London remains the vibrant literary center of the nation as a whole, the Welsh and Scottish literary scenes both compete with and complement it. Both writing in Welsh and translation from and into Welsh has increased considerably, and both Welsh and Scottish publishers also are strongly involved in making foreign literature available in English translation.

In contrast, Irish writers have been able to maintain a more distinct identity, despite their ties to Britain. Irish-language fiction, however, is seldom translated, perhaps because of the great success of so many Irish authors writing in English.

ENGLAND

London's preeminent place as a publishing and literary base, as well as the literary breeding grounds of the English universities, draw writers from throughout Britain and abroad, making England one of the two dominant regions—along with the United States—of English-language writing. American authors, especially of popular fiction, may be even more popular globally, but English writers are nonetheless widely published abroad and make notable contributions to the enormous market share of fiction written in English. Writers born abroad—usually in former British colonies—who have studied or settled in England have long been important contributors to the literary scene, from **Joseph Conrad** (1857–1924) to **V. S. Naipaul** (b. 1932) and **Salman Rushdie** (b. 1947), and in recent years, this class of writers has expanded rapidly, in both size and significance.

Much of the most popular fiction at which English authors excel is strongly rooted in English specifics, most notably mysteries. Although the golden age of English detective fiction reached a peak between the two world wars, modern variations on the mystery continue to enjoy great and deserved success. Writers like **P. D. James** (1920–2014) and the more prolific **Ruth Rendell** (1930–2015) (who also wrote as Barbara Vine) have consistently produced some of the best-crafted works of serial fiction of recent decades. Much of the appeal of mystery novels is that they are dependably formulaic, but the genre has been constantly renewed, from the works of **Derek Raymond** (1931–1994) to **David Peace's** (b. 1967) violent quartet of books covering an era in Yorkshire, the **Red Riding** series, which begins with *Nineteen Seventy-Four* (1999).

Literary standards for the spy thriller tend not to be as demanding as for mysteries, but the novels of authors such as **Eric Ambler** (1909–1998), **Ian Fleming** (1908–1964), and **Len Deighton** (b. 1929) remain impressive foundational texts, and **Graham Greene's** (1904–1991) political thrillers, as well as **John le Carré's** (b. 1931) spy fiction, transcend the genre. **George MacDonald Fraser's** (1925–2008) Flashman is a brilliantly conceived and utilized fictional antihero. The character was a cast-off from **Thomas Hughes's** (1822–1896) classic *Tom Brown's School Days* (1857), who was appropriated by Fraser and featured in a dozen volumes of historical adventures published between 1969 and 2005. Although Flashman may be an almost ridiculously politically incorrect protagonist, Fraser's alternative versions of colonial Victorian history are nonetheless entertaining.

The recent young adult fiction series like **J. K. Rowling's** (b. 1965) Harry Potter saga (1997–2007) and works by **Philip Pullman** (b. 1946), like his nineteenth-century Sally Lockhart quartet (1985–1994) and the parallel-universe trilogy of *His Dark Materials* (1995–2000), have been immensely popular. Despite the prominent use of magical and fantastical elements in all of these, much about the characters and locales feels very English, such as the boarding school settings, the descriptions of Oxbridge-like academic life, and the very British awareness of social class distinctions. These and similar qualities of

Englishness are widely found in both the English genre fiction that has traveled well and much of the more literary fiction.

Penelope Fitzgerald (1916–2000) began publishing fiction late in life—her first novel appeared in 1977—but her finely hewn short novels are beautiful. A series of works of English life was followed by several with historical or foreign settings, including *The Beginning of Spring* (1988), set in prerevolutionary Moscow, and *The Blue Flower* (1995), her version of the eighteenth-century German poet Novalis's love affair with a young girl.

A. S. Byatt (b. 1936) sometimes gets carried away in presenting period detail—whether of the nineteenth century or the 1960s—but her stories and precise, controlled writing are consistently impressive. *Possession* (1990), her novel of letters, poetry, and love, weaves together the stories of two contemporary scholars and their research on two Victorian poets. It is one of her most appealing works. The quartet of novels of English life and culture in the 1950s and 1960s featuring Frederica Potter, beginning with *The Virgin in the Garden* (1978) and closing with *A Whistling Woman* (2002), is a convincing record of the times.

Ian McEwan (b. 1948) is another careful and precise writer. His early works are dark and unsettling, but his later novels tend to have a more measured approach. Much of his work turns on a single event or circumstance as he explores the ripple effects that these cause. Aside from

---

OTHER ENGLISH WRITERS I

- **Iris Murdoch**'s (1919–1999) elaborate and often profoundly philosophical books offer considerable intellectual satisfaction.
- **Margaret Drabble** (b. 1939), A. S. Byatt's sister, also has written a number of solid works.
- Some of **Kingsley Amis**'s (1922–1995) fiction already is dated, but several works, like the comic *Lucky Jim* (1954), remain entertaining records of their day.
- **David Lodge**'s (b. 1935) fiction, especially his amusing novels of modern academia, also is worth reading.

Amsterdam (1998)—a misstep with an over-the-top denouement, for which he nevertheless won the Booker Prize—most of his work is strong, with his novels about the loss of a child, *The Child in Time* (1987), and about betrayal, *Atonement* (2001), among the best. Some readers, however, find irritating the cloying realism of his most recent works.

Even though his tales often revel in the sordid, the talented **Martin Amis** (b. 1949) has a wonderful way with words and feel for language, which he always makes his own. A great admirer of Saul Bellow (1915–2005), Amis's aggressive, forced style can be both riveting and off-putting. *Money: A Suicide Note* (1984) is narrated by a character named John Self and offers all that Amis does best. While parts of the boozy, self-loathing novel may be hard to stomach, *Money* is also very funny. Amis often toys with formal constraints as well, most notably in the underrated *Time's Arrow* (1991). In this novel, the narrator, a doctor who was involved in the medical experimentation at Auschwitz, recounts his life, but he experiences it unspooling in reverse as he finds himself regressing from old age to infancy. Amis's later work has grown increasingly uneven, however, and includes ambitious failures such as the messy *Yellow Dog* (2003). Among Amis's weakest works are those in which he is unable to temper his polemical streak and feels compelled to tackle the issues of the day, mixing nonfiction and fiction in collections such as *Einstein's Monsters* (1987) and *The Second Plane* (2008).

OTHER ENGLISH WRITERS II

- **Julian Barnes**'s (b. 1946) creative, varied output—including the quartet of crime novels featuring the bisexual former policeman Duffy, published under the pseudonym of Dan Kavanagh—is consistently rewarding.
- The prolific **Peter Ackroyd** (b. 1949) writes much nonfiction, but the best of his imaginative works, such as the alternative-history novel *Milton in America* (1997) and the speculative *The Plato Papers* (1999), are fascinating.
- **Howard Jacobson**'s (b. 1942) powerful writing and his darkly comic novels that often feature Jewish characters inevitably draw comparisons to Philip Roth.

From the amusing punk and rock music thriller, *The Dwarves of Death* (1990), to a variety of broader examinations of British society, **Jonathan Coe**'s (b. 1961) cleverly constructed novels are both comic and poignant. With a style more subtle than that of most of the best-known British authors, his work has resonated particularly well in the romance-language nations, especially France.

Jeanette Winterson's (b. 1959) elliptical fiction often leaves a great deal unsaid but offers unusual and captivating perspectives. Her coming-of-age debut, *Oranges Are Not the Only Fruit* (1985), features an artless narrator similar to those found in many of her works, typically facing a world in which she discovers she does not quite fit yet becomes confident in her own identity. Storytelling and art are important subjects in nearly all of Winterson's work, dealt with in a variety of forms. The appropriately entitled *Art and Lies* (1994) is one of her most interesting explorations of the subject. Even though Winterson's writing can be pretentious and sententious, it also has a great deal of creativity, and she has a fine ear for language.

The fiction of the extraordinary stylist **Gilbert Adair** (1944–2011) is replete with postmodern trickery. His smart and funny novels often use mystery tropes, whether in a deconstructionist parody like *The Death of the Author* (1992), which is loosely based on the life of literary theorist Paul de Man (1919–1983), or the trilogy of metafictional whodunit pastiches featuring Evadne Mount, beginning with *The Act of Roger Murgatroyd* (2006). Adair's fiction is influenced as well by his fascination with cinema. His novel *Love and Death on Long Island* (1990), which draws heavily on Thomas Mann's *Death in Venice* and describes an aging author suddenly confronting modernity as he becomes obsessed with a young American film actor, successfully integrates his many interests. Adair also wrote *A Void* (1994), the English rendering of Georges Perec's *La disparition*, a novel that infamously does not contain the letter *e*.

J. G. Ballard (1930–2009) is best known for his relatively conventional autobiographical novel *Empire of the Sun* (1984), about his childhood experiences in Shanghai during World War II, but the greater part of his output consists of formally varied and innovative

---

OTHER ENGLISH WRITERS III

- **Angela Carter**'s (1940–1992) groundbreaking fiction, including her many variations on fairy tales and fables, goes well beyond mere feminist interest.
- **Geoff Nicholson**'s (b. 1953) quirky and amusing novels often feature obsessed and eccentric protagonists.
- Among **Scarlett Thomas**'s (b. 1972) promising works are the excellent *PopCo* (2004) and *The End of Mr. Y* (2006).

---

fiction that is brutally critical of modernity. Many of his works can be considered science fiction and depict civilization—on small and large scales—in crisis. Novels like *Crash* (1972) offer clinical examinations of the intersection of sex, violence, and technology. His seminal collection *The Atrocity Exhibition* (1970, revised 1993; first published in the United States as *Love and Napalm: Export U.S.A.* in 1972, two years after publisher Nelson Doubleday ordered the entire print run of the planned first American edition to be destroyed) is a good and disturbing introduction to his work. With its fragmentary, avant-garde approach to narrative and chapter titles such as "Why I Want to Fuck Ronald Reagan" and "The Assassination of John Fitzgerald Kennedy Considered as a Downhill Motor Race," it is a remarkable social- and media-critical text.

Christine Brooke-Rose's (1923–2012) challenging experimental fiction follows more in the modern French tradition than in the English tradition. Her work constantly reinvents narrative possibilities, beginning at the fundamental building-block level of language, as suggested in such titles as *Verbivore* (1990) and *Textermination* (1991).

Will Self's (b. 1961) refined prose makes his relentless satires revolving around outrageous conceits even more effective. In the twin novellas *Cock & Bull* (1992), a female protagonist grows a penis and a man grows a vagina (and that behind his knee), and in *Great Apes* (1997), chimpanzees are civilized and at the highest stage of evolution, and humans are the lesser primates. In *The Book of Dave* (2006), the

---

OTHER ENGLISH WRITERS IV

- **Tom McCarthy**'s (b. 1969) *Remainder* (2005) is an artfully presented novel of memory and artistic creation.
- **Stewart Home**'s (b. 1962) rawer fiction includes pulp parodies and interesting forms of cultural criticism.

---

rantings of modern-day London cabbie Dave Rudman are dug up centuries later and became the foundational text of a new society.

The number of authors from the newly independent Commonwealth nations who attended university and/or lived in England has increased dramatically, feeding the postcolonial internationalization of English literature. Many of them are most closely identified with their national literatures, but several English-born authors have also become part of this wave, including those with an immigrant family background, such as **Hanif Kureishi** (b. 1954), **Hari Kunzru** (b. 1969), and **Zadie Smith** (b. 1975), as well as those who have lived for extended periods abroad, such as **David Mitchell** (b. 1969). Other authors who are part of this broad trend include **William Boyd** (b. 1952) as well as **Kazuo Ishiguro** (b. 1954) and **Caryl Phillips** (b. 1958), both of whom came to England as young children.

The cross-cultural and ethnic mix of **Zadie Smith**'s (b. 1975) impressive first novel, *White Teeth* (2000), as well as *On Beauty* (2005), are typical. The novels, set in London and the Boston area, respectively, have diverse casts of characters. While questions of identity and attachment to nation and culture run throughout them, Smith's works are broader social canvases, going considerably beyond the usual immigrant novel. Her comic touch and assured juggling of numerous story lines and large casts of characters make these exceptional novels.

Whereas Smith localizes her stories in communities, **Hari Kunzru**'s (b. 1969) novels *The Impressionist* (2002) and *Transmission* (2004) feature untethered protagonists. *The Impressionist* is set at the beginning of the twentieth century in the waning British Empire. The main character, Pran Nath, is a figure who repeatedly reinvents himself in futile attempts at adaptation and assimilation. *Transmission* is a modern view of the clash of cultures and the roles of individuals in a globalized economy and interconnected world. Kunzru presents a world in which characters and scenarios can be anything, anywhere—a Bollywood movie is made in the Scottish highlands, an Indian call center employee passes herself off as Australian to callers—yet they find that any sort of true escape and complete transformation is difficult to achieve.

While much fine fiction has emerged from this aspect of the British colonial heritage, other writers have succeeded in becoming part of a larger, transnational literature while sidestepping it. **Kazuo Ishiguro** (b. 1954) was born outside the Commonwealth, and his early fiction deals with his native Japan. His other understated novels, though, such as *The Remains of the Day* (1989) and *Never Let Me Go* (2005), seem typically English. Assimilation and societal roles also are at issue in these works, but it is not ethnic or national origin but social class that is pivotal. In *Never Let Me Go*, this is a new and entirely different order, in which the characters are clones bred to be organ donors.

With its often off-kilter reality and its accessible style, the fiction by longtime Japan resident **David Mitchell** (b. 1969) invites comparison with Haruki Murakami's (b. 1949) works. Mitchell's novels, such as *Ghostwritten* (1999) and *Cloud Atlas* (2004), about the new world order of global interconnections, are steeped in pop cultural (and multicultural) references. In *Black Swan Green* (2006), Mitchell temporarily retreats, presenting a conventional coming-of-age novel set in 1980s England, but his instincts and talents clearly lie with border- and

---

ENGLISH SCIENCE FICTION

England has a long, strong tradition of science fiction.

Douglas Adams's (1952–2001) entertaining series that begins with *The Hitchhiker's Guide to the Galaxy* (1979) has had great success worldwide.

Other contemporary authors worth seeking out are **M. John Harrison** (b. 1945) and **China Miéville** (b. 1972).

The creative work of **Jeff Noon** (b. 1957), which includes the alternative-reality novel *Vurt* (1993), also is intriguing.

tradition-crossing novels like the dream-filled Japanese quest story, *number9dream* (2001).

WALES

Even though the world has fewer than a million Welsh speakers, concentrated in Wales, redoubled efforts at promoting the use and preservation of the language have led to a recent resurgence of Welsh-language writing. A public policy of strong support for translation and publishing has also led to the increased availability of fiction translated into and from Welsh. Nevertheless, fiction originally written in English by Welsh authors still has a much greater reach, both in Britain and abroad.

Caradog Prichard's (1904–1980) *One Moonlit Night* (1961, English 1995, and, incompletely, as *Full Moon*, 1973), set in the early twentieth century, remains one of the most appealing and disturbing works of Welsh fiction. The simple directness of the childish perspective in the novel is deceptive, as Prichard reveals a dark world filled with adult complexity that is anything but idyllic.

In his novels, **Robin Llywelyn** (b. 1958) has turned sharply away from the generic regional fiction widespread throughout Britain. *White Star* (1992, English 2004) is a compact, futuristic fantasy novel. The adventures rush by too quickly for it to be a truly effective allegory, but the imaginative turns and his playful language and names make it an intriguing read. *From Empty Harbour to White Ocean* (1994, English 1996) is more earthbound, though it also uses fictional locales. In this novel, Llywelyn mixes myth, realism, and fantasy in presenting Gregor Marini's odyssey as he goes abroad to look for a better life in the Capital States.

Niall Griffiths (b. 1966) has emerged as one of the leading writers of Wales, though the Liverpool-born author does not originally come from there. Many of the protagonists in his novels are, similarly, drawn to Wales from elsewhere. The powerful *Grits* (2000) brings together disaffected young people who have lost themselves in an excess of

WELSH FICTION

Some English-language fiction is rooted in Wales.

John Williams's (b. 1961) vivid crime fiction is set in the Welsh capital, Cardiff.

Trezza Azzopardi's (b. 1961) *The Hiding Place* (2000) is about a family of Maltese immigrants in 1960s Cardiff that is narrated by the youngest child, the slightly disfigured Dolores.

---

drugs, sex, and crime and are trying to find a way out. The descriptions of the stark Welsh countryside, the use of curt, slangy dialogue, and the characters' overindulgence of alcohol and drugs are typical of Griffiths's rough, brutal, and lyrical fiction. *Sheepshagger* (2001), the story of the murderous Ianto, is a savage and graphic tale but nevertheless a compelling work.

SCOTLAND

The fiction of many of the best Scottish authors, including **Muriel Spark** (1918–2006) and **Ali Smith** (b. 1962), is not particularly Scottish, but issues of national identity nonetheless feature prominently in much contemporary Scottish fiction. Many authors are keen to emphasize the distinctive qualities of their nation and its people, especially in relation to England, while also exploring Scottish insecurities and English political, economic, and cultural dominance.

In recent decades, the use of Scots-inflected English and the Scottish brogue has been prominent in much of the region's best writing, as it is an obvious way of differentiating between English and Scottish identity. **Irvine Welsh**'s (b. 1958) iconic *Trainspotting* (1993), describing the heroin culture of Edinburgh's working-class neighborhoods, was a breakout work in this regard. With much of the text written with idiosyncratic spelling that barely looks like English, the prose and dialogue in *Trainspotting* are nevertheless readily decipherable. Even though the language used in the novel would seem to have a distancing effect on the reader, Welsh's stories have a striking immediacy, in no small part because of the very rawness of the language. The stories are also surprisingly accessible.

Trainspotting remains one of the most successful examples of the extensive use of nontraditional English, but even Welsh largely stopped relying on it in his later fiction. **James Kelman**'s (b. 1946) more discriminating use of the vernacular, with more emphasis on the rhythm of language than on the spelling of the words, in both the dialogue and his Samuel Beckett–like interior monologues, has also proved very effective. Kelman's feel for language is already suggested in the titles of some of his fiction, such as the story collection *Not Not While the Giro* (1983) and the novel *How Late It Was, How Late* (1994). Much of his fiction deals with Glaswegian working-class lives, and his books feature many heavy drinkers. As a consequence, the language is often realistically vulgar. The controversial Booker Prize–winning *How Late It Was, How Late* reportedly contains some four thousand uses of variations on the word "fuck," or an average of more than ten a page. These penetrating texts offer insight into the lives of its characters, though Kelman's plunges into these ravaged depths may be too protracted for many readers.

Alasdair Gray's (b. 1934) fiction often deals with nationalist and social concerns, but he also blends in history, science fiction, and satire. Despite the gloomy elements of many of his stories, they almost always have humor, a sly kind of cheer. A talented painter, Gray has designed the covers of most of his books and illustrated several of them as well. His attention to typography and the text layout embellishes what are often tales of artists. Gray's fiction is often presented in layers as an annotated memoir or with other forms of authorial intrusion into the stories.

Gray's first and greatest novel, *Lanark* (1981), shows the full range of his writing in the story of a Glasgow artist named Duncan Thaw and his later incarnation as Lanark who finds himself in a dystopian city called Unthank. A novel full of doubles and transformations, with Unthank as an allegorical reflection of Glasgow, it is arguably overfilled and overflowing with invention, but most of it is captivating. While Gray spins fantastical conceits appealingly in novels such as *Lanark* as well as the

---

KEEP IN MIND

- While much of **A. L. Kennedy**'s (b. 1965) work is dark, there is also humor to it.
- **Iain Banks** (1954–2013) wrote fiction as well as science fiction published under the name Iain M. Banks.
- **Janice Galloway**'s (b. 1956) novels examine class and personal identity.
- **Ian Rankin**'s (b. 1960) popular Edinburgh police procedurals feature Inspector Rebus.

---

futuristic *A History Maker* (1994) and the wonderful *Frankenstein*-like *Poor Things* (1992), he also handles the contemporary and everyday well in a number of his works, including his many fine short stories.

IRELAND

All of Ireland was part of the United Kingdom between 1801 and 1922, and Northern Ireland still is, but the geographic separation from the other British Isles and a strong and widely recognized literary tradition have made for what above all else seems to be a very self-confident independent writing culture. Even though most of the leading Irish fiction is published by British rather than Irish publishers, it retains a distinct identity. Among its most striking features is the self-assured ease with which writers beginning with **James Joyce** (1882–1941) and **Samuel Beckett** (1906–1989) use the English language, in contrast to what, for example, seems like the artificially refined polish found in so many of the recent works of American fiction by creative writing–program graduates.

Many American and British citizens have Irish ancestry, but much of the most popular and best Irish fiction has been pointedly insular, concerned not with the Irish experience abroad but the domestic one. With its seemingly narrow focus, Joyce's *Ulysses* (1922), the brilliant, exhaustive novel of a single Dublin day, June 16, 1904, is the ultimate exemplar, but the island and its subjects have sustained a great deal of other fiction as well.

The older generation of Irish authors also continues to play a significant role in contemporary literature, with both **Edna O'Brien** (b. 1930) and **William Trevor** (b. 1928) masters of both the novel and the short story. **John McGahern** (1934–2006) was less prolific, but his work is in the same class, and of the writers of the next generation, **Sebastian Barry**'s (b. 1955) fiction (and plays) stand out.

Other Irish authors' works have a more international scope, though it is revealing that **Hugo Hamilton**'s (b. 1953) very good first novels, set in Central Europe, remain underrated and less well known than his popular duo of Dublin crime novels featuring Pat Coyne: *Headbanger* (1996) and *Sad Bastard* (1998). **Colm Tóibín**'s (b. 1955) widely acclaimed work often includes Irish connections, but he also consistently ventures further afield, from his novel about Henry James, *The Master* (2004), to the sad but beautiful *Brooklyn* (2009). **John Banville**'s (b. 1945) stylish novels are generally dominated by lone men of often self-obsessed genius, including historical figures, as in *Doctor Copernicus* (1976) and *Kepler* (1978). Banville's novels also frequently involve issues of art and authenticity, most obviously in the loose trilogy of *The Book of Evidence* (1989), *Ghosts* (1993), and *Athena* (1995), which feature a protagonist, originally introduced as Freddie Montgomery, in different guises. John Banville has also written several earthier crime thrillers under the pen name Benjamin Black, featuring the Dublin pathologist Quirke.

The body of contemporary Irish-language (Irish Gaelic) fiction is relatively small, and of this, only a small amount is available in English. **Máirtín Ó Cadhain**'s (1905–1970) *The Dirty Dust* (1949, English 2015, and as *Graveyard Clay*, 2016), a story consisting almost entirely of the dialogue of the dead and buried in a local graveyard, is the finest and most important example. Other notable modern Irish works, such as **Séamas Mac Annaidh**'s (b. 1961) *Cuaifeach mo londubh buí* (1983), which weaves the Gilgamesh epic into a tale of contemporary Ireland, have not yet been translated. The Catholic priest **Pádraig Standún** (b. 1946) has translated his own work, and his locally popular, straightforward novels offer some insight into the community and social issues, especially those involving the church.

KEEP IN MIND

- **Flann O'Brien** (1912–1966) (the pen name of Brian O'Nolan / Brian Ó Nualláin) wrote clever and allusive humorous fiction, including the modern classics *At Swim-Two-Birds* (1939) and the posthumously published *The Third Policeman* (1967).
- **Aidan Higgins**'s (1927–2015) works of fiction experiment with style and language in the rich Irish tradition.
- **Patrick McCabe**'s (b. 1955) dark fiction includes the twisted novel *The Butcher Boy* (1992).
- **Anne Enright**'s (b. 1962) fiction, especially about family life, is distinctive.
- **Roddy Doyle** (b. 1958) has written several popular novels that also have been filmed, beginning with *The Commitments* (1987).
- **Eoin Colfer**'s (b. 1965) young adult series is based on the antihero Artemis Fowl (begun 2001).

Sub-Saharan
Africa

Southern Africa

Several of the nations in southern Africa were among the last on the continent to gain independence, Zimbabwe in 1980 and Namibia only in 1990. The largest country in the region, South Africa, remained a pariah state until 1994, when it finally ended its policy of racial segregation (apartheid). But even during apartheid, South Africa was a significant political, economic, and cultural power in the region and exerted considerable influence. The most developed regional book market was (and continues to be) in South Africa, but until 1994, due to apartheid, opportunities for authors who were not white were limited. Throughout the area, English-language (and in South Africa, also Afrikaans) writing still dominates the market, though a small amount of fiction from regional languages is available in translation.

SOUTH AFRICA

Olive Schreiner's (1855–1920) novel of frank feminism and theological soul-searching, misleadingly entitled *The Story of an African Farm* (1883; originally published under the pseudonym Ralph Iron), is widely considered the first South African novel. Significant works of the early twentieth century include several written by black authors, such as **Sol T. Plaatje's** (1876–1932) *Mhudi* (1930), set during the regional conflicts of the 1830s, and **Thomas Mofolo's** (1876–1948) classic Sesotho novel *Chaka* (1925, English 1931, 1981), loosely based on the great Zulu leader.

Alan Paton's (1903–1988) *Cry, the Beloved Country* (1948), published while the legal framework for apartheid was being assembled, grapples with many of the issues that would be of concern in the following decades. Depicting disenfranchised and uprooted blacks turning to violence and a white population seeking to preserve its privileged position even at the cost of social unrest and uncertainty, the novel offers only a little hope.

The officially entrenched second-class treatment of blacks was common throughout much of colonial Africa even after World War II, and only with the wave of independence that swept the continent in the 1960s did South Africa's policy of apartheid truly set it apart. Much as almost all the fiction from the Soviet Union that was published in the West either described the shortcomings and horrors of the Communist system or satirized it, the South African fiction published abroad almost inevitably dealt with the consequences and costs of apartheid.

Writers like **Ezekiel (E'skia) Mphahlele** (1919–2008) and **Alex La Guma** (1925–1985) spent much of their life in exile. Mphahlele returned to South Africa in 1977 after two decades abroad, and his major works are informed by his experience of exile. In *The Wanderers* (1971) the protagonist, Timi Tabane, has the same experiences as Mphahlele did, sharing his frustration over the few possibilities for a black man in South Africa but finding conditions elsewhere in Africa to be difficult as well. *Chirundu* (1979), whose central character is a cabinet minister fallen from grace and power, is about the abuse of power in an unidentified newly independent African country, a danger that Mphahlele saw across the continent. Alex La Guma's novella *A Walk in the Night* (1962), published before he left South Africa in 1966, offers a vivid picture of the bustling shady life in District Six, a largely "coloured" (mixed-race) neighborhood in Cape Town. La Guma's tale of murder and criminal activity reveals another dark side of South African life. Although race also plays a role here, it is a secondary one and only a part of these characters' searches for identities.

Awarded the Nobel Prize in Literature in 1991, **Nadine Gordimer**'s (1923–2014) fiction closely mirrors South African conditions since the beginning of apartheid, ranging from her more personal and relatively hopeful realist works in the 1950s to the darker experimental works of the 1970s and 1980s and then novels exploring the new uncertainties that came after the introduction of universal suffrage in 1994. Despite her long-standing opposition to official policies on race, Gordimer always was committed to remaining in South Africa, and almost all her novels are set there. She wrote more than a dozen novels and even more collections of short stories. Often simpler than her longer fiction, her precise realist style works to best effect in her stories.

Burger's Daughter (1979) is one of Gordimer's best novels. Unlike most of her fiction, it is presented in a number of voices and perspectives. The novel follows the lives of both the Communist activist Lionel Burger and his daughter, Rosa, who must decide to what extent she wishes to follow in her father's footsteps. In describing Lionel's political engagement over several decades, culminating with his life sentence and death in prison, Gordimer recounts the history of opposition to official policies. However, Lionel's actions also seem quite paternalistic. After her father's death, Rosa goes abroad to try to distance herself from her homeland and the issues to which her father devoted himself, but she ultimately finds that she must return and become active too.

A Guest of Honour (1970) is one of Gordimer's few novels not set in South Africa but instead in an imaginary African country that has just made the transition to independence. The central character, Evelyn James Bray, is a former colonial administrator, and the scenario in which Gordimer places him allows her to consider the complex relationship between the new and old holders of power. Even though independence allows for local rule, the new leadership displays many similarities with the old, and Bray becomes a pawn between the forces trying to determine the country's future. In *July's People* (1981), Gordimer goes further with her invention, imagining what South Africa might look like when the old order is finally upset, in a vision that is far more violent than what actually came to pass in the 1990s. In the novel, all the characters find their positions radically changed as a civil war rages, with July sheltering the Smales family, for whom he worked as a servant.

South Africa's other Nobel laureate, the brilliant **J. M. Coetzee** (b. 1940), moved to Australia in 2002, the year before he won the prize, and has since become an Australian citizen, but much of his work is explicitly South African. Coetzee's writing is precise, and though his careful exposition can seem coldly rational, he manages to convey deep emotion as well. Despite the similarities in many of his works, including Coetzee's frequent use of obvious alter egos, his writing is varied. He is constantly trying to reshape the novel's form, often with dazzling results.

Several of Coetzee's novels deal with brutality, whether devastating to an entire people or only the individuals on whom he focuses. His books also commonly include writers, diarists, and others who have a story to tell, even though they often are unable to readily do so. This is most obvious in his variation on *Robinson Crusoe*, *Foe* (1987), in which Friday is rendered literally speech-less, having had his tongue cut out. Coetzee also frequently explores the relationship between author and text. In *The Vietnam Project*, the first of the two novellas in **Dusklands** (1974), Eugene Dawn is charged with writing a report on the use of psychological warfare in the Vietnam War, an undertaking that drives him to a nervous breakdown. In **Diary of a Bad Year** (2007), the narrative follows first two and then three different tracks on the same page: essays—both political and personal—running along the top part of each page, with their fictional author providing commentary below, eventually joined by the diary-like comments by Anya, the neighbor whom he employs as a typist and to whom he is attracted. In his frequent use of characters that bear his name—Eugene's supervisor in *The Vietnam Project* is named Coetzee, for example—or bear a strong resemblance to him—from the "Señor C" in *Diary of a Bad Year* to Elizabeth Costello of the eponymous novel (2003) and **Slow Man** (2005)—Coetzee constantly examines questions of personal culpability and the role of the writer.

Coetzee's novels frequently deal with mechanisms for survival, whether in a violent South Africa, in novels such as **Life & Times of Michael K** (1983) and **Disgrace** (1999), or in confronting old age in novels like *Slow Man*. While not necessarily pessimistic, his stories are often very dark. *Disgrace*'s clinical honesty about the characters' failures and suffering is typical. In that novel, David Lurie is a professor whose unwillingness to go through the motions of apology and remorse in a case of sexual harassment leads to his being forced from his university position in disgrace. He flees to his daughter Lucy's farm in the countryside, where she lives and works alongside newly and increasingly empowered blacks. Although she is gang-raped, she, like her father, chooses to avoid allowing the authorities to handle the situation. Despite both being very strong-willed characters, they also can be seen as misguided. *Disgrace* is, among other things, a novel of trying to find one's place in post-apartheid South Africa. Perhaps tellingly, Coetzee himself abandoned the country only a few years later.

Since the mid-1960s, **Zakes Mda** (b. 1948) has lived mainly in both Lesotho, a small landlocked kingdom surrounded by South Africa, and abroad. Best known in South Africa for his plays, Zakes Mda has also published several notable works of fiction, beginning with **Ways of Dying** (1995). Toloki, the protagonist of that novel, is a professional mourner, hired to grieve at funerals in post-apartheid South Africa. Like Noria, the childhood friend with whom he reconnects, and many others encountered in the novel, he is a broken man, but he also manages to channel his despair and retains some sense of optimism. While Mda does not confront sufficiently some of the horrors his characters face, *Ways of Dying* is full of well-conceived scenes and stories. Mda brings Toloki back in **Cion** (2007), in which the now more worldly character changes pace by traveling to the United States. The outsider's commentary on 2004 America and the many stories Mda weaves into the narrative make for an engaging read, but it cannot match the sad charm of *Ways of Dying*.

Several of **Damon Galgut**'s (b. 1963) novels of contemporary South Africa are set in isolated and apparently quiet parts of the country, but Galgut's plots reveal much that at first passes unseen. In *The Impostor* (2008), middle-aged Adam Napier loses his job in the city, replaced by the black intern he trained, and imagines he can reinvent himself by pursuing his old dream of becoming a poet. He moves to the countryside but, rather than finding his muse, drifts into questionable and ultimately dangerous activities, having an affair with his neighbor's wife and then getting drawn into the neighbor's opaque business dealings. Adam's self-deluding attitude is a defensive mechanism in a world in which all the rules seem to have changed and everyone is something of an impostor. *The Quarry* (1995) is even more obviously about an impostor, as it begins with a fugitive hitchhiker killing the minister who picks him up and then assuming his place. Galgut's lean prose adds to the tension in his novels, and both *The Impostor* and *The Quarry* read almost like thrillers. Indeed, the sequence of short chapters at the end of *The Quarry* mirrors the breathless rush toward its conclusion.

Ivan Vladislavić (b. 1957) is another South African novelist in a line that extends from Gordimer through Coetzee, writing fiction that shifts between playful and direct. The narrator of *The Restless Supermarket* (2001) is a retired proofreader living in the Johannesburg district of Hillbrow as apartheid's grip loosens. He is a keen if idiosyncratic observer of details, finding signs of decay—moral and social as well as physical—in everything around him. In *The Folly* (1993), the protagonist, Nieuwenhuizen, imagines building an immense, elaborate house on an empty plot of land. Although this all remains in his head, it takes on a reality of its own in an appealing parable of imagining and constructing something entirely new. It ends, however, with the edifice's destruction. The three-part *Double Negative* (2010), dipping into photographer Neville Lister's life at three points in his life from 1982 to 2009, is a beautifully and subtly wrought character portrait that also addresses issues of identity, the past, and change in contemporary South Africa.

KEEP IN MIND

- **Zoë Wicomb**'s (b. 1948) fiction is set in South Africa.
- The title of **Phaswane Mpe**'s (1970–2004) short, powerful novel of contemporary urban South Africa is *Welcome to Our Hillbrow* (2001).
- **Niq Mhlongo** (b. 1973) wrote *Dog Eat Dog* (2004) and *After Tears* (2008).
- **Lauren Beukes** (b. 1976) cleverly mixes science fiction and thriller elements in novels set in South Africa, such as *Moxyland* (2008) and *Zoo City* (2010).

Njabulo S. Ndebele's (b. 1948) *Fools and Other Stories* (1983) is a collection of stories mainly about childhood and township life, and it continues to be widely read. But his more recent novel mixing fact and fiction, *The Cry of Winnie Mandela* (2003), also deserves attention. The novel describes four women who, for different reasons, have endured the common South African lot of having been separated from their husbands for extended periods of time. They have spent much of their lives awaiting their return, like Penelope waiting for Odysseus. Part of the novel has them each presenting imagined conversations with the mother of the nation, Winnie Mandela, who endured a similar ordeal—but much more publicly. In the time in which the book is set, Winnie Mandela was a fallen idol, and Ndebele's work is a fascinating semifictional exploration of history, personality, and how South African women dealt with the long absences of the men in their lives.

Writing in Zulu

Zulu (or isiZulu) has about 10 million native speakers. There is a fairly extensive body of Zulu literature going back to the early part of the twentieth century, though only a small part is available in English translation. Despite the continuing efforts to encourage and sustain writing in Zulu and other indigenous languages—South Africa has eleven official languages—these have had little success to date. But along with improvements in the educational system, they should eventually help in developing stronger literary cultures in these languages. Certainly, the relatively large number of native Zulu speakers ensures its long-term viability as a literary language.

Much of Zulu literature is based on the strong oral tradition of Zulu culture, and **Mazisi Kunene**'s (1930–2006) two verse epics, which he translated himself, are excellent examples. *Emperor Shaka the Great* (English 1979) offers another reading of the great Zulu leader, while *Anthem of the Decades* (English 1981) is a poetic rendering of the Zulu creation myth.

Writing in Afrikaans

Afrikaans, which is closely related to Dutch, has about 6 million native speakers in South Africa. Several major South African authors write in both English and Afrikaans, most notably **Breyten Breytenbach** (b. 1939), best known for his poetry and autobiographical works, and **André Brink** (1935–2015). Whereas Brink originally wrote most of his fiction in Afrikaans, he wrote his epic thriller, *An Act of Terror* (1981), in English. It is the story of a botched political assassination attempt, which forces the Afrikaner protagonist, Thomas Landman, underground and then increasingly desperately on the run as the police close in. While Brink is not entirely comfortable with the genre, he creates a good deal of suspense and uses this simple and standard plot to present a fascinating picture of many aspects of South African life from an Afrikaner perspective, especially the different shades of resistance, complicity, and guilt. In *A Dry White Season* (1979, English 1979), perhaps his best-known work, Brink presents the dawning of the characters' realization of the true depths and depravity of the state security system.

Several of Brink's novels that do not directly deal with contemporary events are also of considerable interest. *A Chain of Voices* (1982, English 1982) is based on a historical slave uprising in South Africa in the early nineteenth century. The chapters are monologues in which dozens of characters touched by these events tell their stories and reflect on what happened. Brink is less concerned with presenting a realist account here than with exploring the relationships between blacks and whites and the background of slavery and, by extension, apartheid. In his very amusing novella *The First Life of Adamastor* (published in the United States as *Cape of Storms*; 1988, English 1993), Brink goes back further, spinning a ribald myth around the first encounters between Europeans and South Africans in the late fifteenth century. A white woman is abandoned there and Brink's Rabelaisian hero, T'Kama, a local chieftain who is endowed with a very inconveniently oversized sexual organ, falls in love with her. T'Kama narrates the story from the present, looking back on what happened five hundred years ago and describing how he also lost her, which he includes as part of a cycle of black/white encounters that has continued ever since.

Marlene van Niekerk's (b. 1954) huge novels *Triomf* (1994, English 1999) and *Agaat* (published in Great Britain as *The Way of the Women*; 2004, English 2006) offer detailed, intimate pictures of South African lives. *Triomf* is a raw and comic family portrait of an often overlooked social class. The Benades are a white-trash family living in the Johannesburg suburb of Triomf, confronting a rapidly changing world that left them behind a long time ago. This is made all the more obvious now, in 1994, as they anticipate the first post-apartheid elections as well as the fortieth birthday of their son Lambert. In *The Way of the Women*, Milla de Wet is crippled by a degenerative disease that leaves her able to communicate only by blinking. She is cared for by Agaat, the black woman who was both a foster child and a servant in the farming household. As Milla now tries to sum up her life, it becomes even more obvious how intertwined it is with Agaat's. Van Niekerk skillfully overlays five decades of South African history and life onto Milla's own decaying physical and mental state by using the shifts in the uneasy relationship between the two women.

KEEP IN MIND

- **Ingrid Winterbach**'s (b. 1948) fiction is striking.
- **Etienne van Heerden**'s (b. 1954) crowded magical realist novels are *Ancestral Voices* (1986, English 1989) and *The Long Silence of Mario Salviati* (2000, English 2002).

South African Crime Fiction

Much of the African crime fiction known to international audiences has had a significant social and political slant, if only because apartheid South Africa was one of the few areas from which such fiction was available. Expatriate South African **James McClure**'s (1939–2006) Kramer and Zondi series, beginning with *The Steam Pig* (1971), stands out for its depiction of the South Africa of 1970s and 1980s while the apartheid legacy still colored much contemporary crime fiction. **Deon Meyer** (b. 1958) has written, in Afrikaans, some of the most impressive post-apartheid thrillers. Though still prone to letting furiously paced action sequences dominate the resolutions of his novels, in books like the quest tale *Heart of the Hunter* (2002, English 2003), Meyer uses the past that proves so hard to overcome. The imposing character of Thobela "Tiny" Mpayipheli, who also plays a major role in *Dead at Daybreak* (2000, English 2000), is a larger-than-life figure with a shadowy history as a foreign-trained lone assassin who tries to change his life but finds his past catching up with him as he repeatedly is drawn into the problems of the new South Africa. Meyer saddles Tiny with a great deal, as the character becomes a stand-in for so much of South Africa, but the heroic figure can almost bear all of that in these very solid thrillers.

ZIMBABWE

Publishing and writing flourished for some time in Zimbabwe after it became an independent state in 1980, and the Zimbabwe International Book Fair, founded in 1983, was the continent's preeminent book fair for some two decades. Unfortunately, by the early years of the twenty-first century, the policies of Robert Mugabe's regime and the reactions to it had severely undermined the nation's economy, affecting every aspect of local life and making it impossible to maintain this high level of literary culture.

Because Zimbabwe achieved independence only in 1980, Zimbabwean writers continued to intensively explore the legacy of colonial rule—landownership (largely in white hands), the economic gaps between blacks and whites, the civil war—at a time when authors in most other sub-Saharan countries had moved beyond it. In particular, the long-lasting (1965–1979) civil war figures in many works of Zimbabwean fiction. Among the best works directly addressing the civil war are **Stanley Nyamfukudza's** (b. 1951) *The Non-Believer's Journey* (1980), **Shimmer Chinodya's** (b. 1957) *Harvest of Thorns* (1989), and **Alexander Kanengoni's** (b. 1951) works.

Dambudzo Marechera (1952–1987) remains a very influential literary figure in Zimbabwe, possibly as much for his personality and wild life—which included a great deal of drinking and his expulsion from Oxford—as for his writing. His collection of loosely connected autobiographical stories, *The House of Hunger* (1978), was a strong first book. Marechera was more interested in psychological than political insight, and his writing is visceral and raw. The angry-young-men novels written in Africa until that time were directed against colonial and racial injustice, but in *The House of Hunger* and the only other work of fiction published during his lifetime, *Black Sunlight* (1980), Marechera rages much more widely, addressing societal problems and existential questions. *Black Sunlight* is a less cohesive work, as Marechera largely forgoes plot in his increasingly dreamlike odyssey of its photographer-narrator.

Tsitsi Dangarembga's (b. 1959) autobiographical novel, *Nervous Conditions* (1988), is considered the first novel published by a Zimbabwean woman. The life of the narrator, Tambu, who was raised in patriarchal rural Rhodesia, is contrasted with that of her cousin, Nyasha, whose formative years were spent abroad. For Tambu, education is an opportunity, but it also makes her increasingly aware of the backwardness of aspects of her family's life. Nyasha is more obviously torn between cultures, which eventually is manifested in an eating disorder and a nervous breakdown. Dangarembga's penetrating scrutiny of young women determining their identities and roles in an unstable society is one of the strongest novels about African women. A sequel,

---

KEEP IN MIND

- **Yvonne Vera**'s (1964–2005) fiction is lyrical, though it may seem too extravagantly poetic to many readers.
- **Shimmer Chinodya**'s (b. 1957) fiction offers the broadest introduction to Zimbabwean life over the past few decades.
- **Chenjerai Hove**'s (1956–2015) novels are *Bones* (1988), *Shadows* (1991), and *Ancestors* (1996).
- **NoViolet Bulawayo**'s (b. 1981) strong first novel is *We Need New Names* (2013).
- **Solomon Mutswairo**'s (1924–2005) Shona novel is *Feso* (1956, English 1974).

The Book of Not (2006), covers Tambu's high school years, which coincide with the final years of the civil war and culminate in Zimbabwe's independence. With the character of Nyasha much less of a counterpart here, the novel does not work nearly as well as *Nervous Conditions*.

BOTSWANA

Several foreign authors have chosen Botswana as the locale for some of their fiction, most famously **Alexander McCall Smith**'s (b. 1948) series featuring Mma Precious Ramotswe of *The No. 1 Ladies' Detective Agency* (1998). In more than a dozen charming works, Smith's detective tries to set right the small wrongs affecting her clients. Smith uses his appealing protagonist to present all facets of Botswanan life, and he knows how to tell a good story.

American author **Norman Rush** (b. 1933) worked in Botswana in the Peace Corps from 1978 to 1983 and has set much of his award-winning works of fiction there. The stories in *Whites* (1986) explore the experiences of white foreigners who find themselves in Africa. Rush's novels *Mating* (1991) and *Mortals* (2003) are intellectual exercises full of games between men and women. Both are set in Botswana, and

Rush uses the African backdrop well, but his main concern in these novels is his characters' emotional lives.

In 1964, South African–born **Bessie Head** (1937–1986) moved to what is now Botswana. She was born in the mental institution to which her mother had been committed and later also suffered from mental illness herself, as chronicled in her autobiographical novel, *A Question of Power* (1973), and reflected in some of her other fiction. Both her debut, *When Rain Clouds Gather* (1968), and *Maru* (1971) deal with the possibility of renewal and fundamental societal change. In *When Rain Clouds Gather*, the South African exile Makhaya is one of several outsiders who become involved in efforts to reform farming in the village where he settles. Some of the traditional power holders oppose these communal ideals, making the novel an allegory of a young nation (Botswana) and how its future is to be shaped. The racial conflict in *Maru* is between the powerful Batswana and the despised, lowly Bushmen (Masarwa). Margaret is posted as a teacher to a village where Bushmen are still commonly kept as slaves. She too is a Masarwa, but not obviously and immediately identifiable as such. When her identity becomes known, this upsets the local order, especially when two rivals, Maru and Moleka, fall in love with her. Positive change and increased tolerance result, but when Maru wins Margaret, he takes her far away from his homeland, unwilling to confront its deeply ingrained racial tensions.

ZAMBIA

Little fiction from the former Northern Rhodesia has attracted much notice outside southern Africa. **Dominic Mulaisho** (1933–2013) held important political posts in the government of Kenneth Kaunda, and his two novels of political power struggles, *The Tongue of the Dumb* (1973) and *The Smoke That Thunders* (1979), are solid, if somewhat dated, works. The novels by **Binwell Sinyangwe** (b. 1956) deal more directly with the often bleak everyday life in contemporary Zambia, and both *Quills of Desire* (1993) and *A Cowrie of Hope* (2000) focus on the importance of education as an opportunity to be sought at any cost.

MALAWI

Hastings Banda's ultraconservative rule of Malawi lasted more than three decades and ended only in 1994. American author **Paul Theroux** (b. 1941) was deported while working there for the Peace Corps in the mid-1960s, and his novel *Jungle Lovers* (1971) is still among the most insightful into the early years of Banda's rule and conditions in Malawi. Not surprisingly, it was banned by Banda's government. Typical of Theroux, this is a comic novel of failures abroad, the story being about two foreigners who want to effect change—one, Calvin Mullet, by selling the locals insurance, the other, Marais, by inciting violent revolution.

The first Malawian novel, **Aubrey Kachingwe**'s (b. 1926) *No Easy Task* (1966), is a good example of the African novels of that period. The imaginary nation in which it is set is going through the political difficulties common to countries all across Africa as they achieved independence, and the journalist-narrator is an observer who must decide what role he wants to play in the new nation.

In **James Ng'ombe**'s (b. 1949) *Sugarcane with Salt* (1989), the protagonist, Khumbo Dala, returns from England with a medical degree but finds much has changed for the worse in his homeland. Particularly devastating to him is how the strong family unit has been undermined by his brother's and his mother's embrace of modern, self-interested ways. Their willingness to engage in dangerous and compromising activities affects all those around them. Ng'ombe's dark novel explores the tension between traditional social structures and the possibilities in a new world order, which include both the positive—Khumbo Dala's advanced medical training—and the destructive—his brother Billy's drug dealing.

KEEP IN MIND

- **Steve Chimombo**'s (b. 1945) massive novel is entitled *The Wrath of Napolo* (2000).

NAMIBIA

Though large in size, Namibia has one of Africa's smallest populations. Independent only since 1990, its literary scene is underdeveloped. Among the few works of fictions to come out of Namibia is **Neshani Andreas**'s (b. 1964) *The Purple Violet of Oshaantu* (2001). Set in the bucolic hinterlands, the novel is narrated by Mee Ali, who is concerned about her friend Kauna's unhappy marriage, which ends with the suspicious death of Kauna's husband. It is a colorful but typical social novel of contemporary village life, focusing on the role and status of women in an economy in which husbands are often absent for extended periods of time.

MADAGASCAR

A large island off the coast of Mozambique, Madagascar is a former French colony that achieved full independence in 1960. Aside from the work of pioneering poet **Jean-Joseph Rabéarivelo** (1901–1937), who wrote in both Malagasy and French, little literature from Madagascar is available in English.

A bilingual anthology of Francophone writing edited by Jacques Bourgeacq and Liliane Ramarosoa, *Voices from Madagascar* (2002), includes both poetry and fiction, much of it very recent. It is still the best basic introduction to the literature of Madagascar. **Colleen J. McElroy**'s (b. 1935) account of her time on the island, *Over the Lip of the World: Among the Storytellers of Madagascar* (1999), is a personal travel and research narrative, but it also examines the Malagasy oral-storytelling tradition and contains many local stories and poems. McElroy's supporting material provides a useful context, making this a good introduction to a form of narrative that is largely unknown in the English-speaking world.

Central Africa

Conditions in Central Africa have rarely been conducive to the development of any sort of book culture. Dominated by the huge but war-wracked Democratic Republic of the Congo—the successor state to the Belgian Congo, where **Joseph Conrad** (1857–1924) set his *Heart of Darkness* (1902)—much of Central Africa remains unstable, as neighboring states are constantly pulled into the decade-old conflict in the Congo. Some of the nations further removed from those hostilities are arguably too stable, controlled by some of the world's longest-serving autocrats: Equatorial Guinea's Teodoro Obiang Nguema Mbasogo has led his nation since 1979, and Gabon's Omar Bongo held power from 1967 until his death in 2009.

French is the primary literary language of this region, with a few exceptions such as Equatorial Guinea, whose colonial legacy is mainly Spanish.

RWANDA AND BURUNDI

Ethnic tensions between the Hutu and Tutsi tribes have repeatedly led to large-scale massacres in both Burundi (notably in 1972) and Rwanda (1994), a legacy that dominates Western perceptions of these small African nations. Much has been published about the Rwandan massacres of 1994 in particular, though most of it is nonfiction. Among the best of these works are **Jean Hatzfeld**'s (b. 1949) collections of first-person accounts and **Philip Gourevitch**'s (b. 1961) *We Wish to Inform You That Tomorrow We Will Be Killed with Our Families* (1998). Fiction dealing with these events also has been written largely by foreigners. Books such as Canadian author **Gil Courtemanche**'s (1943–2011) *A Sunday at the Pool in Kigali* (2000, English 2003) typically feature a foreign protagonist caught up in events. **Jean-Philippe Stassen**'s (b. 1966) short graphic novel *Deogratias* (2000, English 2006) offers a broader look at the events of those years and their effects on a variety of young characters.

In 1998, Nocky Djedanoum, the artistic director of the annual French Fest'Africa festival, called on African authors to respond to the events in Rwanda, and the resulting project, Rwanda: To Write Against Oblivion (Rwanda: écrire par devoir de mémoire), led to the publication of numerous works. Among the novels that are part of this project are Senegalese author **Boubacar Boris Diop**'s (b. 1946) *Murambi, the Book of Bones* (2000, English 2006) and Guinean-born author **Tierno Monénembo**'s (b. 1947) *The Oldest Orphan* (2000, English 2004). The main character in *Murambi*, Cornelius Uvimana, returns to Rwanda in 1998 after a long absence and tries to come to terms with what happened. Diop's novel is particularly effective in focusing on the ominous uncertainty in the aftermath of the massacres, with the mass flight of much of the population and calls for vengeance and retribution. *The Oldest Orphan* is narrated by the teenager Faustin Nsenghimana, telling his story from prison where he is awaiting his execution. He only gradually reveals both what happened to him and his family years earlier, during those horrible one hundred days of 1994, and his later crime for which he has been sentenced to death. Monénembo affectingly describes a country and a people still crushed by the burden of what transpired there.

DEMOCRATIC REPUBLIC OF THE CONGO

Despite its large population and storied history, relatively little fiction has come out of the Democratic Republic of the Congo. Previously known under, among others, the names Zaïre (between 1971 and 1997, under the rule of Mobuto Sese Seko), and the Belgian Congo, internal conflicts and authoritarian rule have prevented the development of much of a book culture there.

The academic **V. Y. Mudimbe** (b. 1941), who has long lived and taught abroad, is among the few authors to emerge from the Congo. The three novels that Mudimbe published in the 1970s have been translated into English, each offering a different reaction to the postcolonial experience. The most compelling of them, *The Rift* (1979, English 1993), consists largely of the notebooks of a young academic, Ahmed Nana, written shortly before his death. He returned to Africa from France to research the history and customs of a Congolese ethnic group, the Kuba, but has a mental breakdown. The protagonists of Mudimbe's other novels also are unsure of their roles in a postcolonial world, most notably the former Catholic priest turned revolutionary, Pierre Landu, of *Between Tides* (1973, English 1991). Although Mudimbe's cerebral fiction feels dated now, his novels do pose interesting questions about personal and political identity and roles in contemporary Africa.

Fiston Mwanza Mujila's (b. 1981) *Tram 83* (2014, English 2015) is set in an unnamed country that is clearly inspired by the author's native Congo. The local restaurant bar Tram 83 is the epicenter of this raucous novel of contemporary Central Africa.

FICTION IN THE CONGO

From Joseph Conrad's time to the present, the Congo has been a very popular setting for fiction, for fantasy-adventure tales such as **Michael Crichton**'s (1942–2008) *Congo* (1980) and **Albert Sánchez Piñol**'s (b. 1965) *Pandora in the Congo* (2005, English 2008). But writers have also been drawn to the country's explosive politics and history, as well as to figures like the first elected (and later assassinated) prime minister, Patrice Lumumba, and the outrageous dictator, Mobuto Sese Seko. Most of **Ronan Bennett**'s (b. 1956) *The Catastrophist* (1998) takes place during the tumultuous years of 1959 and 1960, telling the dirty story of how Mobuto came to power. **Barbara Kingsolver**'s (b. 1955) best-selling novel *The Poisonwood Bible* (1998) also begins in 1959 with the arrival of a missionary family in the Congo and covers decades of their experiences in the country.

CONGO-BRAZZAVILLE

Even though the Republic of the Congo, a former French colony generally known as Congo-Brazzaville, contains only a small fraction of the population of its southern neighbor across the Congo River, the Democratic Republic of the Congo, several well-known authors are closely linked to this country. **Sony Labou Tansi** (1947–1995) most obviously straddles the river divide, born in the Belgian colony to a local father and a mother from the French colony before moving to Brazzaville in his youth. The best of his novels available in English, *The Seven Solitudes of Lorsa Lopez* (1985, English 1995), is typical, with its fantastical exaggerations. Like almost all his work, the novel is set in a fictional troubled African country, and even though Sony heaps misery upon misery, it also is a comic farce. Straying far from conventional realism, Sony's cry of outrage goes beyond much political African fiction in its incorporation of myth and fantasy.

    Henri Lopes (b. 1937) also was born in the Belgian colony but has held numerous positions in the Congo-Brazzaville government, including that of prime minister and ambassador to France. His novel *The Laughing Cry* (1982, English 1987) is a satire of an outrageous African dictatorship, presented from shifting narrative perspectives. In its self-reflexive parts, it is reminiscent of Milan Kundera, right down to the prominent use of Diderot, and its comic approach is closer to that of the Soviet satirists than what was generally found in Africa at that time. Even though Lopes is a major author, his only other work available in English is the early story collection *Tribaliks* (1971, English 1987).

Emmanuel Dongala (b. 1941) taught chemistry for two decades at the University of Brazzaville but fled the country for the United States in the wake of the violent civil conflict that erupted in 1997. His books are among the most approachable fictions of Africa for foreign readers, covering progressively narrower slices of recent history. *The Fire of Origins* (1987, English 2001) follows its larger-than-life protagonist, Mandala Mankunku, from the arrival of the French colonialists to the period after independence, a quick sweep through the history of twentieth-century Congo. Dongala does not identify Congo as the setting of **Little Boys Come from the Stars** (1998, English 2001) and **Johnny Mad Dog** (2002, English 2005), but both are clearly based at least in part on Congolese experiences. The teenage narrator of *Little Boys Come from the Stars*, Matapari, allows Dongala to present his story from a perspective that retains some innocence, making for a gentle satire that manages to land solid hits on many targets, including both authoritarian and democratic rule. The alternating narrators of *Johnny Mad Dog* also are in their teens but quickly lose their innocence when they are caught up in a violent rebellion in which child soldiers play a major role. One, a girl, Laokolé, is studying for her final school exams when war breaks out; the other is the thuggish Johnny. Cutting back and forth between the two sides in this fast-paced story, Dongala presents a riveting picture of the horrifying brutality and human toll of these civil conflicts in parts of Africa, including Rwanda, Liberia, Sierra Leone, and Congo-Brazzaville.

The attention-seeking narrator of **Alain Mabanckou**'s (b. 1966) *African Psycho* (2003, English 2007), Grégoire, whose idol is a brutal killer, hopes to find fame in notoriety but fails miserably. *African Psycho* sits uneasily between comic grotesque and moral tale. Mabanckou's approach works better in **Broken Glass** (2006, English 2009), a barroom novel steeped in alcohol, personal stories, and, above all else, cultural and literary references. From the names—the bar where most of the action takes place is the Credit Gone Away, and the narrator is the eponymous Broken Glass—to the tall tales themselves, Mabanckou's style ultimately triumphs over substance. Clearly, Mabanckou is one of Africa's most promising Francophone authors.

CAMEROON

Both French and English are official languages of Cameroon, which is among the region's most politically stable nations. With **Ferdinand Oyono** (1929–2010) and **Mongo Beti** (1932–2001), it also boasts two of the most important African writers of their generation. Although Oyono largely abandoned writing to serve in several government and diplomatic posts, two of his darkly comic novels from the 1950s, **Houseboy** (1956, English 1966) and **The Old Man and the Medal** (1956, English 1969), are some of the best about the final years of French colonial rule. Beti's **The Poor Christ of Bomba** (1956, English 1971) addresses the failures of missionary work in Africa, and his **Mission to Kala** (published in the United States as *Mission Accomplished*; 1957, English 1958) is a sharp critique of the colonial educational system. Beti moved to France before Cameroon achieved independence in 1960 and did not return until the early 1990s, but after a lengthy silence, he did resume writing. His later fiction is more overtly political, beginning with a loosely connected trilogy strongly inspired by the revolutionary figure killed by the French, Ruben Um Nyobé (1913–1958). Beti continued to be highly critical of how African leaders failed their states in the decades after independence, with **The Story of the Madman** (1994, English 2001) the best example of Beti's style of mixing anger with the comic as it addresses postcolonial chaos and dictatorship in an African state.

A CAMEROONIAN WRITER

Calixthe Beyala (b. 1961) moved to France when she was seventeen and has become a prolific, prize-winning author. In the mid-1990s, however, she was accused of and charged with plagiarism from the works of authors that include Ben Okri and Paule Constant. Her often fragmentary and nonlinear narratives contain graphic descriptions of raw violence and sex. While many of her works are set in Africa, her story of an immigrant family in Paris, *Loukoum: The Little Prince of Belleville* (1992, English 1995), largely narrated by a young boy, has the most obvious appeal.

ELSEWHERE IN CENTRAL AFRICA

Some fiction from the other Central African nations is published in France, but almost nothing is available in English translation. Sparsely populated, autocratically governed, and generally very poor (with the exception of oil-rich Gabon and Equatorial Guinea), little fiction has emerged from the mainly Francophone nations of the area, including Chad and the Central African Republic. Gabon-born **Daniel Mengara**'s (b. 1967) *Mema* (2003), in which a son chronicles his mother's difficult life in an African village, is among the few novels available in English written by someone who had lived in the region. Spanish-writing **Juan Tomás Ávila Laurel**'s (b. 1966) novel takes place on his native island of Annobón, in Equatorial Guinea. It is entitled *By Night the Mountain Burns* (2009, English 2014) and is the first of this prolific and highly regarded author's works to be translated.

A PRIX GONCOURT–WINNING AFRICAN WRITER

René Maran (1887–1960) was born on the Caribbean island of Martinique but spent much of his life in Africa. His novel *Batouala* (1921, revised 1938, English 1922, 1932, 1972), set in what would later become the Central African Republic, was widely praised (by Ernest Hemingway, among others) and awarded the Prix Goncourt, making Maran the first black author to win the prestigious French literary prize. Of more historical than literary interest now, its attack on French colonialism and the authenticity of the author's perspective made it a seminal work of the period; it also was soon banned in the French colonies.

East Africa

In the 1960s, East Africa—particularly Kenya and Uganda—became a hub of early postcolonial literature in Africa. A local publishing industry and a relatively large readership helped foster a writing culture, and the University of East Africa, specifically the campus of what is now Makerere University, was a major African literary center at that time. In the late 1960s, the future Nobel laureate V. S. Naipaul was a writer in residence in Makerere, and Paul Theroux taught there. But now only a few writers from the region are well known outside Africa, principally Kenyan **Ngũgĩ wa Thiong'o** (b. 1938) and Somali **Nuruddin Farah** (b. 1945), and younger authors are still largely overshadowed by those from elsewhere in Africa or the former Commonwealth.

KENYA

Ngũgĩ wa Thiong'o (b. 1938) published his first works under his Christian name, James Ngugi, and wrote in English, but in the 1970s he first reverted to his traditional name and later also began to write in Gikuyu, the language of the largest ethnic group in Kenya. (Ngũgĩ, however, continues to translate most of his own work into English himself.) Spanning nearly half a century, Ngũgĩ's works address much of modern Kenyan and African history, often in highly critical terms. In the 1970s, Ngũgĩ was jailed without charge, and in 1982, he left the country during a time of considerable political unrest and instability; he has lived abroad ever since, most recently in the United States.

Early novels by Ngũgĩ, such as the autobiographical *Weep Not, Child* (1964) as well as *A Grain of Wheat* (1967, revised 1986), are anchored in Kenyan history and conditions. *Weep Not, Child* is set during the Mau Mau uprising of the 1950s. In this novel, Ngũgĩ shows the devastating cost of the conflict on families when its protagonist, a young boy named Njoroge who is concentrating on his education, gets caught up in the conflict, both affecting his ability to get a decent education and fraying family bonds. *A Grain of Wheat* takes place in the days leading up to Kenyan independence in 1963, though many of the flashbacks look at the four protagonists' earlier experiences. This nonlinear, almost jumbled approach is frequently found in Ngũgĩ's fiction and is particularly effective here, with the pivotal point of a new dawn always on the horizon, even as each of the main figures confronts betrayals from his or her past. The polemical and polyphonic *Petals of Blood* (1977) is a critique of the failures of postindependence leadership, set in the town of Ilmorog. All of its four principal characters are outsiders there, and Ilmorog itself is representative of the destructive changes that have taken place in Kenya. In addition, the four are suspects in a murder case, with the investigation into it being one of the threads that holds together this fairly loose narrative.

Devil on the Cross (1980, English 1982), written while he was in jail, was the first novel Ngũgĩ wrote in Gikuyu. Fiercely political, it is also a far more fantastical satire than his earlier work and paved the way for his greatest novel to date, the massive satire *Wizard of the Crow* (2004–2006, English 2006). Set in the fictional African republic of Aburiria, this novel features an inept leader known simply as the Ruler who is interested only in money and personal glory and is indulged by his sycophantic and power-seeking advisers. The "Wizard of the Crow" of the title is a creation of two desperate characters who assume the role of an invented spiritual healer-cum-sorcerer and soon find their services in great demand. The comedy here is lighter than that in most of Ngūgĩ's earlier works, and the novel has a generous spirit, even when it ridicules the excesses of the ruling class.

Meja Mwangi (b. 1948) is an author attuned to popular international fiction but writing primarily for a local audience. The variety of his large output, which includes thrillers and young adult fiction, makes it difficult to classify him. Several of Mwangi's gritty urban novels from the 1970s attracted considerable attention, and works such as *Going Down River Road* (1976) and *The Cockroach Dance* (1979) are powerful depictions of the lives of the Nairobi protagonists with little chance of escaping to something better. More recently, Mwangi has tackled other social issues, as in *The Last Plague* (also published as *Crossroads*; 2000), a novel set in the town of Crossroads that has been decimated by AIDS.

British-born **Marjorie Oludhe Macgoye** (1928–2015) moved to Kenya only in 1954 but, after her marriage, became fully integrated into the Luo community. Most of her novels are not, however, primarily rooted in her distinctive background but offer more general depictions of Kenya. *Coming to Birth* (1986) begins with the newly married sixteen-year-old protagonist, Paulina, coming to Nairobi to join her husband a few years before independence. Already pregnant, she quickly miscarries, and the novel is full of difficult birth pangs, ranging from that of the nation itself to Paulina's own maturation. *The Present Moment* (1987) ranges even further, with the old women who have come to a Christian old-age home known as the Refuge talking about their lives, allowing Macgoye to reflect on the changes in Kenya during their long lifetimes. A much younger generation of nurses with different experiences gives the novel an intriguing contrast.

Grace Ogot (1930–2015) is a popular writer whose stories are well known. While much of her fiction explores the role of women in contemporary Kenyan society, one of her most interesting works is *The Strange Bride* (1983, English 1989), a variation on a Luo myth that

---

THE TRIAL OF CHRISTOPHER OKIGBO

Ali A. Mazrui's (1933–2014) only novel, *The Trial of Christopher Okigbo* (1971), is a worthwhile oddity. It is a novel of ideas, set in an after-Africa where its dead protagonist, Hamisi, must pass a test to fully cross over into the afterlife. His own fate is, however, overshadowed by that of another new arrival, the great Nigerian poet Christopher Okigbo (1932–1967), who died fighting in the Nigerian civil war and stands accused of being reckless with his great artistic talent. A programmatic novel, the audacity of *The Trial of Christopher Okigbo* is fascinating, provoking questions about the role of the artist in society.

---

explains the origins of agricultural cultivation. Unlike Ogot's other works, written in English, *The Strange Bride* was written in Luo, and its reliance on oral-storytelling traditions make it a good example of the blending of different approaches to fiction.

UGANDA

A burgeoning literary scene in Uganda in the 1960s was largely quelled by the despotic rule of Idi Amin, which lasted from 1971 to his overthrow in 1979. Although Amin's rule continues to cast a long shadow over Ugandan writing, its monstrosity has also inspired foreign authors in such different works as one of **Donald E. Westlake**'s (1933–2008) best thrillers, the heist tale *Kahawa* (1982); **Giles Foden**'s (b. 1967) novel of a hapless Scottish doctor drawn into Amin's house of horrors, *The Last King of Scotland* (1998); and **Rosa Shand**'s (b. 1937) *The Gravity of Sunlight* (2000), the story of a young American couple and their three children living in Uganda when Amin came to power.

Ugandan authors have also written extensively about the Amin years, both directly or in more allegorical works such as **John Nagenda**'s (b. 1938) *The Seasons of Thomas Tebo* (1986). Whereas **Moses Isegawa**'s (b. 1963) sprawling novel *Abyssinian Chronicles* (1998, first English-language publication 2000) stretches from the 1960s to the present, his *Snakepit* (1999, first English-language publication 2004) focuses on Amin's rule. The autobiographical *Abyssinian Chronicles* is typical of fiction that seeks to mirror a nation's recent history, from independence to the present, in the experiences of a single character— in this case, the narrator, Mugezi. Isegawa ultimately overextends himself in following Mugezi to Europe, but otherwise this far-flung family tale is carried along very well by Mugezi's driven narrative. In *Snakepit*, the protagonist, Bat Katanga, returns to Amin's Uganda after getting his degree from Cambridge University, hoping to work for the good of his country in the civil service but finding much more difficult conditions than he anticipated. Essentially a thriller, the novel presents the elaborate and brutal but often futile power games that a number of characters try to play, and in its messy and rushed uncertainty, the narrative gives a good sense of Ugandan life under Amin.

Founded in 1996, the Uganda Women Writers' Association (also known as Femrite) has been very successful in fostering and advancing the writing of fiction in Uganda. The members of the association have published several books and anthologies, and several authors associated with the organization, such as **Doreen Baingana** (b. 1966) and **Monica Arac de Nyeko** (b. 1979), have also begun to find success abroad. The main characters in Baingana's loosely connected *Tropical Fish: Stories Out of Entebbe* (2005) are three sisters. Their different paths and stories in the aftermath of the Amin years reveal many of the complexities facing young women in modern Africa. Although Arac de Nyeko's prize-winning stories have not yet been collected in a single volume, she is one of Uganda's several promising young authors.

TANZANIA

Aniceti Kitereza (1896–1981) wrote his epic novel *Mr. Myombekere and His Wife Bugonoka, Their Son Ntulanalwo and Daughter Bulihwali* in Kikerewe in 1945, but it remains unpublished in that language. The author's own Swahili translation was published in 1980, followed by translations in German, French, and, finally in 2002,

OTHER AFRICAN WORKS

Okot p'Bitek's (1931–1982) landmark *Song of Lawino* (English 1966, and as *The Defence of Lawino*, 2001), originally written in Acoli, is one of several works that p'Bitek wrote in verse. They are meant to be sung as much as read, as they are close to the African tradition of oral storytelling. In *Song of Lawino*, the title character complains about her husband, Ocol, abandoning his heritage in favor of the colonialists' ways. Despite being widely read and influential, *Song of Lawino* also marks a path not taken in African writing, of asserting the primacy of native languages and of narratives built on oral traditions. There are exceptions, ranging from South African author **Mazisi Kunene**'s (1930–2006) Zulu verse epics, *Emperor Shaka the Great* (English 1979) and *Anthem of the Decades* (English 1981), to Kenyan **Muthoni Likimani**'s (b. 1926) light-verse narrative, *What Does a Man Want?* (1974). Nonetheless, the European novel and story remained the model for most fiction.

English. The novel tells the story of a devoted couple who have difficulty conceiving children, but it is also a meticulous account of local society and tradition. It is one of the most underappreciated works of African literature. Kitereza's novel was translated into English by **Gabriel Ruhumbika** (b. 1938), whose *Village in Uhuru* (1969) was only the second novel written in English by a Tanzanian author ever to be published. Ruhumbika's later fiction is written in Swahili, and only *Silent Empowerment of the Compatriots* (1992, revised 1995, English 2009) has been translated. This historical novel of Tanzania in the second half of the twentieth century provides a good overview of the social and economic changes the nation has gone through.

Peter K. Palangyo's (1939–1993) only novel, *Dying in the Sun* (1968), was also the first to be published in English by a Tanzanian writer. This powerful, short, modernist novel depicts the crushing poverty and alienation through which the protagonist journeys to see his dying father. It is a significant work of this period, especially in its portrayal of disillusionment in postindependence Africa.

Both of the best-known writers with ties to Tanzania, **Abdulrazak Gurnah** (b. 1948) and **M. G. Vassanji** (b. 1950), have long lived abroad.

Gurnah emigrated to Great Britain in 1968, and many of his works deal with the East African immigrant experience in England. Vassanji was born in Kenya and raised in Tanzania before pursuing his higher education in the United States and Canada, where he eventually settled. Several of Vassanji's works, including the novels *The Gunny Sack* (1989) and *The Book of Secrets* (1994), describe the lives of the Indian community in East Africa during the past century. Both these novels use relics from the past—a sack full of objects the narrator inherits from his great-aunt in *The Gunny Sack*, and a diary from the colonial period in *The Book of Secrets*—which allows Vassanji to nest stories within stories, as well as contrasting past and present. *The In-Between World of Vikram Lall* (2003) is narrated by a Kenyan exile in Canada and is particularly good in showing how Asians existed "in between" blacks and whites in East Africa.

ETHIOPIA

Ethiopia is Africa's second most populous nation, but dictatorial rule under Emperor Haile Selassie (1892–1975) and then a military junta called the Dergue, led by Mengistu Haile Mariam, hampered the development of a modern book culture. Ethiopia also was never colonized so, unlike nearly all other African nations, had no lingering connection to any European country, culture, or language. This limited the opportunities for Ethiopian writers to advance their education or publish abroad. Amharic is the most widely used language, but it is far from dominant in a country with dozens of ethnic and linguistic groups.

Berhane Mariam Sahle Sellassie (b. 1936) has written a variety of works in Chaha, Amharic, and English that present different facets of Ethiopian life and history. *Firebrands* (1979) explores the 1974 transition from the sclerotic imperial regime to what quickly became merely a different oppressive dictatorship. **Hama Tuma**'s (b. 1949) collection of almost two dozen stories, *The Case of the Socialist Witchdoctor* (1993), is a dark satirical view of the misrule of Ethiopia, especially under the Dergue. Half the collection has the same narrator recount

AN ETHIOPIAN STORY

Polish writer **Ryszard Kapuściński**'s (1932–2007) riveting account *The Emperor: Downfall of an Autocrat* (1978, English 1983) describes the rule of Haile Selassie and his overthrow in 1974. It is a great introduction to the country, even though Kapuściński is widely thought to have elaborated much of his documentary writing far beyond what is usually tolerated in journalism.

the court cases he witnesses, amusingly presenting both their absurdity and how justice is meted out.

The only novel that **Daniachew Worku** (1936–1994) wrote in English, *The Thirteenth Sun* (1973), is one of the finest works to come out of Ethiopia in modern times. It is the story of a son taking his sick father, the Fitawrary, and his father's illegitimate daughter, the beautiful Woynitu, to a mountainside monastery seeking a cure. The novel is clearly allegorical, with the Fitawrary a stand-in for the emperor in his waning years. The conflict between the generations mirrors that faced by Ethiopia at the time, torn between a past of strict but outdated tradition and belief and a desire to charge ahead into the new, but without enough certainty about how to shape that future, as represented by the intellectual but ineffectual son, Goytom.

Several recent works of fiction have been written by authors with ties to Ethiopia who have resettled in the United States and Canada. Among the best of these, **Dinaw Mengestu**'s (b. 1978) *The Beautiful Things That Heaven Bears* (published in Great Britain as *Children of the Revolution*; 2006), is narrated by Sepha Stephanos, an Ethiopian exile in Washington, D.C. The neighborhood he lives in is undergoing gentrification, but he still has not adjusted to leaving Ethiopia behind him seventeen years earlier. Mengestu captures how the ground and any sense of support seem to be continuing to shift under this passive, lonely, man's feet.

Nega Mezlekia's (b. 1958) *The God Who Begat a Jackal* (2001) is a vivid historical novel set in Abyssinia some two hundred years ago. Centered on a love story, it is an appealing if somewhat simplistic

AN ERITREAN NOVEL

Eritrea became an Italian colony in 1890 and officially became a part of Ethiopia in 1952. A long struggle for independence ended in 1991, with Eritrea attaining nationhood in 1993. Arabic-writing **Abu Bakr Khaal**'s powerful and topical migrant novel, *African Titanics* (2008, English 2014), is one of the few works of fiction by an Eritrean author available in English.

novel replete with stories from Ethiopian history and legend. **Abraham Verghese** (b. 1955) is a doctor who is better known for his nonfiction. While his first novel, ***Cutting for Stone*** (2009), gets bogged down by medical procedures, it is an often compelling story of the lives of identical twins born in Ethiopia in 1954 who later have careers in medicine.

SOMALIA

British and Italian Somaliland were united in 1960 to form independent Somalia. Led by Mohamed Siad Barre since 1969, civil war broke out in 1991 when he was deposed. Since then, it has been one of the world's most unstable countries. Its dominant language is Somali, and it has a strong oral literary tradition, with written Somali not standardized until the early 1970s.

Faarax M. J. Cawl's (1937–1991) ***Ignorance Is the Enemy of Love*** (1974, English 1982) is one of the few works of fiction to have been translated from Somali. Set in the early twentieth century and based on actual events, Faarax's novel is sympathetic to women's rights and makes education central to the story: the hero's illiteracy prevents him from reading the message his beloved sends him, so he cannot save her from the marriage into which she is forced. Following Somali oral tradition, Faarax also uses verse and song throughout the novel, adding both charm and a sense of singularity to what is basically a didactic work.

Nuruddin Farah (b. 1945) went into exile in 1974, during the Siad Barre regime, but Somalia has always figured prominently in his work. The multilingual author writes mainly in English, and his work has always been noted for its sensitive portrayal of female characters, beginning with his early novel, *From a Crooked Rib* (1970). In this novel, Farah addresses issues that recur throughout his work, including the inequitable treatment of women through practices such as female circumcision and arranged marriages, while his protagonist, Ebla, represents the nation as whole and the struggles it is going through. Most of Farah's later—and increasingly political—fiction is grouped together in trilogies, the first of which is *Variations on the Theme of an African Dictatorship* (1979–1983). Often rooted in family and the search for identity, Farah's fiction remains intensely personal even when addressing the political. *From a Crooked Rib* is straightforward, but in his later novels Farah experiments with style and form. In *Maps* (1986), the narrative voice shifts among the first, second, and third person, suggestive of the orphan Askar's attempts to confront his own life story. Even when he uses similar themes, Farah constantly finds new means of expression in his books, and his language is always rich and evocative. While his fiction is worthwhile alone for its depictions of Somalia, first under the Siad Barre dictatorship and then in the seeming chaos after 1991, Farah's work rises considerably beyond this, and he remains one of Africa's leading authors.

DJIBOUTI

Djibouti is one of Africa's smallest countries but has a strategic port on the Horn of Africa. It did not gain its independence from France until 1977. French-writing **Abdourahman A. Waberi** (b. 1965) is Djibouti's leading writer, and his collection of stories *The Land Without Shadows* (1994, English 2005) is an excellent introduction to the country and the author. Waberi's most appealing novel to date, *In the United States of Africa* (2006, English 2009), imagines an inverted world order and history from which Africa has emerged as wealthy and stable, and Europe and the United States are backward and underdeveloped. Waberi's Africa is not superior to the actual developed world; instead, he ridicules familiar prejudices and preconceptions by relocating them in his alternative world. The story itself, about a European girl who has been adopted by an African but goes in search of her birth mother, is merely a framing device allowing Waberi to describe this different universe, but this short novel has enough thought-provoking material to make it well worthwhile.

West Africa

Nigeria is the dominant power in West Africa, in literary and in almost all other respects, but it is far from the only country in the area from which significant fiction has emerged. Political instability and undemocratic rule have obviously hindered economic and cultural development in many West African nations since independence and, in some cases, have completely stifled artistic work. Paris and London remain the literary conduits for the best-known writers from the region, but local publishers and cultural centers also are helping sustain writing there.

NIGERIA

Nigeria is by far Africa's most populous nation and has long been one of its literary centers. **Wole Soyinka** (b. 1934) won sub-Saharan Africa's only Nobel Prize in Literature outside South Africa. Despite civil war in Biafra, extended periods of military government, and often shaky and corrupt democratic rule, Nigerians have consistently produced a large body of fiction, albeit often while living abroad. Several path-breaking authors came of age in the colonial era, including Soyinka, **Chinua Achebe** (1930–2013), and **Cyprian Ekwensi** (1921–2007), and a new generation, which includes writers **Chris Abani** (b. 1966), **Helon Habila** (b. 1967), and **Chimamanda Ngozi Adichie** (b. 1977), has now been established.

English is the unifying language in multiethnic and multilingual Nigeria, but three other major languages—Hausa, Igbo, and Yoruba—have some 20 million native speakers each. Although these and many other languages have their own unique literary traditions and cultures, essentially none of the Nigerian fiction originally written in any language other than English is readily available outside Nigeria. The work of Nigerian writers published in Europe and the United States also tends to be by authors with strong ties to either Great Britain or America, where almost all of them now reside. Several had at least some success while still living in Nigeria—notably Achebe, who moved to the United States in 1990, and younger writers such as Abani and Habila—but much of the work of those in the younger generation is almost predictably multicultural. Raised and educated in two cultures, their fiction often relies on Nigerian subject matter and themes while also being comfortable with Western literary traditions, offering something new but not too new, much like the successful fiction by a slightly older generation of writers from India a few decades earlier.

The Trail Blazers

Amos Tutuola's (1920–1997) quest tale *The Palm-Wine Drinkard* (1952) was one of the first African novels to be widely acclaimed and read abroad. The narrator of the novel relies on a palm-wine tapster to provide him with his beloved intoxicating drink, and when the tapster dies, he cannot find anyone to take his place. Because the narrator heard that some people who die do not go directly to heaven, he hopes to find his dead tapster somewhere in this world, and the novel

MARKET LITERATURE

So-called market literature—mainly pamphlets of self-help and advice but also including the local equivalent of pulp fiction, as well as drama and poetry—flourished in the Nigerian city of Onitsha during the 1960s. While the literary quality was generally not very high—**Cyprian Ekwensi** is the only major writer to have emerged from this scene—it demonstrated the viability of a large domestic market for popular literature in Africa. Unfortunately, the industry was devastated by the Biafran war. The anthology of pamphlets *Life Turns Man Up and Down* (2001), edited by Kurt Thometz, is the best introduction to Onitsha's market literature.

A YORUBA CLASSIC

Wole Soyinka translated **D. O. Fagunwa**'s (1903–1963) *The Forest of a Thousand Daemons* (1938, English 1968) from the Yoruba, helping bring the work of this influential author to a larger audience. In Nigeria, **Amos Tutuola**'s work is widely considered to be a pale imitation of Fagunwa's.

recounts his adventures as he looks for him. With its use of Yoruba myths and idiosyncratic English, the book has a ring of authenticity of a sort rarely found in earlier African fiction. Ironically, it initially enjoyed much greater success abroad than it did in Nigeria itself, where critics were less receptive to the liberties Tutuola took with English and to his borrowings from familiar folktales. None of Tutuola's later, often very similar, works had the same impact, and *The Palm-Wine Drinkard* remains a classic of African fiction.

Chinua Achebe (1930–2013) is the most important figure in modern African literature, and his first novel, *Things Fall Apart* (1958), marks the beginning of modern African writing. With far more than 8 million copies sold, *Things Fall Apart* is also by far the best-selling work of African fiction. Achebe has written a number of other excellent works of fiction, and he is also an accomplished poet and important essayist. As the founding editor of the Heinemann African Writers Series—long the leading outlet for African writing in English—which he oversaw from 1962 to 1972, Achebe played a central role in fostering new talent and recognizing new African authors.

Things Fall Apart is a novel about Igbo village life at a time when the white colonizers' influence is just beginning to spread. The protagonist, Okonkwo, has risen from humble beginnings to become an important figure, but over the course of the novel, his life is marked repeatedly by the demands and expectations of tradition. Among the several violent deaths in the novel is that of a boy who had been delivered to the village as a sacrificial lamb in recompense for another murder. The boy is raised in Okonkwo's household for several years but ultimately has to be put to death. Okonkwo also accidentally kills another youth, which forces him to flee his village. When he returns after the appointed seven years of exile, he finds Christian missionaries have spread their word and undermined the foundations of his society. He tries to combat their influence but fails and is ultimately reduced to committing the shameful act of suicide. Even though Okonkwo is the central figure in the novel, Achebe's intention is clearly to describe a tribal way of life and how it was upset by foreign interference. Village life is far from idyllic, and the villagers display universal human weaknesses, but they live on their own terms—until the white man's terms are dictated to them. Achebe wrote the novel in part as a response to what he considered the superficial portrayal and understanding of African life in novels like **Joyce Cary**'s (1888–1957) *Mister Johnson* (1939), and *Things Fall Apart* succeeds particularly well in validating a largely African perspective.

In the 1960s, Achebe published several other novels dealing with conditions in Nigeria during the twentieth century, but he has written little fiction since then. His last novel, *Anthills of the Savannah* (1987), was also his most stridently political. Achebe set the story in a fictional nation, Kangan, but as in many other African novels attacking dictatorships, the real-life counterparts to the nation and some of the figures are readily identifiable.

Nobel laureate **Wole Soyinka** (b. 1934) is best known for his plays and autobiographical writing, but he has also written some fiction. His most important novel, *The Interpreters* (1965), can seem almost willfully obscure, yet the constant talk of the group of intellectuals

---

KEEP IN MIND

- **Cyprian Ekwensi** (1921–2007) was one of the first, and perhaps the greatest, exponents of popular fiction in Africa, for both adults and children. He wrote a number of rather sensational works about urban life in Lagos, most notably the prostitute tale *Jagua Nana* (1961).
- **T. M. Aluko's** (1918–2010) novels often reflect his experience as a civil servant.
- **Elechi Amadi's** (b. 1934) novels describe village life.

---

at the center of the novel yields a rich picture of newly independent Nigeria and the opportunities for a new generation—and the costs of those opportunities.

The New Generation

Ben Okri's (b. 1959) first novel, *Flowers and Shadows* (1980), was written when he was still a teenager, and this shows in its somewhat contrived and melodramatic plot as well as in his still unsure style. Nevertheless, it is a forceful bildungsroman set in the Nigeria of that time. Its protagonist, the teenager Jeffia, has lived a protected and privileged life, thanks to the success of his ruthless and corrupt father. As his father's life comes undone, Jeffia faces several crises that mark a transition from innocence to experience. Here and in his other early work, especially the collection of stories *Stars of the New Curfew* (1988), Okri's portrayal of Nigerian urban life and corruption is striking. In the long novel *The Famished Road* (1991), Okri continues to move away from strict realism. This novel, which won the prestigious British Booker literary prize, is narrated by an *abiku* named Azaro. He is a spirit child who has gone through many cycles of life and rebirth and now clings to a place in the real world in which he does not entirely belong. Okri imposes his imagined spiritual world on the raw Nigerian reality in a surreal and fantastical mix reminiscent of magical realism. Although he strikes a good balance between the spiritual elements and their connection to the real in

The Famished Road, too many of Okri's later works are skewed entirely toward the spiritual, and while the lyrical language of *The Famished Road* is still controlled, in his more recent novels, it seems excessive.

Helon Habila's (b. 1967) debut, ***Waiting for an Angel*** (2002), describes life under the rule of Sani Abacha in the 1990s. It begins with its protagonist, Lomba, in prison, with the later, largely self-contained, chapters describing the conditions and circumstances that have shaped Lomba's life and finally led to his arrest. If occasionally too grandiloquent, the overall impression is strong. ***Measuring Time*** (2007) is a more ambitious novel covering several decades of recent Nigerian history. Its main characters are twins from a small Nigerian village. One brother, LaMamo, leaves while the sickly one, Mamo, stays behind. Reports from abroad—mainly LaMamo's—bring home some of the larger problems Africa faces, and Mamo becomes a local historian. ***Oil on Water*** (2010) is set in the Niger Delta where the oil industry has brought great corruption and destruction along with vast wealth. The kidnapping of the wife of a foreign oil executive brings two journalists—one legendary but over-the-hill and the other young and just beginning his career—into this contemporary heart of darkness in which they are confronted with conditions that are far more complex and ambiguous than they appeared from a distance.

Biyi Bandele (b. 1967), whose earliest works were published under the name 'Biyi Bandele-Thomas, is better known as a playwright, but he has written several entertaining novels. All are very funny. Even his novel ***Burma Boy*** (published in the United States as *The King's Rifle*; 2007), about African soldiers fighting in Asia during World War II, is leavened by humor. While the way his novels unfold has a jittery quality, with stories within stories and episodes veering and breaking off in all directions, they hold together sufficiently and often are excellent. Bandele has a good ear for language, and his prose is playful without being too ornate. As might be expected from someone used to writing for the stage, it reads aloud very well. With its descents into madness, ***The Sympathetic Undertaker and Other Dreams*** (1991) conveys the unreal and unpredictable world of contemporary Nigeria particularly well, but all of Bandele's novels are worth reading.

KEEP IN MIND

- **Festus Iyayi** (1947–2013) wrote socially and politically engaged fiction.
- **Buchi Emecheta's** (b. 1944) work, especially her fiction, is based on her own experiences in Nigeria and London.
- **Chris Abani's** (b. 1966) poignant tales are about African lives, most memorably that of Elvis in *GraceLand* (2004).

The Next Wave

Chimamanda Ngozi Adichie (b. 1977), **Helen Oyeyemi** (b. 1984), and **Uzodinma Iweala** (b. 1982) already have shown great promise in their first books, among which Adichie's ***Purple Hibiscus*** (2003) and ***Half of a Yellow Sun*** (2006) stand out. *Purple Hibiscus* has many of the elements typical of a coming-of-age novel, but it is the father figure—a devout Christian, widely admired as generous and public minded but a strict brute at home—that makes compelling the narrator, his teenage daughter Kambili, trying to become independent. Unlike many recent African novels dealing with war and rebellion, Adichie's *Half of a Yellow Sun* does not focus on current conflicts but, rather, the Biafran war of the late 1960s. Many English-writing authors of her generation from the Commonwealth countries have written novels about defining periods in their homeland's recent histories of which they have no firsthand knowledge, often in what is clearly an effort to construct a foundation for their own understanding of their country's present. *Half of a Yellow Sun* is such a novel and shows that this exercise can be rewarding for readers as well. In closely following the lives of several protagonists—including a houseboy ultimately drawn into the fighting, a university lecturer, and an Englishman who finds himself in the role of an observer in this war—Adichie offers many perspectives on the conflict and its personal toll. Less focused on the actual combat than how it influenced, disrupted, and destroyed so many lives, it is an affecting novel of Nigerian history that also contrast with the starker works written decades earlier by those directly touched by events in Biafra.

GHANA

Ama Ata Aidoo's (b. 1942) fiction examines the lives of African women, from the young protagonists in her collection of stories *The Girl Who Can* (1997), to Esi, a woman trying to balance career and a second marriage in the novel *Changes* (1991). In *Our Sister Killjoy* (1977), the protagonist, an African student named Sissie, travels through 1960s Europe. Sissie goes to Europe on a scholarship for travel, not for study, making her a cultural observer and ambassador very different from the protagonists of so many African-in-Europe novels. In visiting not only England but also, for example, Germany, she ventures farther afield than do the characters in most novels of the period. Aidoo's presentation mirrors her character's efforts to digest and find the words for what she experiences, ranging from straightforward prose to correspondence to verse. While the novel as a whole has a pieced-together feel suggesting that Aidoo is more comfortable with the story form, it is a unique documentation of those times—and could have been a first step in a direction that one wishes more authors (Aidoo included) had followed.

With its harsh appraisal of the promise that came with independence—Ghana was the first sub-Saharan state to break free of British rule, in 1957—quickly dashed by corruption and an unnamed character referred to simply as *the man*, **Ayi Kwei Armah**'s (b. 1939) *The Beautyful Ones Are Not Yet Born* (1968) is a classic of African anomie. Armah's bleak, almost despairing novel is a wallow in filth, the protagonist literally surrounded by decay, with little hope for renewal or cleansing even in its conclusion.

The Beautyful Ones Are Not Yet Born and the Harvard-educated Armah's next two novels all were first published in the United States, a trilogy of works with autobiographical elements and African settings that strive for universality. The third, *Why Are We So Blest?* (1971), is more polemical and political, but all are highly critical of the roads taken in Africa. While not disassociating himself from the continent, Armah arguably chose to write from a distance, publishing for a primarily Western or Western-educated audience, a path that other postcolonial authors, such as Salman Rushdie, would soon take. Instead of continuing on this course, however, Armah abruptly turned inward. *Two Thousand Seasons* (1973) and *The Healers* (1978), both first published in Africa, are much broader in their historical scope and, in effect, reimagine African history. As the title *The Healers* suggests, Armah's outlook in these works is also more optimistic.

Settling in Senegal, Armah established his own publishing house and has continued to publish fiction, much of which is strongly anchored in classical African myth. While the lyrical intensity impressive in his early work can still be found, Armah's mythmaking and didacticism weigh down his more recent work. In recent decades, Armah has written himself into a corner, cutting himself and his fiction off from the global writing and reading community. Works such as *Osiris Rising* (1995) and the epistemic novel *KMT: In the House of Life* (2002) are of interest but also unpolished by contemporary standards. Without constructive engagement with the literary community, Armah has become a peripheral figure despite the talent that, in his early works, suggested a far more prominent position for him.

B. Kojo Laing (b. 1946) is another Ghanaian author whose leap onto the world stage has so far proved to be only a tentative one. Also a poet, Laing's fiction is noteworthy for its linguistic reach. Incorporating African language and expressions, veering into the poetic, and allowing sentences to run on at considerable length, Laing's prose is among the most distinctive of that of contemporary African writers. Beginning with his novel of Ghanaian corruption, *Search Sweet Country* (1986), his novels can be seem glutted, especially as they rarely contain a story arc that leads to a satisfying resolution. Rather, the pleasure of Laing's tales is found in the often satirical and surreal way they unfold. Always interested in the clash of technology and tradition, several of Laing's works have elements of both magic and science fiction. *Major Gentl and the Achimota Wars* (1992) is a futuristic vision of an idealized African metropolis, set in the year 2020. Like Armah's novels, Laing's early works were first published by American and British publishers; his more recent *Big Bishop Roko and the Altar Gangsters* (2006), an

KEEP IN MIND

• **Mohammed Naseehu Ali**'s (b. 1971) collection of stories about Ghana and Ghanaians in the United States is entitled *The Prophet of Zongo Street* (2005).

unwieldy but remarkable novel that mixes religion and genetic engineering, has been published only in Ghana.

CÔTE D'IVOIRE

All of **Ahmadou Kourouma**'s (1927–2003) few novels are political, ranging from his first, *The Suns of Independence* (1968, revised 1970, English 1981), about the transition from colonialism to independence, to one of the major child-soldier tales to come out of Africa, *Allah Is Not Obliged* (2000, English 2007). A Malinké, Kourouma has skillfully incorporated his native language and storytelling into his fiction. For example, the title of his novel *Monnew* (1990, English 1993), representing the defiance and contempt that dominates it, is a Malinké term with no exact French (or English) equivalent.

Kourouma's novels are set in fictional West African countries, yet the real-life counterparts of both the nations and their rulers are often readily identifiable. His finest achievement is the satirical *Waiting for the Vote of the Wild Animals* (1998, English 2001, and as *Waiting for the Wild Beasts to Vote*, 2003), which brings together many of Africa's worst despots in a gathering to reflect on the life and sing the praises of a dictator named Koyaga, a thinly veiled portrait of Togo's Gnassingbé Eyadema. The presentation, in the form of this very traditional gathering and ritual accounting of Koyaga's life and feats, mixing fantastical embellishments and horrifying realism, produces a devastating critique of both Eyadema's rule and, in the many asides, his fellow despots. It is, along with Ngũgĩ wa Thiong'o's *Wizard of the Crow*, the strongest—and funniest—satirical novel to come out of Africa.

KEEP IN MIND

- **Bernard Binlin Dadié's** (b. 1916) offers creative impressions of an African traveling abroad in works such as *One Way* (1964, English 1994).
- The novels of Côte d'Ivoire–born **Véronique Tadjo** (b. 1955) show an impressive range.
- Côte d'Ivoire–born **Marguerite Abouet** (b. 1971) wrote a series of Aya graphic novels, beginning with *Aya* (2005, English 2007), which is set in the Ivory Coast starting in the 1970s, with illustrations by Clément Oubrerie.

Born in Cameroon, **Werewere Liking** (b. 1950) founded the artistic center Ki-Yi M'Bock in Abidjan in 1985. She is involved in many of the arts, principally theater and painting, but has also written several works of fiction. Some of her unconventional works are "song novels," using oral traditions while also showing obvious theatrical influences. Even a weighty autobiographical coming-of-age novel like *The Amputated Memory* (2004, English 2008) has the feel of a performance piece. The often experimental nature of works such as the hodgepodge *It Shall Be of Jasper and Coral* (1983, English 2000) can be exasperating, yet Werewere's inventiveness is admirable. Certainly, how she mixes genres—and pushes them to their limits—makes her one of Africa's more intriguing avant-garde writers.

SENEGAL

Senegal has produced several notable authors, including the filmmaker and writer **Sembene Ousmane** (1923–2007). Sembene's socially engaged fiction includes *God's Bit of Wood* (1960, English 1962), based on an actual railway strike in the late 1940s. This richly populated novel is as much about community as it is about a labor dispute and remains a landmark of African realist fiction. *Xala* (1973, English 1976) is somewhat overshadowed by Sembene's film version of the same name, but this comic novel about a corrupt, Europeanized member of the new

---

KEEP IN MIND

- **Cheikh Hamidou Kane**'s (b. 1928) *Ambiguous Adventure* (1961, English 1963) stands out among the many African novels about Africans traveling to Europe to advance their studies. The novel focuses on the religious, with its protagonist, Diallo, firmly rooted in Islamic tradition and always drawn back to it.
- The protagonist of France-based **Fatou Diome**'s (b. 1968) *The Belly of the Atlantic* (2003, English 2006) is torn between Senegal and France and recognizes how difficult it is for her countrymen to fulfill their dreams abroad.

---

bourgeoisie who continues to serve French interests rather than those of his countrymen and who finds himself afflicted by impotence (the "xala" of the title) when he takes yet another wife is an enjoyable satire. Sembene's fast-paced, dialogue-heavy *The Last of the Empire* (1981, English 1983) is his most direct attack on Senegalese politics. While its specifics make it somewhat dated, it still holds up well as a thoughtful political thriller.

Mariama Bâ's (1929–1981) first novel, *So Long a Letter* (1979, English 1981), is presented as a letter from the recently widowed Ramatoulaye to her friend Aissatou. The lives of both were marked by their husband's taking second wives, and while Ramatoulaye remained with her husband, Aissatou divorced hers. The novel offers a sharp criticism of the practice of polygamy and convincingly conveys the human toll it takes.

GUINEA

Guinea is one of several West African countries that have been largely under totalitarian rule since independence. Its most famous author, **Camara Laye** (1928–1980), served in several government positions under the dictatorship of Ahmed Sékou Touré, who ruled the country from 1958, when it became independent, until his death in 1984. But after publishing his novel critical of Touré's regime, *A Dream of Africa* (1966, English 1968), Camara went into permanent exile. His masterpiece, and one of the great works of African fiction, is *The Radiance of Kings* (1954, English 1956). The novel's main character is a white man, Clarence, who finds himself down and out in an African country after gambling away his last money and believes his only hope for bettering his situation is to obtain an audience with the king. With little understanding of the society and culture in which he finds himself stranded, Clarence is slowly drawn into it in the fantastical journey he takes to reach his objective. The beautifully written novel is an ambiguous tale that can be seen as anything from an allegorical quest to a surreal and Kafkaesque nightmare. Camara wrote only a few works of fiction, but they are commendable, from his autobiographical *The Dark Child* (published in Great Britain as *The African Child*; 1953, English 1954) to *The Guardian of the Word* (1978, English 1980), his retelling of the life of Sundiata, who became the first emperor of the Malian empire.

MALI

Mali—and its fabled city of Timbuktu—was long a literary and intellectual center and still has a strong tradition of oral literature. The performances of *griots*—a mixture of bards, poets, and singers—continue to influence many of the region's writers. The works of some contemporary writers from Mali have been published in French but not in English, and only a few older titles by Malian authors are available in translation. These include significant novels such as **Amadou Hampaté Bâ**'s (1901–1991) sharply humorous story of the cost of colonialism, *The Fortunes of Wangrin* (1973, English 1987), and **Yambo Ouologuem**'s (b. 1940) only full-fledged novel, the controversial but influential *Bound to Violence* (1968, English 1971).

Covering more than seven hundred years of the history of the fictitious African Nakem Empire, from the thirteenth century onward, *Bound to Violence* is a wildly uneven and often unfocused novel, as Ouologuem rushes through some parts and lingers over others. Driven by a furious energy, it is also a very violent account. Questions arose about the authenticity of his text, as Ouologuem was accused of plagiarism and clearly incorporated passages from other writers' work into his novel, most notably from Graham Greene's *It's a Battlefield* (1934). But even if seen as merely an enhanced collage of other works, it is an often dazzling novel.

ELSEWHERE IN WEST AFRICA

Military rule and civil wars in several of the other western African nations have limited the development of a literary culture, and even though fiction is being published throughout the region now, little of it is ready for the world stage. Among the exceptions is the work of Mauritanian author **Moussa Ould Ebnou** (b. 1956), but much is not yet available in English translation.

Bai T. Moore's (1916–1988) short novella *Murder in the Cassava Patch* (1968) is among the few well-known books from Liberia. Set in 1957, the novel begins with its narrator, Gortokai, in jail, accused of the murder of his fiancée, Tene. Gortokai's account of his life and what led up to Tene's death provides some insight into Liberian culture and tradition, and with the murder mystery framing the story, it is an enjoyable small work.

Sierra Leonean author **Syl Cheney-Coker** (b. 1945) is better known for his poetry, but his ambitious novel *The Last Harmattan of Alusine Dunbar* (1990) also is noteworthy. Taking place in the fictional city of Malagueta, which was founded by freed slaves, it is a work of historical fiction with a strong magical realist inflection that resembles a West African version of Gabriel García Márquez's *One Hundred Years of Solitude* (1967, English 1970). Cheney-Coker's penchant for florid and poetic language can make it seem overwritten, and with characters like the poet named Garbage Martins, it is occasionally forced, a fanciful variation on Sierra Leonean history. Cheney-Coker returns to Malagueta in the similarly ambitious *Sacred River* (2014).

A journalist and outspoken critic of the regime in his native Burkina Faso (previously called Upper Volta), **Norbert Zongo** (1949–1998) was brutally murdered. His novel *The Parachute Drop* (1988, English 2004), about a Mobuto-like dictator in a fictional African country, is the most significant to come out of Burkina Faso.

KEEP IN MIND

- **Wilton Sankawulo** (1937–2009) wrote traditional tales and folklore and also was briefly Liberia's effective head of state in the mid-1990s.
- **Tété-Michel Kpomassié's** (b. 1941) wonderful account *An African in Greenland* (1981, English 1983) is nonfiction but one of the few literary works to come out of Togo.
- **Ebou Dibba's** (1943–2000) fiction is from Gambia.

Lusophone Africa

Long after most of the French and British colonies in Africa had gained independence, Portugal still clung to the scattered territories it nominally controlled. Guinea-Bissau was the first to break free, in 1973, and after the Portuguese Carnation Revolution of 1974 that finally saw the overthrow of the fascist government in Portugal, the other colonies also gained independence. Stability was more elusive. The insurgencies that had started in 1961 were succeeded by the devastating civil wars that persisted in Mozambique until 1992 and in Angola, with a brief hiatus after 1991, until 2002. Not surprisingly, under these conditions, these countries in recent decades have had only limited literary production. Much of what has been translated into English focuses on the struggle against colonial rule, as well as the enormous toll in these countries' long periods of political instability.

ANGOLA

With its use of the local Kimbundu creole and realistic depiction of contemporary Angolan life under Portuguese rule, **José Luandino Vieira**'s (b. 1935) collection of stories *Luuanda* (1964, English 1980) was considered subversive enough for the book to be banned until 1974. The more overtly political *The Real Life of Domingos Xavier* predates it but was first published in French only in 1971, before becoming available in Portuguese (1974) and then English (1978). Both books offer a good impression of the conditions of and opposition to Portuguese colonialism. In *The Loves of João Vêncio* (1979, English 1991), a prisoner awaiting his sentence recounts his life and loves. Even though only his voice is presented, João Vêncio is responsive to the reactions and questions of the other prisoner to whom he is telling his story, thus enlivening the text.

The few novels by **Pepetela** (b. 1941) that have been translated give the best insight into Angolan history and conditions, ranging from *Mayombe* (1980, English 1983), immersed in the Angolan guerrilla war, to the sweeping *Yaka* (1984, English 1996), a novel spanning the colonial period from 1890 to 1975 and using both African and European mythology. In *The Return of the Water Spirit* (1995, English 2002), a "Luanda Syndrome" strikes the capital city, with buildings on a central square collapsing in an allegory of corruption. The novel is a vivid indictment of postcolonial Angola. Pepetela also offers an amusing contemporary local spin on the police procedural in *Jaime Bunda, Secret Agent* (2001, English 2007), one of the few African thrillers. With its good-natured but far from heroic protagonist, *Jaime Bunda, Secret Agent* is the most enjoyable and current of Pepetela's works.

Younger authors **José Eduardo Agualusa** (b. 1960) and **Ondjaki** (b. 1977) are the leading voices of the generation emerging after the end of Portuguese colonial rule, and much of their fiction depicts the struggle for national stability and identity in the newly independent nation and southern Africa generally.

KEEP IN MIND

- **Uanhenga Xitu**'s (1924–2014) *The World of "Mestre" Tamoda* (1974, English 1988) takes place before the civil war dominated local life and is an amusing clash of colonial education and traditional suspicion with an appealingly pompous protagonist in Tamoda.
- **Manuel Rui**'s (b. 1941) *Yes, Comrade!* (1977, English 1993) is another interesting collection of stories about the revolutionary period.

Ondjaki's novels about childhood in Luanda near the end of the civil war, ***Good Morning Comrades*** (2001, English 2008) and ***Granma Nineteen and the Soviet's Secret*** (2008, English 2014), as well as the slightly overwrought village fantasy, *The Whistler* (2002, English 2008), with its almost too colorful cast of characters, display a light, playful touch of an author just beginning to mature. In *The Whistler*, a traveling salesman and a stranger with an extraordinary ability to whistle come to a sleepy town, shaking and waking things up. A charming lyrical fantasy, it is—with the epigraphs opening its chapters from authors ranging from Jorge Luis Borges and Pepetela to Friedrich Hölderlin and Henri Michaux—also a text in which Ondjaki's many ambitions sometimes get the better of him.

Agualusa is perhaps the most pan-Lusophone of authors. He is an Angolan-born writer living also in Portugal and Brazil, and his early novel *Creole* (1997, English 2002) covers at least part of all those worlds, based on the nineteenth-century slave trade reaching from Angola to Brazil. ***The Book of Chameleons*** (2004, English 2006) is narrated by a gecko who lives in the house of a "seller of pasts" (which is also the original Portuguese title, *O Vendedor de Passados*), creating entirely new identities for people in a world where many are in need of such personal re-creation. On a much larger scale, ***My Father's Wives*** (2007, English 2008) reaches from Angola across southern Africa to Mozambique in the story of a musician who had many women in his life. Much of the novel involves the story of the film-maker Laurentina, the youngest of the many daughters of the famed musician Faustino Manso, as she travels to meet her relations, but her story is nested in Agualusa's own story of traveling with another filmmaker, Karen Boswall, collecting material for a documentary film. It is a thoroughly engaging novel full of invention and lies, despite its sometimes bewildering shifting narrative voices.

MOZAMBIQUE

Since the end of the civil war in Mozambique, **Mia Couto** (b. 1955) has established himself as a major author with several works of fiction that combine linguistic and other elements of magical realism, African folklore and mythology, and European literary traditions. In the haunting *Sleepwalking Land* (1992, English 2006), a boy and an old man take shelter in a burned-out bus and find the notebooks of one of the dead passengers, whose stories of his life then meld with those of the boy and the old man. *Under the Frangipani* (1996, English 2001) is an exotic variation on a murder investigation with too many willing suspects, with the form of police procedural becoming completely warped in Couto's fantastical presentation. *The Last Flight of the Flamingo* (2000, English 2004) has an even more far-fetched premise, an investigation into the bewildering phenomenon of UN soldiers who are spontaneously exploding, making for a surprisingly effective picture of contemporary Mozambican conditions and the role of outside agents, including those from the UN and NGOs, who have replaced the colonial masters.

KEEP IN MIND

- **Luís Bernardo Honwana**'s (b. 1942) collection of straightforward stories *We Killed Mangy Dog* (1964, English 1969) gives a good sense of Mozambique under Portuguese rule.

CAPE VERDE

Not much fiction from Cape Verde is available in translation, even by the country's leading author, **Germano Almeida** (b. 1945). His novel *The Last Will and Testament of Senhor da Silva Araújo* (1989, English 2004) nonetheless provides both local color and an appealing story, told almost completely in the modern European tradition. Only with his death do the details of Napumoceno da Silva Araújo's life emerge, and it turns out there was more to him than was commonly known, surprises that Almeida relates in an engaging fashion.

North Africa, Middle East, and Turkey

Arabic-Speaking Countries

Arabic is only one of the official languages in a wide corridor of countries stretching from Morocco to Iraq, and these countries' cultural, historical, and political differences have, in turn, led to different literary traditions. Poetry was long the preferred literary form, and even though the region's storytelling tradition extends far beyond the *Arabian Nights*, the novel is considered a relative upstart. Until recently, little contemporary fiction of any kind had emerged from the Arab Gulf States. In the nations of the Maghreb, French remains the dominant literary language in regard to the fiction that reaches Europe and America. Egypt, with the region's largest Arab-speaking population and a geographically central position, has generally been the hub of Arabic literature and also where the novel first took hold in the Arab world. Throughout the region, civil unrest and political crackdowns, along with a tradition of very harsh censorship, also have forced many writers to work in exile.

Local political censorship, too, has had a chilling effect on writers in the region. Ironically, those works that are critical of Arab regimes, often by authors in exile and published abroad, are those most likely to reach Western audiences, giving a somewhat misleading impression of the Arabic literary scene. A relatively underdeveloped and fragmented publishing industry and a small book-buying public have also limited the growth of Arabic literature and literary culture. Religious pressure continues to have some influence over what is published and can be sold, but in the modern global economy, writers and readers are increasingly able to circumvent many of these controls. While outright risqué or blasphemous works may not be readily available in many Arabic markets, more and more Arabic writers seem to be testing the boundaries of the permissible. The wave of popular revolt across the region that began in December 2010 and saw the overthrow of several long-established regimes, including that of Hosni Mubarak in Egypt, will certainly lead to changes in publishing and book selling. The resulting wider availability of a far greater range of titles, coupled with greater artistic freedom and less censorship, may well lead to a literary boom similar to the one that began in China in the early 1980s.

The written language used in the Arabic-speaking states is essentially the same, but the spoken vernacular varies greatly, and recently more authors have turned to the local street Arabic in their writing, rather than the standard Arabic that has long dominated the literature. Unfortunately, these differences are almost completely lost in English translation, even though they are very obvious to native readers.

Until **Naguib Mahfouz** (1911–2006) was awarded the Nobel Prize in Literature in 1988, only a few contemporary works of Arabic fiction (many of them by Mahfouz) were being translated into English annually—an average of fewer than three a year since the end of World War II. This number has increased considerably since 1988, and since the American-led invasion of Iraq in 2003 and now the Arab Spring, interest in the region and its literature has grown. Whether this burgeoning Arabic literature will now truly establish itself in the global literary market, however, remains to be seen.

EGYPT

Naguib Mahfouz (1911–2006) remains the towering figure of Arabic fiction, especially when considered from an outside vantage point. Extensively translated, the breadth of his work is remarkable and ranges from historical fiction of the Pharaonic age to realistic novels of twentieth-century Cairo life such as *The Cairo Trilogy* (1956–1957, English 1989–1992) to more experimental fiction. His work is truly representative of an astonishing variety of Arabic fiction.

Beginning with *Khan al-Khalili* (1945, English 2008) and *Midaq Alley* (1947, English 1966, 2011), Mahfouz wrote several social realist novels set in specific neighborhoods (hence the titles) in present-day Cairo. His greatest success was his broader view in *The Cairo Trilogy*, consisting of *Palace Walk* (1956, English 1989), *Palace of Desire* (1957, English 1991), and *Sugar Street* (1957, English 1992). With its resemblance in both volume and manner to the long Russian and French novels of the nineteenth century, *The Cairo Trilogy* is the most readily approachable of Mahfouz's novels and a good place to start for either Mahfouz or Arabic fiction in general.

The Cairo Trilogy is a sweeping epic set in twentieth-century Egypt. It is a family saga, with a father, al-Sayyid Ahmad Abd al-Jawad, who is strict in his own household but much more liberal in his indulgences outside it. His family's home at Palace Walk is both fortress and cocoon, especially for the overprotected women who can barely venture from it, but even here a rapidly changing world cannot be kept at bay. Even though al-Sayyid Ahmad tries to steel the household against the changes all around, he is ultimately largely unable to, the fates of the various family members being a microcosm of Egypt in those decades. Mahfouz slowly and steadily stirs this swirl of stories, the turbulence of the times, in both the neighborhood and all of Cairo, preventing the home and family from remaining completely isolated. *The Cairo Trilogy* is both one of the great family-novels and one of the great city-novels of the twentieth century. Beginning with the Egyptian Revolution of 1919, Mahfouz's deliberate pace allows even those unfamiliar with those events to get a sense of what the country and its citizens went through and the various forces at play, from Islamic fundamentalism to a Western-oriented secularism.

Several of Mahfouz's earliest novels were set in the Pharaonic period, but in works such as *Khufu's Wisdom* (1939, English 2003), he is not overly concerned about historical accuracy. Instead, Mahfouz is more interested in myth and telling a good story, unlike the detail-obsessed historical fiction more common nowadays. Mahfouz also explores a Pharaonic subject in the far more mature work *Akhenaten: Dweller in Truth* (1985, English 1998). This novel looks at the obsession with faith as the pharaoh Akhenaten renounces the state's pantheistic religion and tries to impose his own monotheistic vision, catastrophically undermining the established order. Despite some repetition in the accounts of Akhenaten's life, Mahfouz is skilled enough to use the narrator, Meriamun, to collect information about the pharaoh from different sources in order to balance these complementary accounts to make a greater whole.

The historical echoes in other novels are even fainter. In *The Journey of Ibn Fattouma* (1983, English 1992), Mahfouz sends his narrator, nicknamed Ibn Fattouma, on a journey reminiscent of *Gulliver's Travels*. The societies and political regimes that Ibn Fattouma encounters serve as slightly simplified and exaggerated counterparts of those in the contemporary world. Though sometimes too quickly sketched, this is, along with *Arabian Nights and Days* (1982, English 1995), one of Mahfouz's most appealing works. *Arabian Nights and Days* draws on its literary antecedent, using characters and familiar stories from the original *A Thousand and One Nights* but weaving them into a new variation on the original's premises by having the sultan agree to marry Shahrazad, thereby ending the threat of murder that always hung over her storytelling.

All of Mahfouz's panoramic realist novels, including *Midaq Alley*, *The Beginning and the End* (1949, English 1985), and the allegorical *Children of the Alley* (1967, serialized 1959, English 1995, previously translated as *Children of Gebelawi*, 1981, revised 1997), are worthwhile. His later, less expansive novels offer interesting slices of Egyptian life as well. *The Thief and the Dogs* (1961, English 1984) is a revenge thriller with an ambiguous hero, marking a shift from a realist to a more impressionistic style. Many works revolve around a group of individuals brought together, rather than a single family. *Miramar* (1967, English 1978), for example, takes place at a boarding house, and in *Adrift on the Nile* (1966, English 1993), a group of friends frequently gather on a houseboat. The changing social and political situation is reflected most explicitly in works like *Karnak Café* (1974, English 2007), about the 1967 War, and *The Day the Leader Was Killed* (1985, English 1997), the story leading up to the 1981 assassination of Egyptian president Anwar Sadat. Elsewhere, Mahfouz zeroes in on the more mundane, as in his tale of the career of an ambitious bureaucrat, *Respected Sir* (1975, English 1986).

In many of his works, Mahfouz presents the story from different perspectives, and in *Wedding Song* (1981, English 1984), which is set in the theater world, he uses this technique to emphasize the overlap between art and reality. The multigenerational saga *Morning and Evening Talk* (1987, English 2007) goes considerably further. Each of its sixty-seven chapters is a biography of one member of the three families that dominate the book, arranged not chronologically but alphabetically according to the names of the characters. Although the stories overlap, as certain facts are recounted from different perspectives, the presentation is discontinuous, reminiscent of Julio Cortázar's *Hopscotch*. Covering two centuries of Egyptian history, *Morning and Evening Talk* is like an album of randomly ordered snapshots, with the larger picture emerging as the connections accumulate. A far cry from the Pharaonic novels, *The Cairo Trilogy*, or *Children of the Alley*, this is a remarkable late-career effort of an author still seeking new paths in his fiction.

Despite its specific references to Egyptian conditions, the atmosphere in **Sun'allah Ibrahim**'s (b. 1937) novella *The Committee* (1981, English 2001) resembles Kafka's *The Trial*, with its uncomprehending individual confronting a bureaucratic apparatus. Trying to please, he can never be sure that his answers are those wanted, and this allegory suffers from stretching too far, as Ibrahim mocks everything from the

---

KEEP IN MIND

- **Tawfiq al-Hakim** (1898–1987) and **Yusuf Idris** (1927–1991) were early influential Egyptian authors almost completely overshadowed by the prolific Mahfouz. Al-Hakim remains better known for his plays, and Idris is best known for his short stories.
- *The Lamp of Umm Hashim* (English 2004) is a collection of **Yahya Hakki**'s (1905–1992) stories.

---

state to that ultimate capitalist symbol, Coca-Cola. Most of Ibrahim's fiction has an ideological element, but his presentation of his political positions is creative. The chapters of *Zaat* (1992, English 2001) alternate between describing the life of the eponymous protagonist, a representative middle-class woman, and documentary material of late-twentieth-century Egypt in the form of newspaper clippings— headlines, reports, quotations. This layering of personal and public creates a full portrait of Egyptian life, especially in its constant reminder of the burden of widespread corruption on society.

Gamal al-Ghitani's (1945–2015) *Zayni Barakat* (1974, serialized 1970–1971, English 1988) is set in the sixteenth century. It is about a powerful state official's attempts at reform and the suspicion with which it is met, which has parallels with Gamal Abdel Nasser's rule during the 1950s and 1960s. This is imaginative historic fiction at its best. *The Zafarani Files* (1976, English 2008) is al-Ghitani's own entertaining version of the Cairo neighborhood novel. The more elusive, often almost mystical, *Pyramid Texts* (1994, English 2007) is built up in pyramid form, with the first chapter—base and foundation—being the longest and each successive one becoming shorter until a final peak of only three words.

Alaa Al Aswany's (b. 1957) *The Yacoubian Building* (2002, English 2004) quickly became one of the most popular modern Arabic novels, both in the region and in translation. In it, Aswany follows the daily lives of several of the residents of the once grand but now somewhat rundown Yacoubian building, ranging from the servants who live on the roof to politicians and businessmen. Mildly sensational, with sex and other intrigues, Aswany's novel is consistently gripping. The short chapters jump from story to story, constantly leaving the reader dangling, curious as to what will happen next. Aswany is not a great artist, and much of the book is simplistic but still has more than enough to please. A similar template does not work nearly as well in *Chicago* (2007, English 2008), a novel about Egyptians abroad. The individual and overlapping stories—of students, émigrés, and their various and often ambiguous relationships with Egypt and the Egyptian authorities— are interesting, but Aswany's Chicago is flat and unconvincing, especially compared with the vivid, dusty Cairo that is such an impressive backdrop in *The Yacoubian Building*.

KEEP IN MIND

- **Nawal El Saadawi**'s (b. 1931) passionate fiction is about women victimized in systems dominated by men.
- **Mohamed El-Bisatie**'s (1937–2012) creative fiction is frequently about Egyptian village life but often with unusual spins. An example is the novel *Over the Bridge* (2004, English 2006), in which a bureaucrat invents a town on paper, thereby allowing him to embezzle government funds meant for it, only to soon find matters getting out of hand.
- **Ibrahim Abdel Meguid**'s (b. 1946) realist novels are about Egyptian life in different eras of the twentieth century.
- **Miral al-Tahawy**'s (b. 1968) early novels use her Bedouin background, while *Brooklyn Heights* (2010, English 2012) explores the contemporary immigrant experience.
- *Rama and the Dragon* (1980, English 2002) is the title of **Edwar al-Kharrat**'s (1926–2015) demanding avant-garde classic.
- **Ahmed Alaidy** (b. 1974) uses fast-paced, youthful experimentation in his *Being Abbas el Abd* (2003, English 2006).
- Each of the fifty-eight chapters in *Taxi* (2007, English 2008, revised 2011), by **Khaled Al Khamissi** (b. 1962), is an encounter with a different Cairo taxi driver, each with his own story to tell.
- The English-language fiction by Egyptian-born **Ahdaf Soueif** (b. 1950) includes *The Map of Love* (1999), in which the Egypt of the late twentieth century is an echo of that of the late nineteenth century.

LIBYA

Many Western readers think of Muammar el-Qaddafi when they think of Libya, but little available contemporary Libyan fiction offers much insight into his regime or the nation as it adapts to life after Qaddafi. Libyan-raised **Hisham Matar**'s (b. 1970) *In the Country of Men* (2006) presents a child's perspective of life under Qaddafi in 1979, but while the nine-year-old protagonist's incomprehension of much around him adds to the novel's ominous feel, Matar falls short in both his approach and his description of conveying much that is unique to Libya.

The fiction of the Tuareg author **Ibrahim al-Koni** (b. 1948) does not directly touch on the political, but its evocation of desert life in all its surprising variety is some of the most compelling Arabic fiction being written today. Al-Koni's allegorical tales are dominated by their setting, which is spectacularly different from what most readers have ever known and far from the monotone one might expect regarding the desert. The dominance of and respect for nature are brilliantly reflected in the human relationships and interactions depicted in his work, as it necessitates a mutual dependency unlike that in an urban setting. Both the difficulty of striking a balance and the dangers posed by the intrusion of and change expected by those unfamiliar with the ways that have long ensured survival frequently figure in al-Koni's works. Many of his novels also have a mystical element, as in *The Seven Veils of Seth* (2003, English 2008) and *Anubis* (2002, English 2005), mixed with enough realism—and magical realism—to strike the right balance.

Ethan Chorin's anthology *Translating Libya* (English 2008) introduces a larger number of modern Libyan writers, and it differs from most anthologies in giving a more personal perspective on the material through Chorin's extensive editorial descriptions of his efforts to put together the collection. This adds another dimension to the anthology and helps better acquaint readers with the country.

THE MAGHREB

As in many of the former French colonies in Africa, French continues to be widely spoken and read in Morocco, Tunisia, and Algeria, especially in higher education and business. Much of the fiction by writers from the Maghreb nations is written in French as well, and the Algerian author **Assia Djebar** (1936–2015) was even admitted to the Académie française and made one of its so-called immortals who are charged with overseeing the language.

Kateb Yacine's (1929–1989) *Nedjma* (1956, English 1961) is a foundational text of Maghreb literature. The title character is an elusive figure, her mixed and uncertain parentage and the destiny which some of the men obsessed with her seek to impose on her meant to make her representative of Algeria itself. Kateb's presentation, which mixes the realistic and allegorical, is often said to resemble William Faulkner's. The novel blurs chronology and facts and shifts perspectives, giving it an occasionally frustrating opacity, though the dialogue and scenes have poetic power. Moreover, Kateb's ambiguity is clearly intended, and the book's shift in styles enabled North African fiction to move away from a strictly realistic mode. Nedjma, meaning *star* in Arabic, is also the pseudonym of the Moroccan author of the sensationalistic best seller *The Almond: The Sexual Awakening of a Muslim Woman* (2004, English 2005). One of the more explicit novels to come out of the region, it offers an uneasy mix of female empowerment and exotic soft porn.

Tahar Djaout (1954–1993) was among the many prominent intellectuals who fell victim to the Islamic fundamentalist terror in Algeria in the 1990s, and several of his novels capture the atmosphere of violent disintegration during those years, most notably in his posthumous *The Last Summer of Reason* (1999, English 2001). More sad than angry, this incomplete text describes the slow crushing of all freedoms under totalitarian rule. The story revolves around a bookseller who tries to maintain his way of life and his trade even while everything around him succumbs to the oppressive burdens of life under totalitarian rule.

The novel is all the more poignant because of Djaout's own fate, and for an unfinished work, it is surprisingly effective and compelling. *The Watchers* (1991, English 2002), an allegory of an individual's limited power against the state, was written and takes place in a time when terror was not yet omnipresent (as it was with the outbreak of civil war in 1991), but suspicion and fear already are widespread. The protagonist, Mahfoudh Lemdjad, invents a loom, a modernization that religious fundamentalists see as a threat. The state apparatus obstructs Mahfoudh at every turn, but he perseveres and is able to present his invention at an international fair, where it is hailed as great advance. This validation forces the government to switch tacks, but instead of admitting fault, it places the blame elsewhere.

Kamel Daoud's (b. 1970) *The Meursault Investigation* (2013, English 2015) builds on Albert Camus's classic novel *The Stranger* (also published as *The Outsider*; 1942, English 1946, 1982, 1988 [2], 2012). In *The Stranger*, Meursault kills a man who is identified only as an Arab. In *The Meursault Investigation*, Daoud gives the victim a name—Musa—and a younger brother. Many decades later, it is this brother, Harun, who reclaims the story in describing the events and their consequences from his family's perspective. Daoud's story goes considerably beyond a simple critique of colonialism, as Harun's indictment of conditions goes on to include those in independent Algeria.

Yasmina Khadra's (b. 1956) popular novels are set in present-day places of conflict. *The Swallows of Kabul* (2002, English 2004), *Cousin K* (2003, English 2013), *The Attack* (2005, English 2006), and *The Sirens of Baghdad* (2006, English 2007) all revolve around characters driven to extremes by extreme conditions. Khadra balances his stories with characters who desperately try to cling to their humanity, using plausible and understandable cases of radicalization in almost intolerable conditions. The didactic intent is often too obvious in these tales, as the events are too carefully arranged to convey his messages. Nonetheless, his gray—rather than black-and-white—pictures of Islamic fundamentalism are a welcome contrast to the many one-sided accounts in circulation. Even though the books are rather simplistic, Khadra is a good storyteller, and his writing is polished if not entirely natural. Rougher and more hard-boiled, Khadra's series of crime novels featuring Inspector Llob, take place in a violent Algeria where politics is part of every crime and determines how justice is served. They feel more convincing and present a conflict that is not as well known. *Dead Man's Share* (2004, English 2009), set in 1988, a few years before the Algerian civil war, is a good introduction to the character and series. The novel describes the pervasive corruption in a deceptively tranquil Algiers that has taken hold of all aspects of Algerian life that Khadra clearly sees as the root of the unrest that later permeated the country.

Although **Driss Chraïbi** (1926–2007) left Morocco at the end of World War II and eventually settled in France, his fiction is largely set in his homeland and often deals with the tensions between French and Moroccan culture and the lingering effects of colonialism. *The Butts* (1955, English 1983), a frequently grim novel, is one of the first fictional accounts of North African immigrant life. A recurring character in his fiction, Chraïbi's Inspector Ali, a Moroccan policeman, is introduced in *Flutes of Death* (1981, English 1985), in which he is sent on a mission in the mountain region. The novel contrasts urban and very rural life and pits the would-be modern state apparatus, itself hardly an inspiring institution, against Morocco's ingrained and ostensibly backward traditions. The center of *Inspector Ali* (1991, English 1994) is the fictional author of the Inspector Ali books, Brahim Orourke, and his family. This is one of several comic installments in a series in which Chraïbi plays with the detective-story genre.

MYSTERIES WRITTEN IN ARABIC

Although there have been several crime series by Francophone Arab writers like **Yasmina Khadra** and **Driss Chraïbi**, until recently almost no mysteries were written in Arabic. Moroccan **Abdelilah Hamdouchi's** (b. 1958) *The Final Bet* (2001, English 2008), which criticizes the still prevalent systems of law and order and their travesties of justice, is the first Arabic detective novel to be translated into English.

In *The Sand Child* (1985, English 1987) and its sequel, *The Sacred Night* (1987, English 1989), **Tahar Ben Jelloun** (b. 1944) offers an uncommon exploration of gender roles in the Arab world. The novels' central figure is a girl who was raised as a boy named Ahmed before eventually reassuming a female identity and taking the name Zahra. These are among the more intriguing novels focusing on this aspect of Moroccan Islamic society, touching on everything from inheritance laws to violence against women. Ben Jelloun's other novels also tackle social issues, from the insidious rot presented in *Corruption* (1994, English 1997), in which the protagonist tries to avoid being part of a system in which bribery is nearly universal, to the harrowing prison account found in *This Blinding Absence of Light* (2001, English 2002). Despite Ben Jelloun's manifest interest in dealing with social issues—obvious from titles like *Corruption* and the premises of many of his novels—his is considerably more than simply politically engaged fiction.

KEEP IN MIND

- The collection of stories *The Savage Night* (1995, English 2001) is a good introduction to the fiction of **Mohammed Dib** (1920–2003), and his novel in verse, *L.A. Trip* (2003, English 2003), is an engaging (if atypical) curiosity.
- Five decades worth of **Assia Djebar**'s (1936–2015) novels, focused on women's lives in the Maghreb in both modern and historical times, are well worth reading.
- **Bensalem Himmich**'s (b. 1949) historical novels include *The Theocrat* (1989, English 2005) and *The Polymath* (1997, English 2004).
- **Leila Abouzeid**'s (b. 1950) fiction of Moroccan life includes the collection *Year of the Elephant* (1984, serialized 1983, English 1989) and *The Last Chapter* (2000, English 2000).
- **Laila Lalami**'s (b. 1968) fiction about Morocco, *Hope and Other Dangerous Pursuits* (2005) and *Secret Son* (2009), is written in English.

SUDAN

Many twentieth-century African novels center on a protagonist who returns to his homeland, city, or village after studying in Europe or America and is struck by the contrast between the two worlds, finding himself no longer at home in either. Among these often autobiographical works, **Tayeb Salih**'s (1929–2009) *Season of Migration to the North* (1966, English 1969) stands out and is certainly one of the great Arabic novels of recent times. The novel is a doubled tale of the return of both the nameless narrator and Mustafa Sa'eed, who has traveled a similar path from the Sudan to England and back. As he tells his own story, the narrator pieces together Sa'eed's journey. Salih's elliptical presentation reads like a thriller and allows enough ambiguity that no easy lessons or morals can be drawn. Salih's other works, including the two stories from the 1970s collected in *Bandarshah* (English 1996), are worthwhile but do not approach *Season of Migration to the North*.

   Tarek Eltayeb (b. 1959) was born in Egypt to Sudanese parents and emigrated to Austria in the 1980s. His novel *The Palm House* (2006, English 2012) features a narrator, Hamza, whose background is similar to his own. While much of the novel presents the African emigrant experience in Austria, Hamza also describes his childhood and youth in Sudan in a wide-ranging work expanding on Eltayeb's earlier and less polished novel, *Cities Without Palms* (1992, English 2009).

SUDANESE WRITERS

Both **Jamal Mahjoub** (b. 1960) and **Leila Aboulela** (b. 1964) are Anglophone writers who have strong Sudanese ties and emphasize the multinational in their fiction.

LEBANON

Not surprisingly, the Lebanese civil war and the continued political instability feature in much of the recent fiction from the country. In early works like *Little Mountain* (1977, English 1989), **Elias Khoury** (b. 1948) still seems to be deciding how to approach his subject of political turmoil. This short novel is presented from several perspectives and uses repetition as a way to make the events easier to grasp. Khoury's novels rarely unfold in a straightforward manner and often come together as collections of stories and episodes that meld together on his large canvases. The broadest of these, *Gate of the Sun* (1998, English 2005) and *Yalo* (2002, English 2008), about the Palestinian and Lebanese experiences of recent decades, include tales that spiral far beyond the individuals at their centers. While Khoury's lyrical language can be distracting, it is a style similar to that found in much recent Arabic fiction, and thus his novels are a good introduction to contemporary Middle Eastern fiction.

Rashid al-Daif's (b. 1945) *Dear Mr. Kawabata* (1995, English 1999) is cleverly presented as an epistolary novel addressed to the Japanese Nobel laureate. Left with nothing else but memory, the novel's narrator reflects on his life and is drawn to the distant and dead Yasunari Kawabata whose fictional world stands in such contrast to violent and unsettled Lebanon. As in *Dear Mr. Kawabata*, the protagonist in *Learning English* (1998, English 2007) is named Rashid, and in this novel, the death of the protagonist's father inspires reflection. Though he fully embraces modernity, is eager for the latest technological gizmos, and views English as the must-know language, the Rashid of *Learning English* also finds that he cannot entirely escape his roots and the customs and traditions that define his family. Al-Daif is particularly good at describing the tension between the traditional and the modern world that exists alongside the larger political and religious conflicts in Lebanon. His more abstract novels, such as *This Side of Innocence* (1997, English 2001), in which the narrator is held and questioned by the authorities without fully understanding what they want

KEEP IN MIND

- **Hanan al-Shaykh**'s (b. 1945) novels, such as *The Story of Zahra* (1980, English 1986) and the epistolary *Beirut Blues* (1992, English 1995), are about daily life in Beirut.

from him, feels more generic, but al-Daif generally frames quite well the issues his characters face.

PALESTINE AND JORDAN

Just as the poet **Adonis** (b. 1930) is Syria's internationally best-known author, poet **Mahmoud Darwish** (1942–2008)' is Palestine's most esteemed author. Several other writers from the region deserve attention as well. **Ghassan Kanafani**'s (1936–1972) novellas *All That's Left to You* (1966, English 1990) and *Men in the Sun* (1963, English 1978) are still among the best descriptions of the recent Palestinian experience. Although the symbolism in the memorable *Men in the Sun* verges on being simplistic, Kanafani's story of three men representing three different generations trying to reach Kuwait in the hope of bettering their and their loved ones' lives is still very effective. The three men's motives and hopes differ, but all see their only opportunity elsewhere, and their journey is a devastating allegory of post-1948 Palestinian life.

Kanafani's narratives, with their intentional vagueness, are not conventional realist novels. **Ibrahim Nasrallah**'s (b. 1954) *Prairies of Fever* (1985, English 1993) and *Inside the Night* (1992, English 2007), however, push the novel's form even further, employing a lyrical, fragmentary presentation that often resembles sequences of prose poems. In *Prairies of Fever*, the protagonist, Muhammad Hammad, goes to Saudi Arabia as a teacher. Nasrallah presents his experience in a mix of voices, moving between the real and fantasy, with the two becoming increasingly indistinguishable. *Inside the Night* skips back and forth

---

KEEP IN MIND

- **Emile Habiby**'s (1921–1996) *The Secret Life of Saeed, the Ill-Fated Pessoptimist* (1974, English 1982) is a comic story of a Palestinian who remains in Israel.
- The novels of **Jabra I. Jabra** (1919–1994) are noteworthy.
- Anglo-Jordanian author **Fadia Faqir**'s (b. 1956) novels are insightful works about modern life and culture in the Middle East.

---

between the present and the past in another mosaic of the Palestinian experience. While far from straightforward works of fiction, both novels convey the frustrations of life in uncertain conditions, the characters' alienation as expatriates, and their keen awareness of limitations of life in their homeland.

SYRIA

Rafik Schami (b. 1946) left Syria in 1970 to study in Germany, where he still lives today. Despite completing a Ph.D. in chemistry, he found true success as an author writing in German, his fifth language (along with Aramaic, Arabic, French, and English). Schami's fiction meets the *Arabian Nights* expectations of Western readers, especially in ***Damascus Nights*** (1989, English 1993) and ***The Calligrapher's Secret*** (2008, English 2010). Set in 1959 Damascus, a great storyteller in *Damascus Nights* has lost his voice to a spell, and his friends must spin their own stories in order to help him regain it. Playing with the genre, Schami creates his own agreeable fiction, which includes the typically abstract morals of age-old tales as well as some commentary on the Syrian and Arab politics of the time. Taking place during the short-lived Syrian-Egyptian union known as the United Arab Republic, Nasser's pan-Arab ideals and the realities of a police state make an interesting backdrop to the stories. ***The Dark Side of Love*** (2004, English 2009) is the story of two lovers from rival clans, one Catholic and the other Orthodox,

KEEP IN MIND

• The novels by **Hanna Mina** (b. 1924), the leading Syrian author, include his autobiographical *Fragments of Memory* (1975, English 1993) and *Sun on a Cloudy Day* (1973, English 1997).

which serves as the background for an immense study of Syrian life and politics through 1970. Parts of the protagonist's life story also resemble Schami's own, as Farid Mushtak also was educated in a monastery, is a member of the Communist Party, and eventually flees to Germany. But unlike Schami, Farid was imprisoned in one of Syria's most notorious prison camps. In this novel, Schami is particularly critical of the endless cycle of petty revenge and honor killings that is so deeply ingrained in Syrian life.

Zakaria Tamer (b. 1931) is one of the leading Arabic short-story writers. *The Hedgehog* (English 2009) contains tales connected to the title piece (2005), about a young boy's wildly imagined world, as well as the stories previously collected in *Tigers on the Tenth Day* (English 1985). This is a good example of Tamer's rich satirical talents. The more cohesive collection of more than five dozen very short stories, *Breaking Knees* (2002, English 2008), is almost overwhelming in its quick sequence of scenes from all walks of life, with many of the stories barely a page long and some only a paragraph. Despite the brevity of these tales and the fact that many have no obvious conclusion, they are entirely satisfying. Behind an almost plain style, Tamer slyly inserts his characters and situations into suggestive stories. Often instead of arriving at a neatly tied-together end, enough is left to the imagination for the tale to continue to unfold in the reader's mind.

IRAQ

During the nearly quarter of a century that Saddam Hussein (1937–2006) was the president of the Iraqi state, beginning in 1979, the country became increasingly isolated, first caught up in an almost decade-long war with neighboring Iran in the 1980s and then cutting itself off further from the international community with its invasion of Kuwait in 1990 and its defeat in the first Persian Gulf War in 1991. Since 2003, the American-led invasion of Iraq and the removal of Hussein and the Baath Party from power, the protracted presence of a large number of American and also British troops in the country, as well as widespread media coverage, have led to greater interest in local conditions. Although the increasingly repressive regime limited artistic freedom, the fiction that has recently become available in translation ranges from that by long-time exiles such as **Fadhil al-Azzawi** (b. 1940) to novels attributed to Hussein himself, such as the grotesque allegory *Zabiba and the King* (2000, English 2004).

With its backdrop of the Baath Party's rise to power in the early 1960s, **Fuad al-Takarli**'s (1927–2008) family epic *The Long Way Back* (1980, English 2001) is a good introduction to recent Iraqi history and contemporary fiction. Taking place in a multigenerational household and told from various perspectives and with its focus on domestic life, al-Takarli's novel offers a striking picture of a country in which political instability and uncertainty cloud so much of daily life. Fadhil al-Azzawi's much more imaginative *The Last of the Angels* (1992, English 2007), which combines dark comedy and elements of magical realism, also is set in the time before Saddam Hussein came to power and is one of the region's most impressive works of fiction. The book is set in the northern city of Kirkuk in the 1950s as the monarchy is nearing its end and Britain's control of the oil industry is making it the dominant power in the area. Al-Azzawi's humorous exploration of the conflicts between the authorities and the local community is entertaining and full of colorful characters.

Al-Azzawi's more realist story of life in detention, *Cell Block Five* (1972, English 2008), seems unusual for a Middle Eastern prison novel, especially given the reputation of Iraqi regimes. There is little here that is brutal or horrifying. As in *The Last of the Angels*, al-Azzawi is more interested in presenting community dynamics than in concentrating on the system's repressive aspects, although it is possible

KEEP IN MIND

- **Hassan Blasim**'s (b. 1973) dark stories of contemporary Iraq are collected in *The Corpse Exhibition* (English 2014).
- **Iqbal Al-Qazwini**'s novel *Zubaida's Window* (English 2008) is about an isolated exile's experience of the American-led invasion of Iraq.
- **Haifa Zangana**'s (b. 1950) novel *Women on a Journey* (2001, English 2006) concerns women from different Iraqi backgrounds who have been exiled to London.

to imagine from the system he describes the small steps that led to it. This darker side of Iraqi life and history is clearly presented in **Sinan Antoon**'s (b. 1967) *I'jaam* (2004, English 2007), which takes place in Iraq during the 1980s and offers a more brutal depiction of prison life. Antoon conveys the paranoia of the regime and the viciousness of its often arbitrary justice: almost everyone lives in fear, even though some personal freedom is still possible. A prefatory note explains that in the original Arabic, the prisoner's manuscript that constitutes this account was written without diacritical marks, meaning that there is considerable ambiguity regarding the meaning of many of the words in the text, comparable to when English homonyms are heard rather than seen spelled out. Despite the obvious difficulty of replicating this in translation, the English version of *I'jaam* is fairly successful, and the text mirrors the uncertainties of Iraqi life at that time. Fortunately, the wordplay is not relied on too much, so the novel is a relatively accessible read.

   Betool Khedairi's (b. 1965) novels also depict daily life in Iraq under Saddam Hussein's rule, but with the focus on the personal even when the political intrudes. The narrator in Khedairi's autobiographical coming-of-age novel, *A Sky So Close* (1999, English 2001), is caught between cultures, and the tension between her English mother and Iraqi father is only part of the pattern of difference and alienation that she repeatedly confronts. Despite its often being frustratingly impressionistic, *A Sky So Close* offers insight into Iraqi life in the 1970s and 1980s. Khedairi's more interesting *Absent* (2004, English 2005) is the story of a young orphaned woman and her neighbors living in the sanction-suffering Baghdad of the 1990s. Khedairi captures the uncertainty of their lives, and the narrator's detachment does not detract from the descriptions of the various characters and their straightforward dialogue.

SAUDI ARABIA AND OTHER GULF STATES

Abdelrahman Munif (1933–2004) studied and lived mainly in Iraq and Syria, but his fiction is most closely associated with Saudi Arabia and the transformation of the Gulf States that came with the rapid expansion of the oil industry after World War II. His five-volume *Cities of Salt* is set in a fictional Persian Gulf kingdom and is a thinly veiled history of twentieth-century Saudi Arabia. The novels still stand as the great saga of that region. The first three volumes of the series have been translated, as *Cities of Salt* (1984, English 1987), *The Trench* (1985, English 1993), and *Variations on Night and Day* (1989, English 1993). These books (and the others in the series) do not proceed in strict chronological order, and there is a slight disconnect between the more expansive first volume and the rest. The first two volumes, in particular, can stand on their own. As he already showed in *Endings* (1978, English 1988), Munif has both a deep understanding of and sympathy for traditional Bedouin life and a remarkable ability to convey this. Along with Ibrahim al-Koni, he is one of the great writers of desert fiction. *Variations on Night and Day* may contain too much local early-twentieth-century history and politics to be fully appreciated by Western readers, but both *Cities of Salt* and *The Trench* are accessible accounts of the transformation of the region and the resulting cultural and social turmoil. Munif describes the rapid shift away from traditional ways of life and the imposition of a largely new order, showing how the citizens of the newly oil-rich states have strained to adapt and how their rulers have often failed their subjects and the foreign powers pursuing their own agendas. Munif's familiarity with every aspect of his subject—he was an expert on the oil industry and clearly very politically aware—give the novels a sure authority without being overly programmatic. Ranging from political intrigue to the domestic, along with detailed descriptions of the natural (and then unnatural) world, the novels offer a unique picture of the Arabian Peninsula in the twentieth century.

Munif's *Cities of Salt* quintet was banned in Saudi Arabia, but its significance remains all the greater because essentially no locally written fiction appeared there until very recently. **Yousef Al-Mohaimeed's** (b. 1964) *Wolves of the Crescent Moon* (2003, English 2007) is among the first novels to come out of Saudi Arabia, and in its depiction of three disaffected lives, each physically marked and scarred—one is missing an ear, another is missing an eye, and the third is a eunuch—is more of a universal than a local story, relying on few of the obvious associations that outsiders would make with Saudi Arabia, like religion or the oil-based economy. The characters are outsiders in unusual ways, most notably the one who is a freed slave and a eunuch. Al-Mohaimeed opens new vistas on Saudi society by blending local color with universal themes. Artfully constructed around its three protagonists and their life stories, *Wolves of the Crescent Moon* suggests promising new directions for fiction in the region. Al-Mohaimeed's is a voice to look for in the future.

KEEP IN MIND

- The first two volumes of Saudi author **Turki al-Hamad's** (b. 1953) trilogy about coming of age in Saudi Arabia in the late 1960s and early 1970s are *Adama* (1997, English 2003) and *Shumaisi* (1997, English 2004); the third volume has not been translated.
- **Mohammad Abdul-Wali's** (1940–1973) tales of Yemen, *They Die Strangers* (English 2001), reflect his Ethiopian background..
- The anthology *In a Fertile Desert* (English 2009) is a collection of modern writing from the United Arab Emirates.
- United Arab Emirates author **Muhammad al-Murr's** (b. 1955) regional collections are entitled *Dubai Tales* (English 1991) and *The Wink of the Mona Lisa* (English 1994).
- United Arab Emirates poet **Thani Al-Suwaidi's** (b. 1966) wrote an elliptical novella of societal change and sexual identity called *The Diesel* (1994, English 2012).

A different new direction is also found in **Rajaa Alsanea**'s (b. 1981) ***Girls of Riyadh*** (2005, English 2007), touted as a Saudi *Sex and the City*. The story of four college-age women from relatively privileged families, *Girls of Riyadh* offers a glimpse of the hidden world of Saudi courtship and romance. Unfortunately, the underdeveloped male characters remain mystifying figures, and disappointingly, the narrator is obsessed with romance, despite the female protagonists' educational and professional achievements. *Girls of Riyadh* is far from great fiction, but it has an undeniable novelty appeal.

Israel

Fiction from Israel appears to be better represented, per capita, in English translation than that from any other country or language. The large English-speaking Jewish population that lives outside Israel but maintains close ties to it is a natural audience, but much of the literature also appeals to other readers.

Hebrew became a medium for fiction only in the twentieth century, and in particular with the establishment of the Israeli state, creating a literature that, even with its frequent biblical references and echoes, often feels very young. With successive waves of immigration, most recently from the former Soviet Union, literary movements in Israel have been subject to more and quicker change than elsewhere over the decades. While the nation has enjoyed relatively rapid economic growth and success, the horror of the Holocaust still weighs heavily here, as do concerns about national identity, geographic isolation, and threats from hostile regional regimes. The unresolved Palestinian situation, especially, has an uncertainty that pervades both daily life and the local literature.

S. Y. Agnon (1888–1970) was the first great author writing in Hebrew, but his art is generally not fully appreciated abroad, in part because of the difficulties of adequately translating his allusion- and reference-filled fiction. Even so, his stories and novels, such as *A Guest for the Night* (1939, English 1968), with its depiction of the conditions of east European Jews after the collapse of the Austro-Hungarian Empire, and the massive, rich *Only Yesterday* (1945, English 2000), describing the world of the early Zionist immigrants to Palestine, are fascinating reading. **S. Yizhar** (1916–2006) made an early mark with one of the young state's defining novels, but the massive *The Days of Ziklag* (1958), about a group of Israeli soldiers in an epic battle in 1948, has not been translated yet. After decades of literary silence, Yizhar published his autobiographical work, *Preliminaries* (1992, English 2007), set in the Palestine and Tel Aviv of the earlier part of the twentieth century. Along with the controversial *Khirbet Khizeh* (1949, English 2008), which describes the expulsion of Arabs from a village during the conflict of 1948, *Preliminaries* is the best of the little of his fiction available in English.

The Holocaust remains central to much Israeli fiction, and the work of representatives of the younger, post-Holocaust generations such as **David Grossman**'s (b. 1954) classic *See Under: Love* (1986, English 1989) and **Amir Gutfreund**'s (1963–2015) *Our Holocaust* (2000, English 2006) offer interesting perspectives on the deep and lingering effects even on those only indirectly touched by the Holocaust. **Aharon Appelfeld** (b. 1932), who survived it, began to learn Hebrew only after reaching Palestine in 1946, and it has given him a voice. His novels of great restraint indicate that much remains unsaid, as many of his characters are unable or unwilling to speak, clearly or at all, allowing him to convey some of the Holocaust's horrors. Some of his novels directly recount the experiences of the war years, such as *Tzili* (1983, English 1983); others, such as *The Retreat* (1982, English 1984) and *Badenheim 1939* (1979, English 1980), foreshadow what was to come in a Europe where creeping anti-Semitism was creating an increasingly

KEEP IN MIND

- *Adam Resurrected* (1969, English 1969), **Yoram Kaniuk**'s (1930–2013) best-known work, is a novel about living through the Holocaust and continuing with life after that, its protagonist once a world-renowned clown and now a patient in a mental institution. Kaniuk's *The Last Jew* (1982, English 2006) also plays with memories in fascinating ways, the "last Jew" of the title a man who seems to have no personal memories yet is a cultural repository of the entire Jewish past.

intolerable situation; and his retrospective novels, such as *The Iron Tracks* (1991, English 1998), show that the past is proving difficult to overcome, with its endlessly, futilely, wandering Jew.

Aharon Megged's (b. 1920) fiction is more deeply rooted in the Israeli experience itself. The comic touch he displays in works with writers at their center, such as *The Living on the Dead* (1965, English 1970) and the wonderful *The Flying Camel and the Golden Hump* (1982, English 2007), are great literary entertainment, while works like *Foiglman* (1987, English 2003) consider more expansive horizons. *The Flying Camel and the Golden Hump* is typical of Megged's stories with a premise that easily might be stretched into comic excess, in this case when a detested literary critic moves into the apartment above the writer's own. But Megged does not overdo that part of it—and surprises with the humorous situations he finds elsewhere. His writer-protagonists, with their intriguing unfinished books, are appealingly hapless, if not entirely hopeless, characters.

Both of **Yaakov Shabtai**'s (1934–1981) two novels, *Past Continuous* (1977, English 1985) and the posthumous *Past Perfect* (1984, English 1987), are in a way driven by death. Stylistically, both novels push Israeli fiction in entirely new directions. Much of *Past Continuous* takes place between the death of the father of one of the characters, Goldman, and then Goldman's own suicide less than a year later, packing a great deal of reflection and observation into the dense, free-flowing text. In *Past Perfect*, the protagonist, Meir, like the author himself, faces his own mortality in a variation of a midlife crisis that is both specifically Israeli and generally existential. In a fluid, almost neutral prose, Shabtai unfolds these novels less in time than in space, though the full feel of the stream of consciousness of *Past Continuous*, written as a single paragraph in the original Hebrew, is lost in an English translation that breaks the narrative into more digestible bits.

A. B. Yehoshua (b. 1936) and **Amos Oz** (b. 1939) are the best-known authors of their generation, with much of their work widely available in translation. Particularly impressive among Yehoshua's novels are *A Late Divorce* (1982, English 1984), told from the perspective of various characters, including an Israeli who has moved to America and briefly returns to Israel in order to obtain a divorce from his wife, and the dense, layered *The Liberated Bride* (2001, English 2004), in which a professor explores the reasons for his son's divorce while also studying the roots of conflict in Algeria and their relevance to the Israeli situation. Other notable novels by Yehoshua are the creatively structured *Mr. Mani* (1990, English 1992), in which each of the sections introduces conversation partners but then repeats only the words spoken by one of them in their lengthy dialogues. In addition, the text moves backward in time, with the first conversation in 1982 and the final one in 1848, producing a remarkable reverse chronology of Jewish fates. *A Woman in Jerusalem* (2004, English 2006) is a more conventional tracing of a woman's history, but Yehoshua finds a moving journey of discovery in it.

A Tale of Love and Darkness (2002, English 2004), Amos Oz's grand autobiographical work, is a good introduction to the author and his large body of work. From his kibbutz novel, *Elsewhere, Perhaps* (1966, English 1973), onward, Oz's work has held up a variety of mirrors to Israeli society, showing how it has changed over the last four decades. From the entertaining bumbling title character in *Fima* (1991, English 1993) to the clear-headed retired secret service agent who tries to move on after the death of his wife in *To Know a Woman* (1989, English 1991), Oz constantly adds and uses different and novel approaches in his writing and stories. Among his most successful works are two novels in which he plays with form. In the epistolary *Black Box* (1987, English 1988), exchanges of letters (and telegrams) document a heated relationship, and the novel *The Same Sea* (1999, English 2002) is written in verse and prose poems. *The Same Sea* is only a small, domestic tale but arguably one of Oz's best works.

David Grossman's (b. 1954) sprawling *See Under: Love* (1986, English 1989) is one of the finest and most significant treatments of the Holocaust in Israeli literature, moving in four very different parts and steps, with the final part an attempt to sum up in encyclopedic form, alphabetically arranged, what has come before. *The Book of Intimate Grammar* (1991, English 1994) and *The Zigzag Kid* (1994, English 1997) focus on adolescence, the latter a surprisingly light turn for him. Far more intense is *Be My Knife* (1998, English 2001), a novel in which a relationship is built up entirely around written words, a man baring his soul to a woman in the letters that make up the long first section, with her thoughts written in a notebook then making up the second part of the book before it culminates in an exchange between them.

In Grossman's widely hailed *To the End of the Land* (2008, English 2010), a mother, Ora, sets out on a personal journey to the far reaches of Israel, hoping to avoid hearing the news that her son Ofer has been killed in a military offensive for which he was just been called up. The novel's title in the original Hebrew is literally *A Woman Flees News*. Ora is gripped by the irrational fear that something has happened to her boy, but her journey is also one of personal exploration as she looks back on her own life and on the men who played such large roles in it.

Also known for his children's books, **Meir Shalev**'s (b. 1948) entertaining adult fiction is very popular as well. A true storyteller, his fanciful novels often contain elements of magical realism, particularly in *The Blue Mountain* (1988, English 1991), with its descriptions of three generations of early pioneers in Palestine. The more grounded *A Pigeon and a Boy* (2006, English 2007) artfully brings together the story of a present-day tour guide and events from the war of independence.

Orly Castel-Bloom (b. 1960) is the rare Israeli author whose works are far more widely translated into a language—French, in her case—other than English. Her fiction is more experimental and extreme than that of most Israeli writers, and her shocking *Dolly City* (1992, English 1997) is a graphic allegory of modern Israel in which the title character's gruesome experiments in her home laboratory extend to an abandoned baby she finds. In *Human Parts* (2002, English 2003), Israel is beset by not only terrorism but also bitterly cold weather and a vicious flu epidemic, all in a biting satire of contemporary Israeli society.

The enormously popular **Etgar Keret**'s (b. 1967) work includes several collections of generally very short stories, but he also has collaborated on adaptations of these as graphic novels and films. His fiction has an appealing surrealism and humor, which rarely is overtly political, but even the unexpected can be wearing over the course of so many quick-fire bursts. The patchwork volume *The Bus Driver Who Wanted to Be God* (English 2001), which includes several different people's translations of stories from two early collections as well as the amusingly dark novella *Kneller's Happy Campers* (1998), about the afterlife of suicides, offers the best overview of his talents. Keret's more recent *The Nimrod Flip-Out* (2002, English 2005) is overall, however, a better collection.

Sayed Kashua (b. 1975) offers an Arab-Israeli perspective in the semiautobiographical *Dancing Arabs* (2002, English 2004), the story of a young Palestinian who is accepted at an elite Jerusalem boarding school but cannot live up to his promise and expectations there or later. *Let It Be Morning* (2004, English 2006), in which an Arab-Israeli journalist returns to his small and already far from idyllic hometown, where the situation devolves further when it is sealed off by the Israelis, the worst of the conditions in the occupied territories manifested there. The many personal issues and conflicts in a small community, halfway between Jerusalem and Tel Aviv, are central, too, to **Eshkol Nevo**'s (b. 1971) *Homesick* (2004, English 2008). Escalating with the assassination of Yitzhak Rabin, it nevertheless remains focused on the individuals and their relationships and burdens, related from their various perspectives, one of which is Palestinian.

Crime Fiction

Batya Gur's (1947–2005) Michael Ohayon novels remain the preeminent Israeli detective series. She focuses on particular communities

> KEEP IN MIND
>
> - **Yoel Hoffmann**'s (b. 1937) remarkable works of fiction are built out of small pieces and short fragments, whether in a chain as in *Bernhard* (1989, English 1998), in which the last line of each of chapter is the beginning of the next, or in the looser mosaics of a life presented in *The Christ of Fish* (1991, English 1999) or the love story of *The Heart Is Katmandu* (2000, English 2001), each consisting of more than two hundred chapters.
> - Several of **Yehoshua Kenaz**'s (b. 1937) novels offer microcosms of Israeli society in their focus on small communities, such as *The Way to the Cats* (1991, English 1994), in which an elderly woman recovers from a fall, and *Returning Lost Loves* (1997, English 2001), which tells the different stories of the residents of one Tel Aviv apartment building.
> - **Zeruya Shalev**'s (b. 1959) explicit novels probe relationships. In *Love Life* (1997, English 2000), a self-destructive young woman has an affair with a close friend of her father's. In *Husband and Wife* (2000, English 2002), the breakdown of this marriage is manifested in the husband's psychosomatic paralysis.
> - **Gail Hareven**'s (b. 1959) *The Confessions of Noa Weber* (2000, English 2009) is a beautifully composed novel about obsessive love. In *Lies, First Person* (2008, English 2015), her characters deal in different ways with unforgivable evil.
> - **Yael Hedaya** (b. 1964) novels include *Accidents* (2001, English 2004), in which two writers, one still grieving for his deceased wife, slowly find their way into a relationship. This long book is dwarfed by *Eden* (2005, English 2010), which describes contemporary Israeli life in an emblematic place that might be called Eden but cannot live up to its name.

and fields, such as the literary world and academia in *Literary Murder* (1989, English 1993), the world of classical music in *Murder Duet* (1996, English 1999), and psychoanalysis in *The Saturday Morning Murder* (1988, English 1992).

Haim Lapid's (b. 1948) *Breznitz* (1992, English 2000) is a less conventional but solid police procedural with a driven protagonist, and the short *The Crime of Writing* (1998, English 2002) provocatively ties together crime and literature.

Turkey

Despite a long and rich literary tradition, little Turkish fiction seems to have made much impression abroad until the Nobel Prize in Literature was awarded to **Orhan Pamuk** (b. 1952) in 2006. A recent surge of translation has, however, made clear that a great deal of interesting literature has emerged in Turkey in recent decades.

Among the best-known Turkish authors is the poet **Nazım Hikmet** (1902–1963). His epic novel in verse, *Human Landscapes from My Country* (1967, English 2002), written while he was imprisoned in the 1940s but published posthumously, is a remarkable achievement, delivering on the promise of its title. Its cast of several hundred characters from all walks of life offers a panorama of personal stories and experiences regarding Turkey in the first half of the twentieth century.

Ahmet Hamdi Tanpınar's (1901–1962) novel *A Mind at Peace* (1949, English 2008), which opens with World War II already looming, is tightly focused on a specific era and place. He depicts Turkey as a country that has been undergoing a radical transformation under

Kemal Atatürk after the collapse of the Ottoman Empire. His char-acters talk often about the nature of Turkishness and the possibilities for the nation. *A Mind at Peace* is also about Istanbul and tries, above all else, to be evocative, though Tanpınar's language can be excessively ornate. In *The Time Regulation Institute* (1961, English 2001, 2013), Tanpınar contrasts Ottoman times with the uncertainties faced by modern Turkey, and it is filled with nostalgia. *The Time Regulation Institute* is also a humorous satire of the bureaucratic apparatus of the modern state, with the institute of the title charged with making sure that time is kept properly and uniformly throughout the nation.

Yashar Kemal (1923–2015), the first Turkish author to be widely translated into English, writes politically and socially engaged fiction that is often centered on the lives of Turkish peasants. His most famous creation is Memed, the hero of his two-volume 1955 work translated as *Memed, My Hawk* (English 1961) and *They Burn the Thistles* (Eng-lish 1973) (two later sequels have not yet been translated). Even as a boy, Memed tries to flee the oppressive landowner whose control over the local villages is absolute. When he finally makes good his escape, he becomes a brigand and lives as an outlaw on the fringes of society. With his passion for justice, complicated by the lifestyle he has had to embrace and the vengeance he seeks, Memed is a wonderful fictional creation. A trilogy that features another peasant hero, Long Ali, begins with *The Wind from the Plain* (1960, English 1963). These novels also describe the daily struggles of Turkish peasants, for whom picking cot-ton is their main source of income. Yashar's leftist politics occasionally intrudes too much in his fiction, as his portraits of the ruthless exploit-ing class can be almost cartoonish, but he nonetheless vividly captures both countryside and people.

Nobel laureate **Orhan Pamuk's** (b. 1952) *The Black Book* (1990, English 1994, 2006) is not his first novel but perhaps is his most repre-sentative. In it, Rüya, the wife of the lawyer Galip, disappears, and he becomes obsessed with the idea that the newspaper columnist Celâl has something to do with it. Celâl also has disappeared, and in his search for his wife, Galip increasingly assumes Celâl's identity, even-tually even writing his columns. The chapters of the novel alternate between Galip's quest and Celâl's columns, which allows Pamuk to intersperse personal essays on a wide variety of esoteric subjects in an almost metaphysical mystery. This dense and mystic mix is the clearest expression of most of Pamuk's interests and talents.

Pamuk's *My Name Is Red* (1998, English 2001) is yet another twist on the mystery novel. It begins with a murder and, among the many voices narrating parts of the story, is the long unidentified killer's. The novel is set in the late sixteenth century and centers on a group of painters at the Ottoman court who have very different ideas about art and the representation of reality. Western theories and methods—including the use of perspective—threaten age-old traditions, and the role of art itself is questioned. Combining court intrigue, religious intolerance, and questions of artistic freedom, *My Name Is Red* raises issues that seem more relevant than ever, especially with regard to Islam and its reach into personal lives and the public sphere.

Pamuk's *Snow* (2002, English 2004) takes place in contemporary Turkey. The conflicts between Kurds and Turks used to be the major source of tension in Kars and the rest of the country's far east. Now it is Islamists and their demands for a return to greater religious fundamentalism that are Turkey's biggest provocations. The central figure in *Snow* is a poet named Ka, and one of his reasons for coming to this region is to investigate why so many local girls are killing themselves. A snowstorm cuts off Kars from the rest of the country, adding to the claustrophobic and isolated feel of the novel and making the town a more obvious microcosm of the country as a whole. As in all of Pamuk's novels, the interplay between reality and art plays a major role, as does questions of identity, both personal and national.

The narrator in Pamuk's *The Museum of Innocence* (2008, English 2009) is Kemal, who falls deeply in love with a distant relative, Füsun. He is about to get engaged to someone else when he falls for her, and by the time he is free again, Füsun is married, so for most of the novel they are only friends rather than true intimates. Set in Istanbul in the 1970s and 1980s, Kemal becomes a collector, filling his "Museum of Innocence" with everyday artifacts that are meant to allow him to hold on to each precious moment of the present. He takes this to great extremes—eventually his collection holds 4,213 butts of cigarettes smoked by Füsun—but his insistence on holding so firmly to the past also prevents him from building a future. *The Museum of Innocence* is as much about the Istanbul of that time as about the characters and the city lovingly described and reflected in the bits and pieces archived in Kemal's museum—and, indeed, in Pamuk's own, as he actually built a museum where many of the artifacts from the novel are on display.

With their multiple narrators and perspectives, **Bilge Karasu**'s (1930–1995) novels are anything but straightforward. *Night* (1985, English 1994) depicts a dark and opaque world filled with a sense of Kafkaesque menace. Consisting of 110 chapters, few of which are longer than a single page, *Night* is a novel of willful confusion in which Karasu does not allow the reader any sense of certainty about the encroaching terrors. The author also is a presence in the book, commenting on the writing—and undermining it—in a series of footnotes to the narrative. Similarly, the author steps forward near the end of *The Garden of Departed Cats* (1979, English 2003) to discuss how he went about writing that novel. *The Garden of Departed Cats* is told in chapters that alternate between the story of a visitor to a city who participates in a ritual game resembling human chess that pits locals against tourists once every decade, and a variety of apparently unconnected tales. The novel is often overwritten, and Karasu's playfulness can be frustrating. Karasu also uses a variety of perspectives in the thirteen chapters of the coming-of-age novel **Death in Troy** (1962, English 2002). This is his most approachable work, showing how the central figure, Mushfik, comes to terms with the relationships in his family and his homoerotic desires in 1950s Turkey. In all his novels, Karasu's lyrical use of language both impresses and leads to an opacity that can make the texts difficult to enjoy.

Elif Shafak (b. 1971) wrote her first novels in Turkish, including *The Flea Palace* (2002, English 2004). The rundown Bonbon Palace, an apartment building in Istanbul, provides the novel's structure, with the narrative moving between the flats in the stories of the various tenants in a work that resembles both Georges Perec's *Life A User's Manual*

KEEP IN MIND

- **Orhan Kemal**'s (1914–1970) realist works rely heavily on dialogue to create an atmosphere and convey what his characters are suffering through. Although his protagonists have difficult lives, his often bleak tales nonetheless contain a consoling humanism.
- **Asli Erdogan**'s (b. 1967) *The City in Crimson Cloak* (1998, English 2007) is an evocative city portrait with an unusual mix of cultures. The Turkish protagonist Özgür finds herself down and out (and trying to write a novel entitled *The City in Crimson Cloak*) in Rio de Janeiro.
- **Latife Tekin**'s (b. 1957) fiction is close to standard magical realism, even though she consistently deals with the social tensions of a rapidly developing society in novels such as ***Berji Kristin: Tales from the Garbage Hills*** (1984, English 1993), a portrait of a self-contained society that has been built on top of a large urban garbage dump. The novel is a creative parable of a community arising from the dregs of society and demonstrating human resilience and resourcefulness.
- **Selçuk Altun**'s (b. 1950) novels have soap opera–like titles—***Songs My Mother Never Taught Me*** (2005, English 2008) and ***Many and Many a Year Ago*** (2008, English 2009)—but are surprisingly thoughtful thrillers.
- **Mehmet Murat Somer**'s (b. 1959) **Hop-Çiki-Yaya** series, which begins with *The Kiss Murder* (2003, English 2008), features an unnamed transvestite narrator who is both a nightclub owner and a computer specialist and dabbles in criminal investigation. Not nearly as camp as the premise might suggest, Somer has lots of fun with the milieu in this light but enjoyable crime series.

and the *Arabian Nights*. *The Flea Palace*'s entertaining cast of characters makes for a larger-than-life miniature of Istanbul and Turkey.

Since 2002, Shafak has also been writing in English. Her most controversial work is the novel ***The Bastard of Istanbul*** (2007), which was released in its Turkish translation in 2006 and resulted in charges being filed against her under Turkey's notorious article 301, which makes it a crime to denigrate Turkey or Turkish institutions. Telling the story of two families, one Turkish and one Armenian American, Shafak delves into Turkey's unresolved history at the beginning of the twentieth century, when more than a million Armenians were killed in what is widely considered genocide. A lively novel with several strong female characters, Shafak's overblown language and approach are too much at odds with her serious intent. *The Saint of Incipient Insanities* (2004), describing the cross-cultural confusions of three foreigners attending graduate school in the United States, is a lighter work in which it is easier to make allowances for Shafak's uncertainties in her ambitious use of the English language.

Iran and Afghanistan

IRAN

A theocratic state and self-described Islamic republic since 1979, in which a single government ministry is responsible for (and presumably seeks to reconcile) culture and Islamic guidance, Iran is not a nation where Westerners would expect much artistic freedom or expression. Yet even though censorship and the withholding of publication permits continue to be pervasive, the Iranian literary scene is well developed and very active, especially compared with that of much of the Middle East and Central Asia. Moreover, the Iranian Revolution of 1979 did not mark an abrupt break and reactionary crackdown, just a shift in what would be tolerated. Despite the radical change in the governing ideology, Iran has had considerable continuity during these decades.

Iran is one of the few nations with which the United States does not have diplomatic relations, creating great obstacles to cultural exchange. With the imposition of international sanctions over concern about

Iran's nuclear program, publishers have faced additional hurdles in bringing Iranian fiction to American audiences. Several small publishers (Mazda, Mage, Ibex) that serve mainly the large Persian community in the United States bring out some fiction in translation, but interested readers would do well to turn first to some of the available anthologies. *Stories from Iran* (1992), edited by Heshmat Moayyad, is a collection of fiction by all the major writers from 1921 to 1991, and *Strange Times, My Dear: The PEN Anthology of Contemporary Iranian Literature* (2005), edited by Nahid Mozaffari, offers a generous selection of post-revolutionary prose and poetry. Both volumes are good overviews, but because they contain only excerpts and short stories, they can only suggest much of Iran's literary talent.

FEMALE WRITERS ABROAD

A number of predominantly female authors who left Iran in childhood or early adulthood and settled in America have written Iran-themed books, often dealing with the 1979 revolution.

Nahid Rachlin's (b. 1944) novels, in particular, address the cultural clash and confusion felt by citizens of the two nations. Novels like *Foreigner* (1978), *The Heart's Desire* (1995), and *Jumping over Fire* (2006) describe Iranians' experiences in the United States, as well as Americans' experiences in Iran, with both the upheaval caused by the revolution and the underlying cultural constancy always central.

Dalia Sofer's (b. 1972) *The Septembers of Shiraz* (2007) and **Gina Nahai**'s (b. 1960) *Caspian Rain* (2007) focus on the Jewish-Iranian experience of the revolution, while Nahai's *Cry of the Peacock* (1991) and **Anita Amirrezvani**'s (b. 1961) *The Blood of Flowers* (2007) are set further in Iran's past, as is Israeli author **Dorit Rabinyan**'s (b. 1972) *Persian Brides* (1995, English 1998).

Many memoirs have been written by Iranians in exile over the past few decades, with **Marjane Satrapi**'s (b. 1969) autobiographical French graphic narratives the most successful variation on this form. The simple shaded drawings of *Persepolis* (2000–2003, English 2003–2004), *Embroideries* (2003, English 2005), and *Chicken with Plums* (2004, English 2006) convey life in Iran before and after the revolution better than do most prose accounts.

Under the Shah (1953–1979)

Almost all the classical literature of Iran and Persia is in the form of poetry, from **Omar Khayyám**'s (1048–1123) *Rubáiyát*, best known in the translations by Edward Fitzgerald (1809–1883), and the works of Sufi poet **Rumi** (1207–1273) and **Hafez** (fourteenth century) to verse epics such as **Ferdowsi**'s (ca. 940–1020) *Shahnameh* (English 1925, 2004) and several of the works by **Nizami** (1141–1209).

Only in the twentieth century did fiction in prose become commonplace. **Sadegh Hedayat**'s (1903–1951) hallucinatory first-person narrative by a despairing painter, *The Blind Owl* (1937, English 1957, 1974), is the first great modern work of Iranian fiction. Strongly influenced by avant-garde Western literature, it is nevertheless grounded in Iranian culture (and that of India, where, in fact, the book was first published). In integrating such disparate approaches and influences, the novel opened up new avenues for Persian writing. It remains an authoritative foundational text, as familiar and influential in Iranian writing as, for example, Kafka's work is internationally.

After Prime Minister Mohammad Mossadegh was deposed in 1953, the regime of Mohammad Reza Pahlavi took a heavy-handed approach to cultural expression. Many Iranian authors of the time were politically engaged, which was reflected in their works and made them suspect in the eyes of the authorities.

Jalal Al-e Ahmad's (1923–1969) best-known work is his seminal 1962 essay variously translated as *Weststruckness* (1982), *Plagued by the West* (1982), and *Occidentosis* (1983). Like most of his work, it was banned under the shah but regained currency in the transitional revolutionary period in the late 1970s, as its anti-Western thesis appealed to many of the factions concerned with what they perceived to be the pernicious foreign (and specifically American) influence of the past decades. Much of Al-e Ahmad's fiction exposes social conditions, and his novels, such as *The School Principal* (b. 1958, English 1974), remain of interest for the insight they provide into the still very backward but rapidly modernizing society of the time and the consequences of these many changes. While also depicting Iranian history and conditions, his allegorical *By the Pen* (1961, English 1988) is a more studiously literary work that is not as obviously a product of that era.

Although female poets had established themselves in Iran by the 1960s, most notably **Forugh Farrokhzad** (1935–1967), fiction was almost entirely the province of male authors. **Simin Daneshvar's** (1921–2012) *Savushun* (1969, English 1990, and as *A Persian Requiem*, 1991) was the first novel by an Iranian woman to be published in Iran. Set in Shiraz during World War II, it remains the foremost novel of Iran's transition to modernity, offering a panoramic view of the country. Since then, women have become major contributors to Iranian literature, but with her *Savushun* and story collections like *Daneshvar's Playhouse* (English 1989) and *Sutra* (English 1994), Daneshvar has gone significantly beyond merely playing a pioneering role.

Iraj Pezeshkzad's (b. 1928) *My Uncle Napoleon* (1973, English 1996) is the one notable comic novel to have come out of Iran, a family story set in the 1940s with a large cast of characters and an adolescent love story at the center. It also was made into a very popular television series, and if the broad and repetitive comedy occasionally seems dated now, its enduring popularity among Iranian readers suggests that it reflects a certain national nostalgia.

KEEP IN MIND

- **Hushang Golshiri's** (1938–2000) novella *Prince Ehtejab* (1969, English 1980, and as *The Prince*, 2005) is about the decadent Qajar aristocracy.
- *The Patient Stone* (1967, English 1989) is a representative novel of **Sadeq Chubak's** (1916–1998) socially committed fiction that often focuses on Iran's underclass.
- *Her Eyes* (1952, English 1989), by **Bozorg Alavi** (1904–1997), a founding member of Iran's Communist Tudeh Party, deals with both art and politics, with active opposition to the shah's regime central to the plot. Not surprisingly, the novel was banned during the Pahlavi years.
- The novel *Winter Sleep* (1973, English 1994), by **Goli Taraqqi** ('Taraghi) (b. 1939), is a contemporary look at Westernizing Iran, and *The Pomegranate Lady and Her Sons* (English 2013) is a representative collection of her stories.

After the Revolution

The radical political and cultural upheaval of the 1979 revolution caused a bumpy transition from one repressive regime to the next. Some established authors, such as Golshiri and Daneshvar, remained in Iran, but several emerging authors opted, sooner or later, for exile. **Mahmoud Dowlatabadi** (b. 1940), yet another author who was imprisoned for several years (in the mid-1970s) but has remained in Iran, is the most important figure to bridge the two periods. His long, spare novel of family hardship, *Missing Soluch* (1979, English 2007), is typical of his patient, well-crafted novels of Iranian rural life. In *Missing Soluch*, Mergan, a mother of three living in a village, wakes up to find that her husband, Soluch, has inexplicably left. The novel describes in a simple, plain style how she and her family go on with their lives, and despite the understated presentation and limited action, it is a compelling portrait of country life. Dowlatabadi's novel *The Colonel* (2009, English 2011) takes place on a single night in the 1980s during which a retired colonel tries to see to it that his barely teenage daughter, killed by the authorities, is properly buried. Each of his five children has been crushed in one form or another by the 1979 revolution, and the colonel also carries with him the burden of having killed his wife years earlier in an honor killing. The colonel's tortured wanderings and memories on this one night reflect much that Iran went through during those years.

Shahrnush Parsipur (b. 1946) is one of Iran's principal writers now living in exile. What little of her work is available in English is remarkable. *Touba and the Meaning of Night* (1989, English 2006) uses Persian history, tradition, and mysticism to present a life story that, among much else, portrays the changing place of women in Iranian life over the twentieth century. *Women Without Men* (1989, English 1998, 2011) links the stories of a number of women in a mix of the fantastic (one of the women rises from the dead) and the real. Parsipur describes a world in which any sort of normality or balance to a coexistence of the sexes is barred. This fascinating consideration of women's roles and lives in Iran takes place mostly in the 1950s but is nonetheless timeless.

Even more than two decades after its end, the Iran-Iraq War (1980–1988) is still a common subject in contemporary Iranian fiction, to the extent that the "Sacred Defense" (as the conflict is known as in Iran) literature or, as it is also referred to, "Literature of Perseverance and the Art of Resistance" is a recognized genre. This protracted and traumatic conflict has proved to be a surprisingly adaptable foundation for fiction, in contrast to addressing the facts or consequences of the revolution under a regime that allows for no dissent in this regard. Several examples of Sacred Defense literature have been translated, including **Davud Ghaffarzadegan**'s (b. 1959) novella *Fortune Told in Blood* (1996, English 2008) and **Habib Ahmadzadeh**'s (b. 1964) novel, *Chess with the Doomsday Machine* (2004, English 2008) and a collection of stories, *A City Under Siege* (English 2010). These are not propaganda, and *Fortune Told in Blood* is actually presented from the perspective of Iraqi soldiers. Set on an isolated observation post, far removed from the worst of the fighting, *Fortune Told in Blood* conveys the emotional turmoil, psychological toll, and physical strain that the characters suffer even there. *A City Under Siege* and the more elaborate *Chess with the Doomsday Machine* are set in the thick of some of the worst battles of the war in the south of Iran and shows the effects on a larger number of characters, both soldiers and civilians.

KEEP IN MIND

- **Esmail Fasih**'s (1935–2009) *Sorraya in a Coma* (1984, English 1985) is one of the few translated novels describing the consequences of the 1979 revolution, specifically for the secular classes.
- **Zoya Pirzad** (b. 1952) wrote approachable and moving domestic fiction.
- **Abbas Maroufi**'s (b. 1957) novel *Symphony of the Dead* (1989, English 2007) centers on the conflict between two brothers.
- **Moniru Ravanipur**'s (b. 1954) story collection *Satan's Stones* (1991, English 1996) and her novel *Afsaneh* (1990, English 2013) experiment with magical realism.

AFGHANISTAN

Poetry has long dominated Afghan literature, in both Dari (closely related to Persian) and Pashto. Little fiction from the area has been translated into English, and except for some anthologies and journals, even now only the work of a few expatriate authors is available. One of them, **Khaled Hosseini** (b. 1965), writing in English, achieved great international success with his best-selling *The Kite Runner* (2003) and *A Thousand Splendid Suns* (2007). Both novels cover recent decades of Afghan history, through the Soviet invasion and then the years of Taliban rule, while also focusing on personal stories. Well-told crowd-pleasers, they also provide a good overview of recent Afghan history and culture.

    Atiq Rahimi (b. 1962) left Afghanistan in 1984 but continued to write in Dari, and his novels *Earth and Ashes* (2000, English 2002) and *A Thousand Rooms of Dream and Fear* (2002, English 2006) are among the few novels ever translated from that language. Both are almost hallucinatory voyages, internal and external, taken in extreme conditions. The short *Earth and Ashes* describes the aftermath of a Soviet bombing attack that has wiped out a village, from which only a grandfather and grandson have survived. *A Thousand Rooms of Dream and Fear* also is set during the Soviet occupation, the protagonist finding his life suddenly catastrophically upturned, which leads to a nightmarish flight. *The Patience Stone* (2008, English 2010), the first novel that Atiq Rahimi wrote in French, won the Prix Goncourt, the leading French literary prize, in 2008. It describes a woman tending and unburdening herself to her comatose husband, a severely injured jihadist. Both characters, representatives of their sex, remain nameless, and Rahimi uses the wife to strongly condemn the concepts of male pride and superiority that he sees as so damaging to Afghani society.

Asia

Indian Subcontinent

Since the publication of **Salman Rushdie**'s (b. 1947) *Midnight's Children* (1981), English-language fiction by writers from the Indian subcontinent has enjoyed increasing popularity, but even before then, several authors from the region had become established internationally. Though the relatively widespread use of the colonial language has facilitated access to the wider markets, the first great twentieth-century authors from what was then British-ruled India did not write primarily in English. Bengali author and 1913 Nobel laurcate **Rabindranath Tagore** (1861–1941) did translate some of his own work into English and was best known for his poetry, but he was also a very fine writer of fiction. Hindustani author **Premchand** (1880–1936) wrote fiction in both Urdu and Hindi. He remains the prime chronicler of ordinary and village life in the India of his time, and the stories by the prolific Urdu-writing **Saadat Hasan Manto** (1912–1955) deservedly enjoy continued popularity.

INDIA

The Forerunners

R. K. Narayan (1906–2001) is best known for his novels and stories set in the fictional Malgudi, a town in southern India. Written over half a century, beginning with *Swami and Friends* (1935), each of these works centers on different characters from all walks of life and their everyday fates in this typical Indian town, with relatively little attention to the greater social and political upheavals taking place in India during this period. One of the novels, *A Tiger for Malgudi* (1983) is even narrated by a tiger, now languishing in a zoo. Unassuming, often gently comic, Narayan's works contrast with much of the flashier fiction of the Rushdie age but are worth revisiting for their charming studies of Indian life. *The Guide* (1958), in which a con artist is mistaken for a holy man after his release from prison but then grows into the role, is the most memorable of Narayan's Malgudi works, but almost all his books are worth reading.

Whereas Narayan spent almost his entire life in India, **Raja Rao** (1908–2006) lived abroad for much of his, and his longest novels, the autobiographical *The Serpent and the Rope* (1960) and *The Chessmaster and His Moves* (1988), alternate between India and the West. More closely grounded in India, *Kanthapura* (1938) describes the spread to a southern Indian town of Gandhian nonviolent opposition to the British, while *The Cat and Shakespeare* (1965) is a sort of metaphysical counterpart to *The Serpent and the Rope* in which Rao shows a much lighter touch. Rao integrates Indian philosophy and myth, as well as literary traditions, into his novels, but what is still background in a largely social realist novel like *Kanthapura* becomes central in his later works, taking on a philosophical density that particularly weighs down *The Chessmaster and His Moves*. The more playful *The Cat and Shakespeare* offers the most approachable mix, but all of Rao's works—even his sketchy take on Communism, *Comrade Kirillov* (first published in French, 1965; English 1976)—are worthwhile.

KEEP IN MIND

- **G. V. Desani**'s (1909–2000) irrepressible comic bildungsroman is called *All About H. Hatterr* (1948).

The First Wave of Women Writers

A number of female Indian authors writing in English became established after independence, beginning with **Kamala Markandaya** (1924–2004). *Nectar in a Sieve* (1954) is the first of many of her realist works in which modernization and the continually encroaching Western ways, especially of capitalism, upend traditional lifestyles. English characters often figure prominently in her fiction, as the postcolonial readjustment of the relationship between the English and Indians moves forward only haltingly and is a continuing source of friction. Despite the books' old-fashioned feel, they well describe the permutations of Anglo-Indian relationships.

Much of **Nayantara Sahgal**'s (b. 1927) work is closely tied to historical specifics and contemporary events. A niece of the first Indian prime minister, Jawaharlal Nehru, and a cousin of his daughter and also prime minister, Indira Gandhi, Sahgal writes about the Indian political elites with which she is familiar while maintaining a critical distance in insightful novels such as *Storm in Chandigarh* (1969), which revolves around the internal partition; *A Situation in New Delhi* (1977), about the redrawing of state lines within India itself; and *Rich Like Us* (1985), set during the state of emergency in the mid-1970s.

Anita Desai's (b. 1937) fiction treats a much broader variety of foreign experiences, ranging from *Baumgartner's Bombay* (1988), the story of a Jewish expatriate who escaped the Nazis to live in India, to the entirely Mexican story of *The Zigzag Way* (2004). Desai is particularly adept with characters who are outsiders, such as the Europeans searching for spiritual fulfillment in exotic India in *Journey to Ithaca* (1995).

KEEP IN MIND

- **Shashi Deshpande**'s (b. 1938) southern Indian fiction focuses on the lives of women.
- German-born **Ruth Prawer Jhabvala** (1927–2013) may be best known for her work on numerous Merchant-Ivory films that has earned her two Academy Awards, but she also wrote several novels that consider the role of the foreigner in India, which include the Booker Prize–winning *Heat and Dust* (1975).

Midnight's Children and Beyond

Despite the success of many Indian authors abroad, it was the publication of **Salman Rushdie**'s (b. 1947) *Midnight's Children* (1981) that fundamentally changed Western attitudes toward English-language fiction from the region. Like many of the authors from India familiar to American and British audiences, Rushdie spent a significant amount of time abroad, being sent to England to complete his education when barely a teen and eventually settling there. The resulting familiarity with both Indian and Western cultures seems to have helped him and other Indian writers who followed a similar path; the lack of any comparable success abroad by Indian authors writing in a regional language is striking.

With its narrator born at the moment when India and Pakistan become independent in 1947, *Midnight's Children* is, from the outset, presented as a national epic, though less a mirror than a kaleidoscopic refraction of modern India's history. Rushdie's subcontinental spin on magical realism, which includes giving supernatural powers to his protagonist and the one thousand others born in that first hour of independence, was enormously appealing, though, tellingly, considerably more so abroad than in India itself. A riveting story, *Midnight's Children* is also a linguistic feast, with Rushdie showing a remarkable feel for language by enhancing his narrative with vocabulary and expressions from Urdu and other Indian languages.

Shame (1983), Rushdie's denser and darker novel about Pakistan's recent history and the role of shame in culture, is his most accomplished work, but with its close links to actual but less familiar figures and events, it is not as welcoming as *Midnight's Children*. Meanwhile, even the memorable opening of *The Satanic Verses* (1988), describing two characters hurtling toward earth from nearly thirty thousand feet up after the explosion of the plane they were flying in, has been overshadowed by the fatwa issued by the Ayatollah Khomeini (who, as "the Imam," figures in the novel itself), sentencing Rushdie to death for blasphemy. *The Satanic Verses* follows the two characters who survived the plane's explosion, with one taking on the form of an angel and the other the devil in just one of the novel's magical-realist transformations. The controversial passages dealing with Islam are only one aspect of this very good book, whose themes include the immigrant experience and identity, but it has become almost impossible to read without also taking into account all this distracting extraliterary baggage.

Rushdie has continued to write larger-than-life works of fiction that use both distant and contemporary history and highlight cross-cultural encounters and conflicts, but the impact of much of his writing has worn off, and many of his linguistic tics and tricks and flourishes in his later books have come to feel gaudy and excessive. With novels such as *Fury* (2001) and *Shalimar the Clown* (2005), set largely or partially in the United States, Rushdie exposes a tin ear in regard to American culture, which also makes some of his foreign glitz and exotica suddenly look thinner, too. Much in these later works is often a smoke-and-mirrors show rather than something substantial. Nevertheless, all his books contain at least some passages and often long stretches that do impress, with imaginative leaps that few other authors could handle.

Even though *Midnight's Children* was pathbreaking, the best and best-known Indian authors writing in English fortunately did not choose to follow Rushdie's model slavishly (though quite a few lesser authors did). **Vikram Seth**'s (b. 1952) mostly successful novel written in sonnets, *The Golden Gate* (1986), strikes out in a completely different direction, though it, too, may seem more a display of showmanship than a fully realized novel. Based entirely in California and borrowing more from Pushkin's *Eugene Onegin* than from any traditional Indian work, it is, at best, only remotely Indian. In contrast, Seth's saga *A Suitable Boy* (1993) attempts to be comprehensively Indian. From the setting (the 1950s) to the subject (finding an appropriate husband for one of the characters) to the style, everything about this closely observed realist novel is a bit old-fashioned, but its attention to detail and intricately interwoven plotlines make for a rich picture of the India of that time. Its extreme length—at more than fifteen hundred pages, it claims to be the longest novel ever published in English in a single volume— can be daunting, but Seth manages to sustain interest for the duration. *A Suitable Boy* features a large cast of characters from four families, with the heart of the novel being the search for "a suitable boy" for Lata Mehra to marry. Seth reportedly is working on a sequel, *A Suitable Girl*, which jumps some sixty years ahead and in which Lata is now a grandmother, searching for a suitable girl for her grandson. This presumably will allow him to show the dramatic changes in Indian society over the past half century.

Amitav Ghosh's (b. 1956) varied approaches and novelistic reach, extending throughout the subcontinent and to its edges, as well as to northern Africa and the United States, separates his work from that of other transnational Indian writers. His first novel, *The Circle of Reason* (1986), embodies the restless ambition that has come to define his work. Its protagonist, Alu, is suspected of being a terrorist and is chased abroad, thereby allowing Ghosh to revel in all sorts of encounters and characters. As in many of his later books, even in a more straightforward narrative such as his novel about Burma (now Myanmar), *The Glass Palace* (2000), Ghosh seems torn in different directions, giving in too often to his enthusiasms. Although the incidental occurrences are often well handled, the overall effect weakens the structure as a whole, and the novels feel too frail for all the author's ambitions. The first in a trilogy, *Sea of Poppies* (2008), which begins just before the first of the British Opium Wars against China in 1839, is sturdier but still overloaded. Likewise, *The Calcutta Chromosome* (1996) combines the usual historical sweep of his novels with a few science fiction and thriller elements, but they do not all quite fit together.

Several of **Vikram Chandra**'s (b. 1961) works also tend toward epic sprawl. *Red Earth and Pouring Rain* (1995), a variation on the *Arabian Nights*, features stories within stories artfully mixing myth and history and Indian tradition and modernity. On an even larger scale, *Sacred Games* (2007) is a double character-study of the new India's potential, framed as a mystery and thriller set in Mumbai. Pitting a policeman against one of the city's most notorious criminals, the book delves into both their lives at great length. Chandra's description of urban India's recent rapid transformation and how people have adapted to it is arguably too comprehensive, and with its rather anticlimactic resolution, it is not entirely successful as a thriller but still is entertaining.

In his calm, reflective, and often domestic works like *Freedom Song* (1999) and *A New World* (2000), **Amit Chaudhuri** (b. 1962) does not need to resort to the spectacular, and instead of being action packed, his plots meander. With its meticulously controlled writing, Chaudhuri's fiction is evocative, focusing on expression rather than invention.

Arundhati Roy's (b. 1961) only novel to date is the colorful *The God of Small Things* (1997), which also belongs in the recent Indian tradition of wide-ranging, border-crossing—and overwritten—fiction. About a Syrian Christian family in the southern state of Kerala, it features fraternal twins Rahel and Estha. Burdened by their guilt over a death in which they were involved when they are children and the consequences of what happened in its wake, they were separated for many years and were reunited only as adults. The book is undeniably affecting, but Roy has a few too many tricks up her sleeves, and between the almost circular presentation of events and the occasional linguistic excesses, it too often feels forced.

Roy is among the very few Indian authors who did not study or live abroad for extended periods but who have achieved wider recognition in the West. Most of those whose background is entirely Indian have not fared as well, although **Upamanyu Chatterjee** (b. 1959) has deservedly found a small following. His laid-back civil service novel, *English, August* (1988), sends its protagonist to a small Indian town; it is a small satiric gem of a young man trying to find his place in the world. A broader, less focused sequel, *The Mammaries of the Welfare*

KEEP IN MIND

- **Aatish Taseer**'s (b. 1980) novels *Noon* (2011) and *The Way Things Were* (2014) are ambitious novels about modern Pakistan and India.
- **Tarun J. Tejpal**'s (b. 1963) cleverly presented sweeping novel of contemporary India is *The Story of My Assassins* (2009).
- **Manu Joseph**'s (b. 1974) entertaining novels are *Serious Men* (2010) and *The Illicit Happiness of Other People* (2012), offering insight into Indian society.

State (2000), lacks the original's more immediate appeal but still is an entertaining look at Indian governance. *The Last Burden* (1993) is a more somber Indian family tale.

Other Indians Abroad

Many English-writing Indian authors living abroad continue to situate their fiction in their homeland. The universe of **Manil Suri**'s (b. 1959) *The Death of Vishnu* (2001) is almost entirely restricted to a small Mumbai apartment building whose landing has long been occupied by the dying Vishnu, an alcoholic who did some chores for the tenants. Suri describes everyday life and death, using both Hindu mythology—Vishnu becomes a stand-in for the namesake god—and contemporary mores and attitudes. In *The Age of Shiva* (2007), Suri creates a strong but flawed female protagonist, who lives through and is affected by the conflicts in India between the mid-1950s and Indira Gandhi's term in office.

In *Filming* (2007), **Tabish Khair** (b. 1966) follows the rise of the Indian film industry in the twentieth century for a different perspective on the history and events of those times. **Siddhartha Deb**'s (b. 1970) fiction is tied more closely into the politics of the period and its consequences on his characters. Both *The Point of Return* (2003) and *An Outline of the Republic* (published in Great Britain as *Surface*; 2005) take place in remote northeastern India. The piecemeal and, in part, reverse-chronological presentation of *The Point of*

Return, in which a son puzzles out his father's life, is not entirely easy to follow, but both novels offer fascinating insights into yet another corner of India.

Kiran Desai (b. 1971)—the daughter of Anita Desai—began her writing career with ***Hullabaloo in the Guava Orchard*** (1998), a comic novel about a man who tries to escape from the complications of everyday life by climbing into a tree and winding up being mistaken for a sage. Although she cannot entirely sustain the story, it is an enjoyable effort. Desai shows considerable growth and additional potential in *The Inheritance of Loss* (2006), set in northeastern India in the 1980s. In this novel, the lives of Sai and her grandfather, a retired judge, are affected by the activities of Nepalese insurgents in the area, and their cook places his hopes on his son's ability to achieve the American dream. Both story lines illustrate the difficulty of finding one's place in a community in the modern world.

Popular Fiction

Until recently, most of the Indian fiction that has been published in the West has had literary aspirations, but now more homegrown, purely popular fiction is also reaching audiences outside India. Former model **Shobhaa Dé's** (b. 1948) glitzy and sensationalistic novels were the first local blockbusters of this sort. Although her fiction has never really caught on abroad, ***Bollywood Nights*** (originally published as *Starry Nights*; 1991) is a good example of her pulpy action-romances; all her up-from-the-gutter and high-society stories provide some entertainment value.

More recent novels often depict a rapidly industrializing India and the strains on society. **Vikas Swarup's** (b. 1961) *Q&A* (now also published as the movie tie-in *Slumdog Millionaire*; 2005) is one of several clever concept-novels that tries to show contemporary Indian life as multifaceted. The protagonist is a contestant on a show like *Who Wants to Be a Millionaire?* and has astonishing, and suspicious, success in answering the questions, but his recounting his miserable life story explains how he acquired all this knowledge. Unfortunately,

Swarup crams so much into this book (and his hero's life)—most of it horrific—that it drowns in its own excess.

Swarup's *Q&A* is a good idea gone slightly bad, but **Chetan Bhagat** (b. 1974) shows it can be even worse. His enormously successful books typically describe the lives of a small group of young adults making their way in the new Indian order. *Five Point Someone* (2004) has quickly become the classic modern novel of Indian campus life, describing the overwhelming rigors of the nation's leading university, IIT, and how students deal with them. *One Night @ the Call Center* (2005) was inspired by the rise of outsourced customer support, now employing hundreds of thousands of young Indians. These are parts of Indian life rarely explored as fully in other contemporary fiction—except now in imitation of Bhagat—and are full of potential, but Bhagat's lazily formulaic writing is little more than workmanlike, though at least it is fast paced.

Altaf Tyrewala's (b. 1977) Mumbai novel *No God in Sight* (2005) zips along even faster than Swarup's or Bhagat's, jumping in each short chapter to yet another character, and while his rush leads to some carelessness, this is one of the liveliest and best of all these sweeping novels. The chain of the characters' stories—or, more accurately, vignettes from their lives—moves across class and caste and shows the interconnectedness of contemporary Indian society.

Like *Midnight's Children*, *The God of Small Things*, and *The Inheritance of Loss*, **Aravind Adiga**'s (b. 1974) *The White Tiger* (2008) won the most prestigious British literary prize, the Man Booker. Like those other Indian novels, it relies on a creative concept: it is presented as letters addressed to the premier of China. The statesman's forthcoming visit to Bangalore inspires the protagonist to relate his life story, a rags-to-riches rise in the new Indian economy that shines a light on the dark underside of India's recent success. In exposing the social divides and describing the opportunities and limitations in an Indian society undergoing rapid change and also mired in age-old traditions, *The White Tiger* can be engrossing, but the picture Adiga offers is often too muddled, and his epistolary approach seems pointless.

KEEP IN MIND

- The young protagonist of **Anurag Mathur**'s (b. 1954) *The Inscrutable Americans* (1991) spends a year abroad, trying to make sense of America, and although this book is already a bit dated, it is still an amusing study of cultural differences.

Adiga's *Last Man in Tower* (2011) is very much a Dickensian novel set in contemporary Mumbai, in which a real-estate speculator wants to empty a building, Tower A, in order to develop the property. He offers the tenants large sums of money to leave, but one of them, Masterji, remains a holdout. Tower A is a microcosm of Mumbai and India, a premise that allows Adiga to examine many of the issues facing India today.

Indian-Language Literature

With dozens of widely spoken languages—at least five have more than 50 million speakers each (Hindi, Bengali, Telugu, Marathi, and Tamil)—India is a veritable Tower of Babel. Many of these languages have strong literary traditions, but relatively little fiction from any of them has been translated into English. The recent rapid growth of a pan-Indian publishing industry, with English as the dominant language, has greatly increased the availability of such literature in translation, at least locally. Although English seems still—or perhaps more than ever—to be the first choice for budding authors, a large body of work in regional languages remains to be discovered.

Urdu author **Qurratulain Hyder**'s (1927–2007) *River of Fire* (1959, English 1998) is one of the great Indian novels of the twentieth century, even in its "transcreated" English form, a revision for which the author herself was responsible. Spanning most of India's history, continuity is sustained by its central characters, who reappear in different forms over more than two thousand years. The constant dialogue and interaction between the characters gives the book a sense of great immediacy, so history, even on this scale, is always very personal. While it does not address the most recent decades of Indian history, *River of Fire* is an ideal preamble to everything from Rushdie's *Midnight's Children* and *Shame* to Tyrewala's *No God in Sight*. Hyder's **Fireflies in the Mist** (1979, English 1994) is a three-part novel largely set in Dacca (now Dhaka) that describes this Bengal region as it shifted from being part of British India before World War II to becoming, first, East Pakistan and then the entirely independent Bangladesh in 1971. Despite not having a single dominant character or story line, Hyder repeatedly shows how the characters' different layers of identity—national, linguistic, political, religious—conflict and how they struggle deciding which are most important.

Naiyer Masud's (b. 1936) Urdu stories are told in the first person in collections such as **Essence of Camphor** (English 1998) and **Snake Catcher** (English 2006). Masud, a translator of Kafka, shares some of the Czech master's strangeness, but his tales are also distinctively Indian, especially their fanciful, but not too fantastical, elements.

Vilas Sarang's (1942–2015) Marathi stories, most recently collected in *The Women in Cages* (English 2006) in English versions reworked by the author, take more surreal turns and feel more in the Latin American tradition. Sarang often turns to the Kafkaesque as well, though in his metamorphosis story, the protagonist wakes up to find himself transformed into an erect phallus and is revered as the incarnation of Lord Shiva's *lingam*—before he eventually goes limp.

Hindi author **Nirmal Verma**'s (1929–2005) realist fiction is full of individuals who cannot break out of their isolation or connect with others. The collection *The World Elsewhere* (English 1988) is partly another exploration of the Indian abroad, with stories set in London and Central Europe inspired by Verma's own experiences in Czechoslovakia in the 1960s. His novel **Dark Dispatches** (1989, English 1993) is set during the Indian emergency of the mid-1970s, in which Indira Gandhi's government cracked down on democracy. This novel recounts the widespread fear and paranoia of the time, which underscore the increasing alienation of Verma's protagonist.

O. V. Vijayan's (1930–2005) *The Legends of Khasak* (1969, English 1994) and *The Saga of Dharmapuri* (1985, English 1988) are among the finest postindependence Indian novels. Written in Malayalam, the language of the southern state of Kerala, these are two entirely different works of fiction. *The Legends of Khasak* seems at first to be a conventional tale in which a young teacher, Ravi, is sent to open and run a school in a small Indian village. Vijayan evokes Khasak as skillfully as Narayan did his Malgudi, and similarly, he has many different characters play significant roles in the story. The outsider Ravi has as much to learn from the locals as he has to teach them, in this world where the supernatural also has a place. If *The Legends of Khasak* is charming, *The Saga of Dharmapuri* is brutal in its political satire, with Dharmapuri a place that suggests an alternate India, facing the same problems and issues but on a much more horrific scale. Written in the time leading up to the 1975 emergency (but published only afterward), the author's anger at the prevailing political corruption radiates throughout the text. The explicit language and coarse descriptions were shocking in their time but are entirely appropriate.

It is the high standard of the writing that sets apart **Uday Prakash**'s (b. 1951) Hindi novel ***The Girl with the Golden Parasol*** (2001, English 2008) from other Indian campus novels. *The Girl with the Golden Parasol* also addresses issues of caste and tradition in rapidly modernizing India. In each of the three stories collected in Uday's ***The Walls of Delhi*** (English 2012), the protagonists seem to have an opportunity to escape their poor circumstances but are unable to do so. Uday's sympathetic portrayal of the marginalized here is deeply affecting.

Very little of the crime and other popular fiction written in India's regional languages has been translated. While perhaps of more dubious literary quality, such works often do offer a different kind of local color. **Saradindu Bandyopadhyay**'s (1899–1970) ***Picture Imperfect*** (English 1999) is a collection of stories about an early Bengali detective figure, making it a good introduction to native Indian crime fiction. Famed Bengali filmmaker **Satyajit Ray**'s (1921–1992) thirty-five Feluda stories, narrated by the detective's Watson-like sidekick, Topshe, were intended mainly for a younger audience but nonetheless are fine works in the Holmesian tradition. Meanwhile, ***The Blaft Anthology of Tamil Pulp Fiction*** (English 2008, second volume, 2010),

---

KEEP IN MIND

- **U. R. Anantha Murthy**'s (1932–2014) classic Kannada novel *Samskara* (1965, English 1976) centers on rites and expectations in a Brahmin community.
- **Yashpal**'s (1903–1976) thousand-page Hindi epic centered on the lives of a brother and sister at the time of partition is finally available in English as the two-volume *This Is Not That Dawn* (1958, 1960, English 2010).
- Both Assamese author **Indira Goswami** (1942–2011) and Bengali writer **Mahasweta Devi** (b. 1926) wrote socially aware fiction.

---

edited by Rakesh Khanna, offers a wider sample of more recent popular Tamil fiction that also includes romance and science fiction.

PAKISTAN

Indian fiction has long completely overshadowed that from Pakistan, with only a few Pakistani authors attracting much attention abroad until recently. **Ahmed Ali**'s (1910–1994) *Twilight in Delhi* (1940) is widely considered one of the great novels of that city, but because it was published before Pakistan was an independent nation (and is set in the Indian capital in the early twentieth century), it can hardly be considered a representative Pakistani novel. Although **Zulfikar Ghose** (b. 1935) is sometimes claimed for Pakistan, he is undeniably transnational. His multinational background, which includes a childhood spent in both India and Pakistan, as well as extended residence in England and the United States, is mirrored in *Statement Against Corpses* (1964), a collaboration with the brilliant British experimentalist B. S. Johnson (1933–1973), as well as fiction set in Pakistan like *The Murder of Aziz Khan* (1967) and *The Incredible Brazilian* trilogy (1972–1978).

Among the first prominent fiction to truly come out of Pakistan was that by **Bapsi Sidhwa** (b. 1938), but her Parsi background—she comes from the tiny community of Zoroastrians, whose faith differs markedly from the region's dominant ones—in an Islamic country also make her atypical. Her largely realist novels, beginning with *The Crow Eaters* (1978), are grounded in her unusual Parsi background, which provides a wealth of material about cultural conflict. Rich with comedy, these are entertaining and well-written works.

Mushtaq Ahmed Yousufi's (b. 1923) Urdu novel *Mirages of the Mind* (1990, English 2014) is a big, digressive, and melancholy comic work. The main character is Basharat Ali Farooqi, who moved from Kanpur to Karachi with his family at the time of the Indian-Pakistani partition. Basharat remains nostalgic for the lost old world, which Yousufi uses to good effect in the many situations in which he places Basharat.

Contemporary Pakistani politics and larger geopolitical issues play major roles in the fiction of authors such as **Mohammed Hanif** (b. 1965), **Mohsin Hamid** (b. 1971), and **Uzma Aslam Khan** (b. 1969). Hanif's *A Case of Exploding Mangoes* (2008), which reimagines the possible conspiracies regarding Pakistani president Zia ul-Haq's mysterious death in a 1988 airplane crash, veers uneasily between literary satire and thriller mode. The depiction of the role of the military in Pakistani governance and life, as well as American influence over it, is of some interest, but the points Hanif tries to make feel forced.

Mohsin Hamid is a more assured writer, and both *Moth Smoke* (2000) and *The Reluctant Fundamentalist* (2007) crackle with the tension of contemporary Pakistani life. His narrative voices are particularly unsettling despite seeming so welcoming. Written in the present tense, the reader is drawn close to the action, yet Hamid also erects barriers that hold the reader at bay, a subtle, clever technique that gives his fiction a unique feel. Even though his narrators seem so forthright, the texts are full of ambiguity. *The Reluctant Fundamentalist* is a monologue addressed to an unidentified American, the text solely the narrator's side of the story. A Western-educated Pakistani who grew disillusioned with America and returned to Pakistan, the protagonist has become a popular university lecturer, his popularity due in part to his political engagement and anti-American message. How far that anti-Americanism goes is unclear, but in this post-9/11 world, the

KEEP IN MIND

- The fiction by expatriate authors such as **Adam Zameenzad** (b. 1949), **Kamila Shamsie** (b. 1973), and **Nadeem Aslam** (b. 1966) is well worth a look.

implications of every word and suggestion seem much larger, which Hamid fully exploits.

Written in the second person, Hamid's *How to Get Filthy Rich in Rising Asia* (2013) takes another creative approach, chronicling his nameless protagonist's rise from humble beginnings to great wealth in an unnamed country that resembles Pakistan but could be a stand-in for any number of rapidly modernizing Asian states. Hamid ultimately undermines his work by toying too much with his readers, but his novels are among the most revealing to come out of Pakistan.

Uzma Aslam Khan's broad portraits of Pakistani life, such as the love story *Trespassing* (2004), are personal and family oriented, but she also mixes political and social commentary into her fiction. Her perspective also examines subjects that get less attention, as in *The Geometry of God* (2007), with its multiple strands that address the study and role of science in an increasingly religious society.

BANGLADESH

As part of Pakistan until the violent break in 1971, Bangladesh shares its dominant language—Bengali (Bangla)—and much of its literary tradition with neighboring Indian Bengal. With a large local market—Bengali has some 200 million native speakers—and relatively few authors writing in English, literature from Bangladesh has largely remained self-contained and has made few inroads abroad.

The internationally most famous contemporary Bangladeshi author is **Taslima Nasrin** (b. 1962), whose contentious work led to violent threats and a jail sentence *in absentia*, making it impossible for her to remain in her homeland. Nasrin already was controversial by the early 1990s, largely due to her open discussion of the abuse of girls and women and her condemnation of religion being used to excuse this behavior. Her documentary novel *Lajja* (1993, English 1994, and as *Shame*, 1997) further inflamed Muslim extremists. Its description of the treatment of the Hindu minority in Bangladesh, especially after the destruction of the mosque in India's Ayodhya in 1992 by Hindu fundamentalists, led to reprisals throughout India and Bangladesh. Ultimately, however, this book is of greater historical than literary interest.

Like many of the prominent English-writing Indian authors, **Tahmima Anam** (b. 1975) grew up exposed to a variety of cultures and pursued her higher education in the West. Her first novel, *A Golden Age* (2007), is set in Bangladesh and focuses on the 1971 war of independence. This family tale centers on the widow Rehana and her children, Sohail and Maya, and their growing involvement in this ugly conflict. The first volume of what is a planned trilogy, it is a powerful portrait of maternal love and obligation and the best literary introduction to modern Bangladesh currently available. *The Good Muslim* (2011) continues the story, with the novel shifting back and forth between the mid-1980s and the early period after the end of the war, when Maya went to work in the countryside as a doctor while Sohail retreated into fundamentalist Islamic faith. Without reducing her characters to simplistic types, Anam uses their experiences and attitudes to reflect on Bangladesh's postwar transition.

NEPAL

Nepal is yet another country from which the authors who have received the most exposure abroad are those who write in English and were educated or based in the West. **Samrat Upadhyay's** (b. 1974) first collection of stories, *Arresting God in Kathmandu* (2001), and his novel *The Guru of Love* (2003) provide insight into the country and culture, especially in his depictions of domestic lives. The universal complications of love and lust and family are well handled, and Upadhyay's

KEEP IN MIND

- *Himalayan Voices* (1991) is an anthology of Nepali literature edited by Michael James Hutt. Although it does not offer samples of the newest Nepali fiction, it is a useful introductory text.

interest in this rather than relying on what is alien to Western readers—as authors of fiction set in such an out-of-the-way place often do—is welcome. The more recent stories collected in *The Royal Ghosts* (2006) give a vivid sense of the effects of the long-simmering Maoist insurgency in Nepal and also address such sensational events as the royals' palace slaughter in 2001. **Manjushree Thapa's** (b. 1968) *The Tutor of History* (2001) takes place mostly away from Kathmandu and revolves around an election campaign, revealing more local social and political conditions in Nepal. While successful as such, the subsequent upheaval in Nepali politics, which has seen martial law, the collapse and abolition of the monarchy, and the 2008 election of a Communist Party–led government, overshadow Thapa's depictions.

Among the few works of fiction translated from Nepali is **Lil Bahadur Chettri's** (b. 1933) *Mountains Painted with Turmeric* (1957, English 2008), a social realist work about peasant life. Misfortune leads quickly to misery in this world, where there is little margin for error. Earnest and dark, the relatively simple story skillfully describes traditional rural Nepali life and the locals' limited options. **Narayan Wagle's** recent Nepali best seller, *Palpasa Café* (2005, English 2008), describes the ravages of the Maoist insurgency. Despite being a rather busy novel, the variety Wagle offers is a good overview of the reach and damage wrought in those years, on individuals and the society as a whole.

SRI LANKA

Shehan Karunatilaka's (b. 1975) *Chinaman* (published in the United States as *The Legend of Pradeep Mathew*; 2010) is narrated by a once-successful sportswriter, W. G. Karunasena, now near death from chronic alcoholism. The discursive novel recounts his efforts to complete one important work, a biography of a legendary (fictional) Sri Lankan cricketer—the greatest of whom no one has ever heard—before he dies. The lives and fates of Karunasena, with his many failures (and limited successes) and his complicated relationships with family and colleagues, and cricketer Mathew, falling into and then embracing complete obscurity, also are representative of Sri Lanka itself. Despite its emphasis on cricket, *Chinaman* is also a rare sports-dominated novel that rises far above sports.

Several English-writing authors who left Sri Lanka (formerly Ceylon) in childhood revisited the island state in their fiction. **Michelle de Kretser's** (b. 1957) *The Hamilton Case* (2003), an atmospheric novel about colonial Ceylon, is partly a murder mystery. Rather than a neatly tied-up genre novel, however, the ambiguities that arise as the perspective and narrative voice shift from one section to the next section make a richer and more unsettling read. **Michael Ondaatje's** (b. 1943) *Anil's Ghost* (2000) takes place in contemporary Sri Lanka and investigates murder on a different scale by dealing with the ongoing civil conflict there. Identifying one set of skeletal remains is central to the plot, but the novel is full of characters whose identities and allegiances are difficult to pin down, reflecting the nation's complex recent history.

Although **Romesh Gunesekera** (b. 1954) also left Sri Lanka at a young age, much of his fiction is situated there. In both the stories in *Monkfish Moon* (1992) and the nostalgic novel *Reef* (1994), the

---

KEEP IN MIND

- **Shyam Selvadurai's** (b. 1965) coming-of-age novel is entitled *Funny Boy* (1994), and his novel of 1920s Ceylon is *Cinnamon Gardens* (1999).
- Poet **Jean Arasanayagam's** (b. 1930) collection of stories is *All Is Burning* (1995).

consequences of the civil war overshadow much else, with Gunesekera's evocative and often lyrical prose lending additional force to the stories. Much of *Reef* revolves around food and cooking, and Gunesekera handles this particularly well.

Southeast Asia I

Almost no fiction from the Southeast Asian nations extending from Burma (Myanmar) to Vietnam is accessible to English-speaking readers, despite the strong literary traditions in several of these countries. Political isolation offers a partial explanation, as some of these countries have, to varying degrees, closed themselves off from engaging with the outside world for extended periods of time. Yet even fiction from Thailand, by far the most open of them, is seldom available in English translation. The publishing industry and writing culture are still underdeveloped in relatively small Laos and Cambodia, but both Myanmar and Vietnam have a very active literary scene.

BURMA (MYANMAR)

Burma was under British rule from 1886 until World War II before finally gaining full independence in 1948. Because of the limited foreign investment and industrialization under the secretive military dictatorship that came to power in 1962, the nation has remained in something of a time warp until recently, unable to escape its past, and the literature set there often seems to reflect that. The best-known works set in Burma are colorful historical fictions such as **Maurice Collis**'s (1889–1973) *She Was a Queen* (1937) and **F. Tennyson Jesse**'s (1888–1958) *The Lacquer Lady* (1929). Even more recent novels, like **Daniel Mason**'s (b. 1976) *The Piano Tuner* (2002), take place in the early colonial period. **Amitav Ghosh**'s (b. 1956) *The Glass Palace* (2000) begins with the British takeover, though at least it extends to the present. **George Orwell**'s (1903–1950) *Burmese Days* (1934), inspired by his own years there working for the colonial police, feels dated but remains among the best novels about Burma.

Only a few works of fiction have been translated from Burmese since independence. **Ma Ma Lay**'s (1917–1982) *Not Out of Hate* (1955, English 1991) is set in colonial Burma in the 1930s. In this novel, a very traditional girl marries a ridiculously Anglophile Burmese, who then imposes his ways on her. Well intentioned—as the title emphasizes—he nevertheless crushes the girl's spirits in an obvious allegory of British rule. The depiction of small-town Burmese life and customs is appealing, and the story is engaging, but the writing now feels quaint.

Nu Nu Yi's (b. 1957) more recent *Smile as They Bow* (2007, English 2008) seems to promise something far more exotic, though its real success is how it presents its colorful premises prosaically. The novel takes place in a transvestite milieu, the central figure a *natkadaw* queen named U Ba Si (but known as Daisy Bond) who plays a prominent role in a local annual festival. *Smile as They Bow* shows how deeply rooted superstition and spirituality are in Burmese life, as well as incidentally revealing the everyday hardships of getting by. Nevertheless, the novel is largely apolitical and has a timeless feel, as it could just as well be set during colonial times as the present.

Expatriate author **Wendy Law-Yone** (b. 1947) left Burma in 1967, and her first novel, *The Coffin Tree* (1983), recounts an experience of being an immigrant in America. The more ambitious *Irrawaddy Tango* (1993) is clearly based on conditions in her homeland, though

Law-Yone sets it in a fictional country named Daya. The central figure, Tango, marries a man who becomes the country's dictator, but she is kidnapped by rebel forces and eventually winds up in the United States. With its lively main character and whirlwind story, *Irrawaddy Tango* is ultimately more a novel about personal experience than about Burma.

CAMBODIA

During the horrific reign of the Khmer Rouge (1975–1979), Cambodia had almost no cultural activity, but in any case, until very recently, there have been limited opportunities for writers at any time in Cambodia's modern history. Both under the French colonialists and then, after becoming independent in 1953, under Norodom Sihanouk, as well as after the toppling of the Khmer Rouge by the Vietnamese, political and economic realities prevented the development of an open literary culture. Moreover, what is considered the first modern Khmer novel, **Rim Kin**'s (1911–1959) not yet translated *Sophat* (1941), was first published in Vietnam.

While many memoirs and personal accounts of surviving the Khmer Rouge regime are available in English, almost no adult fiction has been translated. Among the few works available is **Oum Suphany**'s (b. 1946) *Under the Drops of Falling Rain* (1989, English 1997). The novel tells of a marriage arranged by the Khmer Rouge in which the couple docs eventually find true love. Albeit a product of the Vietnamese-installed People's Republic of Kampuchea (as the country was called from 1979 to 1993), where the dominant school of art still was strict social realism, the novel's mix of romance and validation of cultural values after a period when all these had been denied make it an interesting curiosity.

A number of foreign authors have set their fiction in Cambodia, most notably Canadian-born author **Geoff Ryman** (b. 1951). Several of Ryman's award-winning shorter works of fantasy have been inspired by recent Cambodian history, and his novel *The King's Last Song* (2006) is a sweeping portrait of Cambodian culture and history that alternates between the present and the twelfth-century reign of Jayavarman VII.

LAOS

Laos, with by far the smallest population of any of the countries in the region, is also relatively isolated. **Outhine Bounyavong**'s (1942–2000) collection of stories *Mother's Beloved* (English 1999) is a rare sample of Lao writing. Even though the stories are hardly exceptional, they do offer some sense of the country and culture, and Peter Koret's lengthy introduction, a survey of Lao literature, is also very useful.

Despite the paucity of Lao literature in translation, the country has not been entirely ignored by writers from elsewhere, and British-born **Colin Cotterill** (b. 1952) set a series of crime novels featuring coroner Dr. Siri Paiboun in 1970s Laos after the Communist takeover. Using a great deal of local color, ranging from Lao superstition to Communist politics, and with their comic touch, these are entertaining mysteries.

THAILAND

Thai fiction remains largely unknown in the West, and Thai censorship—under its draconian lèse-majesté laws (Thailand is still a monarchy)—is the only aspect of reading and writing in Thailand that gets much attention abroad—and even then, it is usually only when foreign authors or publications are involved. Any writing perceived as in any way insulting to the monarchy is strictly prohibited, and offending journalists and authors have been sentenced to long jail terms. In 2009, Australian author **Harry Nicolaides** pleaded guilty to the offense of slandering the Thai royal family in a passage in his self-published novel *Verisimilitude* (2005) of which only a few copies had been sold; he was sentenced to three years in prison.

Rattawut Lapcharoensap (b. 1979) is one of the few authors with strong ties to the country who have found any recognition in the

English-speaking world in recent years. Born in America, he was raised in Thailand before completing his higher education in the United States, and he writes in English. His collection of stories *Sightseeing* (2005) describes contemporary Thai life and takes in the familiar tourist scene but also delves more deeply into local issues. From a story about evading the military draft to a longer piece about cockfighting, Lapcharoensap sketches his characters simply but effectively.

In the best one-volume introduction to modern Thai fiction, Marcel Barang's *The 20 Best Novels of Thailand* (1994), offers a useful (if very idiosyncratic) contemporary overview as well as excerpts from the twenty selected works. Several of these have also been published in full in translation, including **Siburapha's** (1905–1974) *Behind the Painting* (1937, English 1990), **Kukrit Pramoj's** (1911–1995) *Four Reigns* (1954, English 1981), **Wimon Sainimnuan's** (b. 1958) *Snakes* (1984, English 1996), and **Chart Korbjitti's** (b. 1954) *The Judgment* (1981, English 2001).

Siburapha's *Behind the Painting* is a nostalgic romance that in some ways resembles an Eastern variation of the fin-de-siècle novel. The narrator, Nopphon, looks back on a relationship he had years earlier with an older woman, a newlywed and aristocrat, in Tokyo and what it meant to both of them. Whereas he overcame the passion of youth after they parted, he discovers that she has continued to harbor feelings for him. Nopphon represents a new, forward-looking generation, and his beloved, Kirati, is from an aristocratic class that is literally dying out.

Kukrit Pramoj was a member of the royal family and briefly served as prime minister (1975–1976)—and also played the role of Prime Minister Kwen Sai in the film *The Ugly American* (1963, starring Marlon Brando and based on William J. Lederer and Eugene Burdick's novel about American diplomacy in Southeast Asia). Kukrit Pramoj also was a prolific writer. *Four Reigns* is a historical novel that follows the life of its female protagonist, Ploi, through the reigns of four Thai monarchs—Rama V through Rama VIII—from the late nineteenth century through World War II. Its depiction of court life and Thai customs and its appealing central character make this much-loved Thai classic a fine introduction to the local culture and history, though the English translation can seem prolix.

The vast majority of Thais are Buddhists, and the religion plays an important role in the country. With its depiction of the potential for corruption among the clergy and the abuse of religion by politicians, popular author Wimon Sainimnuan's *Snakes* offers particularly interesting insights into this world.

Chart Korbjitti is the leading contemporary Thai writer, whose breakthrough work was the dark novel of small-minded small-town life, *The Judgment*. In this novel the main character, Fak, gives up a religious life to help his father but becomes the victim of local gossip when he is suspected of having an affair with his beautiful but feeble-minded stepmother. These rumors lead to greater misery for Fak and eventually drive him to his death. Other novels by Chart also rely extensively on short, fast exchanges of dialogue and action. Chart addresses a wide variety of social issues in an entertaining fashion that contrast with the region's otherwise generally earnest and socially engaged fiction (as well as its popular but very light romantic fare). In *Time* (1993, English 2000), Chart experiments with the form of the novel. The narrator of *Time* is a filmmaker getting on in years who is watching a long-winded play about the elderly. He describes what he sees and thinks and also reimagines how he would have the scenes play out if he were filming this story. *Time* is a novel about aging and throughout the cleverly structured narrative are constant rhythmic reminders of time slowly and steadily passing.

VIETNAM

The Vietnam War, which ended in 1975, still casts a long shadow over Vietnam and its literature. All aspects of the prolonged American involvement in the conflict, in which several million members of the military served, have been treated in many works written by Americans, but few Vietnamese works covering this period have been translated. The victorious Communist government that unified Vietnam has restricted what can be written and published in Vietnam. Economic

THAILAND AS A SETTING FOR FOREIGNERS'
FICTION

With its glorious beaches and notorious sex trade, Thailand has also been
a popular setting for fiction by foreigners. **Alex Garland**'s (b. 1970) idyll-
shattering, backpacking novel *The Beach* (1996) remains a favorite among
tourists. A surprising number of mysteries and thrillers also are set in the
region. While the best that one can say about **Dean Barrett**'s (b. 1942)
Thai novels is that they are action packed, Bangkok-based authors **John
Burdett**'s (b. 1951) and **Christopher G. Moore**'s (b. 1952) familiarity with
Thai culture and subculture serve them well in their crime books.

liberalization and reform have accelerated in recent years, however,
and have led to greater cultural freedom, despite reversals. As in China,
there was considerably more openness in the late 1980s, followed by a
retrenchment after the collapse of the Soviet Union. With a majority
of its large population having been born after the end of the war, the
continued shift from politically engaged—and politically correct—
fiction to writing that examines contemporary everyday concerns (as
well as escapist entertainment) seems inevitable.

The Vietnam War dominates **Bao Ninh**'s (b. 1952) stark *The Sorrow of War* (1991, English 1994). From his childhood to his disappointment when he returns to civilian life, the war defines the life of the
protagonist, Kien. Most significantly, it also crushes his hopes for love.
Nguyen Khai's (1930–2008) *Past Continuous* (1985, English 2001) is
another novel presenting the war from the Vietnamese perspective. Its
three main characters, including a secret agent and a Catholic priest,
each engaged in the conflict in a different way, offer a vivid portrait of
the North Vietnamese struggle.

Duong Thu Huong (b. 1947) is among the few Vietnamese authors
whose works have been widely translated. She has long been a prominent and outspoken critic of the regime and was expelled from the
Communist Party and imprisoned for several months in 1991. Several
of her books, including the trilogy that begins with *Novel Without a
Name* (1991, English 1995), were first published abroad, and many are

still banned in Vietnam. One of the major story lines in *The Zenith* (2009, English 2012) focuses on an aging Ho Chi Minh, no longer at the center of government as he was at the height of the Vietnam War.

In Duong's ***Beyond Illusions*** (1987, English 2002), the central character, Linh, is despondent about the compromises her husband and then her lover make, selling out their ideals. Situated in Hanoi in the late 1980s, this novel is a revealing picture of the difficulties of remaining true to oneself and one's beliefs in a totalitarian society that cannot live up to its own slogans and ideology. Several of Duong's novels revolve around difficult personal relationships, often involving degrees of separation between lovers as lives and relationships are made more complicated by the Vietnam War and its aftermath. Although politics is omnipresent in her fiction, her main characters are frequently engaged in the arts. Duong's focus on the creative and the personal—and a powerful, direct style of writing—make for stories that transcend their narrow Vietnamese setting.

In ***Crossing the River*** (English 2003), the most comprehensive collection of his fiction, **Nguyen Huy Thiep** (b. 1950) presents a gritty, realistic picture of postwar Vietnamese society. Many of his characters are far from the Communist ideal found in social realist fiction, and he depicts the failures of the impossible perfect society for which the Vietnamese had fought and the realities his characters now face.

KEEP IN MIND

- **Ho Anh Thai**'s (b. 1960) novels include *Apocalypse Hotel* (2002, English 2012), about fast times in fast-changing 1990s Vietnam, and *The Women on the Island* (1988, English 2000).
- **Pham Thi Hoai**'s (b. 1960) story *The Crystal Messenger* (1988, English 1997) is about of twin sisters in postwar Vietnam.
- **Ma Van Khang**'s (b. 1936) *Against the Flood* (1999, English 2000) is an appealing novel about an idealistic writer, Khiem, undone by the conniving that goes on around him in an increasingly corrupt modern Vietnam. The translation, however, distorts much of the original, including uprooting its Communist foundations.

Southeast Asia II

MALAYSIA

Malaysia is a multiethnic nation in which a quarter of the population is of Chinese descent and which also has a significant Indian (mainly Tamil) minority. While Malay is the official language, English is widely spoken, and there also are numerous outlets for authors writing in Chinese and Indian languages. As with the writing from other countries in the region, fiction by authors who write in English and have spent significant time abroad dominates what is available to English-speaking readers outside Malaysia. Very little has been translated from the other widely spoken languages.

English author **Anthony Burgess** (1917–1993) spent several years in the 1950s in Southeast Asia and wrote three books that form *The Malayan Trilogy* (1956–1959), now published together as *The Long Day Wanes*. The character of Victor Crabbe links the three novels. Like Burgess, Crabbe was a teacher in the Federation of Malaya (as it was then called) in the transitional years leading up to independence in 1957. In describing Crabbe's confrontations with all the contesting ethnic, religious, and colonial groups, as well as the guerrilla movement, Burgess captures the messy jumble out of which the current Malaysian state arose, in a work that has still not been superseded as a fictional account of that time and those events. Burgess became a fluent Malay speaker, and his trilogy is particularly noteworthy for its familiarity with local conditions.

Recent English-language novels by authors with Malaysian backgrounds include **Tash Aw**'s (b. 1971) *The Harmony Silk Factory* (2005) and **Tan Twan Eng**'s (b. 1972) *The Gift of Rain* (2007) and *The Garden of Evening Mists* (2012). The Japanese occupation of Malaysia during World War II figures prominently in these novels, and the suspense revolves around the characters' many betrayals. Both authors put the Malaysian countryside to good use, as the relatively isolated settings of the novels are both paradisiacal and treacherous.

Preeta Samarasan's (b. 1976) *Evening Is the Whole Day* (2008) revolves around an Indian family in Malaysia, the Rajasekharans. Beginning with the ostracism of a maid, the novel is a compelling story of how much identity—and the possibility of self-fulfillment—is based on one's place in a community, ranging from the family unit to an (adopted) nation. With its focus on the domestic and on the Indian community, *Evening Is the Whole Day* offers only a splintered view of Malaysia, but despite the stylistic excesses of Samarasan's lush writing, the novel conveys the complexities arising from Malaysia's ethnic and political mix.

K. S. Maniam's (b. 1942) fiction also explores the Indian experience in Malaysia. The autobiographical coming-of-age novel about the Tamil boy Ravi, *The Return* (1981), is another story of displacement and takes place during the time of independence. Here it is English culture and the English language that the boy sees as an escape but that also reinforces his sense of alienation from his own culture. In the novel *In a Far Country* (1993), the narrator's midlife crisis results from his feeling that he is not truly part of modern Malaysia. Though a successful businessman, Rajan is still trying to find his place in this Malay- and

Islam-dominated environment. In one of the best novels of the nation's multiethnic conditions, the narrator reflects on his past and the Indian experience in Malaysia in general.

SINGAPORE

The city-state of Singapore, at the tip of the Malay Peninsula, declared its independence from British rule in 1963 and became a part of Malaysia. This short-lived union ended in 1965 when Singapore became an independent state. Although its main ethnic groups are the same as those in Malaysia, Singapore's population is predominantly of Chinese origin, with Malays constituting less than 15 percent of the population and those of Indian origin less than 10 percent. Malay is recognized as the national language, but English, (Mandarin) Chinese, and Tamil also are official languages and widely used.

Rapid modernization and economic growth in this small, concentrated area have changed the country dramatically. American author **Paul Theroux** (b. 1941) taught in Singapore from 1968 to 1971, and the world he describes in *Saint Jack* (1973) already is ancient history. Taking place during the Vietnam War, with its American protagonist, Jack Flowers, working as a pimp, the novel presents an older image of the city that the government did not like, and the 1979 Peter Bogdanovich film version was long banned in Singapore.

Goh Poh Seng's (1936–2010) *If We Dream Too Long* (1972) is considered the first truly Singaporean novel. Set in the late 1960s, its protagonist, Kwang Meng, has just graduated from school and works as a clerk. Like Singapore itself, he is uncertain of his future. Although he has some aspirations, his circumstances make it unlikely that he can escape his father's fate of laboring at a tedious, unrewarding job for his entire life. The novel thus suggests both the limits and the possibilities facing the nation and this first generation of citizens.

Gopal Baratham's (1935–2002) novels explicitly address Singapore's authoritarian government. In *A Candle or the Sun* (1991), the protagonist, Hernie Perera, begins as a successful store manager and would-be writer whose world is thrown into increasing turmoil. His mistress is a member of a clandestine Christian group that questions the government's absolute control and the limits placed on free speech. Perera agrees to pass on information about the group to the government but eventually also helps his mistress and the group's leader escape and winds up being arrested. Very loosely based on the events that culminated in the 1987 arrests of more than a dozen people in a so-called Marxist plot, no Singaporean publisher was willing to publish the book, even though it was eventually made available there. The more sensational *Moonrise, Sunset* (1996) begins dramatically—How Kum Menon wakes up on a park bench to find his fiancée murdered in his arms—and uses the conventions of the mystery novel and a colorful cast of characters to present an engaging picture of Singapore's dark sides.

Catherine Lim's (b. 1942) larger body of work includes a variety of popular novels with a regional setting. The most notorious is *The Bondmaid* (1995), which she self-published because its sexual content scared off local publishers. Lim is more concerned with personal dynamics than social or political commentary in this story of a girl sold into what amounts to slavery in 1950s Singapore. Other works, like *The Teardrop Story Woman* (1997), set in 1950s Malaya, and a novel about contemporary Singapore, *Following the Wrong God Home* (2001), also focus on passion and romance but provide more of a local flavor. Lim uses differing cultural expectations, social conditions in the region, and even superstition in fashioning her novels, but much of her writing verges on the melodramatic.

Hwee Hwee Tan's (b. 1974) Generation X novels, *Foreign Bodies* (1997) and *Mammon Inc.* (2001), feature young adults and the clash of cultures in an increasingly globalized world. *Foreign Bodies* is about Mei, a young Singaporean lawyer to whom Andy, an English expat friend of her childhood friend Eugene, turns when he is arrested for allegedly running an illegal betting operation. In the brief time they have to prove his innocence, these three characters must come to terms with the considerable baggage of their own pasts and beliefs. Each character narrates part of the story, creating three very different perspectives. Tan adopts a very hip tone throughout the pop reference–filled

> KEEP IN MIND
>
> - Malaysian-born **Vyvyane Loh**'s *Breaking the Tongue* (2004) is set around the fall of Singapore to the Japanese in 1942. The novel features the family of the protagonist, Claude Lim, which is Chinese but has become completely Anglicized.
> - **Philip Jeyaretnam**'s (b. 1964) satire is called *Raffles Place Ragtime* (1988).

narrative but manages to weave in a number of weighty moral issues as well. The central character in *Mammon Inc.*, Chiah Deng, is torn between academic pursuits—the study of Christian mysticism—and a remunerative job with a giant multinational, Mammon. The position she is offered at the corporate subsidiary, Mammon CorpS, is that of Adapter, helping clients adjust to and blend into foreign conditions. To get the job, she has to transform herself, her sister, and her flat mate. If the lessons are a bit obvious, Tan's comic touch makes for an enjoyable but not entirely lightweight work.

PHILIPPINES

Filipino (which is essentially Tagalog) and English are the official languages of the Philippines, but many others are widely spoken. Spain was the major colonial power in the region until the Spanish-American War, after which the Philippines were ceded to the United States. Even so, Spanish was widely spoken well into the twentieth century, and the first great Filipino author, **José Rizal** (1861–1896), wrote in Spanish his now classic novel *Noli Me Tángere* (1887, numerous English translations, most recently 2006; previously published in English as *An Eagle Flight*, 1900, *The Social Cancer*, 1912, and *The Lost Eden*, 1961). English-language fiction is currently thriving, albeit on a small scale, and few of these novels and story collections are distributed outside the Philippines.

F. Sionil José (b. 1924) is the leading modern Filipino author. His five-volume Rosales saga (1962–1984) covers almost a century of Philippine history, beginning before the Spanish-American War and leading to the early 1970s and the student uprisings against the Marcos regime. Somewhat confusingly, the American edition of the five books of the Rosales saga is published in three volumes, in which the books are arranged in the chronological order of the action, rather than in the original order in which they were written. *The Samsons* (2000), for example, consists of the first book, *The Pretenders* (1962) and the fourth, *Mass* (1979).

Much of this family saga examines the exploitation and oppression suffered by Filipinos during this period. The tensions between land-owners and peasants are explored in the largely rural setting of the first volumes, but class differentiations become blurred in later generations. In *The Pretenders*, Tony Samson escapes his peasant roots and earns a doctorate from Harvard, but the compromises he has to make when he is seduced into becoming part of the nation's elite are too great for him to bear. Throughout the five books, José reveals the cost, both in individual terms and for the country as a whole, of the corruption and greed of the ruling class. While offering some hope that this legacy can be surmounted, the Rosales saga is a strong indictment of the abuse of power by the wealthy in the Philippines during this time. José addresses questions of justice and how to affect change throughout the series, but violence is still the most frequent last resort in these novels filled with tragedy. The scope of the Rosales books make them a compelling national saga, and they serve as a good introduction to the Philippines.

Jose Dalisay's (b. 1954) *Killing Time in a Warm Place* (1992) describes growing up in the Philippines under the Marcos regime and martial law in the 1970s. It is narrated by Noel Bulaong, and as his positions include both opposing and working within the system, the novel gives a good sense of that period of Philippine history. *Soledad's Sister* (2008; published in the United States together with *Killing Time in a Warm Place* as *In Flight: Two Novels of the Philippines*, 2011) opens with the arrival of a casket from Saudi Arabia containing a dead woman, one of the many Filipinos who have gone to the Gulf to work as a domestic servant. Misidentifications of the corpse lead to a number of people getting involved in seeing to it that the body is returned to the rightful family, but the woman's odyssey continues to be complicated. Dalisay mixes stories of the woman with those of her sister, and the policeman who helps transport the coffin to create an intriguing montage of contemporary Filipino fates, enlivened by the vivid urban backdrop.

A United States resident since the mid-1950s, **Linda Ty-Casper** (b. 1931) has written many works of historical fiction covering the major periods of Philippine history. Several of her novels take place during the time of the Marcos regime (1965–1986), but her trilogy of the Philippine struggle for independence against the Spanish and then the Americans at the end of the nineteenth century is noteworthy also. These three novels, *The Three-Cornered Sun* (1979), *Ten Thousand Seeds* (1987), and *The Stranded Whale* (2002), take place during the brief period when self-determination seemed possible in the Philippines. Ty-Casper describes the armed struggle in the Philippines itself and emphasizes foreign perceptions and reactions, using characters such as an American couple who come to the Philippines on their honeymoon in *Ten Thousand Seeds*. Her novel *DreamEden* (1996) covers the rough transition to democracy that began with the "People Power" revolution of 1986 and the removal of Ferdinand Marcos from power. Ty-Casper's painstaking presentation of history in her novels is admirable, but it often overwhelms her fictional lining.

Miguel Syjuco's (b. 1976) exuberant *Ilustrado* (2010) is a storybook first novel by an author with literary aspirations in regard to both its success—it won the prestigious Man Asian Literary Prize—and the text itself. Featuring two writers—the fictional Crispin Salvador, presented as one of the grand old men of Filipino letters, and a young man writing his biography named Miguel Syjuco—*Ilustrado* is an ambitious work that relies greatly on pastiche. Both Salvador and the fictional Syjuco are scions of the politically engaged elite in the Philippines, and both disappoint their families by not going into politics (and by going abroad). Syjuco amusingly shows, and comments on, many aspects of Filipino society and politics through these characters. The novel begins with Crispin Salvador found dead in the Hudson River, and the

---

KEEP IN MIND

- The novels and stories of **Nick Joaquin** (1917–2004) are noteworthy.
- **Alfred A. Yuson**'s (b. 1945) *The Great Philippine Jungle Energy Café* (1988) is a funny metafictional novel.
- Much of the fiction of Filipino-American authors **Paulino Lim Jr.** (b. 1935), **Jessica Hagedorn** (b. 1949), and **Han Ong** (b. 1968) is informed by Filipino history and culture.

---

mystery surrounding his death, including the question of whether it was suicide or murder and a missing manuscript that he had been working on for years, also add suspense to the story.

INDONESIA

While there are hundreds of regional languages spoken in the world's fourth most populous country, Indonesian is the country's official and most widely understood language. Despite a potentially large audience, the number of locally published novels was, until recently, very small, and very few have been translated into English.

Pramoedya Ananta Toer (1925–2006) is the towering figure in modern Indonesian literature. His major work, the *Buru Quartet*, is named after the island on which Toer conceived these stories and where he was held as a political prisoner until 1979. Initially forbidden to write while incarcerated, he related the stories orally to other prisoners. Eventually he was allowed to write them down, and the first volume of the quartet was released in Indonesia in 1980. Shortly thereafter, however, the first and second volumes were banned by the Suharto regime, and little of Toer's work has been officially available in Indonesia until recently.

The *Buru Quartet* begins with *This Earth of Mankind* (1980, English 1982), which introduces the central character, the Javanese youth Minke. It begins at the end of the nineteenth century, when Minke is the only native student at an elite Dutch colonialist school. Minke is from an aristocratic family and moves comfortably within different ethnic and social circles. He falls in love with Annelies, the daughter of a Dutchman and his Javanese concubine. Minke and Annelies marry, but it is not a legal union according to prevailing Dutch law, leading to a heartbreaking ending. Despite being well educated by the colonizers, Minke comes to see that his status remains that of a second-class citizen. With its appealing protagonist, strong female characters—the beautiful Annelies, her remarkable mother, and Minke's own mother—and its dramatic story arc, *This Earth of Mankind* is a wonderful novel. In the later volumes, after his youthful idealism has been shattered, Minke learns more about his own culture and becomes more politically aware and active. While these are also very good novels, they are not as engaging as *This Earth of Mankind*.

Y. B. Mangunwijaya's (1929–1999) *Durga/Umayi* (1991, English 2004) is a fascinating take on more recent Indonesian history. The novel's female protagonist goes by a number of names, reflecting Indonesia's rapid transformation after it became independent following World War II. The title of the novel refers to the wife of the Hindu deity, Siva: as Umayi she is a beautiful woman, but she is also cursed with a monstrous and destructive second form, Durga. Mangunwijaya finds this duality throughout modern Indonesian society. With its runaway sentences, rapid shifts, and multiple identities, *Durga/Umayi* is a challenging but exhilarating short novel.

Eka Kurniawan (b. 1975) explores recent Indonesian history in novels that are, in turn, shocking, poignant, and amusing. He often uses elements of magical realism. **Beauty Is a Wound** (2002, English 2015) begins with the main character, a prostitute, rising from the dead after more than two decades. The story of two families, **Man Tiger** (2004, English 2015) also features a character who is half-human, half-tiger.

After three decades in office, Suharto resigned the presidency in 1998, allowing for more democracy and less censorship in Indonesia, as well as the growth of publishing. Light romances—called *sastra wangi* (fragrant literature)—often written by young women, have been especially popular and have had some success abroad, especially in Malaysia. The best selling of these, **Ayu Utami's** (b. 1968) *Saman* (1998,

English 2005), is one of the more ambitious examples of the genre. It opens in an exotic setting—New York's Central Park—but the heart of the novel concerns social justice in Indonesia. The title character, Saman, is a priest who becomes involved in the cause of farmers whose land is being expropriated. Utami shows how the modern abuses of the state hardly differ from those of the Dutch colonialists, and her novel contains several female characters who test the possibilities and limits of personal freedom in modern Indonesia. The novel's explicitness is hardly shocking by Western standards—one of the women manages to cling to her virginity even while she has an affair with a married man—but was previously unheard of in Indonesian fiction. With its different narrative voices as well as cuts back and forth in time—and a concluding section that is composed of a lengthy e-mail exchange—*Saman* was also groundbreaking in its style and presentation.

Indonesia has the world's largest Muslim population, and **Habiburrahman el-Shirazy**'s (b. 1976) best-selling *Ayat-Ayat Cinta* (*The Verses of Love*; 2004, English forthcoming), which was also made into a very popular movie in 2008, is essentially a romance novel that adheres closely to Islamic principles. Set in Egypt, the Indonesian protagonist, Fahri, is a student at the center of Islamic scholarship, Al-Azhar University. The novel nevertheless is very much the product of a more open Indonesian culture; no Arab author seems yet to have found a way of balancing pulp romance and religious conformity in a similarly appealing fashion.

KEEP IN MIND

- **Andrea Hirata**'s (b. 1967) best-selling *The Rainbow Troops* (2005, English 2009, revised 2013) is the first in an autobiographical quartet. It is a charming, if simple, novel about childhood in rural Indonesia.

China, Tibet, and Taiwan

Mainland China has undergone several radical transformations in little more than a hundred years, from the collapse of its empire through periods of foreign occupation and international isolation to its reemergence as one of the world's great economic powers. The post-Maoist years have seen what seems like nearly unfettered and still accelerating expansion in many spheres of life there. Rapid urban and economic growth are the most obvious manifestations, but this transformation also extends to film, the fine arts, and literature. For centuries, Chinese fiction has reached English-speaking readers only haphazardly, making it difficult to get much sense of this culture's rich literary tradition, but suddenly the uneven trickle has become at least a steady flow.

With new trends following in rapid succession, shifting standards of censorship and permissiveness, and a growing and increasingly prominent number of expatriate authors who write in both Chinese and Western languages, the dull and nearly blank slate that was Chinese fiction at the height of the Cultural Revolution has become a huge, variegated canvas. Yet despite this proliferation of recent fiction in translation, the English-speaking world is still in the process of catching up to older Chinese literature.

CHINA

Classical Fiction

The foremost classical Chinese novels have faced several hurdles in becoming integrated into the body of universally recognized world literature. They do not come from any single era and have little sense of progression. Many are long, with unabridged translations taking up several volumes. The existence of numerous, often heavily edited, translations that appeared throughout the twentieth century and a variety of different English titles for the works—**Cao Xueqin**'s (ca. 1715–1763) *The Story of the Stone* (ca. 1760) is also known as the *Dream of the Red Chamber*, for example—has complicated their reception. Although some of the earlier versions of the classic Chinese novels provided an adequate impression of the originals, it is only relatively recently that even an approximation of novels such as *The Story of the Stone*—one of the great works of world literature—could be appreciated by English readers (in the translation by David Hawkes and John Minford, 1973–1986). Instead, for much of the twentieth century, populist abridged renderings were all that readers were likely to be exposed to: Arthur Waley's *Monkey* (1943), consisting of a few episodes from *Journey to the West* (1592), and Pearl S. Buck's version of *Outlaws of the Marsh* (fourteenth century), *All Men Are Brothers* (1933), remain the best known. They helped introduce Western audiences to classical Chinese fiction, but they nonetheless were fundamentally different from the originals.

Ironically, it is **Pearl Buck**'s (1892–1973) *The Good Earth* (1931) that, in many ways, became the definitive "Chinese" novel of the twentieth century. Buck's familiarity with China resulted in a depiction that was undeniably authentic but also subjective and limited. Buck may not have been a very good writer, but *The Good Earth* remains a much-loved (and best-selling) book. Essentially unchallenged for decades as the peremptory choice of representative contemporary Chinese fiction, at least in the United States, its legacy has cast a long shadow. With such a small amount of fiction being written—much less translated—in the early years of the People's Republic, *The Good Earth* defined China for generations of readers, and even after an increasing amount of contemporary Chinese fiction started to become available in the 1980s, it still was the trusted keystone. Indeed, as late as 2004, Oprah Winfrey fell back on this rather than select a more recent Chinese novel for her television book club.

Several of the leading Chinese writers of the early twentieth century studied or lived abroad, and some specifically tried to present Chinese culture to Western audiences. The versatile **Lin Yutang** (1895–1976) even went so far as to write some of his works in English, including *Moment in Peking* (1938), a historical novel describing China in the first decades of the twentieth century. A better writer, **Lau Shaw** (Lao She, 1899–1966) lived and taught in London for several years in the 1920s but, unlike Lin, did not write for a Western audience, and his works began to appear in translation only years later. Mindful of American readers' expectations, his publishers adapted his starkest novel of the struggles of life in China, *Rickshaw Boy* (1936, English 1945), to foreign tastes. The translation took great liberties, right down to the ending, in which a happy outcome replaced the much darker original. More recent translations, as *Rickshaw* (1979), *Camel Xiangzi* (1981), and *Rickshaw Boy* (2010), are much closer to the original.

The People's Republic of China Under Mao

After World War II, the separation of China from the West in terms of cultural exchange and dialogue grew more pronounced, and with the establishment of the People's Republic in 1949, the rift became nearly absolute. Mainland China turned inward and was, in turn, isolated. Without diplomatic relations with the United States until the 1970s or a seat at the United Nations, there was little practical possibility of much literary exchange. But there was not much to miss. Creative literature was valued in the People's Republic only if it conformed to narrow specifications. Far more quickly and effectively than in the Soviet Union, the Maoist state imposed its ideals and expectations on literary works. This meant that realist fiction—often highly idealized—dominated, focusing on aspects of what was considered the revolutionary struggle, that is, straightforward stories of facing and overcoming hardships, culminating in heroic triumph over the enemy or the elements. Agricultural and military themes dominated this Chinese form of social realism, and even though it was not always crude, most Chinese writing was simplistic and predictable until the fall of the Gang of Four in 1976.

What is most remarkable is how little was published in the People's Republic at all: while short stories continued to be published in widely read periodicals, an average of only a dozen new novels a year appeared from 1949 through 1976. Other countries in the twentieth century had periods of limited literary production due to war or lack of capacity, but this dearth of new book-length fiction is unequaled in modern times. It began with a radical and apparently largely self-imposed break with the past as the old guard largely abandoned fiction in this new society. Many of the leading novelists from the prewar period who remained in mainland China, including **Shen Congwen** (1902–1988) and **Ba Jin** (1904–2005), largely or completely turned away from fiction after 1949. So did **Mao Dun** (1896–1981), even when he served as China's minister of culture for some fifteen years. Meanwhile, relatively few of the authors writing in exile during the Maoist period made much of an impression abroad. **Eileen Chang** (Zhang Ailing, 1920–1995) is the best and most prominent among them, but even some of her works—commissioned by the United States Information Agency—are too obviously calculatedly anti-Communist.

Aside from the practical difficulties, mutual suspicion and paranoia limited the availability of contemporary mainland Chinese fiction abroad. Any Chinese author who was appreciated abroad was suspect; indeed, one of the few whose works continued to be published in the United States after 1949, Lao She, was murdered by the Red Guard in 1966. Meanwhile, Chinese fiction from the People's Republic was generally seen by outsiders as little more than propaganda.

As in other Communist countries, foreign-language publishing houses were established to provide material to readers in other nations. Much of this was outright ideological propaganda, but some fiction was translated, and the Chinese Foreign Languages Press and then the Panda Books imprint offered several representative titles of contemporary fiction from the People's Republic. Most of the titles from the Maoist period are of interest only as historical curiosities, and even as such, they are quickly wearing, with the insistent political correctness of the time crushing most of the creative flourishes. A few works from the tendentious and safely predictable bunch do stand out, including **Yang Mo**'s (1914–1995) *The Song of Youth* (1958, English 1964) and some of the works by **Hao Ran** (1932–2008), but even these have relatively little appeal. Only Taiwanese author **Ch'en Jo-hsi** (Chen Ruoxi, b. 1938), who moved to China in 1966 and lived there until 1973, offered fiction straight out of the Cultural Revolution. Her collection of stories, *The Execution of Mayor Yin* (1976, English 1978), could not be printed in mainland China but remains a powerful record of that period.

China After Mao

With the downfall of the Gang of Four came a turning point in the People's Republic, beginning with a shift in scale: an almost tenfold increase in the average number of novels published annually, to a hundred per year between 1977 and 1986. An accelerating opening to the West also changed foreign attitudes, with 1979 providing a convenient demarcation point both in China and abroad. It is then that Lao She's most famous novel was published in a new English translation, as *Rickshaw*, and this one was true to the original, dark end and all. This was also the year when **Ch'ien Chung-shu**'s (Qian Zhongshu, 1910–1998) *Fortress Besieged* (1947, English 1979) appeared in translation. This portrait of East and West is set in the prewar years, but its broad, packed satire offers a smart, insightful overview of the cultural confluences in 1930s China. Though conditions differ greatly in contemporary China, *Fortress Besieged* remains fresh and has enough basic similarities in the continuing tug between old and new, as well as the domestic and foreign influences that Qian describes, for it to be a pertinent as well as an enjoyable read.

The revised *Rickshaw* and *Fortress Besieged*, both set in pre-Communist times, along with the first volumes of the definitive editions of some of the classic Chinese novels, helped pave the way for English-speaking readers' greater understanding of Chinese fiction. Fiction written by authors working in the People's Republic was slower to gain ground, but by the late 1970s and early 1980s, a profound shift in what was tolerated by the state resulted in writing that was far more palatable to Western audiences.

Wang Meng (b. 1934) is the most interesting figure from the first wave of post-Maoist liberalization that ended with the Tiananmen Square massacre. After some early success as a writer, his story *A Young Man Arrives at the Organization Department* (1956, English 1981) was heavily criticized, and he endured nearly two decades of internal exile and was able to return permanently to Beijing only in 1979. In 1986, he was named minister of culture, only to be ousted in 1989. His novella **Bolshevik Salute** (1979, English 1989) is a milestone, and Wang's stream-of-consciousness experiments and modernist approach mark a radical change from a tradition in which unity was expected and narratives unfolded simply and chronologically. Wang's fictional reckonings with party loyalty and commitment and the personal and introspective focus found in *Bolshevik Salute* and in works such as *The Butterfly* (1980, English 1983) offer a critical examination of recent Chinese history unthinkable even a few years earlier. Yet Wang's break with the past is far from absolute. He remains very much grounded in the ideology and slogans of the Maoist era, with even the protagonists' soul-searching reflecting the self-critical thought that was expected and demanded during that time.

In comparison to the self-absorbed Japanese I-novel or many of the first-person narratives found in modern Western literature, Chinese fiction of the 1980s, which still balanced that long-inculcated concern for the greater good with individual desires and needs, hardly seems self-indulgent. Nevertheless, many of these works have a sense of transgression in showing greater concern for the individual. This creates a heightened tension that gives these works a sense of otherness and casts the universal concerns and feelings in a different light, being situated in a world that had so long insisted on different assumptions. Love, in particular, had had only a limited place in Chinese fiction but now came to the fore. **Zhang Jie**'s (b. 1937) *Love Must Not Be Forgotten* (1980, English 1986) has an indicative title, and though not as sentimental as the title suggests, this story collection represents some of the new directions Chinese writers were taking at this time. More interesting is Zhang's *Leaden Wings* (1981, English 1987, and as *Heavy Wings*, 1989), which combines a focus on the individual and romance as a part of self-fulfillment with the familiar industrial and bureaucratic settings, an opposition that fueled the controversy surrounding the novel. **Zhang Xinxin**'s (b. 1953) *The Dreams of Our Generation* (1982, English 1986) is another novel of the period that explores the role of women and of love that stands out. **Ran Chen**'s (b. 1962) personal and deeply introspective *A Private Life* (1996, English 2004) is a transitional work from after 1989 and before a sex-drenched pop mentality came to dominate the scene.

Wang Anyi (b. 1954) is an author with a particularly broad range, which comes across in even the few of her works available in translation. In her early realist writing, such as *Lapse of Time* (1982, English 1988) and *Baotown* (1984, English 1989), she concentrates on small-town and country life and the lives of women in particular. Her much larger work, *The Song of Everlasting Sorrow* (1995, English 2008), is the story of a strong female figure, this time against a backdrop of four decades of history in Shanghai, from the years just before the People's Republic was founded to the 1980s.

Decade-spanning, panoramic novels that cover large stretches of recent Chinese history have appeared in large numbers, and many make for satisfying reading as comprehensive one-volume overviews of the tumultuous changes the country has undergone. Whereas *The Song of Everlasting Sorrow* is very much driven by personality, a novel like **Zhang Wei**'s (b. 1956) *The Ancient Ship* (1987, English 2008), which describes more or less the same span of history, uses many more strands in weaving its broad tapestry. It is set in the fictional noodle-producing city of Wali, a locale very different from Shanghai, with its days of glory and strategic importance long gone. Several of **Yu Hua**'s (b. 1960) novels are similarly far-reaching: *To Live* (1993, English 2003) offers a much quicker tour of the decades, its protagonist beginning as a ne'er-do-well whose transformations bring only limited redemption, while *Cries in the Drizzle* (1991, English 2007) uses the Cultural Revolution as a starting point. The massive *Brothers* (2005–2006, English 2009) is the most elaborate of his fictions, chronicling the story of two (step)brothers, who, despite their differences, maintain their bond in rapidly modernizing China. The violent, sex-filled narrative provides some insight into recent changes in Chinese society, but by the standards of Western fiction, it is far from straightforward in how the story unfolds.

Among other works of fiction covering a narrower historical time frame, **Bai Hua**'s (b. 1956) *The Remote Country of Women* (1988, English 1995), with its two-track narrative and use of the matrilineal Mosuo ethnic group, is an interesting take on the Cultural Revolution. Meanwhile, the eminent author **Jia Pingwa**'s (b. 1952) *Turbulence* (1987, English 1991), a weighty rural epic of the 1980s, describes a time of uncertainty when corruption is rife and the locals, deprived of the prop of Maoist absolutism, mix old and new superstitions and beliefs. The novel has appeal, but, like too many Chinese novels in translation, both the prose and the plot have a rough feel.

Among Chinese authors working on the mainland, **Mo Yan** (b. 1955)—a pen name meaning "don't speak"—was already one of the best-known Chinese writers abroad even before he was awarded the 2012 Nobel Prize. His novels are ambitious and expansive, as he "with hallucinatory realism merges folk tales, history and the contemporary" (as the Nobel commendation expressed it). The creative reach of his work fulfills many of the expectations of contemporary international fiction. He uses and defies conventions in a variety of colorful versions of China, grounding several of his novels in the same locale (Northeast Gaomi Township in Shandong) and featuring a character named Mo Yan but also constantly spinning out his stories in new ways. Widely translated even before he received the Nobel Prize, all the English versions of his work were translated by Howard Goldblatt, giving them a welcome consistency.

Beginning with *Red Sorghum* (1986, English 1993), Mo Yan has worked on a grand scale, culminating in the most all-encompassing of his novels, *Big Breasts and Wide Hips* (1996, English 2005), a reworking (and summing up) of Chinese history in the twentieth century and a monumental work even its abridged English version. *Life and Death Are Wearing Me Out* (2006, English 2008) leads yet another protagonist through recent Chinese history, this time in several animal reincarnations. *Sandalwood Death* (2001, English 2013) is a more naturalistic novel set in Gaomi around the turn of the nineteenth century. A panoramic historical novel, it also describes German colonial activity in the China of that time, specifically the disruptive construction of the Qingdao–Jinan Railway. Mo Yan's fiction contains much violence and bloody excess. Among the most entertaining of his works is the more tempered, consumption-focused novel *The Republic of Wine* (1992, English 2000), in which he artfully combines the particularly Chinese obsession with food (and alcohol) with sly social and political criticism.

Unlike Mo Yan, **Su Tong** (b. 1963) situates his vivid and brutal fictions largely in the past. The three novellas in the collection *Raise the Red Lantern* (1990, English 1993) are set in the 1930s, and *Rice* (1991, English 1995) and *My Life as Emperor* (1992, English 2005) are also, at least nominally, historical. Setting supplies some of the atmosphere, but Su revels in keen description and storytelling, which produces a jarring effect, given the bleak worlds he presents.

While the realistic and epic are dominant in recent Chinese fiction, some experimental fiction also has been translated. Yu Hua's earliest prose, including the stories collected in *The Past and the Punishment* (English 1996), was considered avant-garde, and by comparison, his better-known later novels are much more restrained and realistic. Tibetan-Chinese author **Zhaxi Dawa** (Tashi Dawa, b. 1959) is one of the authors who has most emphatically embraced magical realism, as in his collection *A Soul in Bondage* (English 1992), and the familiar feel this gives his creative stories, coupled with their exotic local color, makes his work attractive to Western audiences. The leading avant-garde author, and one well represented in translation, is the challenging **Can Xue** (b. 1953). Her work clearly stands apart from most of the available Chinese fiction and, with its detailed focus on the individual, frequently veers into the surreal and feels closer to Western literary traditions. A different and more approachable form of literary experimentation is found in the works of **Han Shaogong** (b. 1953), first in his collection *Homecoming?* (1985, English 1992) but then especially in *A Dictionary of Maqiao* (1996, English 2003), a novel presented in the form of dictionary entries. This record is made by a lexicographer-cum-narrator sent to a remote region in the south of China for reeducation during the Cultural Revolution. As Bai Hua did with the Mosuo in *The Remote Country of Women*, Han uses an ethnic group distinct from the Han Chinese majority to good effect, but his is also a novel about language itself. Despite what is inevitably lost in translation, *A Dictionary of Maqiao* is one of the most impressive contemporary Chinese works available in English, the multilayered text engaging on all its different levels, from its commentary on the policies of the Cultural Revolution to the eye-opening use of language.

   Zhu Wen's (b. 1967) collection of stories *I Love Dollars* (English 2007) describes China in the 1990s when commercialism has moved to the fore. The extremes of this embrace of Western consumerism, coupled with the newfound sexual freedom, can be found in the novels of a number of young women writers, such as **Wei Hui**'s (b. 1973) *Shanghai Baby* (1999, English 2002) and **Mian Mian**'s (b. 1970) *Candy* (1999, English 2003). These are novels of the new international cosmopolitanism, with the great Chinese urban centers now like any other city in the world, right down to the racy chick lit that exposes the (relatively) wild ways of a new generation. Unsurprisingly, Wei's protagonist has a trendy Western name like Nikki—and is known as Coco—and much of the sequel to *Shanghai Baby*, entitled *Marrying Buddha* (2005, English 2005), takes place in New York. While they are of dubious literary value, these works do at least suggest some of the changes Chinese society has undergone.

   Engagement with the past continues as well. **Yan Lianke**'s (b. 1958) winning satire, *Serve the People!* (2005, English 2007), set in the Cultural Revolution, is occasionally crude but describes an isolated corner of that time much more benignly than might be expected.

Yan, however, also goes about smashing the Maoist idol enthusiastically (and literally) in a way that even now must seem shocking in China. Yan's *Lenin's Kisses* (2004, English 2012) features the isolated village of Liven, which is almost entirely populated by the disabled. The novel pits local leader Grandma Mao Zhi, who wants the town to be able to "withdraw from society" and the control of regional authorities, and one of those regional leaders, Chief Liu, who has the harebrained idea of buying Lenin's embalmed corpse and building a new mausoleum near Liven, creating what he believes will be an incredible tourist attraction. The inspired, multilayered satire is amusing and revealing, but *Lenin's Kisses* is unwieldy in size and scope—in contrast to the more pointed *Serve the People!* Another of Yan's novels, **Dream of Ding Village** (2006, English 2011), is partly based on a blood-selling scandal in China from the 1990s. In this work of grim humor, Yan describes a provincial town shattered after the establishment of a blood-plasma collection enterprise there leads to many of the locals becoming infected by HIV and dying of AIDS.

KEEP IN MIND

- *Wang in Love and Bondage* (English 2007), a collection of three short novellas, is the only fiction by **Wang Xiaobo** (1952–1997) that has been translated, but the vigorous style of these creative works suggests an author who should live up to the high reputation that has preceded him.
- **Wang Shuo**'s (b. 1958) cartoonish *Please Don't Call Me Human* (1989, English 2000) and *Playing for Thrills* (1989, English 1998) are too broad in their satire to be entirely satisfying, but for a dizzying spin across large swaths of urban Chinese society, they offer a great deal of material.
- **Mai Jia**'s (b. 1964) *Decoded* (2002, English 2014), the first of this very popular author's works available in English, is presented as a documentary account of a mathematical genius enlisted by the state to work in cryptography. Though unpolished, this narrative offers a fascinating picture of intellectual life in Maoist China.

Jiang Rong's (b. 1946) epic *Wolf Totem* (2004, English 2008) is an astonishingly comprehensive indictment that also largely takes place during the Cultural Revolution. In idealizing the nomadic herdsmen of Inner Mongolia—and the wolf—the novel condemns both the Han Chinese national character and the Communist system. This prescriptive allegory is a difficult and largely unsatisfying read, of interest far more for what its immense popularity says about contemporary China than its literary qualities.

Expatriate Authors

The most pronounced effect of the Tiananmen Square massacre of 1989 and the subsequent government crackdown on Chinese literature was the consolidation of an expatriate establishment. The year 1989 and its aftermath led to a number of authors leaving China, as well as confirming the decision to stay abroad for others, including the 2000 Nobel laureate **Gao Xingjian** (b. 1940).

In his novella *Stick Out Your Tongue* (1987, English 2006), **Ma Jian** (b. 1953) presents simple everyday scenes that are realistic depictions of Tibetan life; considered defamatory, the book was sufficient to make him an author non grata. Now long settled in London, he continues to write in Chinese, and his novels *The Noodle Maker* (1990, English 2004) and *Beijing Coma* (English 2008) remain centered on the mainland. *Beijing Coma*, in which Ma describes both the changing China of the 1990s and the bitter past for a protagonist who has been in a coma since being shot in Tiananmen Square, is one of the major novels of the post-1989 period. Painstakingly detailed, the long novel may, however, seem bloated.

Other authors who have settled in England and the United States have made the transition from writing in Chinese to writing in English. **Geling Yan** (b. 1959) published several novels in China before emigrating, and her novel *The Banquet Bug* (2006) is the first she wrote in English. Its entertainingly spun-out premise of an unemployed worker posing as a journalist to sneak into fancy and elaborate official banquets allows her, like Mo Yan in *The Republic of Wine*, to cleverly mix the Chinese obsession with food with a story of corruption. In an effective twist, **Xiaolu Guo** (b. 1973) made the transition of going from one language to another the basis of the first novel she wrote in English, *A Concise Chinese-English Dictionary for Lovers* (2007). That novel focuses on émigré life, but her *Village of Stone* (2003, English 2004) and *20 Fragments of a Ravenous Youth* (2008), an English adaptation of her first novel, which she had originally written in Chinese, revolve around Chinese conditions.

Both **Ha Jin** (b. 1956) and **Yiyun Li** (b. 1972) write in English and have become critical favorites in the United States. A number of French-writing Chinese authors have achieved considerable international success, including **Dai Sijie** (b. 1954), whose works seem most attuned to the Western reader. *Balzac and the Little Chinese Seamstress* (French 2000, English 2001) is one of the most approachable tales of the Cultural Revolution, and its lessons about the power of literature offer a pleasing affirmation of Western ideals. *Mr. Muo's Travelling Couch* (French 2003, English 2005) is a quixotic comedy of psychoanalysis illustrating how even in modern times East and West still are separated. In her novels, including the somewhat rushed *The Girl Who Played Go* (French 2001, English 2003) and *Empress* (French 2003, English 2006), the much younger **Shan Sa** (b. 1972) prefers to look back to earlier times.

Although **Gao Xingjian** is a well-known dramatist, his two major works of prose, the novels *Soul Mountain* (1989, English 1999) and *One Man's Bible* (1999, English 2002), are intricate and deeply personal quest novels. In both works, Gao experiments with a variety of formal approaches (and narrators) in his philosophical-literary explorations. As such, the works differ from the generally realist fiction that makes up the bulk of Chinese fiction available in translation and, despite their occasional difficulties, are worth reading.

KEEP IN MIND

- **Hong Ying** (b. 1962) spent more than a decade living abroad, starting in 1991, but also continued to write in Chinese. Her novels were controversial for their explicitness in the People's Republic but agreeably sexy by mainstream Western standards.

TIBET AND ELSEWHERE

A significant amount of the Chinese fiction available in translation uses locales and characters outside the traditional Han Chinese heartland. In part, this is a reflection of the experiences of their authors, who were sent to these remote areas during the Cultural Revolution. These experiences range from Wang Meng's long internal exile among the Uighurs to Jiang Rong's familiarity with Inner Mongolia. Authors have also found these isolated pockets of different cultures useful as cover in criticizing that dominant state. Tibet, the most prominent autonomous region in the People's Republic, holds a special place, especially as Chinese primacy over the territory (and culture) is often questioned abroad. The fate of Ma Jian's *Stick Out Your Tongue*, with its depiction of the area and its people that departs from the official line, suggests that fiction dealing with Tibetan issues is subject to closer government scrutiny. Thus **Xinran** (b. 1958) did not finish writing *Sky Burial* (English 2004), which describes life in Tibet in more recent times, until she was established in London. Nevertheless, some works are coming from the mainland about Tibet, like Zhaxi Dawa's stories and **Alai**'s (b. 1959) *Red Poppies* (1998, English 2002), set during the time shortly before the Communist takeover of China, that are of some interest. Coming from a completely different angle, the India-based Tibetan activist **Jamyang Norbu** (b. 1949) creatively re-created Sherlock Holmes's missing years (spent in Tibet, according to Arthur Conan Doyle) in *The Mandala of Sherlock Holmes* (published in the United States as *Sherlock Holmes: The Missing Years*; 1999). Here, Holmes protects the young thirteenth Dalai Lama as

Jamyang mixes fact and fiction in a pastiche that also transposes elements from Rudyard Kipling's (1865–1936) *Kim* (1901).

TAIWAN

Even during the Maoist years, the mainland has remained the focus of foreign literary attention. Although a largely independent literary culture has developed in the Republic of China (Taiwan), it has received considerably less attention in the English-speaking world.

Li Qiao's (b. 1934) trilogy *Wintry Night* (1975–1980, English 2001) is incompletely translated but is an evocative epic covering roughly five decades in the lives of several generations of Hakka settlers in Taiwan through the end of the Japanese occupation of the island. Several works describe the history and post-1949 evolution of Taiwan. **Tung Nien**'s (Dong Nian, b. 1950) *Setting Out* (1993, English 1998), presented in vignettes from a child's perspective, creates an interesting vantage point to look at the Taiwan of the 1960s, while **Pai Hsien-yung**'s (Bai Xianyong, b. 1937) collections *Taipei People* (1971, English 2000) and *Wandering in the Garden, Waking from a Dream* (1968, English 1982) present much larger casts of characters. The two parts of **Chang Ta-Chun**'s (Zhang Dachun, b. 1957) trilogy published in English as *Wild Kids* (1993–1996, English 2000) explore growing up in more recent times, including the attraction of Taiwan's darker underside.

Chu Tien-wen's (Zhu Tianwen, b. 1956) *Notes of a Desolate Man* (1994, English 1999) and Pai's *Crystal Boys* (1983, English 1990) are among a number of Taiwanese works depicting homosexuality, a subject that mainland Chinese authors have been much more reluctant—and, because of disapprobation by the authorities, less able—to address.

Wang Wen-Hsing (Wang Wenxing, b. 1939) is one of Taiwan's leading authors. His *Backed Against the Sea* (1981, English 1993) shows some of the originality that, until recently, seems to have flourished more in Taiwan than on the mainland. The novel consists of a confessional rant by a down-on-his-luck narrator who is on the run and hiding in the Taiwanese boondocks. Both angry and funny, *Backed*

KEEP IN MIND

- **Li Ang's** (b. 1952) *The Butcher's Wife* (1983, English 1986) and **Li Yung-p'ing's** (Li Yongping, b. 1947) *Retribution* (1986, English 2003) are brutal works in which the main characters are driven to murder.
- **Wang Chen-ho's** (Wang Zhenhe, 1940–1990) *Rose, Rose, I Love You* (1984, English 1998) is a rare example of a humorous Chinese novel. The comic relief in its depiction of how the locals prepare for the visit of American GIs is an amusing and insightful view of misconceived East–West cultural expectations.

Against the Sea is also stylistically innovative in trying to convey all this pent-up anger and frustration. The more approachable *Family Catastrophe* (1972, English 1995) also creatively presents a dark story, with the disappearance of the father of the protagonist, Fan Yeh, being the final piece of the long decline and collapse of this family.

Chinese Genre Fiction

Lighter and more popular Chinese fare has recently appeared in translation, but much of it covers old ground. As in most totalitarian states, the People's Republic had no tradition of mystery and detective fiction, and until recently, only a few novels that could be described as crime fiction, such as Wang Shuo's *Playing for Thrills*, have appeared in translation. For now, almost all the mysteries available in English are those written by foreigners or emigrants, with **Qiu Xiaolong's** (b. 1953) Chen Cao series and **Diane Wei Liang's** (b. 1966) Mei Wang series being the most notable examples. Science fiction fares even worse, with Taiwanese author **Chang Hsi-Kuo's** (Zhang Xiguo, b. 1944) ambitious *The City Trilogy* (1984–1991, English 2003) and **Cixin Liu's** (b. 1963) trilogy that begins with *The Three-Body Problem* (2006, English 2014) among the few examples that are of any interest.

One very popular Chinese literary genre that has received limited attention abroad is *wuxia*, martial arts fiction. Fortunately, several works by the master of the genre, Hong Kong author **Louis Cha** (Jin

Yong, b. 1924), are available in English, including the early *The Book and the Sword* (1956, English 2004) and the culmination of his work, the three-volume *The Deer and the Cauldron* (1972, English 1997–2003). Whereas much recent Chinese fiction leans heavily on Western literature and its traditions, Cha's adventure novels are much closer in spirit and style to some of the popular classic Chinese epics. Cha's books are superior historical entertainment and a welcome escapist alternative.

Japan

After centuries of self-imposed and almost complete isolation, Japan signed the first of several treaties in 1854 opening the country to both international trade and culture. By the early twentieth century, contemporary Japanese writing, often shaped by European and American influences, attracted considerable attention abroad. Among the literatures written in non-European languages, Japanese was easily the most prominent abroad during the twentieth century, and with authors ranging from **Yukio Mishima** (1925–1970) to **Banana Yoshimoto** (b. 1964) and **Haruki Murakami** (b. 1949), was the only one from which writers of both literary and popular fiction found large international audiences.

With a large, well-educated population that has sustained a strong reading culture and, for the most part, the absence of governmental interference in the form of radical censorship or suppression, literary production has thrived. Most of what has been translated into English, however, are the works of relatively few authors.

Modern Classics

Ryūnosuke Akutagawa (1892–1927) remains the quintessential Japanese author. His output consists mainly of short stories, ranging from retellings of familiar Japanese tales and myths to introspective confessional accounts typical of the *shishōsetsu* genre—the so-called I-novel. With stories set in many different historical periods, including the two on which Akira Kurosawa's film *Rashōmon* (1950) is based, as well as supernatural tales and contemporary stories of early-twentieth-century life in Japan, Akutagawa's work remains the most accessible introduction to Japanese literature. Nothing resembling a collected edition of Akutagawa's work is available in English, and his best-known stories must be sought out in various collections and renderings. Jay Rubin's new translation in the Penguin Classics collection **Rashōmon and Seventeen Other Stories** (2006) is currently the best available.

Jun'ichirō Tanizaki (1886–1965) bridges several eras, his first works published during the Meiji period (1868–1912) and his last novel, *Diary of a Mad Old Man,* in 1962 (English 1965). In addition, his translation of the great Japanese classic *The Tale of Genji* (early eleventh century) into modern Japanese played a major role in the revival of that text. Fascinated by the novelty and art of the West in his younger years, Tanizaki eventually turned back to Japanese culture and tradition, a shift conveyed in **Some Prefer Nettles** (1929, English 1955), in which the main character, Kaname, is first presented as enamored of Western culture but then finds his interest in Eastern tradition reawakened in a story revolving around the breakup of his marriage. Tanizaki's novel of a family living in 1930s Osaka, **The Makioka Sisters** (1948, English 1957), is his magnum opus and a wonderful, if fairly traditional, work. In the novel, the two eldest sisters of this family in decline already are married, and much of the plot centers on finding a husband for the third while the youngest waits her turn. Tanizaki's narrative is detailed and occasionally slow but offers a vivid portrait of the Japan of that time. Always a sensualist, Tanizaki's late works, **The Key** (1956, English 1961) and *Diary of a Mad Old Man,* are remarkably intimate novels written in diary form—in the case of *The Key*, the diaries of both husband and wife. Both are filled with sexual tensions and frustrations, even though *Diary of a Mad Old Man* is a great comic work.

The first Japanese author to win the Nobel Prize, **Yasunari Kawabata** (1899–1972), may seem to meet Western expectations of Japanese exoticism and sensibilities more consistently than do any of the other major authors, in both content and style, particularly in works like **Snow Country** (1937, English 1956), with its memorable geisha character. Nostalgia for old ideals, purity, and refinement is pervasive in his delicate fiction. Among Kawabata's other novels of note is *The Master of Go* (1954, English 1972), which uses the board game as a metaphor for the contest between the old and new.

The most notorious Japanese author, and one of its greatest, is **Yukio Mishima** (1925–1970). Like Kawabata, he took his own life, but the two acts could hardly have been more different. Kawabata slipped away almost quietly, but after a failed attempt to start a nationalist military uprising, Mishima staged a very public ritual suicide (*seppuku*) as he disemboweled himself and then was beheaded by an acolyte. Not surprisingly, Mishima's fiction is full of tortured souls who act out. A prolific author, he burst on the scene with an impressive autobiographical novel of a man hiding his homosexuality from society, **Confessions of a Mask** (1949, English 1958). Mizoguchi, the protagonist of what is arguably Mishima's best novel, **The Temple of the Golden Pavilion** (1956, English 1959), is an even more tortured outsider, a self-destructive youth who burns down the famous Kinkaku Temple. Loosely based on an actual incident, Mishima fashioned a philosophical novel around this sensational plot, with the temple a symbol of beauty and perfection that the protagonist, an unattractive stutterer, is driven to destroy. The disturbing **The Sailor Who Fell from Grace with the Sea** (1963, English 1965), in which a young adolescent turns on the man who falls in love with his widowed mother, is another fine work. Mishima's tetralogy, **The Sea of Fertility** (1968–1970, English 1972–1974), is his impressive massive final work of fiction. The four volumes, with their different styles and settings, cover much of the twentieth century. One character, Shigekuni

Honda, figures prominently throughout all four, and another character appears in a different reincarnation in each of them.

Despite being Japan's only other Nobel laureate (in 1994), a considerable amount of **Kenzaburō Ōe**'s (b. 1935) writing remains unavailable in English. The variety of what he has written during a career now spanning half a century may have something to with that, as he is an author that is difficult to pin down. With their sometimes bewildering and portentous titles—*Teach Us to Outgrow Our Madness* (1969, English 1977), *The Day He Himself Shall Wipe My Tears Away* (published in *Teach Us to Outgrow Our Madness*; 1972, English 1977)—a number of his books may also seem relatively inaccessible. Uneven and often challenging, and with even more translation issues than usual for Japanese fiction, many of them are nevertheless worth reading.

KEEP IN MIND

- **Saiichi Maruya**'s (1925–2012) *Singular Rebellion* (1972, English 1986) is a broad and gently comic novel of a widower who does not quite fit the expected Japanese mold, especially after he marries a much younger woman, offering amusing insight into Japanese life in the late 1960s. *A Mature Woman* (1992, English 1995), with its newspaper setting, satirizes more recent times, with a variety of organizations and people jostling for advantages in a novel of unexpected turns and consequences.

- **Kōbō Abe**'s (1924–1993) fiction often has science fiction or surreal premises, such as *Inter Ice Age 4* (1958, English 1970), an early novel warning of the effects of global warming. Several works feature alienated protagonists, including Abe's classic *The Woman in the Dunes* (1962, English 1964), in which a man becomes trapped in a sandpit, an outsider in a world cut off from his own, and the unsettling *The Face of Another* (1964, English 1966), in which a disfigured scientist records his attempts to make a lifelike mask that will allow him to face and be accepted in the world at large again.

- **Morio Kita**'s (1927–2011) *The House of Nire* (1964; originally published in English separately as *The House of Nire*, 1984, and *The Fall of the House of Nire*, 1985) is a grand and often humorous family epic spanning much of the twentieth century.

Ōe's oldest son has been brain-damaged since his birth in 1963, and many of Ōe's works feature boys who are similarly handicapped. One of the first of these, *A Personal Matter* (1964, English 1968), is also his best. The novel tells the story of Bird, a father who wants to let his deformed baby die but eventually accepts him. This is an unsparing account of the man's weakness in the face of adversity.

Other works by Ōe are overtly political, focusing on Japanese issues of national identity in a post–World War II world in which the United States wields considerable power. *The Silent Cry* (1967, English 1974), the story of two brothers that bridges contemporary history and an uprising from a century earlier, is the more interesting of these. The dangers of nuclear power and proliferation also have long been of concern to Ōe and inform some of his work. His somewhat long-winded novel about a religious cult, *Somersault* (1999, English 2003), was inspired by the sarin gas attacks on the Tokyo subway carried out by the Aum Shinrikyo group in 1995.

The Next Generation

The old guard of Japanese authors remained dominant well into the 1980s, and only then did a new generation of Japanese authors begin to make their mark in English translation. **Haruki Murakami** (b. 1949) has emerged as the most successful of them, but for a time it appeared that **Banana Yoshimoto** (b. 1964) would be the leading new voice. Her first novel, *Kitchen* (1988, English 1993), was radically different from most of the Japanese fiction to which English-speaking readers had been exposed. *Kitchen*'s charmingly straightforward, almost naive style, contemporary setting, and young woman's perspective were unlike the much more staid writing that heretofore had seemed to be the norm. Here was a story that was unabashedly popular fiction but that had enough pith and resonance to pass as more than just light entertainment. Yoshimoto has continued to find some success with her generally short novels of young protagonists dealing with loss, though in the American market she seems to have rather worn out her welcome. Her style has served her well, but she is best writing in smaller spaces; her one long novel, *Amrita* (1994, English 1997), feels aimless. Her quirky plots also can become convoluted, but works such as *NP* (1990, English 1994), with its cursed story of an author and then three of the story's would-be translators committing suicide, retain some appeal.

It is not surprising that **Haruki Murakami** (b. 1949) is more popular abroad than Yoshimoto. Considerably richer, Murakami's work offers much of what Yoshimoto's does and then some. His protagonists tend to be male and older than hers, and they share some traits with the author. Not quite loners, many live in relative isolation with only a few other significant figures in their lives; they also tend to be fairly passive. Music, especially jazz, figures prominently, and many of Murakami's pop references are to Western authors and musicians, lending the books a comfortable familiarity for English-speaking readers. His fiction often has a sense of nostalgia, too, as well as the melancholy of love that circumstances do not allow to be sustained.

The stories of *Blind Willow, Sleeping Woman* (English 2006), written over a quarter of a century, are a good introduction to Murakami's work, but this collection is a big dose of short pieces by an author who fares better when he has more space to allow his fiction to unfold. The very satisfying *Norwegian Wood* (1987, English 1989, 2000) is a relatively conventional realist novel, centered on the narrator's university years in the late 1960s and the two women who played a significant role in his life as he matured to adulthood. *South of the Border, West of the Sun* (1992, English 1998) is like an echo of *Norwegian Wood*, the focus here on the present, with the protagonist still clinging to some of his past as he faces the uncertainties of the future. *After Dark* (2004, English 2007), set during a single night in Tokyo and full of chance encounters, is still fundamentally realistic, while the airy *Sputnik Sweetheart* (1999, English 2001), a tale about unrequited loves, veers toward the mystic.

Several of Murakami's other works incorporate far more fantastical elements, some closer to science fiction. The very elaborate *Kafka on the Shore* (2002, English 2005) has two alternating plotlines. One follows a teenager running away from home, and the other is about an older man who underwent an unusual experience during World War II. This retiree has the ability to communicate with cats, a typical

Murakami touch that, in his presentation, is not as silly or absurd as it sounds. Even though the English translation of *The Wind-Up Bird Chronicle* (1995, English 1997) is a significantly diminished version of the Japanese original, it is among Murakami's strongest works, his fantastical predilections—which here also include psychic abilities, missing cats, and a dry well in which the narrator likes to spend time— contrast with events from World War II, which Murakami confronts head-on here.

Murakami's massive three-volume (with possibly a fourth to follow) *1Q84* (2009, 2010, English 2011) is the culmination of his work to date. It begins in the year 1984. First one and then both of the main characters, Aomame and Tengo, whose stories are told in alternating chapters, find themselves in another reality that is very similar but not identical to the 1984 they know, with minor (and a few greater) differences in the world around them, from history having taken slightly different courses to some changes in everyday details. (The Japanese word for the number 9 is *kyū*, pronounced like the English *q*, so the title—left unchanged from the Japanese to English version—also is a play on that idea.) Both Aomame and Tengo are loners in their thirties, and both are relatively content with their lifestyles. Tengo is working on a novel and teaches part time, but he finds his life thrown into disarray when he is asked to help polish a manuscript that has been submitted for a literary prize by a teenage girl named Fuka-Eri. The story is based on her own experiences in a cult from which she escaped when she was ten years old, but her novel reads more like an allegory or fable—with two moons in the sky and mysterious and supernatural "Little People"— than a realistic work. As it turns out, her story is not as fantastical as it first seemed, and those associated with it, including Fuka-Eri and Tengo, find themselves threatened. Aomame is a massage therapist, but she also works for a woman who helps women and girls who have suffered domestic violence and abuse and have nowhere else to turn, and it is this sideline that leads Aomame to become involved with the cult and its mysterious leader. It also turns out that Aomame and Tengo knew each other as children, and they seem fated to be reunited as a couple. The path down which Murakami leads them, however, is twisted and complicated, with many surprises. While arguably somewhat long-winded, *1Q84* rewards readers with its slow and steady buildup.

Ryū Murakami (b. 1952)—no relation to Haruki—writes considerably more explicit and rawer fiction, often presenting a darker, even brutal, side of contemporary Japanese life. The autobiographical *69* (1987, English 1993), narrated by a teenager and set in 1969, is not typical, being instead a fine look at life in a small city dominated then by an American military base. The same setting, but with slightly older and not yet wiser youths, figures in *Almost Transparent Blue* (1976, English 1977), which is a more graphic character study of aimless youths experimenting with sex and drugs. *Coin Locker Babies* (1980, English 1995) is Murakami's most complete and expansive critique of modern Japanese society, following the lives of two boys, Kiku and Hashi, who were abandoned by their mothers as infants. They wind up in their teens in a contaminated part of Tokyo called Toxitown and indulge in sex, drugs, rock 'n' roll, and pole-vaulting. Murakami strains mightily for shock effects in a particularly wild and violent ride of a novel, and it is his most impressive work.

More recent novels by Ryū Murakami, including *Piercing* (1994, English 2007) and *In the Miso Soup* (1997, English 2003), explore the duality in Japanese society of a surface that is formal, orderly, and polite, contrasted with a dark underbelly to which many just turn a blind eye. Murakami's fiction shows that underbelly as particularly dark and violent, with characters who find themselves caught up in more than they ever bargained for. *Audition* (2000, English 2009) is the best example of this, with its creepy premise of a widower letting himself be convinced that the way to find a new wife is to hold film auditions as a ruse to meet and audition women for the real-life role of romantic partner. Here again, neither appearance nor reality—both reflecting Japanese society—is what it seems to be, with horrible consequences.

Murakami's satirical farce *Popular Hits of the Showa Era* (1994, English 2011) is the most approachable of his novels, the violence and gore here so ridiculously over the top that they do not feel as real as they do in some of his other works. The novel pits two gangs against each other, each representing a specific demographic: a group of six disaffected and socially inept young men who occasionally get together but hardly consider themselves friends, and a group of divorcees in their late thirties who happen to share the same name, Midori. The two groups tangle, and their conflict quickly escalates into brutal violence (and then to the entirely absurd), the Midoris showing themselves quite capable of holding their own against the young men.

Two of the men from *Popular Hits of the Showa Era* also have cameo roles in Murakami's **From the Fatherland, with Love** (2005, English 2013), another ambitious work on the scale of his *Coin Locker Babies* but taking place mostly in 2011. The premise of the novel is a small group of North Korean infiltrators fixing the groundwork for a take-over of the Japanese city of Fukuoka. This in turn enables Murakami to portray an economically weakened Japan humbled by its relegation to secondary status on the global stage. In this cruelly comic thriller, a traditional culture of deference to seniority and official titles rather than competence undermines most of the Japanese efforts to counter the North Korean threat, thereby facilitating the foreign occupation of Japanese territory. While also offering insight into the rigid absolutism of North Korean society, *From the Fatherland, with Love* is a darkly humorous and blistering critique of modern Japanese society that also works as a traditional national-crisis thriller.

Translations of **Yoko Ogawa's** (b. 1962) fiction have finally started to appear in English, beginning with the three short novellas collected in *The Diving Pool* (English 2007) and the novel **The Housekeeper and the Professor** (2003, English 2009). *The Housekeeper and the Professor* is the story of a professor of mathematics whose short-term memory since an accident he had in 1975 has been limited to an eighty-minute span, after which he again forgets everything. Ogawa spins the clever premise well, although it is more of a conventional crowd-pleaser, and readers should be aware that it is very tame compared with most of her other work.

The stories in *The Diving Pool* display a controlled calm even as the female narrators slowly reveal a world that is ever so slightly and eerily deranged. In the remarkable **Revenge** (1998, English 2013), a cleverly connected cycle of stories that comes full circle, Ogawa manages a similar effect in shorter, sharper episodes. This book, whose pieces ultimately fit together so neatly that it also works as a novel, is the best introduction to the author. *Hotel Iris* (1996, English 2010) is the most deeply unsettling of Ogawa's works available in English. Here, the seventeen-year-old narrator, Mari, becomes involved with a much older man who works as a translator. Their relationship develops into a sexual one in which both of them enjoy her assuming a passive and often humiliated role, but the experimentation gets out of hand, leading to catastrophe. Although Ogawa succeeds in discomfiting readers, her narrator is too young to adequately convey the complexity of her situation.

The calm of **Hiromi Kawakami**'s (b. 1958) understated novels differs from that in Ogawa's, and they contain nothing nearly as sinister. Both *Manazuru* (2006, English 2010) and *The Briefcase* (published in Great Britain as *Strange Weather in Tokyo*; 2001, English 2012) feature female protagonists well into adulthood and their uncertainty about their relationships with specific men. *Manazuru* is narrated by a mother already in her forties whose husband simply vanished from her life more than a decade earlier, a loss that continues to haunt her. Tsukiko, the narrator of *The Briefcase*, describes how, when she was in her thirties, she met one of her old teachers and slowly and tentatively formed a romantic relationship. Kawakami gently and effectively explores in both works how characters who are in one way or another isolated find ways of allowing others into their lives and how they deal with absence.

Minae Mizumura (b. 1951) spent her teen years in the United States and went on to study at Yale but eventually returned to Japan. Her work is explicitly rooted in Japanese literary tradition, beginning with her untranslated first novel, an attempt to complete **Natsume Sōseki**'s (1867–1916) unfinished classic *Light and Darkness* (1916, English 1971, and as *Light and Dark*, 2013). In *A True Novel* (2002, English 2013), Mizumura appropriates the outlines of Emily Brontë's *Wuthering Heights* (1847) for her story but re-creates it in a fashion more reminiscent of Tanizaki than either Brontë's or Mizumura's contemporaries. Its lengthy prologue takes up nearly a fifth of the more than eight-hundred-

---

A JAPANESE EXPATRIATE WRITER

Yoko Tawada (b. 1960) has long lived in Germany and writes in both German and Japanese. *Where Europe Begins* (English 2002) contains work originally written in both languages, providing a good overview of her creative approaches. Two other collections are available in English translated from Japanese: the surreal *The Bridegroom Was a Dog* (1993, English 1998) and *Facing the Bridge* (English 2007), with its stories of foreigners out of place. Chantal Wright's revealing annotated "experimental translation" of one of Tawada's German texts, *Portrait of a Tongue* (2002, English 2013), offers a fascinating look at the process of translating.

---

page novel, in which Mizumura describes growing up on Long Island, as well as how she arrived at the story that is at the heart of *A True Novel*. This introductory section—a story within the story—chronicles the shaping of both the author and the authorial process between cultures. Mizumura's tale is nominally one of a Japanese man who achieves great success and the love of his life but, in its broad sweep, presents a fascinating picture of the changes in Japanese society and culture from the end of World War II to the turn of the twenty-first century.

Surrealism and Beyond

Yasutaka Tsutsui's (b. 1934) fiction is both surreal and comic. The collection *Salmonella Men on Planet Porno* (English 2006) ranges from science fiction to the relatively conventional, and Tsutsui almost invariably takes his tales in unexpected directions. His novel *Hell* (2003, English 2007) is a creative reimagining of what hell might be like, though it feels a bit more like a series of interconnected stories than a full-fledged novel. Tsutsui posits a device in *Paprika* (1993, English 2009) that allows users to see another person's dreams, and he imagines the possible consequences of those abusing it.

Hideo Okuda's (b. 1959) fiction is more realistic but also has a comic touch. Japanese humor does not always translate well, but

Okuda's work is among the funniest available in English. His stories of neurologist (or, rather, all-around head-case doctor) Dr. Irabu and his idiosyncratic treatment methods, *In the Pool* (2002, English 2006), are very enjoyable. *Lala Pipo* (2005, English 2008) is a cleverly structured novel of six episodes loosely but ingeniously connecting the lives of a number of rather sad and lonely figures, with a heavy emphasis on sex.

Many Japanese writers continue to rely a great deal on the supernatural, extrasensory, and paranormal, with **Koji Suzuki** (b. 1957) the best known of them. Several of his novels have been filmed in both Japan and Hollywood. Suzuki is best known for his **Ring** series, beginning with *Ring* (1991, English 2003), with its infamous videotape that promises that those who have watched it will die exactly a week later. This strained premise has a surprisingly clever resolution, and it is a passable thriller. The sequels *Spiral* (1995, English 2004) and *Loop* (1998, English 2006) have some promising twists, but Suzuki is less successful here. With its religious and personality cults, his most realistic novel, *Promenade of the Gods* (2003, English 2008), offers some insight into Japanese society but feels far too safe in what little it exposes and criticizes.

KEEP IN MIND

- The colorful but messy *Dream Messenger* (1989, English 1992) by **Masahiko Shimada** (b. 1961) is full of ideas, from an orphanage that rents out its wards to the protagonist's alter ego–cum–guardian spirit and some special dreaming talents.
- **Chiaki Kawamata**'s (b. 1948) science fiction novel *Death Sentences* (1984, English 2012) is a surreal literary thriller about the power of the written word.
- **Taichi Yamada**'s (b. 1934) fiction has a touch of the supernatural, as in *Strangers* (1987, English 2003), *In Search of a Distant Voice* (1986, English 2006), and the unsettling tale of a woman who grows younger and younger by stages and the impossible love affair she has with the narrator of *I Haven't Dreamed of Flying for a While* (1985, English 2008).

Young and Female

Japanese I-novels (self-absorbed fiction written in the first person) have recently become popular again, especially those featuring young women in a society that still emphasizes tradition but also in which traditional roles and both expectations and opportunities—for career and family—have changed for both men and women. The mix of innocence with spiritual and moral corruption in **Ami Sakurai**'s *Innocent World* (1996, English 2004) is typical. Its narrator, a girl cramming for her university entrance exams, also juggles a phone-sex job, an entirely inappropriate lover, and a number of family issues. **Mari Akasaka**'s (b. 1964) slightly confusingly entitled *Vibrator* (1999, English 2005)— it does not refer to the device—is not nearly as sensational, portraying a more mature young woman and focusing on the sense of isolation so prevalent in contemporary Japan. **Hitomi Kanehara**'s (b. 1983) work resembles that of Ryū Murakami, albeit from a younger and female perspective. Her incredibly successful first novel, *Snakes and Earrings* (2003, English 2005), is an effectively raw if somewhat immature text about a disaffected teenage narrator in a milieu of body piercing, tattooing, and casual violence and sex. The narrator in *Autofiction* (2006,

---

CELL PHONE FICTION

Cell phone fiction (*keitai shōsetsu*) is a growing phenomenon, especially in the Far East. These novels, written on and for mobile phones, have been immensely popular, and many of them have continued to sell astonishingly well even when published in traditional book form. The medium demands compression, so these "novels" tend to be simple narratives, heavy on dialogue and skimpy on description. With a predominantly female and young readership, the stories also tend to be variations on romances. As storytelling at its most basic level, most of it is of limited literary interest. Although the Japanese examples seem unlikely to translate well, the genre might very well spread, especially as texting technology improves and is even more widely adopted.

English 2008) is a married woman and a successful author in her early twenties, and the novel unfolds in reverse chronological order, describing how she was marked by earlier experiences.

Crime and Mystery

Crime fiction has long been a popular genre in Japan, and although not extensively translated into English, at least a smattering of the work of the main mystery and thriller writers is available. Still, even a leading writer like **Seishi Yokomizo** (1902–1981) is represented by only a single title in translation, *The Inugami Clan* (1951, English 2003). In addition, delays in reaching English-speaking markets are common, which often gives a dated feel to what crime fiction does become available. Several works by **Seicho Matsumoto** (1909–1992) have been translated, but a work like *Inspector Imanishi Investigates* (1961, English 1989) felt more like a period piece by the time it reached American audiences. Among the works by this older generation of writers, **Akimitsu Takagi**'s (1920–1995) have held up the best, especially the historical exoticism of an underground world shortly after the war, in *The Tattoo Murder Case* (1949, English 1998), and his picture of the Japanese financial world during the 1960s boom, in *The Informer* (1965, English 1971).

Miyuki Miyabe (b. 1960) resorts to the supernatural in novels such as *Crossfire* (1998, English 2006), in which the vengeful murderer has pyrokinetic powers (able to start fires through sheer willpower). Her novels like *All She Was Worth* (1992, English 1996) and *Shadow Family* (2001, English 2004) address, in a reasonably interesting fashion, contemporary Japanese issues ranging from debt collection to online role-playing games and their effect on individuals and society. **Natsuo Kirino** (b. 1951) is even more successful in psychological thrillers such as *Out* (1997, English 2003), with its group of women who work an overnight factory shift and are driven to murder, and the teenage girls in *Real World* (2003, English 2008), who are intrigued by a loser who kills his mother and who do not observe the norms expected of them. Unfortunately, the writing often bogs down these novels, as neither

---

KEEP IN MIND

- **Fuminori Nakamura**'s (b. 1977) philosophical explorations of crime and the individual can be found in his novels like *The Thief* (2009, English 2012) and ***Evil and the Mask*** (2010, English 2013).
- **Keigo Higashino** (b. 1958) has emerged as one of Japan's most popular writers abroad. His novels include ***The Devotion of Suspect X*** (2005, English 2011), in which physicist Manabu Yukawa brings his cerebral approach to the investigation of crimes.
- **Masako Togawa** (b. 1933) wrote elaborate psychological mysteries.
- **Shizuko Natsuki** (b. 1938) wrote thrillers with more sensational premises.

Kirino nor Miyabe seems able to create her stories without an awful lot of effort showing.

Kenzo Kitakata's (b. 1947) varied pulp thrillers with their strong protagonists—the *yakuza* (gangster) insider who narrates *Ashes* (1990, English 2003), the intense painter from ***Winter Sleep*** (1996, English 2005) who has killed before, and the former gang member who now runs a supermarket but still has a taste for his more exciting younger days in ***The Cage*** (1983, English 2006)—are consistently entertaining. Kitakata's tone is by far the most natural and convincing of any of the recent crop of Japanese crime writers.

South Korea and North Korea

A great deal of Korean literature remains inaccessible to English-speaking readers, and while the situation has begun to improve, the amount of modern fiction being translated conveys only a small sense of the very lively contemporary South Korean literary scene (and essentially none of the admittedly well-masked North Korean scene).

Long overshadowed and often dominated by China and Japan, few of the classics from Korea have been able to compete with those of its neighbors for foreign interest. *Three Generations* (1931, English 2005), by **Yom Sang-seop** (1897–1963), one of the leading writers from the time of the Japanese occupation, is one of the few novels of that period that is available in English, and it offers a good picture of Korean life during those years. The Japanese occupation, which lasted for most of the first half of the twentieth century, and then the calamitous Korean War that split the nation also limited the development of a literary culture. Only since the rapid economic expansion in South Korea that started in the 1960s has Korean literature truly begun to assert itself.

SOUTH KOREA

Beginning in the 1960s, a system organized around the family-domi-nated *chaebol* (business conglomerates) fueled South Korea's tremen-dous economic growth. **Cho Se-hŭi**'s (b. 1942) *The Dwarf* (1978, English 2006) is the most significant work of fiction dealing with the consequences of this rapid social and economic change. The linked stories entail characters from all walks of life affected by the shift to an industrial economy and the headlong rush to embrace global capitalism.

The classic novel cycle that **Park Kyong-ni** (1926–2008) began in 1969 and continued to publish over the next quarter century covers much of modern Korean history. The first tenth or so of the completed work was published in English in 1996 as *Land*, which was then reis-sued in 2008 as *Toji I*, along with a second volume. An earlier work, the family saga *The Curse of Kim's Daughters* (1962, English 2004), set in a fishing town in the first half of the twentieth century, is a more manageable size, though it has a similarly deliberate pace. But it is the epic *Toji* cycle, with its immense sweep, that is Park's most remarkable achievement, even though it is only partially accessible to English-speaking readers.

Yi Ch'ŏngjun's (1939–2008) *Your Paradise* (1976, English 2004, previously translated as *This Paradise of Yours*, 1986) is an allegorical novel taking place in the 1960s on an island leper colony. It describes the efforts of a new director to instill a sense of self-respect and worth into the inhabitants, as well as to join the island to the mainland, and how he meets with considerable resistance. This is an entertaining work about a closed society with its own special rules and habits, shaken up by the new administration. Even though parts of the allegory can seem almost painfully obvious—such as the plan to connect the island with the mainland—Yi does not allow everything to fall easily into place. It is a novel about failures, even when it is clear what the right thing to do is. More important, Yi tells a very good story.

Yi Munyol (b. 1948) is one of the leading contemporary Korean authors, and his novella about adolescence, *Our Twisted Hero* (1987,

English 2001), is a Korean version of a tale that in its broader outlines could be set anywhere, the cult of personality that develops around a charismatic schoolboy. Yi's biographical novel about the nineteenth-century poet Kim Pyong-yon, *The Poet* (1991, English 1995), is completely different in tone, but both works subtly address the issues of the authoritarian Korean regime in power when he wrote them.

The liberalization of the South Korean government in 1987 gave writers greater latitude in what they could publish. Even so, **Hwang Sok-Yong's** (b. 1943) visit to North Korea in 1989 was controversial and forced the author to spend several years abroad in voluntary exile. His novel *The Guest* (2001, English 2005) is set in the present but focuses on the still festering wounds of the Korean War, taking its protagonist to present-day North Korea. *The Old Garden* (2000, English 2009) is a fascinating look at the recent transformation of South Korea, even though this is just the backdrop for what is basically a love story. The main character was imprisoned in the wake of the 1980 Kwangju uprising and was released eighteen years later. He then learns from the diaries of his now dead lover about what he missed in the years while he was in prison. Although it is not available in translation, Hwang's much more circumspect ten-volume epic *Chang Kil-san,* written between 1974 and 1984, a period of strict censorship, is a historical bandit tale that enjoys continued popularity and is noteworthy because it is one of the few modern Korean works that have been successful (and tolerated) in both South and North Korea.

Jang-Soon Sohn's (b. 1935) *A Floating City on the Water* (1999, English 2004) is a curious South-meets-North novel that begins with a murder confession in 2014 before revealing something far more sensational that happened twenty years earlier when a South Korean and a North Korean met in Paris and fell in love. It is not ideology that forced them apart, but something equally divisive, and as with the two Koreas, the separation is not absolute but instead intimately connects them.

The very popular **Young-ha Kim** (b. 1968), who already has a large body of work, will likely become the most translated author of his generation. The narrator of his novel *I Have the Right to Destroy Myself* (1996, English 2007) is very detached and leads and pushes people toward suicide. *I Have the Right to Destroy Myself* is an existential novel of contemporary Korea with all the modern frills. Here the civil war and the military rule that had long overshadowed civilian life have been superseded by a culture and economy integrated into the global community, which nevertheless brings with it similarly fundamental concerns of identity and one's place in the world. With its cosmopolitan awareness, Kim's book is a transnational work, but it also reflects its specific locales, the clearest example to date of a Korean work of fiction that fits neatly in the international library. His more recent novel *Your Republic Is Calling You* (2006, English 2010) is a fascinating take on the North–South split and the Korean psyche. The main character, known as Kim Ki-yong, is a sleeper spy who infiltrated South Korea as a student. For two decades he has lived as a South Korean, with a wife and daughter, and in recent years he lost all contact with his northern handlers. The novel presents a day in the life of the family—the day when Kim suddenly receives an e-mail summoning him back to the North. Mixing everyday routine with these extraordinary circumstances allows the author to present issues of Korean identity and culture, as well as the divergent paths of South and North, in a novel that also works as a spy thriller.

Kyung-Sook Shin's (b. 1963) tale of a family reflecting on a mother's sacrifices, *Please Look After Mom* (2008, English 2011), is crushingly sentimental but certainly strikes many chords and has proved to be enormously successful, both in South Korea and abroad. The very popular author's *I'll Be Right There* (2010, English 2014) takes place in the 1980s and early 1990s and is a similarly broad exploration of family and personal connections.

NORTH KOREA

North Korea is one of the most isolated nations in the world, its official *juche* ideology of self-reliance precluding almost all foreign contact. Little of the literature from the country has leaked out over the decades, and almost none has been translated into English. **Han Sŏrya**

KEEP IN MIND

- The great **Ko Un** (b. 1933) is South Korea's foremost modern poet, but he has also written some fiction. *Little Pilgrim* (1991, English 2005) is his major prose work. Loosely based on an ancient Buddhist sutra, the novel describes the spiritual journey of a young boy and his encounters with fifty-three beings who guide him toward enlightenment. For a time, Ko Un was a Buddhist monk, and *Little Pilgrim* is somewhat weighed down by its spiritual earnestness but is still well worthwhile.
- Perhaps **Choi In-hoon**'s (Ch'oe In-hun, b. 1936) best novel is *The Square* (1961, English 1985, 2014), which examines the Korean War and the North–South split. His *A Grey Man* (1963, English 1988) also is worth reading.
- Two novellas by **Lee Oyoung** (b. 1934) are collected in *The General's Beard* (English 2002). The title piece (1967) is a variation on the detective story involving a novel also entitled *The General's Beard*. The second novella, *Phantom Legs* (1969), is a story in which a work by Stendhal functions as a constant frame of reference and counterpart.
- **Jang Eun-jin**'s (b. 1976) *No One Writes Back* (2009, English 2013) is a well-crafted and moving road novel that slowly reveals itself to be more than it initially seems.
- The collection of three longer stories by **Ch'oe Yun** (b. 1953), *There a Petal Silently Falls* (English 2008), addresses some of the major Korean issues: the 1980 Kwangju uprising in one story and the consequences of the divided state in another.
- **Lee Seung-U**'s (b. 1959) *The Reverse Side of Life* (1992, English 2005) is a book about a writer putting together a book about another writer. Its approach is interesting and presents a good picture of Korea.

(1900–ca. 1970) was one of the leading exponents of what was in effect the mandated socialist realist school of writing. His novella *Jackals* (1951) is available in B. R. Myers's study *Han Sŏrya and North Korean Literature* (1994), which itself gives a useful overview of North Korean literature. More recent examples of fiction from the self-styled Democratic People's Republic can be found only in anthologies, notably *Literature from the "Axis of Evil"* (2006), which includes an excerpt from the most discussed North Korean novel of recent times, **Hong**

Seok-jung's (b. 1941) historical novel *Hwangjini* (2002). This is one of the rare pieces of North Korean fiction that was also published in the South, where it was quite successful. If any North Korean novel were to be translated in full into English, it would be this one.

Ironically, the most insightful fictional portrayals of North Korea come from writers working outside its borders, such as Hwang Sok-Yong's *The Guest*. **Hyejin Kim**'s "novel of North Korea," *Jia* (2007), is a workmanlike effort with good local color, especially in its depiction of everyday life after the death of Kim Il Sung in 1994. Perhaps the most appealing works set in North Korea, however, are the pseudonymous **James Church**'s quite convincing Inspector O novels, beginning with *A Corpse in the Koryo* (2006), the mystery genre again proving particularly accommodating to the presentation of the foreign and unfamiliar.

Oceania

Australia, New Zealand, and South Pacific

AUSTRALIA

Australia now has a strong local publishing industry, but for a long time, many local authors depended on publishing abroad to reach a larger and more discerning readership. Indeed, many of the best-known Australian authors have benefited from living in proximity to the English-speaking publishing hubs of London and New York. **Christina Stead** (1902–1983), **Shirley Hazzard** (b. 1931), **Janette Turner Hospital** (b. 1942), and **Peter Carey** (b. 1943) all have spent much of their careers abroad. Even when writing about Australia, they and such best-selling authors as **Colleen McCullough** (1937–2015) and **Morris West** (1916–1999) often enjoyed their first, greater success elsewhere.

For much of the twentieth century, Australian literature seemed to have two tiers, domestic and expatriate, though by the close of the century, this divide had become rather artificial. Nevertheless, a conservative literary culture and insular national pride led to, for example, Christina Stead's being denied a major Australian literary award in 1967 simply because she lived abroad. The separation no longer appears as pronounced in Australia itself, but much of Australia's domestically published fiction remains cut off from the rest of the English-speaking world.

Nobel laureate **Patrick White** (1912–1990) remains, with his imposing personality and large varied output, the towering figure in Australian fiction, even though his fiction has not always been as wholeheartedly embraced in his homeland as it was in the United States and Great Britain. His grand but often dark and critical epics of Australia like *The Tree of Man* (1955), *Voss* (1957), and *Riders in the Chariot* (1961) represented a considerable advance from the straightforward realism that had dominated Australian fiction. *Voss,* based on a real-life explorer who trekked across Australia in the mid-nineteenth century, is a story of mythmaking in a nation that has not yet been completely mapped, both literally and figuratively. *Voss* is also a surprisingly poignant love story, which, since the two lovers are separated, is played out almost entirely in Voss's and Laura Trevelyan's minds.

More experimental novels by White include *The Vivisector* (1970), a fascinating attempt to describe the life and work of a visual artist, and the faux memoirs of the very unreliable Alex Xenophon Demirjian Gray, *Memoirs of Many in One* (1986). Sexual ambiguity and identity are prominent themes in many of the homosexual author's works. *The Twyborn Affair* (1979) is the most intense of White's novels concerning questions of identity, with a protagonist who appears in a different guise in each of the novel's three parts.

Much of **Peter Carey**'s (b. 1943) fiction takes place elsewhere, but Australia nevertheless figures prominently throughout his work. Without detracting from the stories themselves, Australian identity—national and personal—and the country's myths always are central themes.

Many of the protagonists in Carey's novels cannot manage to live entirely within the bounds of law, and as a consequence, they frequently find themselves as outcasts. Several are con men and a few are—at least in the eyes of the law—outright criminals. Carey's characters often have a somewhat hapless yet still noble desperation, as they usually mean well, but their actions, such as the kidnapping in *His Illegal Self* (2008) and the forged poetry in *My Life as a Fake* (2003), seem to spin out of their control. Several of his protagonists admit to being liars, among the many forms of fakery and imposture throughout Carey's fiction—involving paintings, poems, and especially identity—and he is expert at playing with the resulting sense of uncertainty. From the Dickensian *Jack Maggs* (1997), a reworking of Charles Dickens's *Great Expectations* (1861), to the convincingly unpolished voice of Ned Kelly (1855–1880) in his novel about the historic Australian outlaw, *True History of the Kelly Gang* (2000), and the narrator's garrulous flood of invention in *Illywhacker* (1985), Carey displays a remarkable stylistic range.

Most of **Tim Winton**'s (b. 1960) fiction is set in his native Western Australia. He chronicles the lives and changing times in this somewhat remote region in books that strike a chord among Australians and have also been widely embraced abroad. Winton's depiction of his homeland and the language he uses are carefully balanced between the exaggeratedly rough and the romanticized versions of Australia, giving his fiction an air of authenticity. *Cloudstreet* (1991), his saga of two very different families living in the same house for the first two decades after World War II, is among the most popular novels of Australian life and one of the most representative texts to come out of the country.

Although Winton's more narrowly focused novels, such as the coming-of-age surfing novel *Breath* (2008), with its abyss of risks tempting its characters in ever deeper, are satisfying, his broader novels, like *The Riders* (1995) and *Dirt Music* (2001), are better. *The Riders* is a rare foray abroad for Winton. It is a dark, unusual, and uncomfortably revealing novel in which the Australian protagonist, Scully, goes searching for his wife, who disappeared while she was coming with their daughter to join him and begin their new life in Ireland.

Murray Bail (b. 1941) has published only a few novels, but he is a major figure in contemporary Australian literature. Although his fiction, in which storytelling often plays a significant role, has the feel of being carefully constructed, the artificiality of his precise sentences and stories is pleasing. The sense of wonder, and the wonderful, in the

---

KEEP IN MIND

- **David Malouf**'s (b. 1934) large body of work includes his novel about Ovid, *An Imaginary Life* (1978), as well as *The Complete Stories* (2007).
- **Richard Flanagan**'s (b. 1961) work includes the artfully constructed *Gould's Book of Fish* (2001), a "novel in twelve fish," and the Man Booker Prize–winning *The Narrow Road to the Deep North* (2014).
- **Alexis Wright**'s (b. 1950) *Carpentaria* (2006) is an epic of Aboriginal life.
- **Gerald Murnane** (b. 1939) wrote a short but profound exploration, *The Plains* (1982), and also a brilliant meditation on fiction, reading, and writing, *Barley Patch* (2009).
- The great poet **Les Murray**'s (b. 1938) wonderful novel in verse is *Fredy Neptune* (1998).
- **Thea Astley**'s (1925–2004) books are worth reading.
- **Thomas Keneally**'s (b. 1935) fiction, such as *Schindler's Ark* (now published as *Schindler's List*; 1982) and his novel of the Eritrean conflict with Ethiopia, *Towards Asmara* (1989), is often based on real-life events.
- **Christopher J. Koch**'s (1932–2013) novel of the turmoil in Indonesia in 1965 is *The Year of Living Dangerously* (1978).
- **Dorothy Porter** (1954–2008) wrote fiction in verse, including the historical novel *Akhenaten* (1991) and the mystery *The Monkey's Mask* (1994).

---

tales themselves helps. Works like *Eucalyptus* (1998) and *The Pages* (2008) involve unusual obsessions: in *Eucalyptus*, Holland is a father who demands that his daughter Ellen wed only a man who can identify every one of the eucalyptus trees on their property, and in *The Pages*, Wesley Antill devotes himself entirely to philosophy, spending the last years of his life working on a project that never progresses beyond being a collection of fragments and jottings. Even though these stories have a serious side, the situations are also humorous, even comical, and Bail teases the reader by wittily undercutting what he presents as profound.

NEW ZEALAND

New Zealand's geographical remoteness has limited its writers' exposure abroad. Even though many of the country's writers have achieved some measure of recognition in considerably larger, neighboring Australia, the works of only a few have been widely published and read in other English-language markets.

Janet Frame (1924–2004) is the best-known modern author from New Zealand, in no small part because of her autobiographical works and colorful personal history. Mentally fragile and misdiagnosed as schizophrenic, she published her first book while she was institutionalized. Although the mesmerizing poetic language of her fiction is acclaimed, her often loosely structured narratives can be frustrating. Several works, ranging from the autobiographical to highly speculative fiction, explore the mental health issues with which she long struggled. In *The Carpathians* (1988), Frame introduces a "Gravity Star" that destroys humans' perception of distance, an element of science fiction that is only the most overt manifestation of how Frame alters and undermines reality and conventional perception throughout her fiction.

An influential professor of literature whose works of criticism may well have outsold his fiction, **C. K. Stead** (b. 1932) also wrote a number of cerebral but highly entertaining novels that resemble some of those by British author Gilbert Adair. Stead is interested in literary and philosophical issues and adeptly weaves theory into his stories. Writers often figure in his novels, and he experiments with a variety of postmodernist tricks, as in grappling with the mind–body problem in *The Death of the Body* (1986), a novel that also works quite well as a thriller. Other works look at historical events and figures, such as *Mansfield* (2004), describing a short period in the life of Katherine Mansfield (1888–1923), New Zealand's most famous author, and Stead's reimaging of the Christ story in *My Name Was Judas* (2006). His first novel was the dystopian *Smith's Dream* (1971), which imagines New Zealand under totalitarian rule.

Keri Hulme (b. 1947) is the most recognizable New Zealand author with Maori roots, thanks largely to her Booker Prize–winning novel, *The Bone People* (1984). Though often derided as one of that prize's most forgettable winners, *The Bone People* has been surprisingly enduring (and has sold well over a million copies). It is a dark and violent tale of a damaged boy—a mute orphan who had literally washed up on the shore years earlier—the father figure in his life, and the woman whose life they become part of, and the complex relationship that develops between them. Hulme incorporates both Maori myth and contemporary New Zealand life in her story. *The Bone People* has sharply divided readers both because of its subject matter and because so much of the lengthy novel is presented in a stream of consciousness of short paragraphs, many only a short sentence, that can become grating.

The more approachable fiction of **Patricia Grace** (b. 1937) and **Witi Ihimaera** (b. 1944) offers greater insight into Maori culture and history and is worth exploring beyond Ihimaera's *The Whale Rider* (1987), the basis for the excellent 2003 film.

Lloyd Jones (b. 1955) finally achieved greater international recognition with his best-selling novel *Mister Pip* (2006), but that is only a recent peak in an impressive body of work. Jones's quirky *Biografi* (1993) is presented as journalistic travelogue, but it also is a work of fiction. *Biografi* recounts Jones's travels through an Albania still recovering from the isolation and oppression of the Enver Hoxha regime as he searches for a dentist named Petar Shapallo, who was the dictator's body double, standing in for him on some occasions. With his own past and person erased, Shapallo was unable to return to his previous life after the Great Leader's death. Jones uses Shapallo's life and fate as an allegory of how fiction and reality are presented, and while he never explicitly states it, Shapallo himself seems to be a fictional stand-in, an invention of the author.

The Book of Fame (2000) also mixes fact and fiction, Jones using the triumphant European tour of New Zealand's national rugby team (the All Blacks) at the beginning of the twentieth century to create a fascinating study of national pride and sporting fame. *Mister Pip* builds on the blockade of Bougainville by the government of Papua

---

KEEP IN MIND

- Both of **Eleanor Catton**'s (b. 1985) novels, *The Rehearsal* (2008) and the Man Booker Prize–winning *The Luminaries* (2013), are technically very accomplished, showing great skill in the use of language and structure.

New Guinea in the early 1990s as experienced by a young local girl, Matilda. Already set apart from the rest of the world, Bougainville is progressively cut off further during the blockade, the children adapting most readily to the enforced self-reliance. The one white man left there, Mr. Watts (also called Pop Eye), assumes the duties of teacher, using the only book at hand, Dickens's *Great Expectations*, to teach them. Most of the novel is entirely foreign to the children, but Mr. Watts nonetheless reveals to them the worlds of *Great Expectations* and of great literature in general. When their only copy of the book is lost, Mr. Watts has them try to piece the story together again as an exercise in collective memory. Jones's exploration of the clash of civilizations and the power of literature and storytelling is charming and, with its tragic turns, affecting. Despite the premise, the story does not come across as patronizing, owing to how convincingly Jones presents the young girl's perspective.

SOUTH PACIFIC

The island nations of the South Pacific are widely dispersed over an enormous area and have different cultural and colonial histories. Most are too small and isolated for local literature to make inroads beyond their shores, especially when competing with the already popular and existing South Sea tales written by foreign authors such as Robert Louis Stevenson (1850–1894), Herman Melville (1819–1891), Jack London (1876–1916), W. Somerset Maugham (1874–1965), and Pierre Loti (1850–1923). Some institutions, such as the University of the South

Pacific, have tried to foster a regional literary culture, but relatively few writers have found an audience outside Oceania.

Samoan-born **Albert Wendt** (b. 1939) is a leading figure of South Pacific literature as both a writer and a teacher. His collection of stories *The Birth and Death of the Miracle Man* (1986) is a good introduction to his fiction and the region, but his multigenerational *Leaves of the Banyan Tree* (1979) is a more focused, large-scale epic of modern Samoa. In *Leaves of the Banyan Tree*, the ambitious Tauilopepe Mauga achieves material success, but at a cost of betraying family and tradition. His son and grandson each also goes his own way, which Wendt uses to describe the different cultural and economic forces that shaped Samoa over these decades.

Wendt's wildly imagined novel *Black Rainbow* (1992) is completely different, combining science fiction and literary games. It is set in a dystopian alternative world in which the narrator faces a Tribunal that deems him an ideal citizen after he has convinced them that he has destroyed all personal history. With distinctly Orwellian touches and many contemporary cultural references, Wendt has his narrator eventually recognize the mechanisms of this totalitarian and depersonalizing state. Both allegory and thriller, *Black Rainbow* is an occasionally messy but ultimately compelling read.

Tongan author **Epeli Hau'ofa** (1939–2009) relies heavily on humor in his writing. The protagonist of *Kisses in the Nederlands* (1987), Oilei, literally has a terrible pain in his rear, and his search for a cure to his medical ailment makes for a hilarious tour of local mores and ways, allowing for myriad cultural revelations through the different approaches to treating such an indiscreet problem. Hau'ofa's collection of stories *Tales of the Tikongs* (1983) takes place on the fictional island of Tiko, a stand-in for Tonga and many similar Pacific island states. Hau'ofa pokes fun at many of the people found in the region, from foreign-aid advisers to various locals.

Latin America

Brazil

With a population as great as that of all the other South American nations combined and with the next largest, Argentina, having barely more than a fifth as many people, Brazil is the colossus of the continent; it also dwarfs Portugal, whose colony it once was. Despite sharing an Iberian heritage with many of its neighboring countries, Brazil's official language is Portuguese, not Spanish. Demographically, Brazil was shaped by its legacy of historically being the largest importer of slaves in the Western Hemisphere. All these factors have helped develop a strong and self-sufficient literary culture and market.

The Brazilian literary tradition goes back well into the nineteenth century and, in **Joaquim Maria Machado de Assis** (1839–1908), boasts one of the great novelists of that time in any language. Machado was a successful author during his own lifetime and seems destined to remain popular. His ***The Posthumous Memoirs of Brás Cubas*** (1881, English 1997; previously published in English as *Epitaph of a Small Winner*, 1952, and *Posthumous Reminiscences of Braz Cubas*, 1955) and

Quincas Borba (1891, English 1998; previously published in English as *Philosopher or Dog?* 1954) are still fresh and modern in their use of realism and stylistic conceits.

Jorge Amado (1912–2001) was the first Brazilian author to achieve great international success, and his colorful and often rollicking novels of the Bahia region enjoy worldwide popularity. A Communist who briefly served in the Brazilian congress and who won a Stalin Peace Prize in 1951, his work was always socially engaged, but he is best known for the more comic works he wrote after he left active politics, beginning with the entertaining *Gabriela, Clove and Cinnamon* (1958, English 1962). Sex and sensuality are prominent in these later novels, with several, such as *Tereza Batista* (1972, English 1975), featuring protagonists who are prostitutes. His female characters tend to be strong individuals, overcoming the exploitation they are subjected to, though Amado empowers them only to a limited extent and prefers that they ultimately assume more conventional and traditional roles. As suggested in the complete title, which is close to the Portuguese original, of *Tieta, the Goat Girl; or, The Return of the Prodigal Daughter: Melodramatic Serial Novel in Five Sensational Episodes, with a Touching Epilogue, Thrills, and Suspense!* (1977, English 1979), Amado's novels are not understated. Many describe improbable adventures, and some move into the magical and fantastical. For example, one of the husbands is even dead and yet still a posthumous presence in *Dona Flor and Her Two Husbands* (1966, English 1969), one of Amado's best books. Not surprisingly, with so many novels, basic themes and tropes are repeated, and even their exuberance can be exhausting, but for the most part his works are both winning entertainment and memorable portraits of all classes of people, as well as of the Bahia region.

The existential works of **Clarice Lispector** (1920–1977), with their strong feminine perspective and voice, contrast with much of the South American fiction of her time. Many, like *The Stream of Life* (1973, English 1989, and as *Água Viva* 2012) and the disturbing, self-abasing *The Passion According to G. H.* (1964, English 1988, 2012), are introspective first-person narratives. One of her last books, *The Hour of the Star* (1977, English 1986, 2011), a novella about the sorry life

A STORYTELLING MASTERPIECE

João Guimarães Rosa's (1908–1967) *Grande sertão: Veredas* (1956) was translated into English as *The Devil to Pay in the Backlands* (1963), but that rendering has long been out of print and is widely considered inadequate. Prospects for a new translation have repeatedly been dashed, but one will eventually appear. In this seminal work of Brazilian literature, a narrative and linguistic tour de force (hence also the difficulties in translating it), a man recounts his life story, looking for absolution and trying to make sense of what he has lived through and done.

(and tragic death) of a typist with small delusions of grandeur, is a sort of summation of Lispector's work and a good starting point. Narrated by a man named Rodrigo S. M., it is his account of trying to record and understand the brief existence of Macabéa, an ugly girl living in humble circumstances who loses her boyfriend and then her life. As in many of Lispector's novels, the plot is minimal, and instead, *The Hour of the Star* is a work of reflection on life and writing.

Osman Lins's (1924–1978) later novels are interesting experiments with form. The labyrinthine *The Queen of the Prisons of Greece* (1976, English 1995) is the diary of a teacher who, in writing about the unpublished work left by his dead lover, probes his relationship with her as well as the nature of creativity and fiction. The complex structure of *Avalovara* (1973, English 1980) is considerably more challenging, its multiple narratives built up around a palindrome in a novel revolving around the protagonist's pursuit of three different women.

Ignácio de Loyola Brandão's (b. 1936) novels also are far from straightforward, with *Zero* (English 1983) assembled from short sections and fragments and written in a variety of styles. It is a powerful and absurdist indictment of the conditions under military rule in the Brazil of those years. (Unable to find a publisher for the novel in Brazil, *Zero* first appeared in an Italian translation, by Antonio Tabucchi, in 1974.) Brandão's rather cinematic *Teeth Under the Sun* (1976, English 2007) features a protagonist who finds himself increasingly isolated in a town that many have already abandoned. The atmosphere in the novel reflects the repression of the times. Brandão's particularly dark dystopian vision of São Paulo and environmental catastrophe in the futuristic novel *And Still the Earth* (1982, English 1985) still holds up well despite its bleakness.

João Ubaldo Ribeiro (1941–2014) made an early impression on English-speaking audiences with his own translation of his novel about an out-of-control mercenary, *Sergeant Getúlio* (1971, English 1978). *The Lizard's Smile* (1989, English 1994), set on a secluded island, centers on a husband and wife and the strains of their marriage, but it also contains political intrigue and elements of a thriller. Ribeiro cannot quite pull it off cleanly, but comparisons to Graham Greene's books are not unreasonable. The large-scale family epic *An Invincible Memory* (1984, English 1989) chronicles how Brazil was shaped over the past four centuries, and its entertaining presentation of history and changing national identity makes it the most readily rewarding of his novels.

Much of **Moacyr Scliar**'s (1937–2011) fiction deals with Jewish and emigrant themes, most successfully in his novel of assimilation, *The Centaur in the Garden* (1980, English 1985), with its half-human, half-centaur protagonist who must constantly deal with his otherness. Guedali Tartakovsky tells the story of his life inhabiting this hybrid body, from a relatively carefree childhood to a much more difficult adolescence. After spending time as a circus act, Guedali and the female centaur he meets undergo an operation that makes them much more human. Left with centaur legs and hooves but otherwise entirely human bodies, their true identities can be masked and hidden from others but never entirely forgotten. While they continue their transformation into full-fledged human form, Guedali is never entirely certain that he is doing the right thing by not being true to himself (or at least his original form).

Scliar's *Kafka's Leopards* (2000, English 2011) is a tale of misinterpretations, beginning with a young would-be Trotskyist named Mousy making contact with the wrong writer in 1916 Prague and receiving a parable from Franz Kafka instead of the secret missive he had been charged to obtain. The signed text does not yield the secrets that Mousy had been told to expect but nonetheless is still valuable, and

Mousy carries it with him for the next decades. Half a century later, in the mid-1960s, Mousy wants to sell it and use the proceeds to help his grand-nephew escape the brutal crackdown in Brazil, but his intentions are again thwarted by a misinterpretation of the text. A novella that covers just three periods in Mousy's life, this is a charming and amusing work.

Interest in Scliar's *Max and the Cats* (1981, English 1990) revived after Yann Martel's 2002 Man Booker Prize–winning *Life of Pi* (2001) was discovered to be similar to it. Although the very compact three-part novella is of some interest, Scliar's novel about a man discovering his Jewish roots, *The Strange Nation of Rafael Mendes* (1983, English 1988), and also *The Collected Stories of Moacyr Scliar* (English 1999) offer more rewards.

Luís Fernando Veríssimo's (b. 1936) *The Club of Angels* (1998, English 2001) is an amusing novel about a group of friends who meet monthly for a grand dinner, which takes on a whole new meaning when members of this select club begin dying, one after every meal. It is a clever mystery, but Veríssimo's *Borges and the Eternal Orangutans* (2000, English 2005) is much more impressive. A well-crafted homage to Borges and Poe, its construction may be too obviously thought through, as the significance of many of the details becomes clear only retrospectively. The narrator, Vogelstein, attends a conference of Poe enthusiasts and scholars at which there is a murder of the classic locked-room variety. Borges also plays a prominent role in the story and is the author who brings the book to its conclusion.

The few titles by **Rubem Fonseca** (b. 1925) available in English show him to be a master of the intellectual thriller. Although murder and investigation do feature in his novels, they transcend the crime fiction genre. *Vast Emotions and Imperfect Thoughts* (published in Great Britain as *The Lost Manuscript*; 1988, English 1998) involves a Brazilian film director who has an opportunity to film Isaac Babel's *Red Cavalry* and becomes obsessed by Babel's life while also dealing with diamond smuggling and Babel's lost manuscript. *Bufo & Spallanzani* (1985, English 1990) also has strong literary leanings, with an author protagonist who is a suspect in the murder of his lover.

High Art (1983, English 1986) also parodies crime fiction, and *The Taker* (English 2008), a collection of stories, offers more tightly focused versions of Fonseca's visions.

Several widely translated Brazilian authors write crime fiction and thrillers. The cerebral Rio de Janeiro policeman who is easily lost in reverie in **Luiz Alfredo Garcia-Roza's** (b. 1936) series of Inspector Espinosa mysteries, is an appealing protagonist, and the careful, deliberate plots of these books make good reads. As titles like *The Killer* (1995, English 1997), *Inferno* (2000, English 2002), and *Black Waltz* (2003, English 2004) suggest, **Patrícia Melo's** (b. 1962) fast-paced noir thrillers are dark and intense. Her violent psychological thriller about a hit man, *The Killer*, remains her best work, but *In Praise of Lies* (1998, English 1999) amusingly skewers the publishing industry and offers several surprising noir twists.

PAULO COELHO

Paulo Coelho (b. 1947) is a phenomenon, which is perhaps all one should say about him. The pop spirituality of his crudely inspirational tales of journeys of personal growth is general enough that books like his "fable about following your dream," *The Alchemist* (1988, English 1993), have met with incredible success throughout the world, their reach likely extending farther than the work of any other living writer. Such widespread resonance suggests a rudimentary storytelling ability that strikes a common chord. At least his tales appear to have variety, with dashes of the exotic and erotic: *The Zahir* (2005, English 2005) moves from Paris to Kazakhstan and deals with celebrity and wealth; the sex-centered *Eleven Minutes* (2003, English 2004) revolves around a Brazilian woman who becomes a prostitute in Switzerland; and *Veronika Decides to Die* (1998, English 1999) is largely set in a mental institution in Slovenia. Regardless of the frills, however, the story and message remain numbingly the same.

Perhaps some comfort can be taken in the fact that some of Coelho's financial bounty has presumably trickled down to his English translators, led by Margaret Jull Costa, enabling them to turn to other, worthy projects.

KEEP IN MIND

- The novels by the multitalented musician **Chico Buarque** (b. 1944) include a man's dark tour of personal and urban decay across all cross sections of often violent Brazilian life in *Turbulence* (1991, English 1992), as well as *Budapest* (2003, English 2004), with its ghostwriter in very foreign territory, captivated by the Hungarian capital, a woman, and the local language.

- **Hilda Hilst**'s (1930–2004) fiction, including *The Obscene Madame D* (1982, English 2012), *Letters from a Seducer* (1991, English 2014), and *With My Dog Eyes* (1986, English 2014), is compact and poetic.

- **Paulo Lins**'s (b. 1958) gritty epic *City of God* (1997, English 2006) immerses readers in the heart of Rio's favelas. The acclaimed film version does not have nearly the range of the sprawling novel, a densely populated, unremitting account of this slum world.

- **Márcio Souza**'s (b. 1946) works range from those based on historical incidents, such as the artfully presented *Emperor of the Amazon* (1977, English 1980), a bawdy and richly imagined look at imperialism in the far reaches of the Amazon, to the very broad satire of his later novels, like the international thriller *Death Squeeze* (1984, English 1984) and the slightly science fictional *The Order of the Day: An Unidentified Flying Opus* (1983, English 1986).

- **Jô Soares**'s (b. 1938) *A Samba for Sherlock* (1995, English 1997) brings Sherlock Holmes (and Sarah Bernhardt) to Brazil, and his anarchist chronicle, *Twelve Fingers* (1999, English 2001), also mixes fact and fiction, its protagonist crossing paths with Mata Hari, Marie Curie, and Al Capone, among others, in an amusing collection of capers and failures.

South America

Outside the continental giant, Portuguese-speaking Brazil, Spanish is the most widely spoken language in South America. The area has long had a rich literary tradition, though well into the twentieth century much of the fiction was regional (and often outright provincial). **Jorge Luis Borges** (1899–1986) was the first transcendent Spanish-writing author from this hemisphere, coming to international attention in the early 1960s, around the time the Latin American "Boom" began. **Gabriel García Márquez**'s (1927–2014) *One Hundred Years of Solitude* (1967, English 1970) is the landmark text of the Boom, and its magical realism spawned an enormous number of imitators before more or less losing its appeal by the early 1980s. Several writers who rose to prominence in the 1960s, including García Márquez, **Mario Vargas Llosa** (b. 1936), and the Mexican **Carlos Fuentes** (1928–2012), have continued to write well into the twenty-first century and for a long time overshadowed younger talents.

Political repression across the continent—such as in Chile after the Pinochet regime assumed power in 1973 and under the Peronist and then the military regimes in Argentina—appears to have stifled creativity. A few authors broke through during this time, notably the best-selling **Isabel Allende** (b. 1942), but only recently has a post-Boom generation come to the fore. Many writers have now repudiated magical realism and embraced American pop and consumer culture with as much fervor as the older generation denounced American imperialism. The McOndo movement—its name openly mocking García Márquez's Macondo, the setting of *One Hundred Years of Solitude*—is one of the most prominent recent literary trends, beginning with the representative anthology *McOndo* (1996), with contributions from many who have become leading writers today.

The works of the old masters—Borges, García Márquez, Vargas Llosa, **Julio Cortázar** (1914–1984), and a few others—are well represented in English translation, but only a surprisingly small selection of the works by other major as well as younger authors has been translated, giving at best a skewed impression of their talents. This situation is improving, but only gradually.

ARGENTINA

In the early twentieth century, Argentina was one of the world's wealthiest countries. Its export-oriented economy reinforced its strong cultural ties to Europe and the United States, and reading, writing, and publishing thrived there. While the works of some authors from the early part of the century continue to be of interest today, notably those of **Roberto Arlt** (1900–1942), **Jorge Luis Borges** (1899–1986) has emerged as the towering figure of Argentine literature. His masterful short stories, especially those collected in *Ficciones* (1944, revised 1956, English 1962, and in the *Collected Fictions*, 1998), rank alongside the works of Franz Kafka (1883–1924) as among the century's most distinctive and influential fiction. With their philosophical and literary underpinnings, and Borges's ability to take his fantastical premises about language, time, infinity, and identity to their absolute extremes in just a few pages while framing them in what always amounts to a story, his fiction has been widely (if only rarely successfully) imitated.

The circle around Borges included other notable writers, such as his frequent collaborator, **Adolfo Bioy Casares** (1914–1999), and Bioy Casares's wife, **Silvina Ocampo** (1903–1993). Whereas Ocampo's fiction, like Borges's, was almost exclusively in the form of short stories, Bioy Casares wrote a number of novels that often also included fantastical premises. With its more elaborate and drawn-out presentation, the eerily hallucinatory virtual reality tale set on a not quite deserted island, *The Invention of Morel* (1940, English 1964), takes a very different approach to speculative fiction than Borges chose but is a particularly impressive work.

Julio Cortázar's (1914–1984) innovative *Hopscotch* (1963, English 1966) is one of the major novels of the Latin American Boom. The first section of the novel is a conventional story, and Cortázar said that the nearly one hundred supplementary chapters of the second section were expendable. The protagonist of this soul-searching novel is Horacio Oliveira, who describes his unfulfilled life in first Paris and then Buenos Aires. As the author explains, the novel's 155 chapters can be—but do not have to be—read in the order in which they were printed. Cortázar supplies instructions for an alternative sequence, which ultimately leave the reader caught in an infinite loop. While Cortázar's presentation might appear to be a gimmick, it is carefully and well done and allows for different readings of the text, including the traditional one of front to back. His novel *62: A Model Kit* (1968, English 1972) builds on *Hopscotch*, specifically the sixty-second chapter of the earlier novel, putting into practice the theory outlined there, of a new kind of novel. Melding place—the three locales of the novel: Paris, London, and Vienna—and presenting fragmentary material, this novel also demands more active participation by the reader.

Much of Cortázar's other fiction is more conventional in form, although his most political novel, *A Manual for Manuel* (1973,

English 1978), about a kidnapping plot by a group of revolutionaries in Paris, also incorporates other material. Interspersing actual newspaper clippings in the text gives the novel a documentary quality, as it becomes a scrapbook of the injustices and violence in the world of that time. Here, however, the extraliterary embellishment distracts from the strong narrative. Cortázar is more successful in *Fantomas Versus the Multinational Vampires* (1975, English 2014), in which he develops a story based on an actual comic book in which he and other literary figures like Susan Sontag, Alberto Moravia, and Octavio Paz are characters. It is a very amusing, metafictional, political adventure story.

Often consisting of little more than dialogue, **Manuel Puig**'s (1932–1990) novels also use pop culture extensively. Many of his characters are obsessed with the movies, and Puig uses references to films as markers in their lives and in how they relate to others. Even in what is ostensibly a detective novel like *The Buenos Aires Affair* (1973, English 1976), Puig inserts parts resembling excerpts from movies and screenplays. The epigraphs at the start of each chapter also contain dialogue from actual films.

The Kiss of the Spider Woman (1976, English 1979) is the fullest realization of Puig's cinematic vision, essentially a two-hander taking place almost entirely in a prison cell. One prisoner, the homosexual Molina, spends much of the time recounting Hollywood movie plots, on which Puig builds to show how the men's friendship develops. The additional narrative layers—there are scholarly footnotes discussing homosexuality, for example, and the police reports on the two main characters—also are typical of Puig's use of multiple perspectives.

Tomás Eloy Martínez (1934–2010) was one of many Argentine authors—including Cortázar and Puig—who spent much of his life in exile. As is too often the case with many Latin American authors who have lived and taught in the United States for extended periods, surprisingly little of his large output is available in English translation—though ironically, one of the few works that is, *The Perón Novel* (1985, English 1988, 1999), has been translated twice. *The Perón Novel* is a portrait of the dictator Juan Perón, and *Santa Evita* (1994, English 1995) is a novel that explores the worship of his wife, Eva Perón, the other personality who, even after her death, has dominated modern Argentine politics. Both are fact-saturated fiction addressing the Perón phenomena in Argentina in creative ways, especially in using Eva's corpse as a totemic and magical object in *Santa Evita*. *The Tango Singer* (2004, English 2006) is set in more recent but equally unsettled times, in the midst of Argentina's economic crisis in 2001 and 2002. The novel's protagonist, Cadogan, a graduate student at New York University, travels to Buenos Aires to do research on his dissertation on Jorge Luis Borges's essays on the tango. The novel is filled with episodes of people not finding their way, a paean to what Martínez presents as a constantly shape-shifting city.

Martínez's most personal work is **Purgatory** (2008, English 2011). Its narrator strongly resembles the author, but the central figure is Emilia Dupuy, whose husband, Simón, disappeared during Argentina's "Dirty War." Now, thirty years later, she believes she has run into him again in New Jersey where she fled. Amazingly, Simón appears to her exactly as he did thirty years earlier, not having aged or changed at all. As earlier circumstances and events are slowly revealed, it becomes clear what Simón's fate was, yet Martínez generously and persuasively explains that Emilia has convinced herself that she has found Simón after all these decades of uncertainty.

The prolific **César Aira** (b. 1949) has written a strange and wondrous variety of novellas, with the few available in English giving only a hint of his prodigious interests, abilities, and output. Aira's works often have a sense of the ineffable, yet he can make even spectral presences seem almost mundane, as in the hauntingly allegorical yet also down-to-earth **Ghosts** (1990, English 2009). Set on a construction site, the ostensibly simple story of the family of the night watchman living there touches on issues like national and class consciousness and reaching adulthood, yet without ever seeming to *be* about anything specific. The most charming of his works available in English, **How I Became a Nun** (1993, English 2007), is typically ambiguous (the plot has nothing to do with taking religious vows—the title is a typical Aira feint). In the novel, the narrator recalls episodes from his—or is it her?—childhood when he or she was six. Despite the uncertainty about the character's gender, confusion about sexual identity is a relatively incidental issue

---

ARGENTINA'S POLITICAL NOVELS

Many novels address Argentine politics and current events of the 1970s and 1980s.

Osvaldo Soriano's (1943–1997) satire of Peronist enthusiasm and overkill, *A Funny Dirty Little War* (1980, English 1986), becomes almost slapstick in its excesses, while the narrator in **Marcelo Figueras's** (b. 1962) *Kamchatka* (2003, English 2010) recounts his family's efforts to maintain the illusion of normality in 1976, when he was ten, and his own childishly limited awareness of the larger world around him.

Works such as **Elvira Orphée's** (b. 1930) *El Angel's Last Conquest* (1977, English 1985) and **Alicia Kozameh's** (b. 1953) *Steps Under Water* (1987, English 1996) are realist depictions of the brutal treatment of those deemed opponents of the regime during the time of the Dirty War. Kozameh's fragmented *259 Leaps, the Last Immortal* (2001, English 2006) is an autobiographical work that also explores exile.

In **Rodolfo Fogwill's** (1941–2010) *Malvinas Requiem* (1982, English 2007), a group of deserters try to survive during the 1982 Falkland Islands war with Great Britain; it is one of the few war novels about that conflict.

---

here: in Aira's world, the narrator can simply claim to have been both a boy named César Aira and an innocent young girl and leave it at that. Aira succeeds in superbly evoking both childhood and childishness in his narrative and offers a surprisingly action-packed plot.

Written during the military dictatorship's Dirty War—the often violent oppression of citizens that lasted from about 1976 to 1983, during which time some thirty thousand Argentines were made to "disappear," as the euphemism has it—**Ricardo Piglia's** (b. 1940) *Artificial Respiration* (1980, English 1994) is one of the most interesting reactions to that period. While pointedly beginning the story at the outset of the Dirty War, in April 1976, and also having one of the central characters go missing, most of the novel ostensibly depicts a more distant history. It is a multilayered and very literary thriller of reconstructing the past and of revealing the state's threat to the creative individual. Piglia also uses Argentine and European intellectual and political figures such as the nineteenth-century Argentine dictator Juan Manuel de Rosas, as well as Kafka, Wittgenstein, and Hitler. With other works that show considerable range, such as the slightly futuristic Buenos Aires novel, *The Absent City* (1992, English 2000), and *Money to Burn* (1997, English 2003), based on a notorious 1965 bank robbery, Piglia has proved to be one of Argentina's most significant contemporary authors.

The works of some of the younger Argentine authors are only beginning to appear in translation: **Rodrigo Fresán**'s (b. 1963) first novel to appear in English was *Kensington Gardens* (2004, English 2005), perhaps in the hopes that the English setting would ease foreign readers into his work. The narrator is a writer of children's books who uses the pen name Peter Hook, and the novel itself is a dual biography of Hook and the creator of Peter Pan, J. M. Barrie, neatly contrasting Victorian times and the swinging 1960s of Hook's childhood. The first of **Pablo De Santis**'s (b. 1963) works to be translated, *The Paris Enigma* (2007,

---

KEEP IN MIND

- Prolific old master **Juan Filloy** (1894–2000) is famous for the many thousands of palindromes he devised and for his tale of precision thrown out of kilter, *Op Oloop* (1934, English 2009).
- **Ernesto Sábato** (1911–2011) is known for *The Outsider* (1948, English 1950, and as *The Tunnel*, 1988) and his masterful *On Heroes and Tombs* (1961, English 1981).
- **Luisa Valenzuela**'s (b. 1938) provocative fiction is noteworthy.
- **Juan José Saer**'s (1937–2005) fiction features many recurring characters and themes.
- **Federico Andahazi**'s (b. 1963) controversial novel *The Anatomist* (1997, English 1998) is about sixteenth-century sex research and reactions to it.
- **Sergio Chejfec**'s (b. 1956) *My Two Worlds* (2008, English 2011) and *The Planets* (1999, English 2012) are reflective, meandering novels of memory and observation.
- **Andrés Neuman**'s (b. 1977) *Traveler of the Century* (2009, English 2012) is a leisurely paced novel set in nineteenth-century Germany (and reminiscent of German novels from that time).

English 2008), is an homage to the detective novel taking place during the 1889 Paris World's Fair, where the "Twelve Detectives," an elite club of the world's leading sleuths, become involved in a network of conspiracy and crime. The story is narrated by a young wannabe who is thrown into the middle of all this, and even though he is in way over his head, he proves resourceful and observant, finding that some of the great detectives also have their own secrets. Much of De Santis's other fiction, such as *Voltaire's Calligrapher* (2001, English 2010), also uses historical settings and figures and is even more concerned with linguistic and literary references.

A trained mathematician, **Guillermo Martínez** (b. 1962) has written several cerebral mysteries that have been influenced by Borges. With its autobiographical elements, academic backdrop, and the clever but never abstruse integration of mathematics, *The Oxford Murders* (2003, English 2005) is the most appealing of his novels.

CHILE

Chile has produced many fine novelists, but until recently its poets easily outshone them. **Vicente Huidobro's** (1893–1948) *Altazor* (1931, English 1988, revised 2003) is an early landmark text and a remarkable epic poem. Chile has two Nobel laureates (1945 and 1971, respectively), **Gabriela Mistral** (1889–1957) and **Pablo Neruda** (1904–1973). The overthrow of the democratically elected government of Salvador Allende in 1973 had a profound effect on Chilean writers, with many of the most prominent and promising spending in exile most or all of the years that Augusto Pinochet was head of state (until 1990). Among them were **Ariel Dorfman** (b. 1942) and **Isabel Allende** (b. 1942), both of whom have settled in the United States and taken American citizenship, as well as **Antonio Skármeta** (b. 1940) and **Roberto Bolaño** (1953–2003).

José Donoso (1924–1996) was Chile's major "Boom" author, and his novel *The Obscene Bird of Night* (1970, English 1973) can be considered the ultimate outgrowth of that literary trend. The novel has a nightmarish quality, and the narrative is easily taken for hallucinatory, with much in the jumbled story remaining ambiguous. Even Boy, the creature at the novel's center, is monstrous, an entirely deformed being who is the last in the line of an aristocratic family.

Donoso also wrote in a more realist vein. The autobiographical *The Garden Next Door* (1981, English 1994) is about a writer's experiences in Spanish exile as he tries to write the great Chilean novel, allowing Donoso to write about both the Boom and recent Chilean history. Typically, Donoso upends expectations with his ending, in which he reveals that the narrator and author Julio is not the one behind this work. Touching on both politics and literature, the two novellas published together in *Taratuta / Still Life with Pipe* (1990, English 1993) sum up many of the issues Donoso addresses in his fiction. Here Donoso has his protagonists become obsessed with other characters—one with a terrorist from Russian revolutionary times and the other with a painter—and in both he offers lessons in trying to come to grips with art and history.

Isabel Allende (b. 1942) is among the globally most widely read Latin American authors. Her multigenerational saga of the Trueba family, *The House of the Spirits* (1982, English 1985), is her most agreeable read. While Allende employs some magic realism in the novel, her strengths are in the very personal evocation of (slightly disguised) twentieth-century Chilean history. Her novels range from the reimagining of a fictional character in *Zorro* (2005, English 2005) to young adult fiction. Allende displays a sure hand and keeps her stories rolling along, yet only at its most personal is her work truly memorable.

Diamela Eltit (b. 1949) is among the most prominent authors who remained in Chile during the Pinochet years. Her aggressively confrontational fiction often challenges the prevailing social order and system, especially patriarchy, at the most basic level. *The Fourth World* (1988, English 1995) begins in the womb, each of the two parts of the novel narrated by one of a set of twins who remain intimately connected later in life. Eltit's most intriguing work is *E. Luminata* (1983, English 1997), which is presented in a variety of forms, including sequences of poetry, but most frequently resembles a film script. Eltit consistently undermines any developing sense of story in *E. Luminata*, which is essentially an experiment in narrative and language, yet the nightmarish vision of an oppressed woman (and victim), brutally exposed in an ominous square, is compelling.

Barely registering outside the Spanish-speaking world before his death, **Roberto Bolaño**'s (1953–2003) meteoric posthumous rise in reputation and popularity are almost unheard of for a writer of literary fiction. In recent decades, only W. G. Sebald (1944–2001) burst on the scene anywhere near as spectacularly, but given the breadth of Bolaño's work, the Chilean looks likely to enjoy even greater success. Raised in Chile and Mexico, Bolaño spent essentially all his adult life abroad, first in Mexico and then Spain, but Chile figures prominently in several of his works. Exile, dictatorship, unfathomable evil, and the possibilities of the metafictional are among the dominant and recurring themes in his work, but Bolaño is almost impossible to pin down, and his remarkably varied fiction is full of the unexpected. If there are weaknesses in his sometimes rushed fiction, such as in his limited, underdeveloped female characters, the scale of his invention and the richness of his creations still mark him as the region's most striking and original writer since García Márquez.

Bolaño's posthumous magnum opus, *2666* (2004, English 2008), may be his most representative work, as its five separate parts show off many of his different interests and approaches. The book's longest and most notorious section, "The Part About the Crimes," is an extended cycle of brief descriptions of the fates of several women, the victims of a massive brutal murder spree inspired by the actual unsolved murders of hundreds of women around Ciudad Juárez in Mexico that began in the early 1990s. Such sequences of short, biographical snapshots are found in a number of Bolaño's books—particularly in the bizarre fictional encyclopedic tour de force that is *Nazi Literature in the Americas* (1996, English 2008)—and the individual vignettes and the cumulative effect in *2666* are particularly effective. Other parts of *2666* center on academia and the literary life, and even though the nominal unifying presence is the elusive author Archimboldi, Bolaño unfolds his stories indirectly. The narrative seems to drift off on tangents, and the connections remain subtle and often incidental. Typically, the novel never explains or alludes to the meaning of the title—the date or

KEEP IN MIND

- Although best known for his play *Death and the Maiden* (1991), **Ariel Dorfman** (b. 1942) has written several novels, including the multilayered *The Last Song of Manuel Sendero* (1982, English 1987).
- The fiction of **Luis Sepúlveda** (b. 1949) is worth a look.
- **Antonio Skármeta**'s (b. 1940) novels include, especially, *Burning Patience* (now published under the Oscar award–winning movie tie-in title, *The Postman*; 1985, English 1987).
- **Alberto Fuguet**'s (b. 1964) novels *Bad Vibes* (1991, English 1997) and *The Movies of My Life* (2003, English 2003) describe pop culture as seen from a Chilean perspective.
- **Roberto Ampuero**'s (b. 1953) *The Neruda Case* (2008, English 2012) introduces his private investigator Cayetano Brulé to English-speaking audiences when he is hired for his first case by a dying Pablo Neruda in 1973.

number *2666*. Even so, *2666* adds up to a satisfying and largely cohesive whole, albeit one that leaves much unexplained.

The Savage Detectives (1998, English 2007) is Bolaño's other large-scale work. With its authorial alter ego in the form of Arturo Belano, as well as descriptions of the Mexican literary scene and the "visceral realist" poetry movement (the fictional counterpart to Bolaño's own infrarealism), it is a more revealing road-trip novel. Like *2666*, *The Savage Detectives* can seem like a jumbled assemblage, but Bolaño throws in so much and keeps the narrative going so well that it easily sustains the reader's interest. Other works, including Bolaño's story collections, offer more compact if not necessarily more satisfaction. Even the shorter novels colored by the repression of the Pinochet regime, such as the monologue by a dying Jesuit priest in *By Night in Chile* (2000, English 2003) and *Distant Star* (1996, English 2004), with its murderous skywriting air force poet, move along unusual arcs. Underlying—and bubbling forth in—these novels, as in so much of his work, are failed poets and their poetry, and terrible violence.

The first examples of **Alejandro Zambra**'s (b. 1975) work suggest a promising talent who is cautiously expanding his horizons. Zambra's

Bonsai (2006, English 2008) is a novella about a relationship that is doomed from the start, with much of its charm and effectiveness coming from Zambra's forthrightness, as he makes clear from the opening of the story that there can be no happy end here. *The Private Lives of Trees* (2007, English 2010) is another short book with a similarly wistful edge. For much of the brief narrative, the main character, Julián, is waiting for his wife to come home and is trying to entertain his stepdaughter, Daniela. This novella also reflects on the past and the future, as Julián imagines future stages of Daniela's life (including, eventually, reading this very book).

COLOMBIA

Gabriel García Márquez's (1927–2014) novel *One Hundred Years of Solitude* (1967, English 1970), about the rise and fall of the Buendía family and the town of Macondo, is one of the great works of the twentieth century. A novel filled with ghostly presences and preordained and inescapable fates, García Márquez's skillful conflation of time provides the novel's essential foundation. With the fantastic presences of the lingering dead and the brilliantly conceived passions of the living, *One Hundred Years of Solitude* is the highpoint of magical realism.

One Hundred Years of Solitude cast a long shadow over Latin American fiction. Despite the many imitators, few approached it in quality. Even much of García Márquez's other fiction, including his dictatorship novel, *The Autumn of the Patriarch* (1975, English 1976), and his creative variation on the detective novel, *Chronicle of a Death Foretold* (1981, English 1982), pales by comparison. Of his later novels, *Love in the Time of Cholera* (1985, English 1988) is perhaps his greatest accomplishment. Essentially realist, it is a decades-spanning love story in which Florentino Ariza remains determined to win the girl, Fermina Daza, he fell in love with in his youth. Theirs was an almost childish passion, with only a few brief encounters and little opportunity for any sort of relationship to develop beyond that in their imaginations. The magic of the novel is found in Florentino's ability to sustain—and be driven—by that same youthful romantic desire throughout his life and into old age when he finally meets Fermina again.

Álvaro Mutis (1923–2013) has been overshadowed by García Márquez. The longtime resident of Mexico is best known for his poetry, little of which has been translated into English. His stories featuring Maqroll the Gaviero (Lookout) (1986–1991, collected in *The Adventures and Misadventures of Maqroll*, 2002) also form a remarkable chapter in recent Latin American fiction. Maqroll was a recurring character in Mutis's poetry long before Mutis chronicled his stories in prose. A fatalistic wanderer and adventurer, Maqroll travels around the world, yet it is not the adventures but the characters—foremost, the philosophical Maqroll himself—that fascinate. With poetic precision, Mutis brings to life an elusive dark hero who rambles and drifts across the globe and through life, rarely finding much success and, yet in his own often dispirited way, is still curious what the future holds.

Manuel Zapata Olivella's (1920–2004) *Changó, the Biggest Badass* (1983, English 2010) is an epic of the African diaspora in the Americas. Beginning with a section in verse, the entire narrative is creative in its use of different literary forms and voices, as well as its blending of different actual historical events, basing episodes on real occurrences but also shaping them to fit the story. Zapata Olivella leads the readers through the centuries of the African slave trade and then contemporary history, using both familiar and invented historical figures, including the larger-than-life spirit of the title, in a grand panoramic consideration of the entire African American experience throughout the Americas.

The works of some significant younger Colombian authors have not yet been widely translated, most notably those of **Fernando Vallejo** (b. 1942). His novel *Our Lady of the Assassins* (1997, English 2001), the only one available in English, is one of several in which he confronts the drug war–fueled violence of his native Medellín. In this compact, nihilistic work full of operatic violence whose title echoes Jean Genet's (1910–1986) *Our Lady of the Flowers* (1943, revised 1951, English 1949), a writer named Fernando returns after thirty years abroad to a city now

> KEEP IN MIND
>
> - **Jorge Franco**'s (b. 1962) violent novel about Medellín is entitled ***Rosario Tijeras*** (1999, English 2004), and his tale of loss and longing (and living illegally in the United States) is ***Paradise Travel*** (2001, English 2006).
> - **Juan Gabriel Vásquez** (b. 1973) contrasts the long shadow of Nazism and modern Colombia in *The Informers* (2004, English 2008). His *The Secret History of Costaguana* (2007, English 2010), featuring a narrator obsessed with Joseph Conrad and his novel *Nostromo*, is both a historical commentary and a multilayered literary game.

entirely in the grips of the drug trade and has a doomed affair with a teenage boy.

Laura Restrepo's (b. 1950) novels have a great deal of violence, as they also describe some of the darker sides of Colombian life, but they are not as brutal as Vallejo's and offer at least some hope at their conclusions. *Delirium* (2004, English 2007) is set in 1980s Bogotá, where the former literature professor Aguilar finds that his wife, Agustina, has been reduced to madness, a symptom of both the times and her upbringing. *The Dark Bride* (1999, English 2002) takes place deep in the Colombian countryside among the oil workers and the prostitutes who serve them. The narrator is a journalist who, in conversations with the locals, learns the story of a legendary prostitute, an Indian girl who adopted the working name of Sayonara. Restrepo tries too hard with her premises of madness or a prostitute's passions, but her novels offer interesting glimpses of otherwise unseen Colombian life.

PERU

The prolific and widely translated **Mario Vargas Llosa** (b. 1936) has been the dominant figure in Peruvian writing for more than four decades. As his failed but very serious candidacy for the Peruvian presidency in 1990 suggests, Vargas Llosa has always been politically engaged, more so than any of the other prominent authors of the Latin American "Boom." Remarkably, despite Vargas Llosa's ideological shift from socialism to neoliberal conservatism, and from being under the spell of Jean-Paul Sartre to embracing the ideas of Friedrich von Hayek, his own politics have not tainted his fiction. His very naturalistic realism has little magic, and while condemning Peruvian and Latin American politics in many novels that have a historical basis, he lets the facts and situations speak for themselves rather than use his characters as mouthpieces for his politics.

Vargas Llosa's books are among the most approachable by all the Boom authors. Several feature autobiographical elements, including his most entertaining novel, *Aunt Julia and the Scriptwriter* (1977, English 1982). Its teenage protagonist who is an aspiring writer named Mario and falls in love with his aunt makes a wonderful comic novel. The story is told in chapters alternating between the narrator's account of this time of his life and the soap opera inventions of the scriptwriter, Pedro Camacho, who works for the same radio station young Mario does. This kind of twin narrative is typical of much of Vargas Llosa's fiction. Here reality (Mario's life) and fantasy (the soap opera plots) initially seem divergent, but the distinctions between the two finally blur, allowing Vargas Llosa to address some of his favorite themes, such as the pull and distraction of erotic passion and the barriers to a productive, creative life as an artist.

Many of Vargas Llosa's novels are historical, and *The Way to Paradise* (2003, English 2003) is the most successful in marrying all his interests and showcasing his favorite literary tricks. The alternating chapters in this novel move back and forth between the lives of the nineteenth-century Peruvian social activist Flora Tristán and the French painter Paul Gauguin (a grandson she never knew), each in her and his way abandoning comfortable bourgeois lifestyles for what seems like a greater cause.

Peru is central to many of Vargas Llosa's works of political fiction and the massive *Conversation in the Cathedral* (1969, English 1975), which is the culmination of Vargas Llosa's early novels dealing with his homeland. The novel is framed as a conversation between two men,

KEEP IN MIND

- **Alfredo Bryce Echenique**'s (b. 1939) charming and insightful novel *A World for Julius* (1970, English 1992) is about a young boy from an aristocratic family in 1950s Peru.
- Quechua-speaking **José Maria Arguedas**'s (1911–1969) fiction offers awareness of and insight into Peru's indigenous population.
- Peruvian-born but English-writing **Daniel Alarcón**'s (b. 1977) novel *Lost City Radio* (2007) is set in an unnamed, civil war–wracked South American country. *At Night We Walk in Circles* (2013) is noteworthy as well.

Santiago and Ambrosio, over drinks in a dive called La Catedral. Centered on events under the dictatorship of Manuel Odría in the 1950s, it explores the pervasive human corruption of those times and the toll it takes on individuals and society. Vargas Llosa's layering of dialogue in the novel in recalling the past is one of his more ambitious stylistic experiments. Other, more straightforward novels, are based on foreign events. In *The Feast of the Goat* (2000, English 2002), he examines the phenomenon of the Latin American dictator, the case study here being of the Dominican dictator Rafael Trujillo. *The War of the End of the World* (1981, English 1984) describes the historical rebellion in Canudos chronicled in Brazilian author **Euclides da Cunha**'s (1866–1909) classic account *Rebellion in the Backlands* (1902, English 1944 and as *Backlands*, 2010). Set in the backlands of late-nineteenth-century Brazil, Vargas Llosa sees what happened here as representative of the South American experience, the anarchic Canudos a place undone by both fanatic zeal and the violent reaction to it. With its colorful characters and dramatic action, *The War of the End of the World* is a grand epic of the times and the continent and one of Vargas Llosa's greatest achievements.

The first of **Santiago Roncagliolo**'s (b. 1975) novels to be translated, *Red April* (2006, English 2009), is a political thriller and mystery. Its protagonist, the lowly but dutiful district prosecutor Félix Chacaltana Saldívar, is assigned to investigate a horrific murder and soon finds himself in way over his head. The legacy of the long-lasting and violent Shining Path Maoist insurgency and the corrupt authorities who obstruct much of the increasingly deadly investigation result in a twisty, compelling thriller, even if Roncagliolo ultimately heaps too much onto the story.

BOLIVIA

Much of the domestic fiction by authors from many of the smaller South American nations has not circulated widely beyond their borders, much less in translation. The works by Bolivia's **Juan de Recacoechea** (b. 1935) and **Edmundo Paz Soldán** (b. 1967) are among the first to reach larger foreign audiences.

In Juan de Recacoechea's *American Visa* (1994, English 2007), both the author and his protagonist, Mario Alvarez, borrow from American noir fiction. Alvarez is desperate to get to the United States, but when he fails to obtain a visa directly from the U.S. authorities, he tries to get one by paying off the right people. Short of funds, he tries to use what he has learned from the detective novels he has read to pull off a robbery, but like the heroes of his favored fiction, he ends up making his situation more complicated. Recacoechea's account of a 1952 train trip and its attendant mysteries and murder in *Andean Express* (2000, English 2009) adds a dose of Agatha Christie to his repertoire. Despite the stock characters and situations, the distinctly Bolivian spin and jovial approach to both these novels make it enjoyable fiction. Too mild and humorous to be considered Latin American noir, Recacoechea has nevertheless found a winning formula.

Longtime U.S. resident Edmundo Paz Soldán continues to write in Spanish, and Bolivia—and the fictional town of Rio Fugitivo—figures in much of his work. The narrator of *The Matter of Desire* (2001, English 2003), Pedro Zabalaga, bears many biographical similarities to the author, but in addition to a predictable account of a campus romance and an academic torn between two worlds, Paz Soldán leaves considerably more for his protagonist to uncover back in Bolivia. Moving

KEEP IN MIND

- **José Wolfango Montes's** (b. 1951) *Jonah and the Pink Whale* (1987, English 1991) is an amusing look at the absurdities of life in Bolivia.
- **Jesús Urzagasti's** (1941–2013) creative introspective novel *In the Land of Silence* (1987, English 1994) has three narrative voices—Jursafú, the Other, and the Dead Man, all of whom are variations of the same protagonist.

in with his crossword puzzle–writing uncle, David, Zabalaga begins looking into his dead father's activist past and finds a much more complicated picture of the man. One apparent key to the many mysteries surrounding the man is the cult novel he wrote, *Berkeley*, and Paz Soldán's multilayered puzzler offers decent rewards, even if it cannot live up completely to its great ambition. *Turing's Delirium* (2003, English 2006) also comes with several puzzles. A kind of cyber thriller, it pits the experts running the government's intelligence-gathering "Black Chamber," which employs both the newest technologies and older, more basic approaches, against the hackers trying to undermine the repressive government. With its political, social, and technological criticism tackling everything from globalization to virtual reality, Paz Soldán throws more into his story than the novel can ultimately sustain, but it is an intriguing read.

URUGUAY

In the English-speaking world, **Juan Carlos Onetti** (1909–1994) has long had the reputation of being the least-known and read of the major modern Latin American writers. Onetti's distinctive works stand apart from both the dominant magical realist and the naturalistic schools. Both in staking out his own territory—most of Onetti's novels about the River Plate region take place around the fictional port city of Santa María—and in constantly shifting the points of view in his nonlinear narratives, Onetti's writing is frequently compared with William Faulkner's. A sense of fatalism prevails in much of Onetti's fiction, leading to a sense of resignation and passivity among his characters, but these existential works are not as overtly introspective as those of contemporary European authors. Onetti's prose is rich and evocative yet can be frustratingly elusive, with the narratives often appearing to run in place. *The Shipyard* (1961, English 1968, 1992) is typical in its premise, that when the protagonist, Larsen, takes a job running a rundown and bankrupt shipyard, any and all prospects he might have are illusionary.

Presenting "a life in stories," *Voices of Time* (2004, English 2006) is illustrative of **Eduardo Galeano**'s (1940–2015) approachable creative writing. The collection of more than three hundred vignettes— stories, reflections, musings—is more a kaleidoscope than a mosaic, but Galeano's often lyrical style and variety make it a thoughtful collection. His *Memory of Fire* trilogy of *Genesis* (1982, English 1985), *Faces and Masks* (1984, English 1987), and *Century of the Wind* (1986, English 1988) takes a similar, if more controlled, approach and on a much larger scale. With each of the many short pieces with which he builds these fictions based on extraneous sources, Galeano rewrites the history of the Americas, from creation to modern times. It is, as Galeano acknowledges, a very subjective rendering, but it is also a powerful collage.

ECUADOR

Jorge Icaza's (1906–1978) social realist novel *Huasipungo* (1935, English 1962, and as *The Villagers*, 1973), about the exploitation of the indigenous Quechua Indians, may be the most famous Ecuadorean novel, but other Ecuadorean authors have produced much more innovative fiction. **Demetrio Aguilera-Malta**'s (1909–1981) *Don Goyo* (1933, English 1980), with its 150-year-old protagonist who communes with nature, is among the earliest examples of a kind of magical

KEEP IN MIND

- **Mario Benedetti**'s (1920–2009) representative story collections are *Blood Pact* (English 1997) and *The Rest Is Jungle* (English 2010).
- **Carlos Martínez Moreno**'s (1917–1986) novel of political terror is entitled *El Infierno* (1981, English 1988).
- **Cristina Peri Rossi** (b. 1941) wrote intense and poetic fiction.

realism, and Aguilera-Malta continued to experiment with new styles late in his career. Although Aguilera-Malta's fiction does not have the sustained coherence of García Márquez's, he lags only a little behind the Colombian master in his lyrical evocation of the slightly unreal. *Babelandia* (1973, English 1985) is one of the most colorful novels of dictatorship in Latin America. This is a satire with absurdist flair, in which the Babelandian ruler is a robotic skeleton named Holofernes Verbofile, but it is grounded in the prevailing unsettled autocratic Ecuadorean political situation and centers on the real-life case of the kidnapping of a general (as the far more prosaic original Spanish title *El secuestro del general*, *The Abduction of the General*, also emphasizes). Aguilera-Malta takes even greater liberties in Santorontón, the fictional setting of *Seven Serpents and Seven Moons* (1970, English 1979). This allegorical novel overflows with mythical creation and invention, including a speaking Christ figure on a crucifix, and even time and place are largely an indistinct blur. The great Spanish translator Gregory Rabassa translated the novel and cited it as the definitive example of magical realism.

Alicia Yánez Cossío's (b. 1929) novels of life in the Andean highlands, such as *Bruna and Her Sisters in the Sleeping City* (1973, English 1999) and *The Potbellied Virgin* (1985, English 2006), as well as her novel about the Galápagos Islands, *Beyond the Islands* (1980, English 2011), are a restrained amalgam of Latin American styles. She resorts to devices like the familial insanity in *Bruna and Her Sisters in the Sleeping City* and the inertia (and all it symbolizes) of the town

---

AN ECUADORAN NOVEL

Poet **Jorge Enrique Adoum**'s (1926–2009) playful but complex post-modern novel of Latin America, *Entre Marx y una mujer desnuda* (1978), is one of the region's major works of fiction not yet translated into English.

---

against which her protagonist wants to rebel, but the more fantastical elements in Yánez Cossío's fiction are rarely flashy. Her novels have a gentle humor and also a cumulative, poignant power.

VENEZUELA

Rómulo Gallegos (1884–1969)—who was elected president of Venezuela in 1948 but was overthrown in a military coup after only a few months in office—is the only Venezuelan author to have found much of an audience in the English-speaking world. His frontier novel of the Venezuelan plains, *Doña Bárbara* (1929, English 1931), is typical of his regional and realist fiction. Its depiction of taming the prairie is more compelling than that found in most such novels, in no small part because of the powerful and cruel female lead, Bárbara. Gallegos's fiction could not compete abroad with the then more fashionable Boom authors and those who came afterward, but ironically, the Spanish-language literary prize with the most impressive record of recognizing the highest achievement in modern fiction is named after him.

Ana Teresa Torres's (b. 1945) century-spanning *Doña Inés vs. Oblivion* (1992, English 1999) is apparently based on an actual court case that took nearly three hundred years to resolve. The novel's narrator, Doña Inés, begins her account early in the eighteenth century and continues her single-minded pursuit of her family land long after her death, haunting the rapidly changing Venezuela. This short novel is packed with incident and characters, and the monomaniacal Doña

Inés is not the most agreeable guide, but in its depiction of the dramatic transformation of Venezuela and Caracas, as well as the history that shaped the country, it has considerable appeal.

PARAGUAY

The leading Paraguayan author is **Augusto Roa Bastos** (1917–2005), best known for his classic novel *I the Supreme* (1974, English 1986). A standout among the many novels about the region's dictators, the story is closely based on the life of one of the continent's first authoritarian leaders, José Gaspar Rodríguez de Francia (1766–1840), who ruled Paraguay from 1814 to 1840. The novel is presented as a compilation composed mainly of this El Supremo's dictated accounts. The voice of the amanuensis, Policarpo Patiño, is integrated into his dictation, but The Supreme's voice is the controlling one. The compiler, who provides editorial notes, is a subtle yet significant presence throughout, and among the connections between the original writing and the compiler's addenda is the use of the same memory pen in both the original nineteenth-century manuscript and then the edited modern one. *I the Supreme* is about the written interpretation of facts and history, and from the very beginning, Roa Bastos constantly questions both the authenticity and the objectivity of any account. The symbolic memory pen is partially broken, for example, and words are erased at the same time as they are written. Similarly, the account itself ends in an illegible, fragmented mess.

Paraguay is the only Latin American country in which an indigenous language, Guaraní, has maintained its dominant position. Despite a strong tradition of Guaraní poetry, it has not become widely established as a medium for fiction. In this comprehensive social-historical novel about Paraguay, the bilingual Roa Bastos invokes Guaraní oral traditions, adding another literary dimension to a novel that is as much about writing as it is about a dictator.

Mexico and Central America

Mexico is the northern giant of Latin American literature. Its sheer size, cultural and educational infrastructure, and comparatively stable and moderate political climate contribute to its dominant position in the region. Many authors from other Latin American countries, including the Colombians **Gabriel García Márquez** (1927–2014) and **Álvaro Mutis** (1923–2013), Honduras-born Guatemalan **Augusto Monterroso** (1921–2003), and Chilean **Roberto Bolaño** (1953–2003), settled there or had strong ties to the country, enhancing its position as a literary center.

Although the much smaller Central American countries have long literary traditions, they have been much more isolated, with little available in English translation. Most of the few authors that have achieved greater recognition abroad have also spent much of their lives abroad, including Guatemala's Nobel laureate, **Miguel Ángel Asturias** (1899–1974).

MEXICO

Juan Rulfo's (1918–1986) *Pedro Páramo* (1955, English 1959, 1994) is one of the books that set off the wave of popularity of Latin American fiction abroad. The short work follows Juan Preciado's quest for traces of his father, Pedro Páramo, in desolate Comala. Exploited and ruined by Páramo, Comala is a place permeated by death. The novel is a mix of the realistic and the hallucinatory, with the dead presented as real presences. Much of the fragmentary and elusive narrative seems uncertain and uneasy, but this precursor to magical realism is distinctive in its presentation and treatment of the supernatural.

Almost all of **Carlos Fuentes**'s (1928–2012) fiction concerns Mexico, and a number of his novels synthesize large swaths of Mexican history. The most sweeping of these efforts is the massive *Terra Nostra* (1975, English 1976), which tries to encompass all the recent centuries of Spanish and Latin American history. In large part an exposition of the forces that shaped the Spanish domination of Mexico, this is a complex novel of clashing ideologies and traditions. As in other works, such as *Christopher Unborn* (1987, English 1989), a novel more closely focused on Mexico itself, Fuentes does not end in the present but looks slightly ahead: *Terra Nostra* leads up to the millennium, a quarter of a century in the future, while *Christopher Unborn* culminates in the celebration of the five-hundredth anniversary of Columbus's discovery of America in 1492. His more political novel *The Eagle's Throne* (2002, English 2006) takes place in 2020, and even *The Years with Laura Díaz* (1998, English 2000) is extended to the turn of the century. Typically, Fuentes's fatalistic historical accounts imagine the future as an inevitability similar to what has happened so far, with little improvement possible. His dark visions are also warnings, of course, and can be taken as suggestions that the course of history should be changed.

Fuentes repeatedly examines the Mexican Revolution of the early twentieth century and its legacy, most notably in one of his best books, *The Death of Artemio Cruz* (1962, English 1964, 1991). The title figure

personifies many of the changes that Mexico underwent in the twentieth century, with Cruz graduating from being a poor young idealist
to being a powerful industrial magnate, having brutally and cynically
climbed to the top. A dying man now, the novel describes his painful
physical and mental decline while also looking back on the different
stages in his—and Mexico's—past. Cruz's present is narrated in the
first person, and the past is considered more dispassionately in the
third. In addition, there are sections in which a voice in the second
person admonishes and accuses him. Artemio Cruz is among Fuentes's
more convincing human creations in a body of work in which characters almost inevitably represent something and therefore often can
seem less than entirely lifelike.

Two of **Fernando del Paso**'s (b. 1935) major works are available
in English, covering very different periods. Like Fuentes's largest
works, Paso's novels try to encompass a great amount of history and
material. *News from the Empire* (1987, English 2009) centers on
the brief, ill-fated reign of the Austrian Archduke Maximilian, who
was installed as emperor of Mexico in 1864 and executed when the
republic was restored under Benito Juárez in 1867. Maximilian's wife,
Empress Carlota, lost her mind but lived, in Europe, until 1927, still
believing herself to be the empress of Mexico. *News from the Empire*
is presented in chapters that alternate between the madwoman's personal ravings from 1927 and more neutral accounts of Maximilian's
brief reign and its aftermath. This almost farcical interregnum did
not mark the end of European imperialism per se, but Paso's examination of this colorful episode in history from both the European
and Mexican vantage points clearly shows the dawning of a new
political age. A lively text that shifts between the documentary and
the freely imagined, it succeeds as a historical novel, personal saga,
and political commentary.

The rapid shifts and larger ambitions of Paso's *Palinuro of Mexico*
(1977, English 1989) make it a similarly busy novel. The main characters are the medical student Palinuro and his cousin Estefania. In
a section presented as a drama (or, rather, a dark comedy), Palinuro
is shot during the 1968 massacre at Tlatelolco Square, but the novel

is not primarily political, focusing instead on Palinuro's personal and visceral quests for knowledge and understanding. The novel has been compared with James Joyce's *Ulysses*, and given its humor, linguistic contortions, and anatomical detail, the comparison is not unreasonable.

Several women are among the Mexican authors who have had success both in Mexico and abroad. In ***Like Water for Chocolate*** (1989, English 1991), **Laura Esquivel** (b. 1950) cleverly integrates into her story the pleasures of cooking and eating, literally imbuing the food cooked by the protagonist, Tita, with her emotions. A charming example of thoughtful popular fiction, it is a story of a grand, unfulfilled passion, as Tita is expected to remain single and care for her aging mother while the love of her life marries her older sister. Esquivel has not managed the same happy balance of gimmicks like the recipes in *Like Water for Chocolate*, imaginative premises, and a good story in her later fiction, though not for want of trying. Much of ***The Law of Love*** (1995, English 1996), for example, is set in the twenty-third century, and the book comes with a CD of accompanying music.

Carmen Boullosa's (b. 1954) cross-cultural fiction, which includes creative historical works like her novel ***Cleopatra Dismounts*** (2002, English 2003); and works by **Ángeles Mastretta** (b. 1949) such as those about the Mexican Revolution, ***Mexican Bolero*** (1986, English 1989, and as *Tear This Heart Out*, 1997) and ***Lovesick*** (1996, English 1997), all feature strong female characters. Though best known for her documentary work on the 1968 clashes between students and the authorities, ***Massacre in Mexico*** (1971, English 1975), French-born **Elena Poniatowska**'s (b. 1932) larger body of work contains several novels based on such famous artists as Diego Rivera (***Dear Diego*** [1978, English 1986]) and Tina Modotti (***Tinisima*** [1992, English 1996]).

Daniel Sada (1953–2011) used and manipulated language and style expertly in his fiction, creating considerable problems in attempts to translate it. The mischievous and circuitous courtship novel ***Almost Never*** (2008, English 2012), set in a slowly changing Mexico after the end of World War II, offers some sense of his abilities. Despite relatively little plot, Sada's off-beat style easily carries the reader through this amusing and sex-filled tale.

The younger authors **Jorge Volpi** (b. 1968) and **Ignacio Padilla** (b. 1968) are part of a Latin American trend of writing less fixated on the national. In Volpi's dialogue-heavy novel of ideas, ***In Search of Klingsor*** (1999, English 2002), a scientifically minded American named Francis Bacon becomes obsessed after World War II with learning the identity of a Nazi known as Klingsor. A mix of spy and scientific fiction, the novel revisits German efforts to make an atomic bomb. Ignacio Padilla's stylish if thin stories collected in ***Antipodes*** (2001, English 2004) are exotic in locale and invention, but his novel ***Shadow Without a Name*** (2000, English 2003) is considerably better. This novel of identity and role-playing begins with a high-stakes game of chess during World War I: two men play for their identities and the future that each of these seems to hold, one assured of a life of safety and security and the other surely doomed. Both men, in fact, survive, and identities prove surprisingly elusive as the story progresses in what turns out to be a chesslike game that stretches over decades (and also involves Nazism). Four different narrators recount parts of the story, each shining a different light on events in this clever puzzler.

KEEP IN MIND

- **Alberto Ruy Sánchez's** (b. 1951) novels using his fictional Moroccan setting include ***Mogador*** (1987, English 1993) and ***The Secret Gardens of Mogador*** (2001, English 2009).
- The novels of **Jorge Ibargüengoitia** (1928–1983) are worth reading.
- **Homero Aridjis's** (b. 1940) historical novels are ***1492*** (1985, English 1991) and his "visions of the year 1000," ***The Lord of the Last Days*** (1994, English 1995).
- **Paco Ignacio Taibo II** (b. 1949) writes politically engaged crime fiction.

GUATEMALA

Despite being awarded the Nobel Prize, **Miguel Ángel Asturias** (1899–1974) remains an underrated precursor of the Latin American Boom. His grotesque satire based on the Guatemalan dictatorship of Estrada Cabrera, *The President* (published in the United States as *El Señor Presidente*; 1946, English 1963), is at least acknowledged as one of the first and finest of the region's dictator novels. A more remarkable achievement is the complex *Men of Maize* (1949, English 1975), a novel pitting indigenous culture against outside influences and might that is deeply rooted in local myth and oral storytelling. A dedicated follower of the surrealist movement when he lived in Paris in the 1920s and 1930s, Asturias is notable for his linguistic creativity and his integration of many literary traditions, ranging from the European avant-garde to Mayan storytelling.

Despite being born in Honduras and having spent the last five decades of his life in exile in Mexico, **Augusto Monterroso**'s (1921–2003) life was also closely tied to Guatemala, and he is considered one of its greatest writers. A master of the succinct, he is famous for his micro-tales, with some of his stories only a sentence or paragraph long. The title of his 1959 collection, *Complete Works and Other Stories* (English 1995, in a translation that also includes *Perpetual Motion*, 1972) reflects some of his playful attitudes, from suggesting comprehensiveness and finality when in fact he is just getting started, to immediately undermining the claim to absoluteness. Monterroso's elegantly crafted fables are remarkable pieces of concision that nevertheless seem full-bodied; they also are both profound and humorous.

Rodrigo Rey Rosa (b. 1958) is unavoidably linked to American author Paul Bowles (1910–1999), who influenced and translated several volumes of Rey Rosa's fiction. Rey Rosa's spare, restrained stories and novellas often depict great violence, the dispassionate prose of the surface ultimately revealing great turmoil beneath. *Severina* (2011, English 2014), a short but action-filled tale of human and literary passions in which the narrator becomes obsessed with a woman named Severina, is a fine example of Rey Rosa's work.

NICARAGUA

Nicaragua boasts several of Latin America's finest poets, beginning with the father of modernism, **Rubén Darío** (1867–1916). **Ernesto Cardenal** (b. 1925) is a Catholic priest who also became the minister of culture under the Sandinista government, which came to power in 1979. His epic *The Doubtful Strait* (1966, English 1995) is a verse narrative about the Spanish conquest of Central America that prefigures more recent Nicaraguan history and the Somoza dictatorships. Cardenal weaves quotations from historical documents, including accounts by Christopher Columbus and Bartolomé de las Casas, into a critical rewriting of the early experiences of the Spanish in the New World. **Gioconda Belli** (b. 1948) also is a noted poet who has written several conventional novels, including a retelling of the story of Adam and Eve, *Infinity in the Palm of Her Hand* (2008, English 2009). Her most compelling work of fiction is *The Scroll of Seduction* (2005, English 2006), with its dual narratives of obsessions. A professor, Manuel, recounts the story of the crazed love between the mad queen Juana of Castile and her husband, Philippe the Handsome, to the teenage Lucía. The retelling gets out of hand, with Manuel and Lucía completely embracing the old tale in an intriguing take on passion.

Closely involved with the Sandinista cause, **Sergio Ramírez** (b. 1942) served as vice president of Nicaragua from 1985 to 1990, but he has also long been one of Central America's leading writers. Ramírez already displays considerable storytelling talent in his early representative collection, *Stories* (English 1986), even if some of the satirical pieces critical of the United States and its influence in Latin America in it are rather obvious. In one story, a Nicaraguan emulates bodybuilder Charles Atlas (a stand-in for the United States), only to be disillusioned when he meets the dying man himself. In another story,

Ramírez describes the ridiculous preparations made by Nicaraguan high society anticipating a visit by Jackie Onassis, who never shows up.

Ramírez's later novels are more complex and nuanced. *Margarita, How Beautiful the Sea* (1998, English 2008) moves back and forth between the lives (and legacies) of the legendary Rubén Darío and the dictator Anastasio Somoza. The two poles of the story are Darío's triumphal return to Nicaragua in 1907 and the 1956 assassination of Somoza, but Ramírez's crisscrossing story is full of connections between the two in a small country where everyone seems to know everyone else. With its assassination plot, *Margarita, How Beautiful the Sea* has elements of a thriller, but the broader picture of the novel is of Nicaraguan life in the first half of the twentieth century. With its melding of personal fact and fiction, *A Thousand Deaths Plus One* (2004, English 2009) is a novel in the style of Spaniards Enrique Vila-Matas and Javier Marías. The novel alternates between first-person accounts by a narrator much resembling Ramírez and the man whose life he is trying to piece together, an obscure photographer named Juan Castellón. Ramírez comes across traces of Castellón while traveling in his official political capacity, and over the years of his obsession, a fascinating picture emerges. The two tracks of the narrative cover more than a century of Nicaraguan history but also address issues such as how to capture history and convey individual lives. Ramírez's novel suggests that neither photography, even from the very midst of history (where Castellón often found himself), nor a written record or re-creation seems able to ever grasp all the essentials.

ELSEWHERE IN CENTRAL AMERICA

Several of the most prominent authors from the other Central American countries, including **Claribel Alegría** (b. 1924) and **Horacio Castellanos Moya** (b. 1957), have led very peripatetic live. Although she is best known for her poetry, the Nicaraguan-born Claribel Alegría has also written several works of fiction. *Luisa in Realityland* (1987,

English 1987), inspired by Lewis Carroll's *Alice* books and based on her own childhood in El Salvador, alternates between short prose sections and poems in a tapestry of myth, history, and remembrance that is a good introduction to the author. Horacio Castellanos Moya was born in Honduras but grew up in El Salvador. Strongly influenced by the Austrian writer Thomas Bernhard, Castellanos Moya's novels, such as *The She-Devil in the Mirror* (2000, English 2009) and *Senselessness* (2004, English 2008), feature obsessive narrators confronting violent Central American society in Bernhardian monologues. *Senselessness* is set in an unnamed country that is nevertheless readily identifiable as Guatemala. The narrator, who hastily fled his own homeland after publishing a piece of writing that generated a very critical reaction—much as Castellanos Moya went into permanent exile after the publication of his controversial novel *El asco* (1997, not yet translated)—has agreed to edit an eleven-hundred-page report detailing atrocities committed by the army against the indigenous population. The Bernhardian style of run-on sentences and relentless self-reflection, even in light of all these horrors, is very effective.

KEEP IN MIND

- **Manlio Argueta**'s (b. 1935) novels about El Salvador are noteworthy.
- **Zee Edgell**'s (b. 1940) English-language fiction is from Belize (formerly known as British Honduras and achieving full independence only in 1981).
- *Costa Rica: A Traveler's Literary Companion* (1994), edited by Barbara Ras, contains more than two dozen stories from all parts of Costa Rica.

Caribbean

With its many dispersed islands and languages, the literary world of the Caribbean—extending to the Dutch-, French-, and English-speaking outliers of South America (Suriname, French Guiana, and Guyana)—is an enormous hodgepodge. Although Cuban literature is a significant part of the Latin American tradition, until recently the country's isolation from the United States has led to a relatively muted reception of Cuban fiction in the English-speaking world. Despite some sense of community in the Caribbean, fostered by regional publishers and organizations, its linguistic, cultural, and economic differences—in some instances, as in the case of Haiti and the Dominican Republic, all even on the same island—have limited the rise of a more unified literary marketplace. With only a small local base of readers, an underdeveloped publishing market that often can offer only little editorial support, and few venues providing useful critical feedback, a healthy literary culture has been difficult to sustain in most of the Caribbean nations. Not surprisingly, many authors from the island states are best known for their work created abroad, most famously the Trinidad and Tobago–born Nobel laureate **V. S. Naipaul** (b. 1932).

CUBA

Cuba's experience with authoritarian rule is not unusual in Latin America but has, under Fidel Castro and now his brother Raúl, lasted longer and been more stable than elsewhere. The totalitarian regime that took power in 1959 continues to limit freedom of speech, but as in the Soviet Union, a high regard for culture has provided fertile ground for authors, and the literary output by those in Cuba itself and writers who have gone abroad has consistently been impressive.

Cuba's greatest novelist, **Alejo Carpentier** (1904–1980), spent much of his life abroad. A dedicated leftist, he fled the country in 1928 after being blacklisted and spent most of the next decades in Europe and Venezuela before settling in Cuba again after the revolution in 1959. Despite a comfortable and privileged life in Cuba under the Castro regime, he accepted a diplomatic posting to Paris in the late 1960s and lived there until his death. Carpentier's fiction is a fascinating amalgam of his cultural and political influences. He also frequently relied on music for his fiction, most obviously in the grand Stravinsky-suffused *La consagración de la primavera* (*The Rite of Spring*; 1978, not yet translated).

Carpentier is perhaps best known as the originator of what is now known as magical realism. This was not a term he himself used but was taken from the notion of *lo real maravilloso* (the marvelously real), which he described in conjunction with his novel *The Kingdom of This World* (1949, English 1957). In *The Kingdom of This World*, Carpentier examines the transition from colonial French to local rule in Haiti at the turn of the eighteenth century through the Haitian revolution and its messy aftermath in which the regime of Henri Christophe (the black self-proclaimed king of the northern part of the new nation) proved to be as delusional as that of the Europeans. The four short parts of *The Kingdom of This World* offer a fragmented view of this period of Haitian history. Ti Noël is a unifying figure across the different sections. He starts out as a slave, and like most Haitians, his lot is little improved by the political changes. It is Carpentier's embrace of what he saw as "the marvelously real" that is the novel's most striking feature, with its reliance on native Haitian custom, including voodoo, in an eerily dreamy presentation verging on the surreal. *Explosion in a Cathedral* (1962, English 1963) broadens the themes of *The Kingdom of This World*. Taking place during the French Revolution, the novel is a more expansive examination of how these transformations affected the Old and New Worlds.

Carpentier's most acclaimed work, *The Lost Steps* (1953, English 1956), offers a more radical contrast of civilizations. In this novel, a composer living in a large city in the United States who has more or less sold out to commercial interests takes up an offer to travel to the isolated backlands of South America to collect musical instruments used by the indigenous population. There he finds a culture still largely existing outside history. Its simplicity and purity attract him, but in his attempt to capture his experience in a musical composition, he leaves it. Then, after returning to civilization, he cannot find his way back. *The Lost Steps* is a fascinating allegory of the artist in the modern world.

Though best known as a poet, **José Lezama Lima** (1910–1976) wrote one of the great novels of Cuba, *Paradiso* (1966, English 1974). More than simply a coming-of-age novel, it artfully traces protagonist José Cemí's maturation into a poet. Sexually charged and explicit, and with its baroque evocation of old and contemporary Cuba as well as its immersion into the poetic, *Paradiso* is a challenging but rewarding work.

Guillermo Cabrera Infante's (1929–2005) fiction is among the most comic to come out of Latin America. The wordplay and puns in his novels of pre-Castro Cuba, such as *Three Trapped Tigers* (1965, English 1971) and *Infante's Inferno* (1979, English 1984), are very difficult to translate. Laurence Sterne's *Tristram Shandy* (1759–1767) is one of the most obvious and strongest influences on his work (right down to the use of entirely blacked-out pages). Fluent in English, Cabrera Infante collaborated on the English versions of *Three Trapped Tigers*

and *Infante's Inferno*; both are re-creations rather than strict translations. Appropriately, *Three Trapped Tigers* begins with a master of cere-
monies' bilingual introduction to the show to come, just as might have
been heard in the 1950s on many of Havana's nightclub stages catering
to both local and U.S. audiences. Speech and conversation continue to
dominate in the work, with multiple perspectives and many voices, but
the novel also uses letters and even texts on the death of Leon Trotsky,
written as a parody of seven of Cuba's best known authors (including
José Lezama Lima and Alejo Carpentier). *Infante's Inferno* is a coming-
of-age novel that deals with sexual awakening and obsession even more
intently than does Lezama Lima's *Paradiso*.

   José Manuel Prieto (b. 1962) left Cuba after high school to spend
more than a decade in the Soviet Union before moving to Mexico in
the mid-1990s, and his books reflect some of those international experiences. His trilogy of novels with Russian themes, **Encyclopedia of a
Life in Russia** (1997, English 2013), **Nocturnal Butterflies of the Russian Empire** (1999, English 2000), and **Rex** (2007, English 2009),
are exciting works with flighty narrators who get caught up in shady
business dealings, and they are strongly rooted in other works of modern fiction. *Nocturnal Butterflies of the Russian Empire* and *Rex* build
on Nabokov, Borges, and Proust. The narrator in *Rex* is obsessed by
Marcel Proust's *Remembrance of Things Past*, to which he refers as "the
Book." Hired as a tutor for a young Russian boy, he relies on it as an all-
encompassing textbook. In *Nocturnal Butterflies of the Russian Empire*
the narrator, J., reflects on his life as a smuggler. Among the objects he
pursued and wanted to bring across international borders were both
rare butterflies and V., a prostitute with whom he had fallen passion-
ately in love. The novel follows his attempts to frame a perfect letter to
V., who has escaped his grasp, adding a literary dimension to his story.
Prieto's novels might seem too allusive, but the underlying stories of
international intrigue and personal quests make them better than most
such referential fiction.

   Leonardo Padura Fuentes (b. 1955) is among the few internationally recognized and successful authors who have remained in Cuba.
Six of his crime novels featuring Mario Conde have been translated

into English, and they offer a surprisingly unvarnished picture of contemporary Cuba. Conde was introduced as a policeman with literary aspirations in a quartet of novels covering a year at the end of the 1980s in Conde's life, each of the four volumes devoted to a different season and crime: *Havana Blue* (1991, English 2007), *Havana Gold* (1994, English 2008), *Havana Red* (1997, English 2005), and *Havana Black* (1998, English 2006). In the later volumes, *Adiós Hemingway* (2001, English 2005) and *Havana Fever* (2005, English 2008), the middle-aged Conde has retired from his job and works as a middleman in the used-book trade but again finds himself caught up in detective work. While all these novels are solid and satisfying police procedurals, their greater appeal is Conde's descriptions of a country that seems to be all faded glory.

In a more ambitious work, *The Man Who Loved Dogs* (2009, English 2014), Padura revisits the assassination of Leon Trotsky. This three-tiered novel recounts the stories of Trotsky; his assassin, Ramón Mercader; and a once-promising Cuban writer, Iván Cárdenas Maturell, who went too far in challenging the authorities with a story he wrote.

KEEP IN MIND

- **Reinaldo Arenas** (1943–1990) wrote challenging but rewarding fiction.
- **Pedro Juan Gutiérrez**'s (b. 1950) *Dirty Havana Trilogy* (1998, English 2001) is a vivid depiction of the misery in 1990s Havana.
- Among **Zoé Valdés**'s (b. 1959) noteworthy novels is the lively *I Gave You All I Had* (1996, English 1999).
- **Antonio José Ponte**'s (b. 1964) collections of short stories include *Tales from the Cuban Empire* (2000, English 2002).
- Uruguayan-born **Daniel Chavarría** (b. 1933) has lived in Cuba since 1969. He shows a lighter, more humorous touch than does Leonardo Padura in his thrillers set in Havana, *Adiós Muchachos* (1994, English 2001) and *Tango for a Torturer* (2001, English 2007). This classics scholar has also written *The Eye of Cybele* (1993, English 2002), set in ancient Greece.

OTHER SPANISH-SPEAKING NATIONS
AND TERRITORIES

Much of the literature available in English by writers from the other major Spanish-speaking nations and territories in the Caribbean, the Dominican Republic and Puerto Rico (a territory of the United States), reflects their close connection to the United States. A growing number of acclaimed U.S.-based English-writing authors have Puerto Rican or Dominican ties, including **Julia Alvarez** (b. 1950) and **Junot Díaz** (b. 1968), both of whom spent parts of their earliest childhood in the Dominican Republic and use their family and cultural backgrounds in their fiction.

The Cuban-born **Mayra Montero** (b. 1952) is the most significant and sure-handed contemporary Puerto Rico–based author. With a novel of Haiti that echoes the work of Alejo Carpentier, *In the Palm of Darkness* (1995, English 1997), and other novels such as *Last Night I Spent with You* (1991, English 2000), her fiction also is oriented to the larger Caribbean region. Her novels often have an erotic tinge, and the most salacious, *Deep Purple* (2000, English 2003), is also wonderfully comic. In that novel, music critic Agustín Cabán finds he is not quite ready for retirement and keeps busy by writing his erotic memoirs in installments. Here Montero combines two of her favorite themes, music and sex, and Cabán's various sexual conquests offer appealing erotic entertainment.

Old Cuba also features in several of Montero's novels. *The Messenger* (1998, English 1999) is based on a historic event, the explosion of a bomb in a Havana theater during Enrico Caruso's 1920 performance of *Aida*. *Dancing to "Almendra"* (2005, English 2007) is set in the late 1950s and begins with the death of a hippopotamus that had escaped the Havana zoo and the murder of a mafioso in New York, two separate violent deaths that turn out to be connected. The young journalist who pursues the story, Joaquín Porrata, finds himself drawn into a complex and dangerous tangle of events that involve both Havana's strong Mafia influence and the revolution. Although Montero overdoes the bizarre—Porrata's love interest is a one-armed circus performer calling herself Yolanda, and she is far from the only colorful character—she spins a tale of intrigue and historic ambience.

FRANCOPHONE CARIBBEAN

The Caribbean's French-speaking nations and territories stretch from Haiti to French Guiana. The so-called overseas departments, including Martinique and French Guiana, are still officially parts of France and remain closely tied to it, which is reflected in much of the literary production there. Haiti was the first Latin American colony to gain independence, during the French Revolution, and its cultural development has followed a very different arc, which has repeatedly been stunted by extended periods of political instability and militant authoritarian rule. Creole (Kreyòl) is, along with French, Haiti's official language, and even though most of the Haitian fiction that reaches an international audience—mainly in France but also in English translation—is written in French, much of it has Creole influences.

René Philoctète's (1932–1995) *Massacre River* (1989, English 2005) explores the infamous 1937 massacre ordered by Dominican dictator Rafael Trujillo in the border region dividing Haiti from the Dominican Republic. The protagonists are the Dominican Pedro Brito and his Haitian wife, Adèle, caught up in the events, but Trujillo also figures in the novel. In scenes that shift between the real and the surreal, the poet Philoctète vividly portrays the madness of the times. Language plays a central role in the massacre, with a quick test of the Spanish pronunciation of the word for *parsley* (*perejil*) determining who is to be spared and who is to be killed, in the absence of any other means of differentiating between the nationalities of those in the area. Philoctète's extensive use of a mix of French, Spanish, and Creole reflects the communal attitude of the locals that readily transcends nationalist fervor. It is the outsiders, led by the authoritarian Trujillo, who seek to impose notions of difference and racial superiority where there are none.

Lyonel Trouillot's (b. 1956) compact novel *Street of Lost Footsteps* (1996, English 2003) compresses Haiti's violent history into an account of a single brutal night in a dark ride reminiscent of Louis-Ferdinand Céline (1894–1961). Trouillot's dense yet lyrical style can be difficult to fully appreciate in translation, but he is an important author who should make a larger mark as more of his work becomes available in English.

Martiniquais author **Édouard Glissant** (1928–2011) was a highly influential critic and intellectual and a major poet. He also wrote several novels, including *The Fourth Century* (1964, English 2001) and *The Overseer's Cabin* (1981, revised 1997, English 2011), both of which tell the often violent and dark history of the island, with an emphasis on voices and stories that have long been lost or overlooked.

Another author from Martinique, **Patrick Chamoiseau** (b. 1953), is among the region's most innovative. His use of Creole in his French texts is particularly noteworthy, as he is less concerned with authentically representing local speech than with the new puns and different formulations that Creole offers. The wonderful *Solibo Magnificent* (1988, English 1998) is nominally a mystery, but the investigation into the death of its storytelling title character is also an allegory of the demise of the local oral tradition. From the crisp precision of the police incident report that opens the novel to the freewheeling dialogue, Chamoiseau's narrative is an often amusing flood of miscommunication as the different ways of telling stories and conveying information clash. The enormous *Texaco* (1992, English 1997) is a beautiful panoramic novel covering more than a century of the history of Martinique in which Chamoiseau employs his trademark approaches to good effect.

ANGLOPHONE CARIBBEAN

The British West Indies extend from Bermuda to Guyana, and while interesting fiction has been produced across the entire region, much of the best has emerged from Trinidad and Tobago and Guyana. Many authors have moved throughout the region as well as farther abroad, with the Nobel Prize–winning poet **Derek Walcott** (b. 1930)—who was born in St. Lucia, studied in Jamaica, and worked in Trinidad and the United States—being typical. Several of the region's countries also have sizable populations with roots in the Indian subcontinent, producing a different cultural mix than that elsewhere in the Western Hemisphere.

V. S. Naipaul (b. 1932) left Trinidad to study at Oxford and then settled in England, and his novels, set in the Caribbean, Africa, India, and England, reflect his international background and experience. Naipaul's characters often find themselves strangers in strange lands, the colonial legacy skewing worlds in which his characters cannot find a proper hold. Several of his works feature would-be revolutionaries, but at best, his protagonists are drawn into the action as inadvertent followers and witnesses, not leaders. Despite a surprisingly sure comic touch and some genuinely humane humor, Naipaul's fiction is often bleak and sour. However, his supremely elegant style—one of the finest of any contemporary author writing in English—and penetrating character studies redeem most of the faults in his fiction.

A House for Mr. Biswas (1961) is the longest but also one of the simplest and most generous of Naipaul's novels. The title character, Mohun Biswas, is loosely based on Naipaul's own father, and the novel describes how he stumbles through life (and into his marriage). Mr. Biswas clings to the ambition of owning his own house, a symbol of what otherwise eludes him: accomplishment and independence. After numerous failed attempts, he finally meets with success, yet what Naipaul allows him looks like only a hollow victory. The overwhelmed protagonist of this tragicomic story is typical of Naipaul's fiction, but the attentive portrait of him is also a particularly warm one.

Naipaul offers grim portrayals of the postcolonial world in politically charged novels such as *Guerrillas* (1975), set in the West Indies, and *A Bend in the River* (1979), set in Africa. Here, as elsewhere in his work, Naipaul is not nihilistic or simply cynical—except regarding those characters who claim to be able to orchestrate social and political change—but he ruthlessly deflates almost any idealism his characters might harbor. The two novels about Willie Somerset Chandran are the most compelling late-career synthesis of Naipaul's outlook on life and the world. *Half a Life* (2001), a novel of half-lived lives and incompleteness, portrays Willie as he drifts from India to England to Africa to Berlin. One of Willie's failures is his halfhearted attempt at becoming an author, and part of the book's power comes from the fact that his fate seems to be one that Naipaul could have envisaged for himself. Naipaul's cool and controlled account of Willie's life continues in *Magic Seeds* (2004), a summation of Naipaul's worldview presented in spare prose. In *Magic Seeds*, Willie seeks to make his life whole by joining a guerrilla movement in India but finds no radical redemption. *Magic Seeds* is a devastating, pitch-perfect meditation on contemporary anomie.

The entire range of Naipaul's fiction is worthwhile, but among his other works deserving closer attention are two with strong autobiographical elements: *A Way in the World* (1994)—called a "novel" in the American edition and a "sequence" in the British edition—and *The Enigma of Arrival* (1987). Naipaul's superb (if often frustratingly opinionated) nonfiction is also reflected in these close-to-life novels.

The leading Guyanese authors **Roy Heath** (1926–2008) and **Wilson Harris** (b. 1921) emigrated to England in the 1950s, but much of their work is set in Guyana. Heath's *The Murderer* (1978) is a penetrating psychological study of a man driven to kill his wife. In the comic novels *Kwaku* (1982) and *The Ministry of Hope* (1997), the misadventures of Kwaku Cholmondeley, first in the countryside and then in the city, offer an entertaining overview of Guyanese society, life, and political corruption. Wilson Harris's novels range more widely across Guyana and also are more stylistically varied; his writing career also had several distinct phases. Much of his fiction is experimental and his narratives are often nonlinear, but it also has connections, as characters and themes appear again in later novels. None of his many novels can be considered representative, but *Resurrection at Sorrow Hill* (1993), about the residents of an asylum in the depths of the Guyanese jungle, with its reworking of both European and indigenous myths and the use of both simplistic allegory (characters with names like Christopher

---

KEEP IN MIND

- V. S. Naipaul's younger brother, **Shiva Naipaul** (1945–1985; emigrated to Great Britain), and their nephew **Neil Bissoondath** (b. 1955; emigrated to Canada) also wrote fiction.
- Trinidadian author **Earl Lovelace**'s (b. 1935) *Is Just a Movie* (2011) is a novel of late-twentieth-century life in Trinidad.
- Jamaican author **Marlon James**'s (b. 1970) rich novel *A Brief History of Seven Killings* (2014) deservedly won the Man Booker Prize.
- The writer **Caryl Phillips** (b. 1958) was born on St. Kitts but raised in Great Britain. Several of his books are about different forms of the African diaspora.

D'eath) and philosophical argument subtly woven into the narrative, serves as an excellent introduction to his work. Harris is also one of several authors who has written about the 1978 mass suicide of more than nine hundred followers of Jim Jones in Jonestown, in his novel *Jonestown* (1996). **Fred D'Aguiar** (b. 1960) also wrote about these events in his narrative poem *Bill of Rights* (1998).

DUTCH-SPEAKING NATIONS AND TERRITORIES

Dutch is the official language of the Caribbean's Netherland Antilles, as well as the South American nation of Suriname. Only Suriname is large enough to have developed a modestly self-sustaining domestic literary culture, though some of its writers, like **Astrid Roemer** (b. 1947), emigrated to the Netherlands. **Cynthia McLeod** (b. 1936) is the most prominent local author whose work is available in English. Her novel *The Free Negress Elisabeth* (2000, English 2004) is a fascinating historical work based on the eighteenth-century figure Elizabeth Samson, who attained considerable wealth and social standing, even though she was barred from marrying a white man.

North America

United States and Canada

UNITED STATES

In almost every nation in the world, fiction from other countries makes up a significant portion of the local market, but not so in the United States. Although English-language fiction from abroad, especially Great Britain, has a place, otherwise only a little foreign fiction is readily available or widely read. The vast annual output by American authors easily crowds out most foreign competition, and American fiction also thrives abroad, in both its most popular form—airport thrillers and the like—and more literarily demanding ones. The spread of English as the internationally most widely used language has also greatly increased the market that American authors can readily reach, and success has continued to breed success. Many foreign authors are popular in the United States and abroad, but worldwide, almost any best-seller list continues to be top-heavy with American writers.

The size and the cultural and social diversity of the United States easily support a much greater amount and variety of fiction than smaller and more homogenous countries could. Even when it is introspective, American fiction seems to have more breadth than that from more uniform cultures. The land of opportunity offers authors a wealth of material, too, to go along with its huge potential readerships. Much of the best genre fiction, from pulp thrillers to science fiction, has long come from American writers, nurtured in a supportive environment that includes large, loyal fan bases and continuity in the publishing industry. America has enjoyed an extended period of stable, democratic government, free press, and comparatively little wartime disruption on American soil, facilitating the development and continuing success of American popular fiction. In contrast, the major European, Asian, and African countries all have suffered major domestic disruptions as well as considerably greater government interference in publishing, which has, over shorter and longer periods, hampered literary production.

If not always better, American fiction certainly seems bigger than that of any other nation. Beside a seemingly limitless amount of genre fiction, it includes distinctive regional literature as well as many stabs at the "great American novel." The sheer scale of output can also mask passing fads and occasional lulls in creativity and originality in certain areas while others continue to thrive. Beyond its popularity, contemporary American writing also has considerable depth, with a more vibrant writing culture—or several overlapping ones—than any others in the world. There is some truth to American writing's being particularly market oriented and populist, but much of considerable value also rises out of that. Even in summary, the amount of notable American fiction is staggering.

The works by an old guard of authors, including **Saul Bellow** (1915–2005), **John Updike** (1932–2009), and **Philip Roth** (b. 1933), are pillars of the modern canon. Even though Updike's and Roth's fiction is often colored by their personal experiences, depicting WASP and Jewish life in the Northeast, it speaks as well to readers beyond ethnic or local lines in a way peculiar to American fiction. The works by authors like the underappreciated **Cynthia Ozick** (b. 1928) or the last

American to win the Nobel Prize in Literature, **Toni Morrison** (b. 1931), which focus more narrowly on the Jewish and the African American experiences, respectively, may not be as easy for all readers to identify with but are, by any measure, major literature.

William Gaddis (1922–1998) and **William H. Gass** (b. 1924), who often are confused with each other, unfortunately reach only small audiences with their more challenging fiction. Gaddis wrote just a few novels, but each of the two-time National Book Award–winner's works is worthwhile, especially his satire of American capitalism and finance, *J.R.* (1977). William Gass's major work is *The Tunnel* (1995), one of the peaks of American fiction from the 1990s. It is a beautifully written but horribly bleak book about confronting history, narrated by Frederick Kohler, a professor who is trying to write the introduction to his life's work, *Guilt and Innocence in Hitler's Germany*, while also looking back on his own life.

Thomas Pynchon's (b. 1937) *Gravity's Rainbow* (1973) is in the tradition of the big, complex American novels that began with Herman Melville's (1819–1891) *Moby-Dick* (1851). Taking place mainly at the end of World War II, the novel centers on the German V-2 rocket project but in fact spins wildly around many subjects, characters, and themes in a true *tour de force*. Pynchon's other fiction also is intriguing, but only the massive *Against the Day* (2006) has a similarly broad sweep.

KEEP IN MIND

- **Raymond Carver**'s (1938–1988) minimalist realist short fiction was, for a time, tremendously influential, but the lure of more intricate fiction has proved irresistible for most American writers.
- **Don DeLillo**'s (b. 1936) stylized postmodern works offer a variety of critical takes on contemporary America.
- **Cormac McCarthy**'s (b. 1933) novels of male lives in a harsh and bleak world, often set in the Southwest and full of brutality, can seem overwritten but have been popular.

Paul Theroux (b. 1941) is best known for his travel writing, but he is also a fine creative writer, the sense of humor and self-absorbedness familiar from his travel books serving him equally well in his fiction. Many of his novels draw on his own experiences, and several, such as *My Other Life* (1996), are clearly autobiographical. Theroux is generally least successful when straying farthest from what he is familiar with—the futuristic *O-Zone* (1986) is a dud—but his self-centered autobiographical novels and stories of life abroad and in the United States are almost uniformly entertaining and well written.

Many of **John Irving**'s (b. 1942) novels have a nineteenth-century feel, describing protagonists in unusual circumstances trying to make their way in the world. Even though his fiction contains recurring locales (New England, Austria) and quirky elements (an obsession with wrestling, unusual physical characteristics), Irving continues to be inventive in his agreeably old-fashioned entertainments. But he seems to be trying too hard to keep the quirkiness going in his most recent works. The comic novel *The World According to Garp* (1978), describing the life and times of T. S. Garp, is his most successful work, but other novels, such as *The Cider House Rules* (1985), which treats the subject of abortion, are also very good.

Much of **William T. Vollmann**'s (b. 1959) fiction deals with marginalized people or classes of people, prostitutes being a favorite. The continuing series of historical novels he began in 1990, **Seven Dreams: A Book of North American Landscapes**, reconsiders significant

---

KEEP IN MIND

- The sheer mass of superprolific **Joyce Carol Oates**'s (b. 1938) body of work is daunting, but her approachable fiction has considerable appeal.
- The exclamation-point-happy **Tom Wolfe** (b. 1931), a much louder author, brings his journalistic background and style to bear in fat sociocultural novels in the grand old tradition. No master of subtlety, only his first novel, the entertaining period piece *The Bonfire of the Vanities* (1987), a tragic-comic romp set in 1980s New York City at the height of the greed-is-good era on Wall Street, looks likely to endure.

KEEP IN MIND

- **David Foster Wallace**'s (1962–2008) mammoth *Infinite Jest* (1996)— nearly a thousand pages of text plus almost a hundred pages of notes and errata—is another American piece of superfiction. Set in the near future, it is a digressive novel that seems to try to do it all.
- **Jonathan Safran Foer**'s (b. 1977) first novels have proved to be very popular.

periods and events of American history. These often weighty novels are notable for their attention to detail, though all the research that went into them is frequently too apparent.

Jonathan Franzen's (b. 1959) ambitious, sprawling realist novels of the American condition are among the best by any author of the generation after Roth and Updike. His story of the midwestern Lambert family, *The Corrections* (2001), is a particularly impressive slice of contemporary Americana. **Jeffrey Eugenides**'s (b. 1960) more eccentric, all-American tale, *Middlesex* (2002), has a unique twist with its hermaphrodite narrator, Calliope "Cal" Helen Stephanides, but is the sort of novel that has been written several times too often (by John Irving, among others). Nonetheless, Eugenides's *The Virgin Suicides* (1993) is a memorable and original take on adolescence and American life. Its effective use of the first person plural, with a chorus of now adult men who narrate the story, is remarkable.

Native American Fiction

Among the fine regional literature from throughout the United States, the most distinctive is that from Polynesian Hawaii, with its geographical and cultural links to the South Pacific and East Asia, as well that by Native American authors.

N. Scott Momaday's (b. 1934) *House Made of Dawn* (1968) was among the first novels about the modern Native American experience of reservation and urban America to gain a larger readership,

---

KEEP IN MIND

- The younger generation of Native American authors includes **Louise Erdrich** (b. 1954) and **Sherman Alexie** (b. 1966).

---

and it remains a template for much Native American fiction. **Gerald Vizenor**'s (b. 1934) works are playful and inventive, with his satirical novels often incorporating the Native American trickster figure. *The Heirs of Columbus* (1992) is a wildly imagined contemporary story in which one of the many fantastical premises is that the famous explorer had Mayan roots. In *Hiroshima Bugi: Atomu 57* (2003), Japanese culture and history are incorporated into a story about the atomic age, in which the destruction of Hiroshima and its aftereffects mirror the destruction wrought on Native Americans over the centuries.

Foreign-Born Writers

Foreign-born authors are not as prominent in the contemporary American literary scene as they are in Great Britain (or Canada), but several have made significant contributions here. **Vladimir Nabokov** (1899–1977) is certainly the leading example. He began writing in English only after he had already established himself as a Russian author, but he wrote his best works in this second language, with *Lolita* (1955) one of America's greatest novels.

Nabokov grew up multilingual and was comfortable reading and speaking English long before he turned to writing in it, whereas English is more obviously a second language for authors such as **Aleksandar Hemon** (b. 1964), **Ha Jin** (b. 1956), and **Yiyun Li** (b. 1972), who learned it only later in life. Although their prose is somewhat stilted, its different feel and sound can be quite effective. Hemon, in particular, is very attentive to language and the possibilities of English, which contributes to the success of his fiction. Ha Jin's plainer prose also suits his fiction, which focuses on the Chinese experience in both China and the United States.

As in Great Britain, a large number of foreign authors live and work in the United States but remain much more closely associated with their national literatures; the African trio of **Chinua Achebe** (1930–2013), **Wole Soyinka** (b. 1934), and **Ngũgĩ wa Thiong'o** (b. 1938) are prominent examples. Those who came to the United States at a very young age, like the talented British-born **Jhumpa Lahiri** (b. 1967), have been the most successful in navigating two (or more) cultures and the immigrant experience in their work.

Genre Fiction

An immense amount of popular and genre fiction, of widely varying quality, is produced by American authors. Sales and circulation figures suggest that much of it has tremendous appeal and entertainment value. Much, however, is essentially disposable and has little literary worth, and some, like **Dan Brown**'s (b. 1964) sensationally successful *The Da Vinci Code* (2003), has none at all.

Of the consistently best-selling authors, the multitalented **Michael Crichton** (1942–2008) at least impressed with the variety of his work and the ideas he worked into his fiction, including the implications of rapid technological innovation. The versatile **Stephen King** (b. 1947), best known for his horror and supernatural suspense fiction (as well as his prodigious output), is a better writer, at least in some of his books. King can be especially good on the minutiae of everyday American life, including pop and consumer culture, and uses this to good effect in his often unsettling works. More baffling is the success of legal thriller author **John Grisham** (b. 1955). He manages to build some suspense in his novels, but with their limited prose and barely plausible plots, they hardly stand above the many other unremarkable books in the genre, unlike **Scott Turow**'s (b. 1949) well-written and more credible legal thrillers.

The often serial nature of genre fiction, with a stream of books featuring the same protagonist as well as the relentless pace of production, with authors often churning out more than one book a year, can result in very uneven quality. Even though he took his time between books, **Thomas Harris**'s (b. 1940) Hannibal Lecter novels are prime examples: *Red Dragon* (1981) and *The Silence of the Lambs* (1988) are among the best suspense procedurals of recent decades, but the subsequent novels about Lecter are inferior.

The vast expanse of American mystery and crime fiction contains a great deal of fine writing. **Raymond Chandler**'s (1888–1959) fiction and a few of **James M. Cain**'s (1892–1977) works are still the gold standard—and the most widely imitated—but much else, from the pulp fiction of **Jim Thompson** (1906–1977) to **Charles Willeford**'s (1919–1988) and **Donald E. Westlake**'s (1933–2008) works, is impressive as well. American crime fiction writing today has extraordinary variety, and among the most interesting authors are **Elmore Leonard** (1925–2013); **Walter Mosley** (b. 1952), with his Easy Rawlins novels; and **James Ellroy** (b. 1948), with his machine-gun-fire prose.

Science fiction writing can get bogged down in elaborate premises and inventions (and the efforts to explain them), but even a stylistically ragged writer like **Philip K. Dick** (1928–1982) can carry readers through with the audacity of his creations. **Neal Stephenson**'s (b. 1959) massive *The Baroque Cycle* trilogy (2003–2004) and the nearly thousand-page *Anathem* (2008) are typical of the best and worst in science fiction, fascinating in their meticulous research and intellectual reach and filled with rollicking adventures but ultimately glutted. Stephenson's cyberpunk classic *Snow Crash* (1992) is just as richly imagined but much more manageable.

Some very good fiction has also come from authors who move between genres, like **Kurt Vonnegut** (1922–2007). He used elements of science fiction in his classic war novel *Slaughterhouse-Five* (1969), about the firebombing of Dresden, but his approachable style and mix of the jocular and the serious are what make his books so enjoyable. **Steve Erickson** (b. 1950) and **Jonathan Lethem** (b. 1964) also use science fiction as a foundation for much of their fiction while also moving beyond mere genre writing.

Popular women's fiction, in its countless romance and chick lit iterations, obviously satisfies its large audience but is a literary minefield for those not disposed to its formulas. From **Jacqueline Susann**'s (1921–1974) soft-porn mega–best seller *Valley of the Dolls* (1966), through the works of **Judith Krantz** (b. 1927), **Danielle Steel** (b. 1947), and **Nora Roberts** (b. 1950) to beyond **Candace Bushnell**'s (b. 1958) *Sex and the City* (1996), these works obviously enthrall legions but are hard to regard as any more than overwritten fluff and fantasy. The use of empowered female figures, such as in **Terry McMillan**'s (b. 1951) fiction, may be admirable, but most of the popular women's fiction remains largely an acquired taste.

CANADA

The line between American and Canadian literature may seem blurred, especially when viewed from south of the border, but despite the considerable overlap, much Canadian fiction is distinctive. This is most obvious in what is most unnoticed in the United States: the works by Canada's French-writing authors. The country also has an independent literary and publishing community that is not solely reliant on the U.S. market, so an important separate literary culture has developed there.

With the growing fascination with multiculturalism in recent decades, fiction by the many Canadian authors with some foreign background—from **Michael Ondaatje** (b. 1943) to **Yann Martel** (b. 1963)—has often received more attention abroad than has the CanLit by authors without such apparent international connections. Moreover, much of homegrown fiction has thus been misperceived as one-dimensional and provincial.

Anglophone Fiction

The extent to which Canadian fiction is oriented toward to the United States varies widely. **Douglas Coupland**'s (b. 1961) early works of fiction, such as *Generation X* (1991) and *Microserfs* (1995), are all-American tales about a new generation in which the conditions he describes arose first. His more recent fiction features Canadian settings, such as his Vancouver rewriting of the Columbine high school killings in *Hey, Nostradamus!* (2003) or *JPod* (2006), another working-geek novel. Coupland is more interested, however, in the common issues found in technology-oriented consumer societies in general than in local concerns. **Michael Ondaatje** (b. 1943) fixates on specific American myths and figures in his beautiful works of fragmentary and poetic storytelling, *The Collected Works of Billy the Kid* (1970), and *Coming Through Slaughter* (1976), his fictionalized life of New Orleans jazz musician Buddy Bolden. But he is equally comfortable with other settings, from Canada (*In the Skin of a Lion*, 1987) to Italy during World War II (*The English Patient*, 1992), to contemporary Sri Lanka (*Anil's Ghost*, 2000).

The work of authors like **Robertson Davies** (1913–1995), **Mordecai Richler** (1931–2001), and the 2013 Nobel laureate, **Alice Munro** (b. 1931), is more strongly rooted in Canada but also has broader appeal. Davies's three trilogies are wonderful entertainment. His expansive storytelling resembles that of nineteenth-century English authors, but his novels are modern in their use of symbolism and philosophical underpinnings. Comfortable in theatrical, musical, and academic milieus, Davies leads many of his characters on fascinating journeys, most memorably in the final completed trilogy, *The Cornish Trilogy* (1981–1988).

Whereas Davies puts together his visions in a series of connected novels, Alice Munro is a master of the short story. Her second book, *Lives of Girls and Women* (1971), in which the adolescent Del Jordan describes her coming of age and becoming a writer, is ostensibly a novel—her only one—but even here, Munro is more comfortable presenting her material in distinct stories. A great stylist, Munro's many collections of short but substantial pieces are impressive indeed.

Mordecai Richler was a ferocious satirist whose work arguably occasionally descends into vulgarity. His novels about Jewish and Canadian life, from *The Apprenticeship of Duddy Kravitz* (1959) to *Barney's Version* (1997), are raucous and often overcrowded with incidents but also fun. Furthermore, they have been very popular beyond Canada and the United States.

One of Canada's leading poets and novelists, **Margaret Atwood**'s (b. 1939) books range from realism to science fiction. She regularly depicts women in extreme situations, beginning with *The Edible Woman* (1969), whose protagonist eventually is unable to consume any food when her body seems to rebel against the limited, traditional roles expected of women. Atwood's best-known work is *The Handmaid's Tale* (1985), a dystopian tale of a totalitarian and fundamentalist state in which women are completely subjugated. The state, Gilead, is in what used to be the United States before it was decimated by catastrophe and pollution. The book is chillingly effective because their scenarios, whether regarding the effects of pollution or laws limiting women's rights, can be seen as extrapolations from contemporary reality.

If any single work of Atwood's could be considered representative, it is *The Blind Assassin* (2000). Nesting a novel (another *The Blind Assassin*) within a novel, it is a complex yet satisfying work that, in its various layers, combines many of Atwood's approaches and styles. The presentation ranges from unreliable narrators to strict newspaper clipping reality, and this nested novel contains both historical and fantastical parts in its mysteries, social commentary, and considerations of memory and storytelling.

KEEP IN MIND

- **Alistair MacLeod**'s (1936–2014) small body of work includes his excellent novel tracing a family's history and roots, *No Great Mischief* (1999).
- American-born **William Gibson** (b. 1948) is the author of the science fiction classic *Neuromancer* (1984) (in which he coined the word *cyberspace*) as well as more mainstream novels such as *Pattern Recognition* (2003).
- **Brian Fawcett**'s (b. 1944) creative sociopolitical works, *Cambodia: A Book for People Who Find Television Too Slow* (1986) and *Gender Wars: A Novel and Some Conversations About Sex and Gender* (1994), combine fiction and commentary.
- **Michael Turner**'s (b. 1962) fiction includes the film novel *American Whiskey Bar* (1997) and the poetry-less and explicit novel *The Pornographer's Poem* (1999).

Canadian Writers with an International Background

For several decades now, immigrant fiction has been a significant part of the Canadian literary scene. Michael Ondaatje, from Sri Lanka by way of England, is the most prominent of the current generation of writers born abroad, but others include **M. G. Vassanji** (Kenya, b. 1950), **Rohinton Mistry** (India, b. 1952), **Neil Bissoondath** (Trinidad and Tobago, b. 1955), **Rawi Hage** (Lebanon, b. 1964), and **Hiromi Goto** (Japan, b. 1966). This has resulted in a sizable body of multicultural work—both realistic and, in the case of Goto, closer to fantasy and science fiction—that is revealing about both the authors' homelands and the immigrant experience in Canada. **Yann Martel**'s (b. 1963) own very international background figures less directly in his fiction, but his Man Booker Prize–winning *Life of Pi* (2001) with its shipwrecked Indian protagonist, Pi Patel, is replete with cross-cultural connections.

Francophone Fiction

French is the mother tongue of more than a fifth of the Canadian population, with the French speakers concentrated in a single province, Quebec. While Canada is officially bilingual, the overlap in literary cultures is limited, and many French-writing authors are oriented toward Paris. Some of the most prominent French-Canadian authors have also lived in France for extended periods. Even the works of authors like **Antonine Maillet** (b. 1929), who won the most prestigious French literary prize, the Prix Goncourt, and **Anne Hébert** (1916–2000), whose other fiction is overshadowed by her dark love story *Kamouraska* (1970, English 1973), remain underappreciated in translation.

Raised in Canada and the United States before moving to France as a student, **Nancy Huston** (b. 1953) bridges several cultural divides, writing in both French and English and translating her own work. It can make for an odd mix, as in the talky Thanksgiving-meal novel, *Dolce Agonia* (French 2001, English 2001), set in New England and featuring a number of academics—and with an occasional divine narratorial intervention when God lets readers in on the characters' fates. Its intellectual ambitions make *Dolce Agonia* seem like a typical French novel, but Huston also convincingly grounds it on American terrain. Her most impressive achievement to date is the four-part novel of family history presented in reverse chronological order, ***Fault Lines*** (French 2006, English 2007). Beginning in the present day and concluding near the end of World War II, each section jumps some two decades back in time and centers on a different family member at age six. Although Huston's young narrators' voices are not entirely realistic, their childish literalism and limitations serve exceptionally well her story of a family with many fault lines and some dark secrets.

Many of the protagonists in **Jacques Poulin**'s (b. 1937) fiction have a sense of wide-eyed wonder, and Poulin lavishes attention on their fascination with place and surroundings. This is especially true in *The "Jimmy" Trilogy* (1967–1970, English 1979), in which the central characters are, in different ways, still impressionable and young—or are literally young at heart, since the narrator of the third novel in the trilogy, Noël, has received a heart transplant from a teenage girl. Poulin's works also contain a mix of purpose and aimlessness as he explores personal and national identity and history, most obviously in ***Volkswagen Blues*** (1984, English 1988), a quintessential road novel in which the protagonist, Jack, sets out through the United States in search of his brother.

Jacques Godbout's (b. 1933) fiction has a playful way with language, especially in ***Hail Galarneau!*** (1967, English 1970) and its sequel, ***The Golden Galarneaus*** (1993, English 1995), but Godbout's work is also political and often virulently satirical. Written shortly after the 1980 referendum in which Quebecers voted not to move toward secession from Canada, Godbout's untranslated allegorical satire ***Les têtes à Papineau*** (1981), is the story of a man with two heads. His two identities, Charles and François, represent anglophone and francophone Canada. The novel builds toward the operation that is to fuse the two heads together, and a postscript, written in English, reveals that because the operation was a success, the protagonist is now unilingual. His French side has been almost entirely subsumed, as is evident even in the character's closing signature: Charles F. Papineau.

Godbout's *An American Story* (1986, English 1988) places Quebec Canadian Gregory Francoeur (with his suggestive surname) on trial in California for rape and arson, in a broad indictment of the United States that is tempered by Godbout's sense of the absurd as well as exotic elements such as the connection to Ethiopia, where, like his protagonist, Godbout spent time teaching.

Haitian-born author **Dany Laferrière**'s (b. 1953) often autobiographical works are both amusing and provocative in their examination of racial issues in the Americas, as well as stereotypes of identity. They usually feature first-person narrators with a background similar (or identical) to that of the author, who recount their experiences in Haiti, Canada, and the United States. With titles like *How to Make Love to a Negro Without Getting Tired* (1985, English 1987) and *Why Must a Black Writer Write About Sex?* (1993, English 1994), many offer a mix of observation, commentary, and fictional embellishment rather than simply a straightforward story. *I Am a Japanese Writer* (2008, English 2010) is a particularly entertaining twist on Laferrière's favorite themes. The narrator tries to come up with a book to go with the title that just popped into his head when his publisher asked him to describe his new project. Although the narrator struggles with the project, the idea is enough for Laferrière to go off on his usual riffs on everything from writing to identity issues.

Inuit Fiction

A small amount of Canadian First Nations and Inuit fiction is available, with the anthology *Northern Voices* (1988), edited by Penny Petrone, providing a good historic overview of and introduction to Inuit writing in English. **Mitiarjuk Nappaaluk**'s (1931–2007) novel of Inuit life, *Sanaaq* (1984, English 2014), is the most important work originally written in Inuktitut and available in English.

APPENDIX 1

Translation into English, by the Numbers

The claim that only about 3 percent of all books published in the United States (with Great Britain occasionally thrown in for good measure) are translations has gained a great deal of currency over the past decade and continues to be widely cited. It appears, however, to be an essentially anecdotal statistic, only very roughly based on any actual data and, beyond its shock value, is of only limited use.

Even a baseline—a percentage of what, exactly?—is difficult to determine with any accuracy. The "traditional print book output" in the United States was estimated in 2011 to be 347,178 (translations are not counted separately). This includes new editions of previously published work, including paperback editions of last year's hard-covers.[1] Self-publishing and print-on-demand, the bulk of it being public domain works, accounted for more than a million additional titles published in 2011, further inflating and complicating the numbers.

UNESCO's Index Translationum is billed as a World Bibliography of Translation but is marred by the often inadequate data submitted to it.[2] In 2008, the most recent year for which data are available, the United States had 1,431 translated titles. Year-to-year disparities (2,195 translated titles in 2007), which are even more pronounced in the case of other nations, also suggest that the database is, at best, incomplete. In addition are the many duplicate entries and new editions of previously published translations. All in all, the Index Translationum offers only very limited guidance as to how much—and what—has been translated into English in any given year.

The Translation Database kept at Three Percent is currently the most comprehensive effort to track translations in the United States.[3] Maintained since 2008, the database counts all new translations of adult fiction and poetry that are published in the United States. This is by no means a complete register, however, as it does not include any nonfiction, children's literature, cookbooks, or religious and reference works, which account for a significant number of translations annually. It also does not include either new editions—or new translations—of previously translated work, which make up a large percentage of the titles in translation published each year. Because the database is limited to titles that are published or have a distributor in the United States, it also does not include many titles translated into English but published elsewhere, even though many of these books are readily available to American readers via online vendors and distributors.

Nevertheless, the database offers a good crude idea of how much new trade fiction is published in translation in the United States every year—the books that you might find at your local bookstore or that your library stocks. Astonishingly, for 2014 only 494 works of fiction, including anthologies, are listed; in 2013 there were only 448. In addition, translations from three languages—French, German, and Spanish—dominate, routinely accounting together for more than 40 percent of all translations.

Additional translations into English that are published abroad—mainly in India, but also elsewhere—add to the worldwide total, but by any calculation, translation into English lags far behind that into other major languages. Precise foreign data also are difficult to find, but by comparison, the German Publishers and Booksellers Association, for example, reports that out of 81,919 new releases in Germany in 2013, 10,731 were translations into German—although these totals include nonfiction and children's literature.[4]

NOTES

1. "Publishing Market Shows Steady Title Growth in 2011 Fueled Largely by Self-Publishing Sector," June 5, 2012, Bowker, http://www.bowker.com /news/2012/290244861.html (accessed August 4, 2015).
2. United Nations Educational, Scientific, and Cultural Organization, Index Translationum, www.unesco.org/xtrans (accessed April 27, 2015).
3. Translation Database, Three Percent: A Resource for International Literature at the University of Rochester, www.rochester.edu/College/translation/threepercent/index.php?s=database (accessed April 27, 2015).
4. "Economic Figures for the Industry, 2013," Börsenverein des Deutschen Buchhandels, http://www.buchmesse.de/images/fbm/dokumente-ua-pdfs /2014/buchmarkt_deutschland_branchenkennziffern_2014_englisch .pdf_45273.pdf (accessed October 16, 2015).

APPENDIX 2

Supplemental Resources

PERIODICALS AND ONLINE RESOURCES

Major American newspapers and magazines do cover some international fiction, but they generally review very little fiction in translation. British periodicals are somewhat better in both regards. Among publications primarily available in print (almost all now also have an online presence, though not all material is fully and/or freely accessible), the best coverage of foreign titles and authors can be found at:

- *World Literature Today* (www.worldliteraturetoday.org)
- *Review of Contemporary Fiction*
- *Times Literary Supplement* (www.the-tls.co.uk)
- *Bookforum* (www.bookforum.com)

Several websites also offer extensive reviews of foreign works, notably:

- *Complete Review* (www.complete-review.com)
- *The Modern Novel* (www. themodernnovel.org)
- *Quarterly Conversation* (www.quarterlyconversation.com)
- *Three Percent* (www.rochester.edu/College/translation/three percent)

In addition, a steadily increasing number of blogs offer news about and reviews of international literature.

Other websites with a focus on international literature with both original content and essays and reviews include:

- *Words Without Borders* (www.wordswithoutborders.org)
- *Asymptote* (www.asymptotejournal.com)

Smaller literary magazines such as *Mānoa* (http://manoajournal.hawaii .edu/) often devote issues to specific regions or languages.

Many countries have national book offices and organizations that promote domestic literature abroad, and most of these now have an online presence that also provides at least some information in English. These sites vary greatly in quality but are often very useful; a good example is *Dutch Foundation for Literature* (www.letterenfonds .nl/en/).

The excellent independent regional resources online range from the *Literary Map of Africa* (https://library.osu.edu/literary-map-of-africa) to *Albanian Literature in Translation* (www.albanianliterature.net).

Various organizations that are dedicated to cross-cultural exchange, such as *Literature Across Frontiers* (www.lit-across-frontiers.org), also provide information and material of interest.

A comprehensive list of all these sites can be found at www .complete-review.com/guide.

Foreign publishers' websites often provide information (almost always in English) about titles they would like to sell or for which they have sold the foreign rights. This can be a useful way of learning about new titles that are not yet available in the United States or Great Britain or that have not yet been translated into English.

PUBLISHERS

The major publishing houses in the United States and Great Britain do publish some foreign literature, including most of the biggest block-busters, but the smaller independents publish the bulk of foreign fiction, especially in translation.

Many independents have carved out niches for themselves:

AmazonCrossing	Popular contemporary fiction in translation
American University in Cairo Press	Contemporary Arabic fiction
And Other Stories	Contemporary international fiction
Archipelago Books	Twentieth- and twenty-first-century international fiction
Ariadne Press	Austrian fiction
Dalkey Archive Press	Mainly twentieth- and twenty-first-century international fiction
Dedalus	Mainly twentieth- and twenty-first-century international fiction
Deep Vellum	Contemporary international fiction in translation
Europa Editions	Mainly contemporary international (largely European) fiction
Frisch & Co.	Contemporary fiction (solely in e-book format)
Gallic Books	Popular contemporary French fiction
Glas	Twentieth- and twenty-first-century Soviet and Russian fiction
Green Integer	Twentieth- and twenty-first-century international fiction and poetry
Hispabooks	Contemporary Spanish fiction in translation

Host Publications	Contemporary international fiction
Interlink	Contemporary international fiction, especially from the Middle East
New Vessel Press	Twentieth- and twenty-first-century international fiction
New York Review Books	Twentieth- and twenty-first-century international fiction
Open Letter Books	Contemporary fiction in translation
Peepal Tree Press	Mainly Caribbean fiction
Peirene Press	Contemporary European fiction
Pushkin Press	Twentieth- and twenty-first-century European fiction
Seagull	Twentieth- and twenty-first-century international fiction
Telegram	Contemporary international fiction
Twisted Spoon Press	Twentieth- and twenty-first-century Central and Eastern Europe fiction

Other noteworthy commercial publishers that publish significant amounts of fiction in translation are New Directions, Marion Boyars, and Peter Owen.

Several publishers specialize in genre fiction:

Bitter Lemon Press	Mainly contemporary crime fiction in translation
Haikasoru	Contemporary Japanese science fiction and fantasy
Soho Press	Contemporary English-language crime fiction with foreign locales
Vertical	Contemporary popular Japanese fiction

Many American university presses have series devoted to contemporary as well as classical fiction in translation, covering specific regions, languages, and genres. These often are small series, with, at best, a few titles added annually, but many are very strong, such as Northwestern University Press's *Writings from an Unbound Europe*.

Relatively few books published abroad are widely distributed in the United Stated and Great Britain—your local bookstore is unlikely to carry many—but Internet booksellers and lower postal rates have made obtaining them easier and cheaper. Publishers in countries such as Australia, India, and South Africa bring out many worthwhile titles that do not find American or British publishers but can be ordered directly from them or local booksellers. Among the most impressive outlets of titles published abroad is the African Books Collective (www.africanbooks collective.com), which has made available an incredible variety of contemporary African writing at reasonable prices.

LITERARY PRIZES

International literary prizes may help identify authors and books that are not yet well known in the United States and Great Britain. Foreign literary prizes can also help bring works and authors to the attention of publishers as well as American and British readers, and winning works are much more likely to be published here and, when necessary, translated into English.

Prizes Awarded to Authors

Nobel Prize in Literature

Awarded annually since 1901, "to the person who shall have produced in the field of literature the most outstanding work in an ideal direction." The winner is selected by the Swedish Academy. Sometimes controversial, the Nobel Prize is the world's highest international literary honor. Some winners are primarily poets or dramatists (and several have produced only nonfiction), but writers of fiction dominate, and the prize continues to be a good guide to the leading authors of the times.

Neustadt International Prize for Literature

Awarded biennially since 1970 "in recognition of outstanding achievement in poetry, fiction, or drama," the winner is selected by an international jury of leading writers. Four Neustadt laureates have gone on to win the Nobel Prize, and it has consistently high standards.

Jerusalem Prize

Awarded biennially since 1963 "to a writer whose work best expresses and promotes the idea of the 'freedom of the individual in society.'" Four Jerusalem Prize–winning authors have later won the Nobel Prize.

Austrian State Prize for European Literature

Awarded annually since 1965 to a European writer whose work has received significant international recognition. The prize is restricted to European writers and has consistently high standards.

Premio Cervantes

Awarded annually since 1976, this is the leading Spanish-language literary honor. It is limited to authors writing in Spanish and has a very good track record.

Georg-Büchner Prize

Awarded annually since 1923 and limited to writers since 1951, this is the prize of the German Academy and is the leading German-language literary prize.

Prizes Awarded to Individual Books and Translations

Man Booker International Prize

Awarded annually, beginning in 2016, for a work of fiction in translation published in the United Kingdom. The Man Booker International Prize supplants the Independent Foreign Fiction Prize, which was awarded annually from 2002 to 2015 (as well as from 1990 to 1995), and replaces the previous incarnation of the Man Booker International Prize, which was awarded biennially from 2005 to 2015 "to a living author who has published fiction either originally in English or whose work is generally available in translation in the English language."

International IMPAC Dublin Literary Award

Awarded annually since 1994 to a work either written in or translated into English, the prize winner is selected from nominations by libraries in capitals and major cities throughout the world. The list of nominated books, which generally is more than a hundred titles, tends to be very uneven, but overall the prize is a good indicator of the best internationally popular works available in English.

Best Translated Book Award

Awarded annually since 2008 for the best original work of translated fiction published in the United States over the previous year. Unlike the Independent Foreign Fiction Prize, the BTBA does not consider works that have previously been translated but are now also available in a new translation. Its annual long list provides a good overview of the best fiction in translation published in the United States that year.

PEN Translation Prize (formerly PEN / Book-of-the-Month Club Translation Prize)

Awarded annually since 1963, with the award going to the translator, this award has a good track record of rewarding important translations.

Oxford-Weidenfeld Translation Prize

Awarded annually since 1999, for "book-length literary translations into English from any living European language." Not limited to prose.

National Translation Award

Awarded annually since 1998 by the American Literary Translators Association "for the best book-length translation of a work into English," this award is not limited to prose.

Several translation prizes also are awarded for works translated from specific languages into English: the **Saif Ghobash–Banipal Prize for Arabic Literary Translation** (established 2006), the **French-American Foundation Translation Prize** (established 1986), and the **Helen and Kurt Wolff Translator's Prize** (for works translated from German, established 1996) are some of the more important ones. The finalists and winners of these prizes, even though they are not as well publicized as the larger prizes, offer readers a good indication of the best, recently translated works from these languages.

Other International English-Language Book Prizes

Caine Prize for African Writing

Awarded annually since 2000 to a short story by an African writer published in English, this prize also includes translations. Despite being given only for short stories, the prize does offer a good overview of current African writing, mainly but not exclusively in English.

DSC Prize for South Asian Literature

Awarded annually since 2011 to any novel or novella with predominantly South Asian themes, this prize includes translations too.

Man Booker Prize for Fiction

Awarded annually since 1969, this prize is for a novel written in English. Before 2014, the prize was open only to citizens of the United Kingdom, the Commonwealth, the Republic of Ireland, and Zimbabwe.

Several national English-language book prizes are also awarded in countries other than the United Kingdom and the United States. Among the leading ones are the **Miles Franklin Literary Award** (Australia, established 1957), the **Governor General's Literary Awards** (Canada, with prizes for both English- and French-language fiction, as well as translations, established 1936), and the **Crossword Book Awards** (India, with prizes for English-language fiction as well Indian-language fiction translated into English, established 1998).

Foreign-Language Book Prizes

Some of the many national and international foreign-language literary prizes are highly remunerative: the Spanish-language **Premio Planeta** (established 1952) awards a staggering €601,000 to the winning book. Although these prizes are influential in domestic literary markets, only a few help propel an author's work to be translated into English.

The best-known foreign-language literary prize is the French **Prix Goncourt** (established 1903). The winner receives only a token €10 in prize money, but the Goncourt is by far the most influential French-language literary award, and more than half the winning titles have been translated into English.

No other foreign-language literary prize has anywhere near as much clout with American and British publishers and audiences as does the Prix Goncourt, but other notable ones are the **Akutagawa Prize** (Japan, established 1935), the **Nordic Council Literature Prize** (Scandinavia, established 1962), and the **German Book Prize** (Germany, established 2005)

Several foreign-language literary prizes include as part of the award the guarantee of translating the winning work into English. Among the most notable of these is the American University of Cairo Press's **Naguib Mahfouz Medal for Literature** (established 1996).

BOOKS

General Reference Works

Casser, Vincent, and Nik Kalinowski, eds. *The Bloomsbury Good Reading Guide to World Fiction*. London: Black, 2007.

A handy guide to world fiction since 1900, arranged by region and nation.

Classe, Olive, ed. *Encyclopedia of Literary Translation into English*. Chicago: Fitzroy Dearborn, 2000.

This two-volume work with more than six hundred entries covering 1,700 pages in small print, two columns per page, is truly encyclopedic and is the standard reference work covering translation into English. Not limited to contemporary literature or fiction, it is comprehensive and thorough. Besides the topical and national entries are many for individual authors, providing biographical information, bibliographical information about available translations, a concise consideration of those translations, and suggested further reading. Highly recommended, but note that it is a scholarly reference work.

Dilevko, Juris, Keren Dali, and Glenda Garbutt. *Contemporary World Fiction: A Guide to Literature in Translation*. Santa Barbara, Calif.: Libraries Unlimited, 2011.

A good, far-ranging overview of translations from 1980 to 2010, with detailed annotations of translated titles and useful bibliographic information. Clearly targeted at librarians and library users, this is a useful reference work.

France, Peter, ed. *The Oxford Guide to Literature in English Translation*. Oxford: Oxford University Press, 2000.

Another encyclopedic survey of literature in translation, this single-volume work is more concise and not quite as comprehensive as the *Encyclopedia of Literary Translation into English*. It also is not limited to contemporary literature or fiction but does provide a good general historical overview and bibliographic information.

Morgan, Ann. *The World Between Two Covers: Reading the Globe*. New York: Liveright, 2015. (Published in the United Kingdom as *Reading the World: Confessions of a Literary Explorer*. London: Harvill Secker, 2015)

In 2012, Morgan read one book from each country in the world, chronicling her progress at her blog *A Year of Reading the World* (http://ayear ofreadingtheworld.com). This book is an account of her undertaking and also examines many of the issues surrounding international writing and publishing.

Sturrock, John, ed. *The Oxford Guide to Contemporary World Literature*. Oxford: Oxford University Press, 1997.

First published as *The Oxford Guide to Contemporary Writing* (1996), this guide contains twenty-eight essays by leading critics and scholars, such as Robert Irwin, James Wood, Wendy Lesser, and Michael Wood, who describe contemporary literature in twenty-eight essays about individual regions (examples are "African Countries," "Spanish America") and nations ("Brazil," "France," "United States"). The volume is particularly useful in giving a sense of domestic literary culture, since it includes extensive discussions of all a given region's literary output. But because it also discusses works not available in English translation, it is not ideal as a reader's guide. At fewer than five hundred pages, it is a manageable volume, and each chapter also includes a short "Further Reading."

National and Regional Reference Works

Columbia University Press publishes the series Columbia Guides to Literature Since 1945, which consists of encyclopedic reference works for specific regions and literatures. These are thorough introductory overviews and recommended for readers interested in more information about specific regional literature. Nine volumes have appeared, including Oyekan Owomoyela, *The Columbia Guide to West African Literature in English Since 1945* (2008); Raymond Williams, *The Columbia Guide to the Latin American Novel Since 1945* (2007); and Eric Cheyfitz, *The Columbia Guide to American Indian Literatures of the United States Since 1945* (2006).

Cambridge University Press publishes the extensive series Cambridge Companions to Literature, which includes many volumes on specific national and regional literatures as well as individual authors. These collections of essays in books of manageable size—generally fewer than three hundred pages—are good surveys of a wide variety of contemporary and classical literature. Representative volumes include John N. Duvall, ed., *The Cambridge Companion to American Fiction After 1945* (2012); Graham Bartram, ed., *The Cambridge Companion to the Modern German Novel* (2004); and Philip Swanson, ed., *The Cambridge Companion to Gabriel García Márquez* (2010).

Numerous books by leading translators contain in-depth discussions of the specific literatures that they translate. Along with offering insight into the translation and publishing process, these also serve as useful guides. Among them are:

Johnson-Davies, Denys. *Memories in Translation: A Life Between the Lines of Arabic Literature*. Cairo: American University in Cairo Press, 2006.
Levine, Suzanne Jill. *The Subversive Scribe: Translating Latin American Fiction*. St. Paul, Minn.: Graywolf, 1991.
Rabassa, Gregory. *If This Be Treason: Translation and Its Dyscontents*. New York: New Directions, 2005.

General Works

Among the best accessible academic works dedicated to defining and analyzing world literature are:

Casanova, Pascale. *The World Republic of Letters*. Translated by M. B. DeBevoise. Cambridge, Mass.: Harvard University Press, 2004.

Casanova gives a history of the global literary marketplace and analyzes why some national literatures succeed in establishing themselves abroad while others find it much more difficult to do so.

Damrosch, David. *What Is World Literature?* Princeton, N.J.: Princeton University Press, 2003.

Damrosch makes the case for world literature as "a mode of circulation and of reading," rather than its being based on canon.

Moretti, Franco, ed. *The Novel*. Princeton, N.J.: Princeton University Press, 2006.

The two-volume English-language edition is a condensed version of the collection first published in Italian in five volumes but still has a fascinating global historical and theoretical overview of every aspect of the novel in dozens of essays by noted scholars.

Many works provide additional insight into the history, craft, and business of translation, including:

Allen, Esther, and Susan Bernofsky, eds. *In Translation: Translators on Their Work and What It Means*. New York: Columbia University Press, 2013.

Allen, Esther, Sean Cotter, and Russell Scott Valentino, eds. *The Man Between: Michael Henry Heim and a Life in Translation*. Rochester, N.Y.: Open Letter, 2014.

Bellos, David. *Is That a Fish in Your Ear? Translation and the Meaning of Everything*. New York: Faber & Faber, 2011.

Eco, Umberto. *Experiences in Translation*. Translated by Alastair McEwen. Toronto: University of Toronto Press, 2001.

Grossman, Edith. *Why Translation Matters*. New Haven, Conn.: Yale University Press, 2010.

Venuti, Lawrence. *The Scandals of Translation: Towards an Ethics of Difference*. New York: Routledge, 1998.

Venuti, Lawrence. *Translation Changes Everything: Theory and Practice*. New York: Routledge, 2013.

Index